CW01185497

Postwar Taxation And Economic Progress

You are holding a reproduction of an original work that is in the public domain in the United States of America, and possibly other countries. You may freely copy and distribute this work as no entity (individual or corporate) has a copyright on the body of the work. This book may contain prior copyright references, and library stamps (as most of these works were scanned from library copies). These have been scanned and retained as part of the historical artifact.

This book may have occasional imperfections such as missing or blurred pages, poor pictures, errant marks, etc. that were either part of the original artifact, or were introduced by the scanning process. We believe this work is culturally important, and despite the imperfections, have elected to bring it back into print as part of our continuing commitment to the preservation of printed works worldwide. We appreciate your understanding of the imperfections in the preservation process, and hope you enjoy this valuable book.

POSTWAR TAXATION
and
ECONOMIC PROGRESS
By HAROLD M. GROVES

This book provides the reader with a new perspective and a clearer understanding of the long-range factors involved in a planned tax structure. The purpose of the study is to develop recommendations for a postwar tax system which will increase production and consumption, conserve natural and human resources, and encourage saving and investment.

A continuation and expansion of the author's earlier book, PRODUCTION, JOBS, AND TAXES, the present report offers a more comprehensive treatment of the subject, with additional evidence for the conclusions arrived at, and a critical analysis of several proposed tax systems. It summarizes and defines all of the qualifications that emerge as essential for postwar taxes in a long-run national program dedicated to the interests of all groups.

The author provides a thorough appraisal of federal postwar taxes and their effects on business and industry, government fiscal policy, state and local taxation. Bearing in mind postwar revenue needs, the report includes quantitative estimates of income tax yields under varying conditions of national income, rates, and exemption, together with a critical evaluation and rating of various proposed systems and a detailed presentation of the author's recommendations to the Committee for Economic Development.

COMMITTEE FOR ECONOMIC DEVELOPMENT
RESEARCH STUDY

POSTWAR TAXATION AND
ECONOMIC PROGRESS

COMMITTEE FOR ECONOMIC DEVELOPMENT
RESEARCH STUDIES

THE LIQUIDATION OF WAR PRODUCTION
By A. D H Kaplan

DEMOBILIZATION OF WARTIME ECONOMIC CONTROLS
By John Maurice Clark

PROVIDING FOR UNEMPLOYED WORKERS IN THE TRANSITION
By Richard A. Lester

PRODUCTION, JOBS AND TAXES
By Harold M. Groves

INTERNATIONAL TRADE AND DOMESTIC EMPLOYMENT
By Calvin B Hoover

AGRICULTURE IN AN UNSTABLE ECONOMY
By Theodore W. Schultz

POSTWAR TAXATION AND ECONOMIC PROGRESS
By Harold M. Groves

SUPPLEMENTARY RESEARCH PAPERS

PERSONNEL PROBLEMS OF THE POSTWAR TRANSITION PERIOD*
By Charles A. Myers

THE ECONOMICS OF A FREE SOCIETY*
By William Benton

WORLD POLITICS FACES ECONOMICS
By Harold D. Lasswell

* *Published by C E.D.*

COMMITTEE FOR ECONOMIC DEVELOPMENT
RESEARCH STUDY

Postwar Taxation and Economic Progress

BY

HAROLD M. GROVES
Professor of Economics
University of Wisconsin

First Edition

McGRAW-HILL BOOK COMPANY, Inc.
NEW YORK AND LONDON
1946

POSTWAR TAXATION AND
ECONOMIC PROGRESS

COPYRIGHT, 1946, BY THE
COMMITTEE FOR ECONOMIC DEVELOPMENT

PRINTED IN THE UNITED STATES OF AMERICA

All rights reserved Permission to reproduce material from this book may be secured by writing the publisher

THE MAPLE PRESS COMPANY, YORK, PA

The Trustees of the Committee for Economic Development established the Research Committee "to initiate studies into the principles of business policy and of public policy which will foster the full contribution by industry and commerce in the postwar period to the attainment of high and secure standards of living for people in all walks of life through maximum employment and high productivity in the domestic economy" (From C.E.D. By-Laws)

The studies are assigned by the Research Director to qualified scholars, drawn largely from leading universities. Under the by-laws "all research is to be thoroughly objective in character, and the approach in each instance is to be from the standpoint of the general welfare and not from that of any special political or economic group."

The reports present the findings of the authors, who have complete freedom to express their own conclusions. They do not purport to set forth the views of the Trustees, the Research Committee, the Research Advisory Board, the Research Staff, or the business men affiliated with the C.E.D. This report is the second volume on taxation as related to economic progress and the tenth in the series.

The Research Committee draws on these studies and other available information in formulating its recommendations as to national policy for the problems examined. Its policy statements are offered as an aid to clearer understanding of steps to be taken to reach and maintain a high level of productive employment and a steadily rising standard of living. The statements are available from the national or any local C.E.D. office

FOREWORD

THIS study was undertaken to develop recommendations for a postwar tax system patterned genuinely in the public interest. The objective was not a blueprint for temporary transition policy but rather the specifications for a permanent tax structure toward which we should be working. While the book does illuminate transition issues, its main value lies in its contribution to perspective and understanding regarding long-run problems.

Fiscal-monetary policy is not considered extensively here. This subject will be dealt with in a forthcoming C.E.D. report, *Jobs and Markets in the Transition*, and in a later volume addressed to long-run fiscal problems.

As a companion piece to Groves' report, the reader will be interested in the policy statement by the Research Committee, *A Postwar Federal Tax Plan for High Employment*. This statement, based on a preliminary study by Professor Groves of the relationship of taxation to incentives and to employment, as well as other materials, parallels closely Groves' conclusions in this final study.

The various research projects, completed and in process, that comprise the C.E.D. research program are outlined on pages 406–410.

THEODORE O. YNTEMA,
Research Director

PREFACE

A PRELIMINARY report based upon tax studies conducted by the author under the sponsorship of the Committee for Economic Development was published in 1944. The report, entitled *Production, Jobs and Taxes*, stated that the conclusions offered were tentative and incomplete; that a more comprehensive treatment of the subject with additional supporting evidence for these conclusions or some revision of the latter would be forthcoming. This book is the later report there promised.

The first study was confined mainly to federal postwar taxes and gave little attention to the larger issues of fiscal policy and of state and local taxation. The present study includes this territory although it was not possible to treat it all exhaustively. This study also includes quantitative estimates of income-tax yields under varying conditions of national income and income-tax rates and exemptions. Some estimates of the yield of the proposed tax system are also presented. A further addition is an appraisal and rating of other taxes not recommended.

Chapter VIII includes a discussion of joint returns and net income not arising from exchange. Chapter IX covers in some detail the loopholes in our present death and gift taxes. Chapter XI adds a much fuller discussion of incentive taxation proposals and of their application to unemployment compensation.

Most of the conclusions offered in the earlier work are included here without revision except in the presentation and emphasis; some, however, have been revised considerably and new conclusions have been added. Additional evidence and analysis are submitted.

Preface

Among the most important revisions in the conclusions are the elimination of the earlier proposal to credit "advance payments" on corporate reinvestment in reckoning taxes on capital gains; the extension of the privilege of tax-free reinvestment to all new small business, unincorporated as well as incorporated; and a modification of the proposed averaging feature, confining it for the lower brackets to a carry-over of unused personal exemptions and losses.

The manuscript was completed before the end of the war and several months before the passage of the 1945 Revenue Act. No attempt has been made to revise it in the light of recent developments. Books on taxation do not long remain current in the sense of stating current tax practice; thus it seemed expedient to date the book as of the end of the war.

Acknowledgments are due to Dr. Oscar Litterer, now on the staff of the Federal Reserve Bank of Minneapolis, and to Mrs. Charlotte McNiesh, who conducted much of the quantitative research and made most of the estimates presented. Dr. William Anderson assisted in the preparation of several chapters, particularly Chap. IX. Edith Green also contributed to several chapters and conducted the sample study on averaging. The Tax Foundation prepared for our use a special study on state business taxes. Russell Briggs contributed to the sections on the property tax and the taxation of cooperatives. Criticisms from Professor Theodore O. Yntema, Professor Henry C. Simons, and the Research Committee of the Committee for Economic Development resulted in many improvements. Valuable assistance in editing the manuscript was rendered by Sylvia Stone and Marion Goetz, and the latter also contributed much in its preparation.

HAROLD M. GROVES.

MADISON, WIS,
September 1, 1945.

CONTENTS

	PAGE
FOREWORD	vii
PREFACE	ix

CHAPTER

I. TAXES AND PRODUCTION IN THE POSTWAR PERIOD . 1
    Introduction. 1
    Goals of the Postwar Period 1
    How the Tax System Can Affect Production . 3
    Other Objectives of Taxation 15
    Harmony and Conflict of Interests in Taxation 16
    Background of the Federal Tax Problem. . 16
    Scope of This Study 18

II. INTEGRATION OF FEDERAL CORPORATE AND PERSONAL
    TAXES. 20
    Survey of Our Corporate Income-tax Experience 20
    "Theoretical" Basis of a Business Tax . . 20
    Incidence of the Corporate Income Tax 27
    Effects of the Corporate Tax upon Incentives . 30
    Bond versus Stock Financing 31
    Equity of the Corporate Tax. 35
    Other Considerations 36
    Conclusion. 37

III. INTEGRATION AND THE TREATMENT OF UNDISTRIBUTED
    PROFITS 40
    The Cause for Action: Tax Discrimination . 40
    The Cause for Action. Tax Avoidance . . . 42
    The Volume of Corporate Saving . 44
    Social and Economic Effects of Corporate Saving . 46
    Survey of Undistributed-profits-tax Experience . . . 49
    Alternative Remedies 55

Contents

CHAPTER		PAGE
	Foreign Experience in the Integration of Corporate and Personal Income Taxes	67
	Maintenance of a Moderate Business Tax as Such	70
	Conclusion	71
	Summary of Chapters II and III	72
IV.	EXCESS-PROFITS TAXES, MONOPOLY, AND SMALL BUSINESS	74
	Introduction	74
	Excess-profits-tax Repeal	74
	Application of Graduation to a Corporate Net-income Tax	83
	Checking Monopoly by Taxing Intercorporate Holdings	89
	Taxation in Its Relation to Small and New Business	96
	Taxes on Size of Business	105
	Conclusion	106
V.	FURTHER PROBLEMS OF SELECTING AND APPLYING A BUSINESS TAX	107
	Introduction	107
	Net- versus Gross-income Taxes	107
	Capital-stock Taxes	114
	Multibase Business Tax	116
	Corporate versus General Business Tax	117
	Application of the Tax System to Cooperatives as Compared with Private Business	119
	Application of Business Taxes to Publicly Owned Utilities	125
	Problems of Administration	127
VI.	PROBLEMS OF THE BUSINESS INCOME-TAX BASE	130
	Business Losses	130
	Inventory Valuation	146
	Depreciation, Obsolescence, and Depletion	153
VII.	ROLE OF AND CHANGES IN THE PERSONAL INCOME TAX	165
	Introduction	165
	Broad Base	165
	Adequate Standard Rate	174
	Surtax Levels	177
	Suggested Schedule of Rates	180

Contents

CHAPTER		PAGE
	Yield of the Rate Scale at Various Levels of Income	186
	Relation of Exemptions, Standard Rate, and Surtaxes	188
	Instability of Yield	189
	Concentration of the Income Tax Among Classes of Income, Sources of Income, and Geographic Regions	192
	Effect of Proposed Changes on the Tax System	197
	Improved Administration	198
VIII.	PERSONAL INCOME TAX (CONTINUED)	200
	Tax-exempt Securities	200
	Capital Gains and Losses	206
	Mitigation of Discrimination against Irregular Income	223
	Problem of Simplification	236
	Miscellaneous Considerations	237
IX.	DEATH TAXATION	243
	General Considerations	243
	Problem of Evaluating Assets	250
	Forms of Death Taxes and Exemptions	259
	Evasion and Avoidance of Estate and Gift Taxes	262
	The Integration of Federal Estate and Gift Taxes	278
	Miscellaneous Considerations	280
	Conclusion	282
X.	SPECIAL EXCISES AND GENERAL SALES TAXES	284
	Introduction	284
	Federal Excises before and during the War	285
	Arguments Favoring Consumption Taxes	287
	Arguments Against Consumption Taxes	288
	Consumption Taxes and the Functioning of the Economic System	290
	Special Excises	292
	The Spendings Tax	294
	Conclusion	295
XI.	INCENTIVE TAXATION	296
	Introduction	296
	Some Incentive Taxation Proposals	297
	Incentive Taxation Proposals Criticized	303
	Classified Income Tax	306
	Functional Approach to Taxation	307

Contents

CHAPTER	PAGE
Social Security Incentive Taxation	317
Conclusion	325

XII. STATE AND LOCAL TAXES AND THEIR BEARING ON PRODUCTION 327

Introduction 327
Criticisms of State and Local Tax Systems as They Affect Economic Progress 329
Selection of a State Business Tax 337
Treatment of Dividends Under State Personal Income Taxes 340
Migration of Business to Escape Taxes: Special Inducements to Locate 341
The Property Tax 344

XIII. FISCAL POLICY AND THE FUNCTIONING OF THE ECONOMY IN THE POSTWAR PERIOD 349

Introduction 349
Tax and Fiscal Policy during the Later Phases of the War 349
Tax and Fiscal Policy during Reconversion 350
Taxes and Fiscal Policy in the Postwar Period following Reconversion 356
Other Factors and Conclusions 371

XIV. CONCLUSIONS 373

APPENDIX A. THE POSTWAR FEDERAL BUDGET 379

Postwar Federal Expenditures 379
Yields of Tax Proposals 385

APPENDIX B 390

Technique Employed to Estimate the Personal Income Tax Revenue 390
Technique Employed to Estimate Capital Gains and Losses . 399

A NOTE ON THE COMMITTEE FOR ECONOMIC DEVELOPMENT AND ITS RESEARCH PROGRAM 403

EXCERPT FROM BY-LAWS 411

INDEX 417

I. TAXES AND PRODUCTION IN THE POSTWAR PERIOD

INTRODUCTION

SINCE the days of Adam Smith it has been recognized that taxes should be levied with as little hindrance to production as possible. The popular version of this proposition is "Don't kill the goose that lays the golden egg." This aspect of taxation took on new significance, however, in the depression of the thirties. Taxation was then elevated from a mere government "meal ticket" to an instrument of grand economic strategy. The critical importance of adequate employment opportunity in the postwar period ensures for taxation a continuation and enlargement of this sphere of influence. From now on, each component of the tax system is likely to be called before the bar of public opinion and asked the question: "Do you seriously impede enterprise, employment, and production?" If the answer is affirmative and especially if there are alternatives that do not offend in this manner, the tax will probably be selected for discard.

GOALS OF THE POSTWAR PERIOD

It is generally agreed that maintenance of adequate employment opportunity will be a major challenge in the postwar decade and that we must meet this challenge without sacrificing the great gains for democracy achieved in the Jeffersonian and Jacksonian revolutions. Different roads to adequate postwar employment are suggested in the economic literature of the past. Karl Marx, the socialist, predicted and advocated the ownership and management of all important businesses by the State. Thorstein Veblen, the technocrat, laid the foundation for the widely accepted view that the government should draw an over-all plan for "all-out" production and should "induce" private industry to comply with the plan. John R. Commons, among others, advocated a "mixed economy," with the government providing rules to ensure the successful operation of private business in the public interest. His was a highly pragmatic view, allowing for many adaptations to time and place. To which of these views, if any, the distant future belongs is unpredictable, but for the immediate future the American public is committed to the third approach. Changes are not likely to take the form of substituting new systems for old; rather they will occur as new modes of functioning for old institutions and perhaps gradual replacement of some institutions. To say the least, our present system is worth a further investment of effort.

Will private business be able to provide adequate employment after the war? There is a reasonably good chance but no definite assurance that it will. In any event, it is desirable that private business carry as much of the load as possible.

Should the efforts of private business prove unsuccessful, they will probably be supplemented by those of the government. After the experience of the thirties, it is unlikely that the government will stand by and do nothing about unemployment during a prolonged depression. If its program does not win support as a compensatory device to correct a maladjusted economy, it will be accepted as a necessary relief measure for the idle. Neither the wisdom of such a program nor the best techniques for its application need be considered here except to say that the government must avoid, if possible, continually enlarging its unemployment problem by discouraging private initiative.

The public has come to expect that the economic system provide not only adequate employment but also high productivity with progressively higher standards of living. *What* we produce is as important as *how much*. Increased production along with well-balanced distribution means more and

Taxes and Production in the Postwar Period

more of the necessities and amenities of life for larger and larger numbers of people. The future economic order will be and should be judged by the housing, health, and nutrition standards attained by the poorest third of the population.

HOW THE TAX SYSTEM CAN AFFECT PRODUCTION

Fostering production through a well-ordered tax system is obviously a large order. In seeking the main objective, several sub-objectives must be considered, among them the following:

1. The conservation of national resources, particularly human resources.

2. The maintenance of proper relations among consumption, saving, and investment.

3. The preservation and development of economic morale among those engaged in production, including management.

Conserving Resources

The importance of conserving resources, particularly human resources, is self-evident. In the last analysis, the people of a country are its most important factor of production. The tax system should not impair the health or morale of large numbers of citizens by cutting more deeply than necessary into income required for adequate living standards or by imposing sales taxes on necessities.

Balancing Consumption, Saving, and Investment

Having inherited from the war an extremely well-developed and highly productive economic machine, the maintenance of an adequate consumers' market will be of especial importance. It would be threatened by a tax system that sought the greatest portion of revenue from the lowest levels of income.

It is frequently argued that a rich country tends persistently to save more than it requires as new capital. Formerly, the ready answer to this was that tendencies toward a redundancy of savings were speedily curbed by falling rates of interest. But it has become evident that the amount of saving does not respond readily to changes in interest rates. Saving is rather determined by the national income, the distribution of that income, and the need and willingness of people to provide for their futures.

In modern societies, individuals will save for various personal reasons, such as future security, future consumption wants, estates for their heirs, and so on, regardless of the magnitude of investment outlets. This inclination to save has been fostered by decades of thrift education. Yet the savings of a great majority of people have never been sufficient to attain their objectives. Were individuals to save as much as they are exhorted (and properly) to save, or were the social security system to assist them in doing so generally, the problem of oversaving would be much more serious.

It is not clearly established that oversaving *is* a chronic problem in a highly developed and highly productive industrial economy. As recently as the twenties, few people considered oversaving any problem at all. Yet the outlets for savings may have been little more promising at the end of the last war than they are now. Oversaving theories came into prominence during the thirties, a period of low business confidence and very low new investment. The postwar period may turn out to resemble the twenties rather than the thirties, but at least it should be recognized that oversaving is not impossible. Indeed, it may become our number one postwar fiscal problem and should be considered in our postwar fiscal planning.

The demand for savings after the war is not predictable, but undoubtedly the anticipated volume of savings will require a scale of investment much larger than that of the prosperous twenties. During the war, total new construction for the peak year, 1942, amounted to less than $14 billion, the bulk of which was paid for by the government. The productivity of existing plants increased substantially. Even during the

Taxes and Production in the Postwar Period

war period, we produced substantially more in civilian goods and services than we did in the late thirties or early forties. A housing program could be an excellent outlet for investment, but an $8 billion-a-year housing program would be something of a housing "boom." How are we going to offset current savings of $15 to $25 billion per year, to say nothing about using the accumulated savings?

Oversaving might be attacked by either decreasing the supply of savings or increasing the demand for capital. It is not easy to check the supply of savings and at the same time stimulate the demand, but the two purposes are not always diametrically opposed. Death taxation, for instance, checks the supply of savings but may have relatively little effect on the initiation of new enterprises and the expansion of old ones.

The author is not disposed toward defeatism with regard to the savings, investment, and consumption problem in the postwar period. With a high rate of expansion, industry can absorb enormous quantities of capital. Prospects of investment abroad are substantial. We do not know that oversaving and underconsumption *are* chronic problems, but the hypothesis has enough plausibility to warrant a tax system that would tend to correct rather than aggravate the problem should it materialize.

Preserving and Developing Morale

The third way in which taxation can affect production is through its influence on morale. Morale may be a matter of confidence in the future, or of the climate in which economic activity is carried on, or of incentives. Obviously these elements are closely related.

Negative effects may result from taxes that reduce the rewards for economic activity; but these effects may be minimized by the strategic selection of taxes and techniques of application. For example, death may be a more strategic time to tax wealthy persons than when they or their fortunes are actively engaged in producing wealth. And high taxes on incomes may have little or no repressive effects if due allowance is made for the deduction of losses.

Importance of Incentives. A common observation of business executives is that talented young men who would have started new enterprises of their own 25 years ago now prefer secure jobs with established concerns and that they also prefer secure investments. Many a young person faces a choice between security on the one hand and economic adventure on the other. The latter is attractive in many respects but carries with it a burden of responsibility, worry, and possible loss. That the financial prospects have some importance in the weighing of these alternatives is hardly open to doubt. It may not be possible nor desirable to recapture the spirit of high adventure that prevailed in our business world 50 years ago, but at least we should try to retain a dynamic economy.[1]

A recent financial statement of the Curtis Publishing Company includes this observation:

> If we made an additional million dollars we would be able to keep currently only about fifty thousand for stockholders. It is probable that that extra million profit might easily require an extra investment in plant and markets of five million. The risks of a five-million-dollar investment are not justified by a fifty thousand dollar net return.[2]

Former Vice President Henry A. Wallace has expressed an interest in incentives as follows:

> My own opinion is that while governmental preparedness of this sort (public works) is an essential safeguard against unemployment,

[1] A recent study, with particular reference to the Lockheed Aircraft Corporation, concludes that it is extremely doubtful if the company would ever have attempted or could ever have achieved a successful development in the face of a 40 per cent corporate tax. (J. Keith Butters and John Lintner, *Effect of Federal Taxes on Growing Enterprises*, Study No. 1, The Lockheed Aircraft Corporation, Graduate School of Business Administration, Harvard University, Cambridge, 1944.)

[2] *Saturday Review of Literature*, June 10, 1944, p. 23.

our first thought should be to preserve the dynamic character of our economy. For example, if we are to maintain full employment in the postwar period, it is important, at the right time and in the right way, to revise our taxation system sufficiently to place an incentive on the investment of capital which furnishes private jobs in the production of needed goods and services. As one of my business friends puts it, a businessman ought to be able to get his "risk money" back before he has to pay too much in the way of taxation Otherwise, how can any new private enterprise employ anybody?[1]

Of course, there is a distinction between gains that constitute a reward for wealth-creating activities and acquisition that occurs without the performance of any socially useful function. A sound tax system need be solicitous only for the former.

The author offers no justification for economic incentives. If everyone would work and invest to the best advantage without these incentives, the world would probably be a better place. The cooperative movement stands as an open invitation for those who wish to engage in economic activity with less emphasis upon monetary rewards. That it is not an "easy road to paradise" is evidenced by long years of experience.

Allowing for incentives in taxation is not synonymous with "pampering the wealthy." It may be difficult, but it should not be impossible, to make allowance for incentives without sacrificing interests associated with a better distribution of wealth and income. Some obvious duplication of taxes and other inequities can be removed. Some distinctions among sources of income and some modifications in the timing of levies can be made to satisfy both objectives. Our task is to make the economic system function at high capacity; and

---

[1] Henry A. Wallace, then Vice President of the United States, "Work, Peace, and Health," address delivered at the American Labor Party dinner, Hotel Commodore, New York, May 16, 1943.

tax relief for the wealthy, at least for its own sake, is certainly not one of our goals.

Moreover, what we are seeking to do cannot fairly be described as an attempt to make the rich more prosperous in the hope that some of this prosperity will trickle down to the poor. It is true that all will prosper together when all elements in the economic system function in a constructive way. But it is not part of our program to shift taxes from the rich to the poor. To do so might lend support to incentives, but it might also undermine rather than promote production by aggravating an oversaving problem and unduly curtailing the postwar market. The problem is to give some support for production without a shift in taxes from the top to the bottom. The shift may well be in the opposite direction, for the tax system is full of loopholes and does a good job· neither as an equalizer nor as a promoter.

There is a distinction between business and wealth, and it is not illogical to advocate lighter taxes for the one and heavier taxes for the other. A dynamic economy is essential; we must depend upon it for our tax base and for adequate employment opportunity. The problem is to achieve it without surrendering other equally important objectives.

Hypotheses Concerning Taxation and Incentives The motives that lead men to venture their earnings and their abilities in new undertakings are not easily catalogued. They are a blend of psychological and social as well as economic interests. Not all profit is monetary. Here we are concerned mainly with economic motivation. Much of what we know about it necessarily comes from observation and opinion which are not rigorously scientific. On the basis of such evidence, the following hypotheses are offered:

1. Other things being equal, the higher the degree of taxation the more likely it is to affect economic motivation adversely. Certainly far less concern for incentives is required when taxation amounts to one-eighth of the national income than when it amounts to one-fourth.

Taxes and Production in the Postwar Period

2. The *form* as well as the *degree* of taxation is important. Everyone knows that by skillful adjustment of a pack to the right location upon his back a hiker can carry a load that would otherwise be unbearable. Proper techniques of taxation can likewise reduce its burden and its harmful effects upon the economy.

3. Taxes levied directly upon business concerns as such are likely to restrain business activity more than corresponding taxes upon individuals. Companies managed by their principal owners are playing a role of decreasing importance in the nation's industrial life. For example, in the Pennsylvania Railway Company a few years ago, not a single officer or director owned as much as 0.1 per cent of the total stock. The interest of management in building a successful business may serve effectively as motivation even though the possibility of high net personal rewards to the stockholder is considerably limited. The effect of taxes on managerial decisions will be certainly less direct and probably less substantial if levies are imposed on shareholders rather than on their companies.[1] Managements will be rated and rewarded by what they deliver in terms of company earnings and not by what these gains mean, net of tax, to stockholders.

4. Fear of losses may be of as much concern to business men as the hope of high profits. The appetite for risk-taking

[1] The impression that business executives are motivated by concern for their companies, independent of that for investors, was strongly supported by the replies to a questionnaire recently distributed by the National Industrial Conference Board. Summarizing this correspondence, Mr Paul W Ellis observes "Several other executives refer to the profit motive, but in every case they appear to consider it subordinate to the security and welfare of the corporation concerned." "Effects of Taxes upon Corporate Policy," *National Industrial Conference Board Reports*, 1943, p 10.)

This view is also confirmed by the observation of Professor Dewing· "Men who can be even broadly classified as business managers and who value success in productive enterprise as something worthwhile in itself—rather than as an insignificant means to a greater end—want the enterprise associated with their efforts to bear the outward signs of successful achievement. Increasing size is the most obvious of these signs. . . . " (A. S. Dewing, *The Financial Policy of Corporations*, 4th ed., The Ronald Press Company, New York, 1941, pp 854–855.)

might persist in the face of severe taxation if due consideration for losses were assured.[1]

5. The rate of tax on the marginal portion of profits or other income—the top bracket—may be more consequential than the average effective rate of taxation. The application of the excess-profits tax at the margin is a case in point. This tax may not represent a high proportion of net income because of the credits allowed and because of the bracket system of graduation; but on any additional increment of income the tax may bear with great severity. It is the net increment of income after tax that is of vital importance in motivation (Thus a 90 per cent profits tax on the income in excess of a 10 per cent return on capital may amount to very little in the aggregate for a concern that has an 11 per cent return, but it may discourage that company conclusively from seeking a return of 12 per cent.)

6. The motivation to risk and initiate is one of the most sensitive to attack. Liquid and relatively secure investments compete effectively with more venturesome undertakings. Of course, the element of gambling is often attractive and the available supply of venturers amazingly large, even though the chance for success in a given line of enterprise is slight and the mortality rate high.[2] Probably the average profit

[1] See Evsey D. Domar and Richard A. Musgrave, "Proportional Income Taxation and Risk-taking," *Quarterly Journal of Economics*, Vol. LVIII, May, 1944.

[2] The role of risk and profit in the oil business has been described by Ronald B Shuman as follows:

"Historically examined, the oil industry, and particularly the production branch, has displayed more than a normal amount of spirit of the game and adventure. The search for what is properly termed 'black gold' partakes of the nature of the hunt for precious stones and metals It is characteristically uncertain, even with modern developmental techniques, offers occasional great rewards for a few, and a mediocre competence, or economic loss, for many. This is believed to represent the general situation, even though the larger and better financed operators may be able to lessen their risks in some degree through diversification. It is generally agreed that more gold has been spent in seeking this valuable metal than has ever come out of the mines Likewise, it is the belief of the industry that much more money has been put into the production

Taxes and Production in the Postwar Period

in venturesome undertakings need not be large. But there must be some substantial prize to be won.

Risk-taking is not necessarily confined to the wealthy. The middle class and even the very poor assume a large share of this social responsibility. Farmers and independent merchants and small landlords are all risk-takers. It remains true, however, that the wealthy have certain unique qualifications for investing in common stocks. They can afford to take risks and they can also afford the facilities to make risk-taking a professional job. The social consequences of forcing wealthy investors into bonds and the lower middle class investors into stocks might not be disastrous, but they would be unfortunate.

It is sometimes contended that taxation may *increase* the appetite for risk-taking, particularly if losses are allowed as an offset against gains. The recipient of a large income may contemplate the prospect of losses with relative equanimity if they can be offset against high positive earnings in which the government would claim a large share. The much-discussed case of Mr. Marshall Field and his newspaper ventures can be cited as an illustration. But, presumably, those who are moved by economic considerations would ordinarily weigh the positive as well as the negative prospects of an undertaking or investment. If there were no positive prospects (profits), the mere fact that losses might take the place of taxes would hardly serve as an incentive. If there were some positive prospects and if losses would be partly relieved by tax offsets,

branch of the petroleum business than has been realized. This statement must be interpreted in a statistical sense, since common observation, in the leading oil producing centers, demonstrates that certain individuals make a great deal of money from the search for, and extraction of, crude petroleum. As with the Irish Sweepstakes, the appeal lies in the chance of winning, not in the mathematically much greater chance of losing. And just as many folk think of the Sweepstakes in terms of the newspaper accounts of families made deliriously happy, so the optimism of mankind causes the investor, or speculator, in crude oil possibilities to remember the instances of those few who 'without a shirt to their backs,' sold out for ten million " (Ronald B. Shuman, *The Petroleum Industry*, University of Oklahoma Press, Norman, 1940, pp 26–27.)

risk-taking might be compatible with relatively high taxes. The progressive rate, however, has a bearing because positive gains might be taxable in a higher bracket than the income offset by losses.

A distinction should be made between waste and risk. When the government takes a high percentage of an individual's marginal dollar, the result may be a waste of resources. Certainly an individual will have little selfish reason for conserving his resources if the tax is confiscatory. Millionaire "play" farms and excessive advertising are cases in point. Recklessness, as distinguished from readiness to take risks, certainly increases as the taxpayer's equity in his money decreases.

It is not true, of course, that the profit urge differs morally or psychologically from the general desire for economic gain. The mere fact that some kinds of income are contractual and others residual is of no significance in appraising the quality of income. Rackets are all too common in business, in labor, and even in religion; no one form of economic activity can be singled out as their special abode.

7. Uncertainty and frequent changes in the tax laws are inimical to business activity. Federal tax laws have been overhauled about eighteen times in the last thirty years. Some of this is the price we pay for democracy. And while one is suggesting further modifications, he cannot stand too staunchly for a program of leaving tax laws undisturbed! Nevertheless, a presumption favoring stability in taxation may be recognized. Retroactive changes, precluding the possibility of corresponding business adjustments, are particularly bad.

8. Commitments for business expansion depend on anticipation of the future. Present experience is important mainly as an indication of future prospects. Tax reductions that are definitely expected may be as stimulating as those which are already realized.

9. Ordinarily, a tax program will facilitate production if

Taxes and Production in the Postwar Period

it leaves business decisions as much as possible to business discretion. Tax consequences enter very heavily into many business decisions at the present time. The decisions to operate as a corporation or a partnership, to distribute dividends or reinvest earnings, to finance with stocks or bonds, and so on, are all likely to be greatly influenced by "advice of counsel" as to the tax consequences. Much of this influence is without any claim to a desirable social objective, although there are, no doubt, cases where the modification of business behavior at the behest of the tax system is in the social interest. The tax system cannot be entirely neutral in its effects on business decisions, but a strong presumption in favor of as little interference as necessary may be recognized. Tax preferments as well as penalties are suspect. In any case, this is not the time to plant a new crop of tax subsidies; the principal task is to weed out the discriminations (largely unintended) in the tax system as it stands.

10. The economic incentives that need to be conserved are by no means confined to enterprisers. Withholding-tax rates can be so high that they affect the workers' interest in higher production and economic improvements. The setup of the social security system can affect the ambition and thrift of the working population. The tax system can weaken the incentive to consume and thus undermine the highly essential postwar market. Consumption taxes and other levies that fall heaviest on the low-income strata are likely to have this effect.

11. The timing of taxes is always important. For instance, in the case of forest resources, tax techniques have been devised which postpone levies on growing timber and recoup when the crop is harvested. In general, much can be accomplished by lightening levies when especially creative economic activities are being carried on and compensating for this leniency when these activities cease. This accounts for the emphasis here given to death taxes and the application of the income tax to capital gains.

Postwar Taxation and Economic Progress

During recent years considerable support has developed for "incentive taxation." This term is used to cover a variety of proposals providing preferred treatment for income from business enterprises and establishing rewards and penalties to stimulate output. Some of the proposals might accomplish their objectives, but in general they do not seem promising for the following reasons:

1. The economic system in its normal operation should generate opportunities and incentives for enterprise. If, under a fair and sensible tax system, it fails to do so, the real causes of difficulty should be sought out and the appropriate remedies applied.[1]

2. A system of bounties and penalties, politically chosen and imposed, is too liable to perversion which can seriously impede the proper functioning of the economy.

3. It is extremely doubtful, to say the least, that business confidence can be fostered by "taxing diffidence."

4. Subsidies for some business are likely to be at the expense of other business—a process resulting in much unfairness and no net gain in initiative.

An economy run by its tax system would indeed be the tail wagging the dog!

That the quantity and particularly the quality of governmental expenditures have influence on incentives is obvious. Most taxpayers have a selfish as well as a philanthropic interest in governmental outlays that help maintain a progressive community. But they are demoralized by "pork-barrel" outlays, handouts to pressure groups, and a philosophy that government expenditures, unlike those of individuals, need not be paid for. Reckless disregard for the value of money by the

[1] Such as reestablishment of balanced international trade and financial relations, agricultural adjustment, both to the domestic and to the world situation; relations of labor and management, maintenance of an effective balance between consumption and productive capacity; and the effective cooperation between government and industry. (This list was suggested in Harold G. Moulton and Karl Schlotterbeck, *Collapse or Boom at the End of the War*, Brookings Institution, Washington, D.C., 1942.)

government is not compatible with maintenance of the economic virtues among individuals.

Morale is a large factor in business motivation, and morale is supported by a sense of fair play and stability in government-business relations. This is a large and engaging subject but it cannot be covered in this report.

OTHER OBJECTIVES OF TAXATION

Giving attention to the impact of taxation upon production and employment does not mean neglecting other objectives of taxation, such as fairness, ability to pay, and the adequacy of revenue yield. A sensible tax program must be based on a balance of all these considerations.

Fairness, or equity, in taxation calls for reasonable classification and like treatment of those in like circumstances. Beyond this, the term is associated with the concept of ability to pay or with a frank interest in reducing inequalities in the distribution of income or wealth.

It cannot be denied that the desire for "equity" will at times conflict with concern for incentives. For example, a 95 per cent tax on a million-dollar income would leave $50,000 after taxes. Those whose concern is solely with "equity" in the distribution of income may approve the results of such a measure. After all, $50,000 is ample to provide the necessities and amenities of life and most of the luxuries that should be of interest to any reasonable person. It provides opportunity for power over others that might, even with this drastic limitation, be regarded as dangerous. On the other hand, those whose concern is for economic motivation will contend that a 5 per cent stake in the product would hardly leave the producer any enthusiasm for effort, initiative, and venture.

Where opposing interests clash, either they must be compromised or one of them must be given the right of way. But there are a surprising number of important tax reforms that involve no clash of interests at all and that will serve both equity and incentives.

Postwar Taxation and Economic Progress

HARMONY AND CONFLICT OF INTERESTS IN TAXATION

Much has been written on the subject of conflict and harmony in economic relations. Particularly in taxation, the element of conflict appears to predominate. Shifting taxes from one group to another often seems to be a clear gain for the first and a clear loss for the second group. But an apparent clash of interests may be resolved into an actual harmony of interests. This is like the difference between selfishness and altruism, a difference which tends to disappear as a longer view is taken. "Good will among various groups in society is necessary to the effective functioning of economic organization. . . . Taxes imposed by the political power of one group may so destroy the good will of other groups that the harm from the resulting noncooperation more than wipes out the advantage to the apparent beneficiary."[1]

Conflicting interests do exist, but there is a harmony of interests in seeking a reasonable compromise of these conflicts. The time has arrived when Adam Smith's rule that one serves the social interest by following his own can be applied in reverse to economic groups. They serve their own interest by serving the social interest. It is in approaching taxation from the angle of maximizing production that the harmonies of interest are strongest. However, maximum production is not the only objective of economic life. Some might prefer greater equality even if it were to mean less income for everyone. It is to be hoped that something like "reasonable taxation"—*i.e.*, the public interest—can be discerned and that it will command enough support from enough sensible people to ensure its adoption.

BACKGROUND OF THE FEDERAL TAX PROBLEM

During much of our history, the federal government relied principally on tariffs and excises to provide its revenue. The

[1] Roy Blough, "Conflict and Harmony in Taxation," an address delivered before the American Philosophical Society, Philadelphia, Feb. 18, 1944

Taxes and Production in the Postwar Period

federal government was a minor enterprise compared with state and local governments. Income and inheritance taxes were not introduced until shortly before our entrance into the First World War These taxes, at first moderately employed, were pushed into high gear to finance the war. To them were added the excess-profits taxes. These business taxes—the corporate income and the excess-profits tax—produced what were then regarded as extremely high financial returns to the government: $3.16 billion in 1918. After the war the excess-profits tax was repealed, and during the twenties the personal income-tax rates were, in successive acts, substantially reduced. In spite of these reductions, a balanced budget was maintained and the debt was cut more than a third.

The financial upheaval of the thirties brought increased tax rates, but revenues did not increase sufficiently to balance the budget. New taxes included an excess-profits capital-stock tax on corporations. This was based on the declared value of capital stock and amounted to an additional levy on net income "estimated" in advance. An undistributed profits tax was introduced in 1936 but was greatly reduced in 1938 and abandoned in 1939. Pay roll taxes to finance Social Security were initiated in 1935.

As the system stood in 1939, the personal income tax carried a personal exemption of $2500 for a married couple, a normal rate of 4 per cent, and a maximum surtax rate of 75 per cent on income in excess of $5 million. The corporate rate was graduated from 12½ to 19 per cent. Together, these two taxes produced about 40 per cent of federal revenue. Consumption taxes (mainly excises on liquor and tobacco) continued to occupy an important place, supplying 29 per cent of the revenue. More was collected from liquor and tobacco taxes than from the personal income tax! Pay roll taxes added 14 per cent to the revenue. Import tariffs had faded into an inconsequential fiscal role; and the estate tax, with a high top rate of 70 per cent, also was relatively insignificant as a revenue producer.

Postwar Taxation and Economic Progress

The Second World War brought tax increases all along the line. Personal exemptions in the personal income tax were substantially reduced (from $2500 to $1000 for a married couple), and the number of income taxpayers increased from 4 to about 50 million. Bottom rates on taxable income rose to about 23 per cent, compared to 4 per cent in 1939, and top rates ranged to about 90 per cent on income in excess of $200,000. Business taxes mounted to a top corporate normal and surtax of 40 per cent in addition to an excess-profits tax of 95 per cent. Neither business tax was deductible in calculating the other, but excess-profits net income was not subject to the corporate tax, an over-all limitation of 80 per cent was allowed, and 10 per cent of excess-profits taxes was earmarked as a postwar credit. The excess-profits tax was levied on the excess of current profits over prewar earnings or a percentage return on capital, at the taxpayer's option. Of $43 billion in revenue for the fiscal year ending June 30, 1944, it was estimated that the corporate profits and income taxes would produce some $14 billion and the personal income tax some $17 billion (including $1.5 billion attributable to overlapping payments attending the introduction of more current collection).

SCOPE OF THIS STUDY

The taxation of business and the relation of taxation to production could be considered as strictly specialized subjects. Certainly, all aspects of the tax problem neither can nor should be included in this study. For instance, choosing at random, it is unnecessary and inadvisable here to consider poll taxes, state gasoline taxes, property tax delinquency, the disposition of state income taxes, and so forth. But it does seem necessary to cover a large part of the tax problem, even though not all of it can be done thoroughly or freshly.

It is obvious enough that no study of the effect of taxes on production can be confined to that alone. From the narrowest view of the subject, the answer might be to eliminate taxes altogether or shift them from business to nonbusiness sectors of the economy. But considerations of adequacy and equity must be weighed. We need a tax program that has some chance of permanent application. None will qualify on this score unless it is acceptable to the conscience of the American people. Irrational proposals supported mainly by opportunistic considerations cannot (and should not) provide the tax system with the element of stability so desirable for postwar prosperity.

In the broad sense, all taxes are business taxes, and it is extremely difficult to justify exclusions from our treatment. Moreover, one tax is an alternative for another. If we are to recommend a reduction of income surtaxes because of their effect on incentives, the replacement problem and considerations of equity oblige us to weigh the death tax as an alternative. Immediately we become involved in the avoidance aspects of an extremely complicated tax field. The excise taxes have no effect, perhaps, on business incentives, but they have an important bearing on the business market.

It is neither possible nor desirable, in this study, to cover the whole "economic waterfront," including all economic factors that affect the quality, quantity, and stability of postwar production. Although taxation is not the only factor affecting production, it is an important factor, and its relation to production affords an ample and challenging field.

A few groups would undoubtedly welcome recommendations that would be of special benefit only to them. Some may argue that postwar employment will be facilitated only by reduced taxes for business or stockholders. But it should be remembered that, in the long run, group interests are closely identified with the public interest, and the public interest requires some tax modifications that are "unfavorable" to business as well as some that are "favorable."

To make the tax system serve at least two masters and do a first-rate job for both is no easy task; but it is one that must be faced in the postwar period.

II. INTEGRATION OF FEDERAL CORPORATE AND PERSONAL TAXES

SURVEY OF OUR CORPORATE INCOME-TAX EXPERIENCE

THE first federal income tax, introduced in 1913, used the corporate income tax chiefly as a withholding levy. The rate of tax on corporate income was the same as the normal rate on personal income. Dividends were exempted from the normal personal tax. Thus double taxation was avoided. This policy was continued through the First World War, although both the normal personal and the corporate rates were raised to 12 per cent during this period. In the early twenties, the relationship between the two taxes was broken when the corporate rate was raised to 12½ per cent and later to still higher figures, while the normal personal tax was reduced to 8 per cent and subsequently to lower levels In 1936, when dividends were made subject to the normal tax, the divorce between the two levies became complete. What had once been a withholding levy was thus converted into a full-fledged business tax. Both before and during the Second World War, the trend in federal taxation was to rely heavily on taxation of business as such.

"THEORETICAL" BASIS OF A BUSINESS TAX

The "theoretical" approach to business taxes is probably less important than an analysis of their incidence and effects However, the effects of a tax depend considerably upon the reasonableness of its imposition. One of the main objectives of this study is to determine what constitutes a rational tax system and to what extent its attainment is practical. When this objective is contemplated it is apparent that the "theoretical" basis of business taxation is of no small importance.

Integration of Federal Corporate and Personal Taxes

A plausible case for business taxes is made by public finance writers who point out that these taxes are an appropriate return for benefits received by corporations from government and for the special privileges that corporations enjoy. Moreover, they argue that corporations have ability to pay quite apart from that of the stockholders and that business taxation affords a needed instrument of social control.

Writing in 1917, T. S. Adams[1] observed that business taxes were "all but universal throughout the world" and showed "no tendency to disappear with the passage of time."[2] It seemed to Adams that business ought to pay its share of the national expense.[3] He considered the property tax inadequate for this purpose and pointed out that the correlation between the volume of business and the quantity (value) of property employed is small. There may be much property with little business, and vice versa.

Adams also expressed the opinion that the ability-to-pay theory should not be confined to individuals in its application. "It is a shallow and narrow interpretation of the ability principle that tests its every application by the effect of the tax on the consumer; which surveys man, the taxpayer, only as one who clothes his back and feeds his body."[4]

Gerhard Colm has expressed views[5] quite similar to those of Adams. Colm refers to governmental services as a factor of production and suggests that business should be expected to pay for this factor[6] as it does for the others. He also stresses the opportunistic grounds for business taxation, observing that "the necessary revenue cannot be derived from ability-to-pay

---

[1] T. S. Adams, "The Taxation of Business," *Proceedings of the National Tax Association*, 1917, pp 185–194

[2] *Ibid*, p 186

[3] *Ibid.*, p. 187.

[4] *Ibid*, p 191.

[5] Gerhard Colm, "Conflicting Theories of Corporate Income Taxation," *Law and Contemporary Problems*, Vol. VII, No 2, Duke University Press, Durham, N.C., 1940, pp. 281–290.

[6] *Ibid*, p 285.

taxes" and that this is "the strongest argument for taxes on business."[1]

Paul Studenski is probably the most unequivocal present-day proponent of business taxation.[2] Observing the wide variety of prevailing business taxes, he concludes that "the time has arrived for the introduction of some order in this medley"[3] and that this requires a more adequate business-tax theory. The argument that this form of taxation is but an attempt to collect indirectly from the stockholders of businesses is deemed fallacious since it fails to recognize business as an important entity. This group entity includes not only stockholders, but creditors, employees, customers—all those interested in the business. It receives governmental benefits and privileges for which it should certainly pay. In addition, the entity has ability to pay. The notion that ability to pay is confined to individuals is "founded on the false association of business with the owners thereof."[4] "The strictly personal or individual concept of ability to pay must be supplemented by an impersonal or group concept of it."[5]

---

[1] *Ibid.*, p. 282.

[2] Paul Studenski, "Toward a Theory of Business Taxation," *Journal of Political Economy*, Vol. XLVIII, No. 5, 1940, pp. 621–654.

[3] *Ibid.*, p 621.

[4] *Ibid.*, p. 633.

[5] *Ibid.*, p 634. Studenski proceeds to enumerate and explain eight theoretical justifications for business taxation, all of which have some validity in his opinion. First, businesses receive *special privileges*, such as the right to operate as limited-liability corporations That these rights are special privileges is generally recognized and not seriously questioned today Some businesses enjoy *special services*. These are discernible special benefits, such as those insurance companies receive (perhaps) as a result of government regulation Businesses also participate in *general services* through the favorable environment provided by government Justification for business taxation may exist in terms of *social costs*. Many problems of society and government undoubtedly arise from the fact that business is carried on and, moreover, that it is carried on in corporate units. The *ability-to-pay* argument has already been discussed It is admitted that business taxes may be shifted to the consumer but it is contended that the consumer should expect to pay, in part at least, for government as for other factors of production This is termed the *general welfare* justification. A *social expediency* justification is derived from the revenue-producing possibilities in a

Integration of Federal Corporate and Personal Taxes

These views are not accepted by all public-finance writers. Some find no logical excuse for the corporate levy and see only duplication, confusion, and discrimination in the combination of a federal corporate income tax and taxation of dividends to stockholders.[1] Business entities as such have no taxpaying significance; they are only associations of individuals.

Analyzing briefly the "theoretical" aspect of business taxation we may observe, first, that most benefits of government are provided in the common interest and are not subject to apportionment. The benefit theory offers support for taxation in general, but it provides no satisfactory clue as to how taxes should be distributed. Relevant here is the conclusion of Edwin R. A. Seligman[2] that taxes are "compulsory contributions levied to defray the expenses incurred in the common interest, without any reference to particular advantages accruing to the taxpayer . . . ." Certainly, business could not thrive in the anarchy that would prevail without government, but neither could the wage earner, professional man, or any other citizen. "Business," says Adams, "ought to be taxed because it costs money to maintain a market and those costs should in some way be distributed over all the beneficiaries of that market."[3] The fallacy lies in the fact that everyone is a beneficiary of a well-maintained market and the relative benefits are indeterminate. There are cases of special benefits, to be sure, but these are usually financed by special assessments. In general, there is no calculus by which to determine what proportion of either the cost or the benefit of government can be justly attributed to each taxpayer. It is impossible to say in what degree various taxpayers benefit from a battleship.

---

business-tax system Finally, business taxation affords government a convenient means of *social control*.

[1] Roswell Magill, *The Impact of Federal Taxes*, Columbia University Press, New York, 1943, Chap. IV.

[2] Edwin R. A. Seligman, *Essays in Taxation*, 10th ed , The Macmillan Company, New York, 1925, p 415.

[3] Adams, *op cit.*, p. 187.

Postwar Taxation and Economic Progress

In a sense, a business institution is an entity distinct from its owners. It can be conceived as an "organic unity," acting in a single capacity and receiving benefits from government in the course of this activity. But it is as logical to identify this entity with its wage earners, creditors, and customers as with its owners. In this conception, everyone "belongs" to many such entities. But everyone bears some part of the business-tax load also, for the incidence (final burden) of business levies is probably not confined to the owners. The amount each person does and should bear, however, cannot be definitely determined.

A personal tax considers the obligation of the taxpayer in the light of his duties as a citizen. A business tax approaches him in terms of "government as a factor of production." It is interesting that the factors of production—land, labor, capital, management, and government—are all, with the exception of the latter, employed voluntarily by the business man. The amount of government and the apportionment of its cost to business are determined by voting. However, in the voting process, business (directly at least) has a minority voice.

In the last analysis, all taxes come out of the income or capital (actual or potential) of individuals. Tax burdens cannot be borne by inanimate objects. Will division among individuals be more equitable or otherwise more desirable if business taxes are levied? This is the important question, and, in searching for the answer, one gets little guidance from a consideration of benefits.

Specific schemes of business taxation based upon the benefit theory are usually vulnerable to attack because they involve arbitrary classification. The corporate net-income tax takes no account of the fact that, whether or not they show a net profit, corporations enjoy the favorable environment created by government. A gross-income tax would therefore seem to be more in harmony with the theory. But a gross-income tax encounters a multitude of variables among corporations and many of these variables would have a bearing on benefit accounting. A business levy confined to corporations can hardly be supported in the name of benefits; yet if the tax is broadened to cover all business, how shall "business" be defined? Shall it include farmers? Professional people? Wage earners? "Coupon-clippers"? For all the guidance we get from the benefit theory, we might resolve the problem by taxing all individuals twice on their personal income, once for the benefits enjoyed in production and once for benefits enjoyed as consumers.

It is not at all clear that we *should* distribute federal taxes according to benefits even if we *could*. A case can be made for pricing governmental services according to the income level of the beneficiary rather than according to the value of the service. The benefit theory is widely applied and firmly entrenched in the tax systems of state and local governments, where circumstances allow less choice than that enjoyed by the federal government. (The latter has the greater power to borrow, is relatively free from threats of taxpayer migration, and need have little fear of unequal competition.) The federal government might well reject this method of tax apportionment even if it had a feasible means of applying it.

Corporations do receive a special privilege in the grant of the right to operate as limited-liability associations. This is the basis of numerous franchise taxes which now confuse and complicate the tax systems of many government units. Under modern general incorporation laws, however, this privilege is available for the asking. If competition were effective, the value of the privilege would be reduced to zero. It is true that competition is not that efficient, but corporate taxes make no pretense of measuring the results of monopolistic practices. Even if it is granted that the privilege of incorporation has some value, measuring this value in any given case is entirely a matter of guesswork. Moreover, the states, not the federal government, grant most corporations franchises. Incorporation laws differ greatly among the various states. For many years the special privileges granted corporations by New Jersey made that state the favorite for incorporation. Later, other states outdid New Jersey in offering attractive advantages to new companies; in recent years, Delaware has outdistanced all others in this competition. There may be some justification for taxing these special privileges, although it would have been better never to have indulged in this sort of rivalry. However, the federal government is not much involved in these special-privilege grants.

It is plausibly contended that business entities have ability to pay independent of that of their stockholders. Businesses do have one important ability in this respect—namely, the power to meet tax bills. And this ability is not identical in all businesses. Here again, when specific application is attempted, the weakness in this approach is apparent. For example, if ability to pay is to serve as the basis of a corporate income tax, can we properly ignore the ratio of earnings to capital invested? If the answer is negative, we are plunged into the realm of excess-profits taxation. Then the question arises: Can we accept the ratio of income to capital as a measure of ability without attention to the varying degree of risk involved in producing the income? Confronted by the obvious impracticability of making due allowance for risk, we return to the question of whether, since all taxes are finally borne by individuals, we gain anything from the standpoint of ability to pay by levying on individuals indirectly through business taxes.

Extended consideration cannot be given here to the use of business taxes for social control. The graduated corporate tax may, through its differentials, aid small business. Because of their importance in small communities and because of their possible value as a check upon monopoly, small companies have a claim for special attention. However, small business should not be confused with new business, competitive business, or business developing new products, all of which are proper objects of social concern. Moreover, the graduated

Integration of Federal Corporate and Personal Taxes

corporate tax aids not only small business but also large business with a small income. The tax on intercorporate dividends discourages holding companies and intercorporate investment, but it fails to distinguish between "good" and "bad" holding companies. There are, of course, other ways of aiding small business and policing holding companies Corporate taxation has been supported on the ground that it checks concentration of control by preventing corporations from becoming too large, but there is no convincing evidence that the tax has been at all successful in this role. The conclusion is that taxation of corporate income is not sufficiently discriminating or otherwise valuable for social control to warrant its retention for this reason alone.

INCIDENCE OF THE CORPORATE INCOME TAX

The view that the incidence, or final burden, of the corporate income tax falls on the stockholders is widely held and is claimed to be in accord with "the dictates of common sense." But many business men and a considerable number of theorists disagree, holding that the tax is shifted, at least in part, and that a reduction in the tax would mean a fall in prices. A few go so far as to call the levy "a sales tax in disguise." Others hold that wages are also affected by the tax.

No useful purpose would be served by reviewing in detail either the intricate theory involved in this question of incidence or the "polls of opinion" that have been taken concerning the proper answer. The prevailing view is that prices are set at a level which will cover or nearly cover the cost of production for marginal concerns or marginal output, the least profitable portion of the supply needed to meet the demand at these prices. Corporate income taxes, as contrasted with many other taxes (such as excises and property taxes), are not paid by these marginal concerns, considered to be the strategic element in price determination. Therefore, the conclusion is drawn that corporate taxes have no effect on prices.[1]

[1] See note on Incidence of Corporate Income Tax, pp 37–39.

Postwar Taxation and Economic Progress

This analysis is far from universally accepted as conclusive, however. When the dynamic aspect of the economy is included in the analysis, different conclusions can be reached. Although many concerns do carry on production without profit most of the time, it is logical to assume that the possibility of realizing positive profits some of the time is an incentive to remain in business. Were it not for this possibility, these firms might discontinue operations. It is reasonable to argue that price is determined by all the producers rather than by the marginal producers alone, and that a tax which is a cost only for the profitable portion of the supply does affect prices. In other words, some positive profit is a social cost of doing business. The distinction often drawn between necessary and surplus profits follows this view.

The corporate net-income tax applies to items of imputed rent and interest—items deductible as costs when management employs these factors on a contractual basis. Thus the tax does reach certain costs as well as surplus.

Suffice it to say that no definite conclusion as to the incidence of the corporate income tax is possible and that not improbably the burden is divided between at least stockholders and consumers.

One of the weakest spots in the armor of business taxes is the obscurity of their incidence. This is less true of the corporate net income than of other business levies but, as explained above, there is much doubt as to the final distribution of burden even in the case of levies on net business income. When the ultimate bearers of the burden and the degree of their participation are indeterminable, it is hardly possible to appraise a tax. If neither the benefits for which compensation is sought nor the ultimate burden of the tax is discernible, the principal characteristic of the levy would seem to be the thick cloud of confusion hanging over it.

The incidence of the corporate income tax is either on the stockholders or on some other element involved in the economic process, possibly wage earners, though more probably

Integration of Federal Corporate and Personal Taxes

consumers. If it falls on wage earners or consumers, there can be no particular logic or equity in the tax, and "happenstance" will determine the division. If the burden is on the stockholders, not only are they being taxed twice, but the division among them is certain to be prejudicial to small stockholders. The fallacy of the corporate tax arises from treating corporations as though they were persons and as though it were possible for corporate entities to bear taxes in their own right.

It is one thing to argue incidence theory in the abstract and another to consider what would happen in 1946, under existing institutions, were the 40 per cent corporate income tax eliminated or substantially reduced. The reduction would occur at a time when profits and wages were tending to fall and prices tending to rise. Particularly if the reduction in tax were gradual it might ease the transition from war to peace. More specifically, the effects of reducing or eliminating the tax might include one or more of the following:

1. A reduction of prices or the foregoing of price increases. Competition for markets might dictate this policy.

2. Expansion. Available funds might be used for new plant and equipment.

3. Increased dividends or the avoidance of a reduction in dividends.

4. An increase in wages. The earnings of labor, as a result of the elimination of overtime and reclassification of workers, will tend to fall after the war. Earnings can be maintained only if there is an increase in prices or a reduction in corporate costs (including taxes). Labor, through collective bargaining, is in a position to exert pressure to maintain standards.

The change might also increase or sustain the value of stocks and the salaries of management.

Whether a monopolistic business would be more or less prone than a competitive one to convert reduced taxes to dividends is not at all clear. There may be many factors,

Postwar Taxation and Economic Progress

political as well as economic, that affect monopoly price. In general, overtaxing competitive business on the off-chance of catching some monopoly profits is not a very enlightened policy.

EFFECTS OF THE CORPORATE TAX UPON INCENTIVES

As previously stated, the common conclusion that the corporate tax is borne by stockholders involves the corollary that two taxes are imposed on the profit element in income, whereas only one is imposed on most other income. The combination of a corporate tax and the full personal tax on dividends places a special penalty upon risk-taking. The results of this double burden at slightly lower than present top rates and at the margin of income can be seen in Table I.

TABLE I
The Effect on Investment Yields of a Profits Tax of 80 Per Cent and a Personal Income Tax of 90 Per Cent at Their Maximum Effectiveness*
(Yield expressed as per cent of corporate investment)

Corporate profits yield before taxes, per cent	Corporate profits yield after taxes, per cent	Net yield to individual after individual taxes, per cent
10	2	0.2
25	5	0.5
50	10	1.0
100	20	2.0
200	40	4.0

* Rates assumed are slightly lower than the maximum provided in the present federal law (Act of 1944)

There is reason to believe that decisions concerning production and expansion are influenced more by management's solicitude for the company's earning record than by hope of a high return for investors. Managers are extremely and sometimes irrationally interested in the growth of their companies; much of the satisfaction derived from business activity is linked with the standing of the company and not with the size of the

Integration of Federal Corporate and Personal Taxes

return to stockholders. To relieve the tax system of repressive effects, first attention should go to the active business man as such; less concern is required for the passive investor. Of course, businesses must have capital, and venturesome enterprises will encounter a scarcity of funds if the rewards to investors are too limited. But management can often acquire the means as well as the incentive to expand from the earnings of the business unit. The company's success, with which management identifies personal success, is measured first by corporate net earnings, next by dividends, and least of all by dividends net of personal tax.

It is said that no proof has been offered that the corporate tax is repressive. It should be evident enough, however, that a double load of taxes on enterprise income, while other income bears only one such load, imposes a special penalty at a particularly strategic spot in the economic process.

BOND VERSUS STOCK FINANCING

The duplication of taxes, discussed above, applies only to investment in stocks. A dollar of income earmarked for the bondholder is paid to him in full, but the profit dollar earmarked for the stockholder is, in effect, cut to only 60 cents. This encourages corporations to issue bonds instead of stock.

That the present discrimination is substantial and that it does, in many cases, exercise an unfortunate influence upon corporate and individual decisions is confirmed by accountants and others close to corporate financing. Obviously, if a company pays out to bondholders half its net income (before federal taxes and the payment of interest), it can save half the corporate tax that would be due were the company to finance itself exclusively with stock. The higher the effective rate of the corporate tax, the greater the saving. With a 40 per cent effective tax rate and average earnings of 5 per cent on capital and with a distribution of half of the net operating income to bondholders, the saving would amount to 1 per cent on the capital (5 per cent $\times$ 50 per cent $\times$ 40 per cent = 1 per cent).[1] A 1 per cent saving annually is certainly worth considering.[2]

Some quantitative evidence concerning the effect of the corporate income tax on stock and bond financing was submitted by J. Keith Butters in his study, *Federal Taxation of Corporate Profits*.[3] Mr. Butters considered the discriminatory effect of the corporate income tax on a small sample of retail trade and iron and steel manufacturing companies for the period 1929 to 1937. The data were taken from the published accounts of these companies. The results were stated in terms of "reduction in tax bill expressed as a percentage of income taxes which would have been assessed if 'interest on funded indebtedness' were taxable income." The results showed a saving ranging, for the retail companies, from zero to 55.60 per cent and, for the iron and steel concerns, from zero to 56 62 per cent.[4] For the majority of companies, the saving was under 20 per cent, but there were a substantial number of conspicuous exceptions. The case of the Woodward Iron Company was submitted[5] as an extreme example. In this instance, the company experienced a net deficit for the period and had an effective corporate income-tax rate of about 78 per cent and a tax reduction of about 57 per cent "upon the assumption that 'interest on funded debt' was taxable and that the statutory rate was 21 per cent." No account was

---

[1] However, in some cases part of the tax saved as a result of bond financing is recovered through increased individual taxes, owing to the distribution by the company of earnings otherwise taken from the corporation as taxes.

[2] Of course, the availability of this avoidance device will depend a great deal on the marketability of bonds. The use of funded debt has always been more prevalent among utility and transportation companies than among other concerns. It is also more feasible for large companies than for small ones. Closely held corporations might use indebtedness rather freely to replace stock financing, although fixed obligations would require at least a partial distribution of earnings which would result in a partial loss of the avoidance that might be had through reinvestment of corporate earnings.

[3] J Keith Butters, *Federal Taxation of Corporate Profits*, doctoral dissertation, Harvard University, 1941.

[4] *Ibid.*, p. 190.

[5] *Ibid.*, p. 192

taken of the increase in personal taxes resulting from increased personal income through the avoidance of the corporate tax. The evidence convinced the author that at least "the discrimination is quantitatively significant for some individual firms."[1]

A recent study of corporate financial structure concluded that in 1937, for all nonfinancial companies, long-term debt amounted to 56 per cent of the outstanding capital stock. The proportion was much the highest for railroads and public utilities, but even for manufacturing it amounted to 19 per cent.[2]

The undesirable effects of excessive bond financing have been described as follows:[3]

> Heavy fixed (or floating) debt is obviously undesirable for the single enterprise in an unstable economy or industry. Any temporary adversity is likely to produce insolvency, with grave losses, not only for the stockholder but also for senior securities and the enterprise as a whole, through the great costs of reorganization and the inevitable disturbances of operations and business relations which insolvency involves. Moreover, even if technical insolvency and

---

[1] Most people assume that interest paid has always been fully deductible in arriving at the federal income-tax base, but this is not true. Limits were placed on the deductibility of interest in the early corporate income-tax statutes. The corporate excise-tax statute of 1909 allowed the deduction of bond interest only on an amount of bonds not in excess of paid-up capital stock. (Act of Aug. 5, 1909, Sec. 38, 36 Stats. 113. Roy G. and Gladys C. Blakey, *The Federal Income Tax*, Longmans, Green and Company, New York, 1940, p 53.) The 1913 law contained a similar provision, limiting the interest deduction to the interest-bearing securities not in excess of half the sum of these securities and the paid-up capital stock. [Act of Oct. 3, 1913, Sec II $G(b)$, 38 Stats 173.] The provision was somewhat liberalized in 1916 [Revenue Act of 1916, Sec. 12 (a), 39 Stats. 768] and the limitation was abandoned in 1918 [Revenue Act of 1918, Sec 234 (2), 40 Stats 1077.] This was justified on the ground that the excess-profits tax removed the advantages of undercapitalization. The issue was not reopened when the excess-profits tax was dropped. The 1936 Act bore indirectly upon the issue by providing that dividends on stock could no longer be excluded from the normal personal tax base.

[2] Walter A. Chudson, *The Pattern of Corporate Financial Structure*, National Bureau of Economic Research, New York, 1945, p. 102.

[3] Henry C. Simons, in a memorandum submitted to the author.

reorganization are avoided, the enterprise and the whole economy may gravely be damaged by the practices necessary in avoiding it. Thus, physical properties may be abused merely to prolong technical, legal solvency, to avoid definitive squeezing out of shareholders, management, or "control" in bankruptcy or reorganization, and thus to gamble (with nothing to lose!) on remotely favorable contingencies. The physical plant may thus be "bled white" to meet current obligations, especially interest payment and bond maturities, in the pursuit of mere liquidity.

These things are doubtless widely understood What is less clearly apprehended is the aggravated instability of the whole economy, and the obstacle to deliberate monetary stabilization, which corporate debt structures produce in their aggregate It should be obvious what desperate and frantic struggles for corporate liquidity mean in total where the economy has slipped into general recession which, debt structures apart, might prove innocuous and short-lived. They may well mean the difference between a mild recession and a precipitous, catastrophic deflation.

There is some support for the view that it is undesirable to use the credit relationship in business transactions otherwise than to facilitate current operations. According to this view, business should operate without long-term dollar loan contracts and avoid the dangers of insolvency and speculation in the value of money which such contracts entail. It is probably wise to conclude that resources may be employed on either a contractual or a contingent basis and that both forms of employment are necessary but the former tends to be overdone.

The Securities and Exchange Commission and the state utility commissions call constantly for a reduction in bonded debt, but they are shouted down by a tax system that has exactly the opposite bias.

The discrimination that favors bond financing could be removed by taxing the operating income of corporations (including the bond interest) instead of the net income. This alleged solution is supported by many competent critics who maintain that the distinction between stock and debtor capital is not one that should be recognized by the tax system. In the development of the large quasi-public corporation, the distinction between creditors and stockholders has become blurred and that between bondholders and preferred stockholders has largely disappeared. However, a tax on net operating income could and would force some concerns into bankruptcy. On the other hand, since part of the income tax would fall on an element of cost as distinguished from final profit, part of the tax could be more easily shifted to the consumer. Moreover, if net operating income were to become the base of the tax, should not rent paid as well as interest paid be disallowed as a deduction? And why stop with rent paid? Why not disallow the deduction of all expenses and have a gross income tax?

Another objection to the taxation of operating income is that the transition to such a basis would involve many difficulties. Since much financing is on a long-term basis, this transition would need to be gradual and, even so, adjustments might disturb the financial and business structure.

A more sensible approach to the problem of eliminating the discrimination between stock and bond financing would be to move in the opposite direction—*i.e.*, to allow a credit against either the corporate or the personal tax for the element of duplication. This would mean that whether the corporation were financed with stocks or bonds, its earnings would be subject to only one tax.

EQUITY OF THE CORPORATE TAX

It has been shown that the duplication of personal and corporate taxes rests with special weight upon the profit and dividend element in income. Since dividends tend to be concentrated in the higher income brackets, the steeply graduated personal tax places on profits an average tax burden in excess of that on other income elements. This is justified as a necessary antidote for concentration in income distribution, but a question may be raised whether the progression should be compounded by doubling up the corporate and individual taxes.

The corporate income tax is as unsatisfactory to those whose principal interest is in the fairness of the tax system as to those whose first concern is for incentives. As we have seen, an unknown but probably considerable part of this tax becomes an element in prices and is paid by consumers in haphazard amounts and proportions. Moreover, the tax is necessarily impersonal in character and makes no differentiation among stockholders according to income status. The small stockholder, sometimes mainly dependent upon a small income from stocks, is subjected to the same treatment as the wealthy investor. It would be better for all concerned were all income to run the gantlet of the tax system only once and at the personal level. Here it could be taxed as severely as the needs of government and the interest in equalizing income distribution might require.

Some justification for corporate income taxation might be based on the fact that corporations often reinvest a considerable portion of their earnings and that this income might escape the tax system entirely were it not for the corporate tax. The problem of taxing undistributed earnings under the income tax, one of the most difficult in the field of taxation, will be considered shortly. It should be observed, however, that the present system, levying two taxes on the distributed portion of earnings and one undifferentiated impersonal tax on the undistributed portion, is an exceedingly crude and unsatisfactory solution of the problem.

OTHER CONSIDERATIONS

Business taxation has been advocated by some as a necessity for adequate revenue. This point will be examined in more detail later. The fiscal necessity of business taxes is not at all established. In spite of heavy governmental costs, the British managed without an independent business tax

Integration of Federal Corporate and Personal Taxes

until 1937 and employed it thereafter only at the nominal rate of 5 per cent.

Duplication of corporate and personal taxes at the state level (where it often but by no means universally occurs) is less difficult to defend than at the federal level. In state tax systems, the corporate levy reaches the net income of absentee investors, and the inclusion of dividends in the individual tax base is necessary for the fair application of the personal tax. This problem will be considered in a later chapter.

CONCLUSION

These considerations lead to the conclusion that there is little, if any, rational basis for an independent corporate income tax; that its incidence is uncertain and confusing; that its effects are discriminatory and probably repressive. The strongest case for it rests on the ground that it yields well and that certain possible substitutes are worse. If for administrative and political reasons the tax system cannot be entirely rationalized, a capricious tax on stockholders may be less undesirable than a capricious tax on consumers. Leaving the question of priorities among irrational and otherwise undesirable sources for later discussion, we may conclude that corporate and personal taxes should be entirely (or at least largely) integrated. It must be recognized, however, that any integration program runs head on into the tax treatment of undistributed profits, a problem to which we now turn our attention.

NOTE ON INCIDENCE OF CORPORATE INCOME TAX: The National Industrial Conference Board completed an extensive statistical survey of corporate profits in 1928. The objective was to throw light upon the incidence of the federal corporate income tax. (National Industrial Conference Board, *The Shifting and Effects of the Federal Corporation Income Tax*, New York, 1928, Vol. 1.) The records of 4,644 corporations, covering the years 1918 to 1925 inclusive, were secured from the files of the United States Treasury Department. The industries represented were manufacturing, retail and wholesale trades, and coal mining The sample included all corporations reporting a net income of $100,000 or more, from 1919 to 1928 inclusive, and having records for all the years from and including 1918. It represented the larger and more successful corporations in each industry.

The significant observation emerging from the study was that a large part of production and sales occurs at the margin of little or no profit. In each year from 1918 to 1925, the largest volume of sales was made at a low profit and an increasingly smaller volume was made at successively higher rates of profit or at a loss. In general, the highest rate of turnover of capital was concentrated at the no-profit margin on sales This provides some evidence of the dominating influence of marginal producers or production in the market No tendency toward the maintenance of a normal rate of return on capital was observed. Production was continued to the no-profit point and, in many instances, it was continued even at a loss in order to retain the market. The conclusion was drawn that, since the federal income tax and the excess-profits tax are levied on net income, they cannot affect the greater portion of the supply by raising costs or reducing profits and thus cannot greatly curtail the total supply, thereby raising prices.

A second statistical study of the shifting and incidence of the income tax was made by W. H. Coates for the Colwyn Committee on Debt and Taxation (*Report of the Committee on National Debt and Taxation*, H.M. Stationery Office, London, 1927, pp. 108–119). In addition to showing that much production is carried on at the no-profit level, the report made a comparison between prewar and postwar profits. In spite of rising taxes, no evidence of a rise in the rate of profit on turnover was found. However, a comparison of this kind can hardly isolate the effect of the tax factor among others, particularly when, as in this case, the prewar and postwar years selected for comparison were in different phases of the business cycle. Some evidence presented indicates the extent to which industries shift among the profit, no-profit, and loss groups. This evidence supports Marshall's doctrine that the least efficient producers are no more "marginal" than any other producers in regard to the determination of price. However, the Committee arrived at the conclusion that "in a free competitive market, with ample supplies in relation to demand, price at any time is measured by the cost of production to the marginal producer." (*Ibid.*, p. 114)

Although Professor Edwin R. A. Seligman, in his analysis of incidence theory, concluded that business profits do not represent an item in production costs but a surplus over costs, he nevertheless conceded that "the continual growth of a country's prosperity depends largely on the readiness of the able and the venturesome to start new enterprises and to take the risk of the unknown Where the hazard is great, the profits must be correspondingly great; for, in the long run, in new and untried fields the profits of some are likely to be counterbalanced by the losses of others. If the government, however, demands too large a percentage of these anticipated profits, the individual may prefer not to subject himself to the risk and may decide to be content with a smaller but a surer return " (Edwin R. A Seligman, "Income Taxes and the Price Level," *Academy of Political Science Proceedings*, 1926, Vol II, pp. 19–20)

According to Marshall's concept of the normal supply, it is the representative firm, not the marginal or the superior firm, that determines the normal supply price. (Alfred Marshall, *Principles of Economics*, 7th ed , Macmillan & Com-

Integration of Federal Corporate and Personal Taxes

pany, Ltd., London, 1916, p. 317. See also Dennis H. Robertson, *Economic Fragments*, P S. King & Son, Ltd , London, 1931, pp 23–41.) The representative firm is the one "which has a fairly long life, and fair success, which is managed with normal ability, and which has normal access to the economies, external and internal, which belong to that aggregate volume of production. . . . " (Marshall, *op cit.*, p 317.)

The normal supply price must include, in addition to the expenses of operation, "interest and insurance on all the capital" and "the gross earnings of management (including insurance against loss) by those who undertake the risks, who engineer and superintend the working." (*Ibid* , p. 343.) The output of the marginal firms, as well as the superior ones, is a factor in the determination of price, but there is no special or exclusive relation between price and the costs of the least efficient producers. There are always some firms that have valid economic reasons for carrying on production at a subnormal profit or even at a loss. For example, a firm may be attempting to secure a large share of the market or operating on the supposition that eventually maximum profits will be realized by a narrow margin on a large turnover. According to this analysis, price is not set by the marginal producers but is set at the margin by the representative producers.

It is generally conceded that taxes are more easily shifted in some phases of the business cycle than in others and that it is especially easy to shift such burdens in a sellers' market when demand is particularly inelastic. Under such circumstances, the imposition of a tax on profits may well afford an excuse for raising the price still higher.

It is also conceded that the shifting of taxes may require time. It is extremely doubtful that, over a long period, the British system of integrated income taxes has resulted in any higher margin of profit than the system employed in the United States.

It is also possible that, insofar as the corporate tax rests upon the stockholder, it may be diffused to some extent among all investors. A special tax impediment on one line of investment tends to check the flow of capital in that direction, resulting in higher rewards to investment there; the increased supply of funds in other fields reduces the rewards to those investments.

III. INTEGRATION AND THE TREATMENT OF UNDISTRIBUTED PROFITS

THE CAUSE FOR ACTION: TAX DISCRIMINATION

DISINTERESTED writers are generally agreed that the present tax treatment of undistributed corporate earnings is unsatisfactory. The present system applies two taxes to income that passes through the corporation and one to income that is reinvested by the company. It allows an individual to become indefinitely rich for an indefinite period without paying any personal-income tax. To be sure, the tax system may "catch up" with such an individual through the taxation of realized capital gains or through application of the death tax to his estate, but the realization of capital gains can be postponed as long as stock continues to be owned by the same stockholder. It may be further postponed as long as the stock is retained by the heirs of the original owner or the heirs of the heirs, and so on.[1] The death tax is only a delayed and partial compensation for privileges enjoyed in the application of the tax system during the life of the deceased. Thus a strong case in terms of equity can be made for a relatively more rigorous application of the tax system to undistributed profits. In addition, the apparent necessity for at least one levy on undistributed earnings has been used to justify the unfortunate duplication of corporate and personal levies.

Some consider it wrong to include savings in the base of an

[1] Moreover, as the law is presently applied, the basis for the gain in the hands of an heir is not the basis of the decedent, nor is the basis for a donee necessarily that of the donor. In the first instance, the value at the time of the death transfer serves as the new basis; in the second, the basis used is that in the hands of the donor in the case of a gain and the donor's basis or the value at the time of the transfer, whichever is lower, in the case of a loss.

Integration and the Treatment of Undistributed Profits

income tax.[1] The theoretical case for this view need not be discussed here.[2] As a practical matter, the full exclusion of savings from the personal-income-tax base has never been seriously entertained either in this or any other important country. "It would undoubtedly be very difficult to convince the public that a man who spends his money on the education of his children sacrifices less and has greater ability to pay when he is called upon to support the government than the bachelor who puts his money into bonds."[2] It is also a well-known fact that savings are largely concentrated in the higher ranges of income. To exclude savings from the personal tax base would seriously impair the effectiveness of the tax in mitigating extreme inequality of incomes. The most realistic concept of income regards it as an accretion to economic power, and this is hardly compatible with the view that savings can be ignored in income taxation

The view that equity requires consideration of undistributed corporate earnings in the personal-income tax was supported by the Committee of the National Tax Association on Federal Taxation of Corporations as follows:[3]

The pressure for revenue means, for one thing, that the personal income tax must be fully exploited and, under the definition of personal income that appears to commend itself to the conscience of the American people, it becomes necessary to make certain that stockholders in corporations which do not fully and promptly distribute their earnings in the form of dividends may not be favored at the expense of other taxpayers.

* * * *

Obviously . . . the personal tax will not be equitable and just if the tax base is so defined as to exclude elements of income that are

---

[1] See Irving Fisher, "Income in Theory and Income Taxation in Practice," *Econometrica*, Vol V (January, 1937)

[2] See Harold M. Groves, *Financing Government*, rev. ed , Henry Holt and Company, Inc., New York, 1945, p. 165.

[3] *Final Report of the Committee of the National Tax Association on Federal Taxation of Corporations*, pp. 6, 8, 9.

substantial and significant factors in the individual's ability to assume a share of the burden of government

* * * *

The savings in question are, in the first instance, of course, the savings of an artificial person known as a corporation. Fundamentally, however, the savings of a corporation are the savings of the individuals who own the corporation.

THE CAUSE FOR ACTION: TAX AVOIDANCE

The present treatment of undistributed corporate income is also objectionable as an open invitation to tax avoidance. Why should corporations declare dividends beyond the consumption needs of their stockholders, when to do so involves much heavier taxes than if management were to do the investing for them?

Various devices have been introduced into the tax laws to check this obvious leakage. Since the inauguration of the federal tax, the possibility of using a corporation as a "savings bank" to avoid personal-income surtaxes has been recognized. Special taxes have been designed to prevent the practice. The acts which were passed prior to 1921 did not attempt to attack the problem through the corporation itself but rather chose to strike directly at the stockholders. This was done by taxing the stockholders (of companies improperly accumulating surplus) on their respective prorata shares of the corporation's earnings. In 1920, however, the Supreme Court decision in *Eisner v. Macomber*[1] raised some doubt as to the constitutionality of this method. The 1921 Act and subsequent acts have imposed "penalty tax rates" for improper accumulation directly on the corporation.

The problem of protecting the revenue without thwarting legitimate corporate expansion is a delicate one. Section 102 of the revenue law, considerably strengthened by the 1938 Act, makes accumulation of surplus beyond the reasonable needs of the business the equivalent of tax avoidance unless the corporation, by a clear preponderance of the evidence,

[1] 252 U.S. 189 (1920).

Integration and the Treatment of Undistributed Profits

proves the contrary. Investment in assets having no reasonable connection with the business is usually ground for applying Sec. 102 of the law. But it is generally recognized that this feature of the revenue law is feeble.[1] Corporate reinvestment is typically the result of mixed motives, and a plausible defense for it is usually not difficult to discover.[2] Logically, avoidance attends all corporate reinvestment regardless of how legitimate it may be. From the standpoint of all parties concerned, the uncertainties connected with this whole procedure are thoroughly bad. Moreover, the administration of Sec. 102 may interfere with legitimate attempts to develop liquid corporate reserves.[3]

---

[1] The reaction of one competent critic to the experience with this feature of the law is as follows. "Through most of our history this approach has just been a farce and beginning in 1938 it began to be an unmitigated nuisance." At one time, the Packard Motor Company had a $14,400,000 investment in government bonds. There was nothing improper in this, and the liquid reserve enabled the company to weather adversity and to maintain its financial and operating strength while shifting production to low-priced cars

[2] The following account of Treasury policy in the administration of Sec. 102 is taken from the National Industrial Conference Board's "Effect of Taxes on Corporate Policy," pp 47–48:

"Treasury Decision Number 4914 directs examining agents of the Bureau of Internal Revenue to give particular attention to the following classes of corporations and to report a recommendation as to whether Section 102 tax should apply:

1. Corporations which have not distributed at least 70% of their earnings as taxable dividends.
2. Corporations which have invested earnings in securities or other properties unrelated to their normal business activities
3. Corporations which have advanced sums to officers or shareholders in the form of loans out of undistributed profits or surplus from which taxable dividends might have been declared.
4. Corporations, a majority of whose stock is held by a family group or other small group of individuals, or by a trust or trusts for the benefit of such groups.
5. Corporations, the distributions of which, while exceeding 70% of their earnings, appear to be inadequate when considered in connection with the nature of the business or the financial position of the corporation or corporations with accumulations of cash or other quick assets which appear to be beyond the reasonable needs of the business"

[3] The attempt to apply penalty rates of tax is irrational and oppressive on small stockholders. The procedure followed before 1918 was much better and

Postwar Taxation and Economic Progress

Another means of preventing improper accumulation of reinvested funds is by the creation of a separate tax classification for companies designated as "personal holding companies." This practice was inaugurated in 1934 and has been continued in later acts. The classification includes closely held companies engaged principally in the investment business. These concerns are subject to a special and severe corporate tax. In contrast with Sec. 102, liability is a matter of objective fact rather than of motivation. Early laws contained loopholes, such as the exclusion of rent, in determining the portion of the business to be classed as "investment." These loopholes were plugged in later legislation. However, the line between "personal holding companies" and "near-personal holding companies" is necessarily arbitrary. An improvement (applying both to holding companies and concerns subject to Sec. 102 penalties) could be made in this field by requiring that the stockholders be taxed on their prorata share of undistributed income (as is now the case with foreign personal holding companies). This would avoid pressure to distribute earnings and would apply tax burdens most equitably among stockholders. The option of using the prorata method should be open to all concerns at all times.

THE VOLUME OF CORPORATE SAVING

The volume of corporate saving has never been precisely measured and it varies with changing business conditions. Available evidence indicates that corporate saving amounts to some 25 per cent of total saving, that about 50 per cent of new equity capital for corporations comes from this source,

---

that of Canada is still better. The Canadian system provides that if, in the judgment of the Minister of National Revenue, the accumulation is unreasonable, he may notify the corporation to that effect and may designate the amount he deems excessive If this amount is not distributed during the year in which the notice is given, the shareholders are presumed to have received it as a dividend on the last day of the tax year, and are taxed accordingly. [Harry J. Rudick, "Section 102 and the Personal Holding Company Provisions of the Internal Revenue Code," 49 *Yale Law Journal* 171 (1939). See also *Canadian Income War Tax Act*, Part IV, Chap. 97, Sec. 13, Revised Statutes (1927).]

Integration and the Treatment of Undistributed Profits

and that corporations ordinarily reinvest from 25 to 40 per cent of their earnings in new plant and equipment.[1] The figures are for gross saving or reinvested earnings and take no account of corporate losses. If net saving is considered, the figure for corporations is not infrequently negative, as was the case during several depression years of the thirties. Even disregarding losses, corporations paid out more than they earned during some of these years.

Most companies depend considerably upon internal sources for their capital, though the contention that expansion of assets is financed to an increasing extent by this means is not established. Large companies rely heavily upon depreciation and obsolescence allowances and reserves. Small and growing companies depend primarily upon reinvested earnings. These small concerns find the issuance of new securities difficult and expensive and depreciation reserves insufficient.[2]

It is customary to use the Ford Motor Company as a conspicuous example of a concern built largely by plowing back

[1] J. E Amos, *The Economics of Corporate Saving*, Illinois Studies in the Social Sciences, Vol. XXII, University of Illinois Press, Urbana, 1937, Chap. III, Alfred G. Buehler, *The Undistributed Profits Tax*, McGraw-Hill Book Company, Inc, New York, 1937, Chap. IV; *Statistics of Income*, 1933–1941, U S. Treasury Department.

[2] Testimony at Temporary National Economic Committee hearings brought out the facts that, up to the time of the hearings, the U S Steel Corporation, during 19 years of experience, had relied on the market for $148 million of new and replacement capital and had obtained $937 million from depreciation and depletion allowances and $191 million from earnings. ("Savings and Investment," *Hearings before the Temporary National Economic Committee*, Vol. 64, Part 9, 75th Congress, 1939, p. 3590) General Electric had been financed entirely from internal sources since 1920. (*Ibid* , p. 3620.) During 18 years, the General Motors Company had retained $490 million from earnings and $520 million from depreciation reserves. (*Ibid.*, p. 3651.) "All manufacturing corporations in the United States which reported a net income, retained a total of $5 6 billion profit in the three years, 1927, 1928, and 1929. They increased their common stock by $1.8 billion during the same three years." (*Final Report of the Committee of the National Tax Association on Federal Taxation of Corporations*, Reprint, p 9, *Proceedings*, 1939, p. 540) Of the industrial groups, manufacturing, trade, and finance rely most heavily upon reinvestment; public utilities, considerably less. See also Albert Koch, *The Financing of Large Corporations*, National Bureau of Economic Research, 1943.

its earnings. One authority concludes from the meager evidence available that the Ford Company paid out in dividends only $100 million over a 23-year period, during which the corporation's profits amounted to $924 million.[1] Another study places the intangible invested capital of the company at $694 million dollars in 1926, of which all except $40,000 was provided by reinvestment of profits.[2]

SOCIAL AND ECONOMIC EFFECTS OF CORPORATE SAVING

The social and economic effects of corporate saving is a broad subject and one that gives rise to controversy at many points. Only a brief inquiry into some of the issues involved can be attempted here. Opinion differs among students of corporate finance as to whether the present power of management to invest corporate earnings, subject to a relatively weak indirect control of the stockholder, is in the social interest.

Those opposed to corporate reinvestment of earnings argue that the temptation is strong for management to gain power and prestige with other people's money and that the present system is not conducive to the best allocation of resources. According to this view, the privilege of corporate reinvestment entrenches "the tyranny of the board of directors." It also deprives investment of the censorship of a free market, a censorship which helps ensure that new capital will be placed only in lines of business warranted by the economic prospects. It is said that the stockholder should have the prerogative of choosing the board of directors under which he wishes to invest. In reply it has been pointed out that many investors give inadequate weight in their decisions to the long-run interests of their company and particularly that they underrate the reserves needed for business stability. These reserves mitigate the business cycle because they enable corporations

---

[1] Edward S. Mead, *Corporation Finance*, rev ed, D. Appleton-Century Company, Inc., New York, 1933, p 343.

[2] L. Seltzer, *Financial History of the American Automobile Industry*, cited by Amos, *op. cit.*, footnote, p. 67.

to continue payments for wages, materials, taxes, dividends, and so forth, during bad times.

Critics contend that corporate savings aggravate a tendency toward overexpansion of productive equipment and that this creates depressions. A prominent authority has expressed the view that "production facilities of the country and of the world had been greatly overexpanded during the twenty years that preceded the depression of 1930. . . . It is certain that the overexpansion of fixed assets was due in no small measure to the disinclination of directors to relinquish earnings to stockholders."[1] However, although the evidence indicates that there was an excess of plant capacity in the late twenties (from 1925 to 1929 manufacturing plants were utilized at about 80 per cent of their estimated capacity),[2] the condition was by no means novel in the history of American industry. We cannot be certain that industrial growth, which in the past has quickly absorbed temporarily excessive capacity, will continue. But the contention is also made that even more investment is needed to provide full employment.[3]

Proponents of corporate saving argue that this source of capital constitutes an important means of business expansion and diversification and that favorable treatment is particularly important in the case of small and new companies to whom the capital market may be prohibitively expensive. For these companies, a new security issue may cost as much as 15 to 20 per cent of the proceeds. The majority of attempts

---

[1] Arthur S. Dewing, *Financial Policy of Corporations*, 3d ed., The Ronald Press Company, New York, 1934, pp. 616–617.

[2] Edwin G. Nourse and Associates, *America's Capacity to Produce*, Brookings Institution, Washington, D.C., 1934, p. 416.

[3] Writing in 1933, Rexford G. Tugwell (*The Industrial Discipline*, Columbia University Press, New York, 1933, p. 204) argued that corporate reinvestment tends to keep prices high because "unused plant and machinery are . . . an almost constant expense, and these 'overhead costs' are necessarily distributed over the whole product, not just part of it." On the other hand, it has been claimed that corporate reinvestment is our best protection against monopoly (also a cause of high prices) because it facilitates the growth of small companies and thus helps to maintain the number of competitors.

to finance with equity capital end in failure or partial failure.[1] To expect the small or even the average-sized company to rely on the investment market every year is fantastic. In almost every hearing on the problems of small business, the major topic has been the difficulty of obtaining capital. During the late thirties, the Reconstruction Finance Corporation and the Federal Reserve Banks were authorized to make so-called intermediary loans to business for covering capital needs. All corporations find it much simpler and cheaper to expand by the use of reinvested earnings than by the issuance of new securities.[2]

Most critics might accept the view that corporate savings are useful and should not be discouraged by the tax system. It is another matter, however, to say that preferred tax treatment is warranted. Except in the case of new small enterprises, where access to capital is extraordinarily limited,

[1] *Investment Trusts and Investment Companies*, Report of the Securities and Exchange Commission, Parts IV and V (1941), pp 344–345.

[2] Because special methods of integrating corporate and personal taxes have been applied in Great Britain, the comments concerning corporate saving, published by the British Committee on National Debt and Taxation (Colwyn Committee), should be of particular interest. The Committee observed (*Report of the Committee on National Debt and Taxation*, Cmd. 2800, H.M. Stationery Office, London, 1927, pp. 145–149):

"An exceedingly important part of national saving is undertaken by companies themselves. It is recognized as a rule of sound finance that a company should withhold some portion of current profits from distribution, putting the amount to reserve in order to strengthen and expand its business

* * * *

... when a company saves by retaining part of its profits, the operation is smooth and simple. In the case of a progressive business the flow of capital is just in the place where it is required, it is at the growing-point of industry, enabling new needs and opportunities to be met without delay as and when they arise. This is true of the new and enterprising business which may as yet be making only small profits, as well as of the established company whose ability to save for development year by year has given proof of efficiency and power of continued expansion. There are cases, of course, where reserves are accumulated out of caution rather than enterprise, and are invested, *e g.*, in the preference shares of outside concerns, but generally speaking, it is true that the Income Tax, when it falls upon company reserves, entrenches upon a form of saving which is of special value to the community."

Integration and the Treatment of Undistributed Profits

corporate savings would seem to have no convincing claim to preference over other saving (by unincorporated companies and individuals). A distinction might be drawn between savings and investment (corporate saving which is converted into plant and equipment, thus providing employment) and the latter might be given preferred treatment over savings held in cash or other liquid assets. But liquid reserves as a contributing factor to business stability are also desirable. On the whole, the safest rule to follow is that of equal treatment for all income, whether saved or invested and whether the disposition is by corporations or by others.

SURVEY OF UNDISTRIBUTED-PROFITS-TAX EXPERIENCE

For many years, business leaders have been told they would be well advised to accept an undistributed-profits tax in lieu of the duplication in corporate and individual levies and in lieu of excess-profits taxation. After the First World War, the undistributed-profits tax was proposed as a substitute for the excess-profits tax, but the latter was replaced instead by duplication in the personal and corporate levies.

In 1919, in an address before the American Economic Association, T. S. Adams put the case for the undistributed-profits tax as follows:[1]

> But it will not suffice merely to abolish the excess profits tax. Corporations, in order to be placed on something like an equality with individuals and partnerships, must bear an additional tax roughly equivalent to the surtax on undistributed profits paid by sole proprietors, the members of partnerships, and the stockholders of personal service corporations. This additional tax should apply only to undistributed profits

Similar views were expressed by Secretary of the Treasury Houston in 1920.[2]

[1] T. S. Adams, "Immediate Future of the Excess Profits Tax," *American Economic Review*, Vol X, Supplement (March, 1920), p. 16
[2] Secretary of Treasury, *Annual Report*, U S Government Printing Office, Washington, D.C., 1920, pp 33–43.

Postwar Taxation and Economic Progress

Many undistributed-profits tax proposals were advanced in Congress before the thirties but none received a favorable vote until 1936. The circumstances for the inauguration were not auspicious. New funds were required to finance a veterans' bonus that had been passed over the President's veto and to replace revenue lost when a Supreme Court decision invalidated the processing taxes used to support a promotional agricultural program. Thus, to critics of these governmental expenditures, the undistributed-profits tax "was conceived in sin." At least, it was inaugurated in an atmosphere highly charged with politics. The President advocated the tax to replace other levies on corporations, which would have been a step toward integration. But, partly because of a need for more revenue and partly because of uncertainty in Congress as to the fiscal effects of such an innovation, this advice was not followed. The result was an undistributed-profits tax superimposed upon the existing corporate levy and the declared-value excess-profits tax.

In brief, the 1936 law added a surtax on undistributed income, graduated according to the proportion of net income undistributed. The rates varied from 7 per cent of the portion of undistributed income representing less than 10 per cent of the net income to 27 per cent of that representing over 60 per cent of the entire net income. For corporations with net income of less than $50,000, the scale was somewhat tempered. The effect of this concession was to tax the first $5000 of retained income at the minimum rate of 7 per cent, regardless of what percentage of retained income this sum represented.

Some of the law's unpopularity was undoubtedly due to flaws in its drafting. Particularly annoying was the pressure to distribute earnings, under threat of taxation, in the case of corporations which had accumulated deficits from past operations and which were not allowed, under many state laws, to declare dividends. The absence of any carry-over provision for losses aggravated this grievance. The law did include a relief provision for companies having contracts restricting the

Integration and the Treatment of Undistributed Profits

payment of dividends, but the proviso was strictly interpreted and not often effective. The requirement that distribution be made before the end of the taxable year was unfortunate since corporations could not always determine that early what their net income would be. The law also brought into sharp focus the differences involved in taxable income, book income, and cash available for distribution. Inventory profits afforded an undistributed income-tax base but no money for distribution to stockholders. Provision of an untaxed bracket for a small percentage of income undistributed or allowance for an inventory reserve would have helped to avoid irritation at this point.[1]

[1] An interesting phase of the experience with the undistributed-profits tax of 1936 was that involving "paper distribution" of profits. Under the law, tax avoidance could be accomplished without loss of assets to the corporation by applying the personal tax to the stockholder's prorata share of company earnings. This might be accomplished by the declaration of certain kinds of stock or other security dividends or (in the 1938 Act) by the unanimous consent of stockholders to include their prorata share of company earnings in their personal returns. Except for closely held companies, this avoidance was confined as a practical matter to the first of these alternatives. By long-standing legal rule, "straight stock dividends" are not taxable to the recipient, but under the *Koshland v. Helvering* [298 U.S. 441 (1936)] decision, dividends which are not a "mere proliferation of existing interests" are subject to the personal tax. Thus, a dividend in preferred stock to common stockholders is usually taxable. Other taxable distributions include an optional dividend declared in cash which may be used to buy stock, or an optional dividend in stock which may be converted into cash ["The Corporate Undistributed Profits Tax," (Legislation) 36 *Columbia Law Review*, 1321-1354, 1329 (December, 1936)]; a dividend declared in rights to receive stock or bonds; dividends in treasury stock bought as an investment or stock of another company, dividends in notes, scrip, and debentures. The valuation of dividends in kind was either the face value or the market value, whichever was lower (Revenue Act of 1936, Sec. 27, 49 Stats, 1665); that of stock dividends, the fair market value.

The limitations in using such methods of distribution will be discussed later. Suffice it here to observe that distribution of obligations may merely postpone a day of reckoning, and stock dividends may be undesirable because they upset a simple capital structure. Only certain companies, usually the strong companies, are in the position to utilize these practices Although the use of "paper distribution" was undoubtedly encouraged by the Act, it did not become widespread Stock dividends accounted for 4 and 2.3 per cent of total dividends distributed in 1936 and 1937, respectively (Clifford J. Hynning and Gerhard Colm, *Taxation of Corporate Enterprise*, Temporary National Economic Com-

Postwar Taxation and Economic Progress

There is evidence that cash dividends were considerably increased by the act. A study of earnings and dividend payments for 42 corporations, made by *Business Week*,[1] indicates that dividends rose from 64.6 per cent of earnings in 1935 to 79.5 per cent in 1936, an increase of nearly 25 per cent. As for the relative distributions among corporations of different size, the study showed that 13, with net incomes of more than $20 million dollars each during 1936, paid out 82.1 per cent of their earnings; 29 companies, with net incomes under $20 million, paid out 73 per cent. However, dividend distribution varies with business conditions, and at least one study of the subject concluded that the undistributed-profits tax had no effect on dividends.[2] The rates upon undistributed income under the 1936 Act were not prohibitively high. That some corporations reinvested earnings in spite of the tax is indicated by the fact that the government collected about $145 million under the undistributed-income tax in 1936.[3] The act was really a compromise between compelling distribution and taxing undistributed earnings on a compensatory basis.

Some of the technical faults of the 1936 Act were corrected in 1938. Permission was given business to regard as dividends amounts used for, or set aside to pay, certain types of indebtedness. A one-year carry-over of losses was added and some modification in the method of calculating inventory profits was provided. However, the changes were not of much consequence in undistributed-profits taxation, for, while the act maintained the principle of the tax, it virtually

---

mittee Monograph No 9, 1941, p. 76). Of stock dividends, only 13.4 per cent were declared taxable in 1936 and 37 per cent in 1937 (*ibid* , p 76)

[1] *Business Week*, Apr 17, 1937, p 57.

[2] See Francis McIntyre, *Econometrica*, Vol. 7 (October, 1939), pp 336–348, for criticism see Harry G Guthmann, "The Effect of the Undistributed Profits Tax upon the Distribution of Corporate Earnings—A Note," *Econometrica*, Vol. 8 (October, 1940), pp 354–356, for reply see Francis McIntyre, "The Effects of the Undistributed Profits Tax—a Reply," *Econometrica*, Vol. 8 (October, 1940), pp. 357–360.

[3] *Statistics of Income for* 1936, U.S. Treasury Department, Bureau of Internal Revenue, Washington, D.C , 1939, Part 2, p. 6 (exact figure is $144,972,284).

Integration and the Treatment of Undistributed Profits

abolished the levy in practice by applying very low rates. The President allowed the act to become a law without his signature. The last vestige of the experiment was eliminated in 1939.

Probably the most appealing and also the most valid criticism of the 1936 Act was that it discriminated against small companies and thus had perverse economic effects. Not only are small companies objects of considerable sentimental attachment but they also provide potential competition in a system tending toward monopoly. The tax probably bore more heavily upon medium-sized than small corporations.[1] But it is clearly established that small and medium-sized corporations are dependent mainly upon reinvested earnings for the sinews of growth. In a debate on the tax, it was brought out that many large companies, such as the American Telephone and Telegraph Company, regularly pay out all or most of their earnings in dividends. Data prepared by W. L. Crum, showing a fairly consistent negative correlation between size of company and reinvestment of corporate earnings, follows:[2]

PERCENTAGE OF EARNINGS PAID AS DIVIDENDS BY INCOME CORPORATIONS, BY SIZE CLASSES

Size*	1931	1932	1933
0–49	41	54	31
50–99	49	61	29
100–249	56	60	33
250–499	62	63	33
500–999	67	65	38
1,000–4,999	71	70	46
5,000–9,999	78	78	53
10,000–49,999	81	82	69
50,000 and above	95	98	91
Total	83	86	67

* In terms of total assets, unit, $1000

[1] Hynning and Colm, *op. cit.*, pp. 78–82.
[2] W. L. Crum, *The Annalist*, May 1, 1936, pp 652–654. Compiled from *Statistics of Income*, 1931, 1932, 1933, U.S. Treasury Department.

In addition, opponents of the undistributed-profits tax argued that it restricted management's freedom in making business decisions concerning expansion solely on the basis of business considerations. It seemed to business men that a tax program which interfered with the policy of setting aside reserves—a policy preached by conservative business financiers, cooperative leaders, and corporation-finance textbooks for many years—was perverse in its intention or at least in its result. It went "against the grain" of traditions regarded as right and sound since Benjamin Franklin's time. The program was regarded as an attempt to reform dividend policy. A law that discouraged direct investment of funds seemed singularly inappropriate at a time when business was being urged to increase employment.

The failure of the economy to revive satisfactorily and the sudden downturn in 1937 were laid in part at the door of the undistributed-profits tax. The law—justifiably or not— became associated with the unbalanced budget, the "purchasing-power theory" of unemployment, the use of make-work and public investment to provide opportunity, and the whole controversial subject of economic planning. This was a far cry from the simple objective of improving the revenue system which had appealed to Adams. Even now it is difficult to convince business men that an undistributed-profits tax need have no ulterior purpose. At all events, in the atmosphere of insecurity and frustration which prevailed in the late thirties, the law, although stanchly defended, became extremely unpopular; it barely weathered the first revenue act after its enactment and it could not survive the second. Thus, the undistributed-profits tax was disposed of by repeal in 1939, but the problem it sought to solve still remains. "Congress merely retreated from this problem without solving it."[1]

[1] *Final Report of the Committee of the National Tax Association on Federal Taxation of Corporations*, p. 49, *Proceedings*, 1939, p. 579.

Integration and the Treatment of Undistributed Profits

ALTERNATIVE REMEDIES

Many modifications of the present treatment of undistributed earnings and the duplication of corporate and individual taxes have been proposed. Three of the most promising will be considered.

Treating Corporations like Partnerships

One solution to the problem of taxing undistributed earnings would require the paper distribution of such income or the assessment of stockholders upon their prorata shares of reinvested earnings. This has strong claim to support from the standpoint of equity. It would apply "proper" taxes to corporate saving without subsidy or penalty. It would free management from pressure to modify any dividend policy that seemed desirable for business needs alone. Corporations would be treated for tax purposes like associations of individuals, as is now the case with partnerships. This procedure has precedent in our Civil War income tax. In recent years it has also been applied to foreign personal holding companies and personal service corporations. However, the procedure involves administrative difficulties, especially in applying it to large corporations, and (as explained later) it jolts the popular conception of the relation of corporation to stockholder.

The legal feasibility of the partnership method in treating undistributed corporate income is open to some question, but there are probably no insuperable legal barriers to this solution of the problem. For 40 years or more, courts have repeatedly pointed out that for certain purposes the corporate entity must be disregarded in order to deal with the rights and responsibilities of the real persons involved. In the field of taxation, there has been a frequent shuffling back and forth from one position to the other in this matter. Persistent efforts to tax stock dividends as income are one symptom of the tendency to minimize the concept of a distinct corporate institution. The *Eisner v. Macomber* decision[1] stands for the separate entity view, but it was made over the protest of a strong dissent and the Court may be in a receptive mood for an invitation to knock down this landmark.

Administrative difficulties in the proposal to treat corporations like partnerships for taxation purposes are formidable, but these, too, have been exaggerated by some critics. It must not be forgotten that, of the 400,000 to 500,000 corporations, only a few thousand are large institutions with long lists of stockholders scattered over the country. For smaller companies, the partnership method of taxation would present no great administrative obstacles. However, for companies with complicated financial structures, it might be difficult to determine how the undistributed profits should be allocated among various classes of stockholders for tax purposes, particularly where several holding companies lay between the operating corporation and the individual stockholder.[2] Funds allocated to common stock in one year might later be distributed to preferred stock. Some embarrassment would be caused if corporations were field-audited some years after income reports had been made and substantial changes in the taxable corporate incomes were to result. Adjustments would be necessary in the income-tax bases of all the stockholders, numbering, in the case of some single corporations, tens or hundreds of thousands. But this hazard would be confined mainly to large corporations and might be minimized (perhaps constitutionally) by altering taxpayers' current income rather than reopening past returns.

Far more significant as objections to the partnership method are the psychological and political impediments. The taxation of corporations as partnerships violates the popular con-

[1] 252 U.S. 189 (1920).

[2] Actually, under modern corporation law, at least in some states, the right of the stockholder to a fixed place in the capital structure is not absolute and a pattern of hypothetical distribution, once announced, might not be followed at a later time (See Adolf A. Berle and Gardiner C. Means, *The Modern Corporation and Private Property*, The Macmillan Company, New York, 1933, pp. 148-151)

Integration and the Treatment of Undistributed Profits

ceptions of income and of the relations of stockholders to corporations. Through decades of custom, corporations have come to be considered as institutions apart from their stockholders, and the income of the former is not regarded as belonging to the latter until dividends are declared.

Closely related to this point is the contention that stockholders would incur a hardship if they were taxed upon what they had not actually received. Corporations might overcome this to some extent by distributing cash or stock dividends to meet the stockholders' tax liability; but the fact remains that requirements of the stockholder, and particularly the minority stockholder, are often not very articulate in corporate policy. The small stockholder is likely to feel that a bird in the corporation bush is far from a bird in his own hand.

It is true that corporations can distribute taxable stock dividends or other taxable securities to make a division of earnings while retaining their profits for reinvestment. This makes it possible for a corporation to have its cake and eat it too, so to speak. But this procedure also has difficulties and limitations. Capital structures of corporations should not be controlled by tax-avoidance considerations. At present, stock dividends are not income to the recipient as long as they do not disturb proportionate equities in the company. The use of stock dividends as a paper distribution of taxable profits for tax purposes would be facilitated if the Supreme Court were to modify its rule that common-stock dividends issued to common stockholders are not income. There is a possibility that the Supreme Court might do this were Congress to express a clear preference for this interpretation.

But a stock dividend is much more than a paper distribution of earnings. It involves a commitment as to the ultimate distribution of and responsibility for capital, which goes considerably beyond the mere building up of surplus. Stock dividends are hardly an available instrument for a concern with an accumulated deficit from past operations. Moreover, they would be inconvenient as a paper distribution of small reinvestments. Finally, they involve difficult problems of valuation. Should the value accepted for tax purposes be the proportionate share of earnings presently added to surplus or the market value of stocks distributed?[1] The last word on the instrumentation of paper distribution of reinvested earnings has not been written, but until better techniques are available it must be concluded that the use of this device does not provide an adequate solution of the problems of "partnership procedure."

It should not be too difficult to convince the owners of thousands of small companies (which are often little more than incorporated partnerships or family groups) that a tax system which treated their companies like partnerships would be a great improvement over the present duplication of personal and corporate levies. Owners of the larger corporations

---

[1] The two figures would seldom correspond, especially if past deficit or surplus were being capitalized along with current reinvestment. *Taxable* stock dividends are considered income at their market value when distributed, which serves as the basis for reckoning any future gain or loss. The basis for the old stock is the cost at time of purchase. The procedure differs in the case of *nontaxable* stock dividends, where part of the value of the old stock is attributed to that acquired by dividend, and the cost basis of the old stock is reduced accordingly. (Thus, if A has two shares of stock that cost him $1,000 each and receives, as a stock dividend, another share of the same value, the valuation basis for each of the three shares thereafter will be $666.66.)

In the case of taxable stock dividends, the problem arises that a corporation might capitalize and "distribute" all its reinvested earnings and the stockholder might receive, in market value, less than the reinvestment. Then, would the corporation still have undistributed earnings? Presumably the answer is affirmative, which means that the corporation may speculate as to how much surplus, if any, should be capitalized to avoid the undistributed-profits tax. The alternative procedure would be to allow the corporation credit for full distribution if the par value of its stock dividend equaled its reinvestment. If the taxpayer were taxed accordingly, he might pay on more income than he actually received. If he were assessed on the market value of his shares, the rather anomalous situation of the corporation distributing more than the stockholder received would arise. This might be justifiable since it would allow a corporation with an accumulated deficit to take advantage of stock dividends as a means of avoiding undistributed earnings. However, an expansion of capitalization on top of a deficit is objectionable, and tax avoidance by the issuance of paper without value is alarming. The conclusion is that the present procedure had better be continued in spite of its disadvantages

Integration and the Treatment of Undistributed Profits

would be more difficult to convince and they would have more valid grounds for objections. The situation might warrant a classification according to size, with small companies being treated like partnerships and large ones paying a compensatory undistributed-profits tax, adjusted as nearly as feasible to exact from the corporation the equivalent of what stockholders would pay were all earnings distributed. But the compensatory undistributed-profits tax would not be a very satisfactory means of tax integration, and chances are that it would incur the same political hostility heaped upon the "noble experiment" of 1936. If undistributed earnings are to receive any favors, it should be in the case of new small companies especially dependent upon this source for new equity capital.

In the political environment following the twenties, when the emphasis was placed on dangers of overexpansion, a solution along the lines just discussed might have had a chance for acceptance. In the political environment which follows the war, with its emphasis upon expansion and growth of industry, a solution of this kind is not likely to be greeted with enthusiasm.

Nevertheless, the partnership method, with or without classification, does have merit, and it might well be considered in seeking a solution of the postwar integration problem. It is the most logical, direct, and uncompromising solution of this difficult issue. Certainly, it should be applied to all personal holding companies and corporations already subject to special laws for improper accumulation; other corporations, with appropriate limitations, perhaps according to size, might be permitted to use the system at their option.

Taxing Undistributed Earnings through Rigorous Taxation of Capital Gains

It has been suggested that the corporate tax be abandoned entirely and that the capital-gains tax be relied upon to reach undistributed corporate earnings. This means taxing at the full personal rate any increase in the value of a security at the time of its sale or transfer.

At present, undistributed profits are taxed once to the corporation through the general corporate income tax and once to the stockholder through the personal tax when capital gains are realized. However, the personal tax does not apply fully to capital gains. To make it do so, the following changes would be required: elimination of ceiling rate and other special rate provisions; removal of limitations on deductions of capital losses; and taxation of gains and allowance for losses on transfer by gift and at the taxpayer's death. Were the corporate tax removed from the picture and were capital gains made fully taxable, undistributed earnings would eventually be subject to the personal tax completely and to it only.

The capital-gains tax, as a means of applying the personal tax to undistributed corporate income, would favor the retention of earnings in the corporation because of the postponement of the tax. The taxpayer would also have some choice as to the time when his share of reinvested earnings would be realized Reinvestments offset by losses would be fully canceled. These advantages would undoubtedly be stimulating to corporate saving and reinvestment. One proponent[1] describes the system as saying, in effect, to the owner of corporate stock:

> Leave your earnings in the business if you so desire. I won't tax you, while you live, on any earnings reinvested. In fairness to other taxpayers, you and I must have a final and comprehensive reckoning sometime (after you are gone or, if you get indolent with age, when you retire from ownership participation in the enterprise). Pending that time, however, you may, as it were, borrow from me without interest what you would pay additionally under partnership procedure. . . . Besides, if you lose the accrued taxes which I'm temporarily foregoing, along with the rest of your reinvested earnings, I'll take the loss myself.

However, as a solution to the problem of applying the

[1] Henry C. Simons, in a memorandum submitted to the author.

Integration and the Treatment of Undistributed Profits

income tax to undistributed earnings, the above proposal has grave limitations. The remedy is contingent upon the acceptance of much more rigorous treatment of capital gains, which might prove about as unpopular as an undistributed-profits tax. Since this is a political objection, it might be discounted if the program were sound on other counts. More serious are the inequities involved in the proposal. Corporate income not distributed in dividends would escape the tax system entirely until, as a result of sale, gift, or death transfer, it was realized by the taxpayer in the form of a capital gain. In many cases this would involve a delay in the taxation of important additions to economic power until the taxpayer's death.[1] The timing of taxation is exceedingly important, and it is doubtful if any burdens imposed upon the dead can make up for immunities allowed the living. The difference between tax forgiveness and this long postponement of tax liability is like that between title to property and a 99-year lease. Furthermore, unless the privilege to be taxed only upon withdrawals were extended to unincorporated business (including farmers), a discrimination would be added to those already in the tax system; and if the privilege were made universal, a long step would be taken toward an income tax applied only to income used for consumption. As previously stated, it is difficult to justify preferred treatment for one kind of saving or investment as compared with another. It is probably impossible to provide identical treatment for accrued and realized economic power, but the distinction is one that should be minimized and not magnified.

The proposal to confine taxation of withheld income to the levy on realized capital gains also involves uncertain and possibly serious adverse effects upon income-tax revenues. To be sure, some gain for total revenues could be expected if all capital gains were taxed eventually at the full schedule

[1] On the other hand, the "penalty" of higher surtaxes on prospective capital gains might exercise considerable restraint on the propensity to postpone the realization of such gains.

of rates. But the capital-gains element in the income-tax base has been notoriously unstable and the realization of capital losses is subject to manipulation. Immediate shrinkage in the tax base as the result of encouraged use of business entities for saving might be considerable.

In spite of these objections, the proposal to tax reinvested earnings only as realized capital gains has merit and deserves consideration in recasting the postwar tax system. At all events, the method might well be applied to small new businesses where maximum assistance in obtaining new equity capital seems especially warranted. The taxation of capital gains at the time an ownership interest is sold, or otherwise transferred, means an ultimate income-tax accounting for reinvested earnings. The necessity of such accounting affords strong support for retaining and strengthening capital gains taxation. It also affords support for death taxation.

Confining the Corporate Tax to a Withholding Levy and an Advance Payment of Taxes for Stockholders If and While Earnings Are Retained by the Corporation for Reinvestment

Explanation. A third proposal for dealing with our problem stems from British experience. The main British tax on corporate income may be described as a combination of a withholding tax and an advance payment of taxes for stockholders, if and while earnings are retained in the corporation for reinvestment. The tax carries the standard or normal rate that is applied to low-bracket personal income, which is one level above the sub-standard rate for the lowest bracket of income. The standard rate in Great Britain has been much higher than the normal rate in the United States, but our own low-bracket rate is likely to emerge from the war at a higher level than prevailed in the past. The British tax system extends a credit to individuals for taxes paid by the corporation upon any earnings distributed. This makes the corporation tax a withholding levy. But the British tax is also paid by corporations on that portion of income which is not distributed. This is an advance payment for stockholders and is credited to them, applying on their personal tax liability if and when dividends are subsequently paid. However, it does not equate the burdens upon distributed and undistributed income. Were the retained income distributed to affluent stockholders, it would be subject to high surtaxes; were it distributed to individuals with large personal exemptions and small incomes, it would be subject to an effective rate lower than that applied to the corporation.

Expressed in another way, the British corporate tax is a flat-rate levy on corporations as such, with a credit against the personal tax on the portion of corporate income distributed as dividends.

More specifically, this proposed combination of withholding tax and advance payment upon retained income would operate as follows: Assume that the low-bracket personal tax rate is 20 per cent. Corporation A earns $1 million in a given year, on which it pays a 20 per cent tax of $200,000. Half of the remaining $800,000 is distributed, and on this the corporate levy is treated in all respects like a withholding tax; no further tax is due unless stockholders are in the higher income brackets and have surtaxes to pay. In the case of stockholders with low incomes and dependents, refunds may be due. For purposes of calculating the base of the personal tax, the withheld tax on dividends is added to the dividends received. On the $400,000 retained by the corporation, the credit for the tax paid will not be taken up until the distribution of dividends occurs.[1]

Instead of applying the lowest bracket rate, an intermediate rate such as Great Britain maintains might be used. One recent observer advocated the application of the highest rate

[1] In the case of capital gains, administrative convenience might dictate some general rule for crediting the corporate tax, such as exemption of all gains on common stock from half the first-bracket tax In view of the concession as to timing on taxes which the proposed system would allow the taxpayer, no great injustice would result were no credit allowed and were all capital gains subject to the personal tax at full rates.

of personal surtax; but this seems unnecessarily drastic. Moreover, when the corporate rate becomes higher than that applicable to the lower brackets of income, the advance payment on undistributed profits acts as pressure upon management to distribute rather than retain and reinvest earnings.[1]

Modification. The proposal is flexible enough to permit several additional features. No advance payment for stockholders would be required if, by a variety of possible methods, the latter assume immediately their full personal tax responsibility upon their share of the undistributed earnings. This could be accomplished by the declaration of taxable stock dividends or the issuance of other taxable securities. Or it might take the form of voluntary consent by the stockholders to taxation upon their prorata shares of corporate reinvestment.[2] In either event, the tax obligation upon the business income involved would be fully satisfied.[3]

As a second special feature, new small enterprises might be allowed to reinvest all (or a specified proportion) of their earnings without any advance payment. This would involve admittedly difficult problems of classification and administration, but it is recommended for consideration and trial in the hope and expectation that these difficulties might be overcome. The development, if successful, would foster new investment and new competition. It would recognize and help to counteract the present competitive disadvantage that handicaps small business in its effort to raise equity capital. Companies of small size and in an early stage of growth find the organized capital market prohibitively expensive and funds from banks often inaccessible. That the growth of new and small enterprises is vitally important to a healthy economy

---

[1] The proposal is compatible with but does not require a tax on intercorporate dividends. The purpose of a tax on this income is mainly to discourage holding companies As previously observed, it is not a discriminating police measure and, if attainable, other ways of controlling overcomplicated corporate structure are preferable

[2] "Consent dividends"—see *Internal Revenue Code*, Sec. 28.

[3] Except for the capital-gains tax, which will be discussed later.

Integration and the Treatment of Undistributed Profits

is a proposition so generally recognized that no argument seems necessary to support it. Provided it does not subsidize smallness or penalize size as such, the tax system should be used insofar as feasible to ease the special difficulties of small business. A more detailed discussion of this special feature will be found in a later chapter.

The first of the above modifications is definitely recommended and the second is offered tentatively for consideration and trial.

Objections to the Proposal Considered. The proposed integration of personal and corporate taxes will be described as an undistributed-profits tax, and business will not like the idea of any revival of this levy. But the proposal is not the undistributed-profits tax of 1936 and it is set into a vastly changed tax system. It involves no duplication and no pressure to distribute rather than to reinvest income. It involves no drain on available capital beyond that already experienced; undistributed profits would be subject to no greater burdens than at present. As compared with the present arrangement, the proposal would eliminate the duplication of taxes; it would do away with the discrimination against stock as contrasted with bond financing; and it would aid in removing serious impediments to production and employment.

The proposal for advance payment and withholding succeeds only partly in integrating corporate and personal taxes and in eliminating the tax advantage of corporate reinvestment where high-income stockholders are involved. It is likely, however, that this is as near to perfect integration as is feasible. The taxation of capital gains at full rates and without loopholes would go far to complete the integration.

There will be legitimate concern that the proposals here made might encourage "corporate hoarding." The quantity of saving depends upon two conditions: the ability to save and the will to save. The proposal might give corporations more ability to save than they now have. But it would leave them with less propensity to save. The present system provides an

Postwar Taxation and Economic Progress

incentive to hoard in its differential tax burden favorable to undistributed, as contrasted with distributed, earnings. Profits that pass through corporations are subject to two levies; earnings that are reinvested, to only one. The proposed integration would, as far as possible, neutralize the tax system in its treatment of distributed and undistributed earnings. Safeguards against excessive corporate saving would be provided in the application of the personal tax to undistributed earnings, to capital gains, and to the prorata shares of stockholders in improperly retained earnings.

The contention will also be made that integration of the corporate and personal tax will let corporate profits "off easy" and result in a shifting of the burdens of government from the rich to the poor, thus aggravating a problem of personal oversaving. Such might conceivably be the result, but it is by no means a necessary outcome of integration. All property and income are attached sooner or later to individuals, and there are no sound objectives of taxation that cannot be achieved with a personal tax system. Double taxation of corporate earnings is partly, perhaps largely, at the expense of relatively wealthy persons. Thus it may provide the tax system with a "progressive" element. But the "progressivity" of the corporate tax is irregular, capricious, and uncertain in any event. (We have already mentioned the possibility of the corporate tax being shifted. In addition, the same rate is paid by the small stockholder as by the large; low-income stockholders pay whereas others with equal incomes do not; and the tax applies to dividends but not to interest.) If a heavier tax on income from property than on that from services is desired, this, too, can be had by favoring "earned income" in applying the personal tax. That it is possible to make the tax system more progressive, even with the elimination of the corporate tax as such, is not open to serious question. Available means to this end are a reduction of sales taxes, a strengthening of the death tax, and plugging the loopholes in the personal income tax.

Integration and the Treatment of Undistributed Profits

A loss of the $3 or $4 billion that might be expected from a peacetime levy on corporate profits in good years may create a problem of fiscal inadequacy. But some compensation for the loss of the corporate tax as such would appear in the application of the personal tax to undistributed earnings, capital gains, and the increased dividends and wages paid. Corporate profits have rarely accounted for 10 per cent of the national income, and the replacement problem involved in foregoing a double tax upon this small sector of the income flow should be of manageable proportions. Both for fiscal and economic reasons, the transition from business to personal taxation should be gradual—perhaps over a period of 3 to 5 years. In the last analysis, personal income and property represent "what there is to tax," and the revenue required to support the government can be had by levies upon these bases, fairly applied.

FOREIGN EXPERIENCE IN THE INTEGRATION OF CORPORATE AND PERSONAL INCOME TAXES

It has been said that a survey of business taxation in other countries "reveals a chaotic state of affairs,"[1] the inference being that there is little by way of example for us to follow. "Every country imposing an income tax has had to face these (integration) problems and has attempted to work out an approximate and practical solution. In view of the varying conditions and varying importance attached to the several objectives in the different countries, the resulting tax statutes show little uniformity."[2]

A business-tax system similar to our own, at least in its duplication feature, was applied in prewar Germany. At the opposite extreme was Great Britain with the most inte-

---

[1] Gerhard Colm, "International Comparison of Corporation Taxes," *Final Report of the Committee of the National Tax Association on Federal Taxation of Corporations*, Appendix 1, p. 55.

[2] *Final Report of the Committee of the National Tax Association on Federal Taxation of Corporations*, pp. 13, 14.

Postwar Taxation and Economic Progress

grated system of business and personal taxes. The difference is illustrated by the way in which the two countries used collection at the source. This has been described as follows:[1]

> Taxation at the source may function in two ways. In Germany it is a method of tax collection and no more. The tax is deducted from dividend and interest distributions to individuals. In Great Britain (as also in earlier years in the United States) corporations pay the tax on all their profits and the individual stockholders receive tax credit on their dividend income. The latter method results not merely in easier collection of individual income taxes but in addition it amounts to a tax on undistributed profits of at present (1940) 35% in Great Britain. Such an approach therefore seems to solve one of the greatest problems of individual income taxation. If a stockholder owns stock in a corporation which distributes only a part of its profits, the equity value of the stock increases. The accretion of "economic power" is not taxed unless the income tax law provides for a capital gains tax and the stockholder realizes the gain by selling his stock. The British method solves this problem as far as the normal tax is concerned but not with respect to the progressive surtaxes.

Of the British system, one observer comments: " . . . it is safe to say that no country has favored business through its tax system as much as Great Britain."[2] Some would argue that the British tax system has erred in this leniency. But why? There is no evidence that the interest in a relatively equal distribution of income has suffered as a result of this policy. Certainly one could say this if the British included capital gains in the base of their personal tax.

The author has been unable to discover any considerable dissatisfaction in Great Britain with its business-tax policy. When the Royal Commission on the Income Tax gave the

---

[1] Gerhard Colm, "Conflicting Theories of Corporate Income Taxation," *Law and Contemporary Problems*, Vol VII, No. 2 (1940), p. 286

[2] Mabel Newcomer, "European Taxation of Business," *How Shall Business Be Taxed*, Tax Policy League, New York, 1937, pp. 72, 73. See also comment by Richard W. Lindholm, *The Corporate Franchise as a Basis of Taxation*, University of Texas Press, Austin, 1944, pp. 219, 220

Integration and the Treatment of Undistributed Profits

British system a thorough examination in 1920, the suggestion was made that a surtax be levied on corporations equivalent to the maximum rate applied to individuals.[1] This suggestion was motivated by the desire to check avoidance of the personal tax. But it was rejected by the Commission on grounds of inequity and adverse effects upon production.[2] As a remedy for avoidance, the Commission recommended stricter application of a rule against improper accumulation of surplus. Beginning with 1920, the British did impose a 5 per cent profits tax on corporate business, which represented a departure from established tradition. This tax was reduced to 2.5 per cent in the Finance Act of 1923 and was abandoned entirely in 1924. However, it was reintroduced in 1937 to finance rearmament and was retained until the war, when it was merged with the excess-profits tax. The Colwyn Committee, in 1927,[3] discussed the proposition that the "corporate levy" was detrimental to corporate saving and to production, but its judgment was adverse to this view and no change was recommended.[4]

---

[1] Royal Commission on the Income Tax, *Minutes of Evidence*, Cmd 288, H M Stationery Office, London, 1919, pp 711–713, Vol 23, *II of C Reports*, p 1

[2] Royal Commission on the Income Tax, *Report*, Cmd 615, H M Stationery Office, London, 1920, p 125, Vol 18, *H of C Reports*, p. 97

[3] *Report of the Committee on National Debt and Taxation, London*, 1927, pp 149–150

[4] Other countries have had some experience with an undistributed-profits tax similar to our Act of 1936. Norway enacted such a program with a 10 per cent rate in 1921 The act proved to be very unpopular with business and the rate was reduced in subsequent acts. (Alfred G Buehler, *The Undistributed Profits Tax*, 1937, pp 56-58) Under the 1931 Act, a refund of the undistributed-profits tax was allowed to stockholders if dividends were paid in a year subsequent to that in which the corporation earned the profit The Norwegian tax "has been criticized because of its tendency to hamper the accumulation of capital, discourage sound financial practices, weaken industrial enterprises by depriving them of savings needed to tide them through bad years and depressions, depress industry, lessen production and employment, and place unequal burdens on corporations and stockholders of large companies." (*Ibid*, p 57) France and Chile also applied a special tax to undistributed profits (Gerhard Colm, *Final Report of the Committee of the National Tax Association on Federal Taxation of Corporations*, Appendix 1, p. 54) Sweden tried the undistributed-profits tax but later abandoned it. On the other hand, Belgium confined its corporate

Postwar Taxation and Economic Progress

Commenting on the propensity of the United States to consider corporations as taxable entities in their own right, Harrison B. Spaulding, in his comparison of British and American income-tax procedure, observed:[1]

> The United States practice of placing heavier rates on corporate income has in its favor little more than the virtue of simplicity, convenience, and ease of collection. . . . It results in discrimination against corporate income and is contrary to the doctrine that taxes should be imposed in accordance with the ability of the taxpayer to pay. If it is desired to discourage the doing of business by means of corporations, it would be much better to do it in some more straight-forward way.

MAINTENANCE OF A MODERATE BUSINESS TAX AS SUCH

The proposal just considered is quite compatible with the levy of a moderate business tax as such.[2] The retention of any business tax is objectionable on many counts previously cited but it also has some advantages, including the following:

1. A moderate business tax could compensate in some degree for the advantage allowed corporations (as compared with partnerships, for instance) in the application of less than full surtax rates to business saving.

2. A moderate business tax would contribute to the revenue substantially and involve comparatively small additional administrative expense.

3. A moderate business tax applied only to corporations

---

levy to undistributed profits and continued to do so until the war (*ibid*). The Netherlands followed an opposite course, imposing a special tax on distributed income. Australia had a federal undistributed-profits tax from 1915 to 1922, but the law followed the British practice in most respects (*Final Report of the Committee of the National Tax Association on the Federal Taxation of Corporations*, p. 22). The present Australian practice applies the "partnership method" to closely held corporations.

[1] Harrison B. Spaulding, *The Income Tax in Great Britain and the United States*, P. S. King & Son, Ltd., London, 1927, p 94.

[2] The British have had such a levy in recent years at a rate of 5 per cent.

Integration and the Treatment of Undistributed Profits

above a certain size would recognize very real differences in the corporate family.

4. A moderate business tax could be used to avoid an excessive increase in the profit margin of corporations during the period of transition to an integrated system. The differing elements in an economic system have a way of adjusting themselves even to bad economic arrangements. Once the adjustment has been made, precipitous changes of wide dimensions are undesirable and unlikely to accomplish their objective.[1] Movement in the direction of integration should be undertaken in several steps. The taxation of capital gains should be strengthened to take account of the capitalization of tax changes favorable to investment.

CONCLUSION

The conclusion is that the nearest approach to a rational business-tax system and the soundest modification of our present system in the interest of production and employment is as follows:

1. Integrate the personal and corporate tax using the latter, insofar as it applies to distributed earnings, as a withholding levy.

2. Apply a low-bracket personal rate to undistributed corporate income.

3. Tax capital gains at full rates and without loopholes.

As a transition program, an independent corporate tax at moderate and decreasing rates is advisable. As a feature of a permanent tax system an independent business levy is acceptable under the following conditions: (1) where, because of administrative and political factors, departure from a rational tax system proves necessary; and (2) where available alternative irrational sources are even more inequitable and repressive than the corporate income tax. These conditions will be examined in considerable detail later.

[1] This is particularly true of public utilities, where taxes have become embedded in rate structures that cannot be changed without a substantial lag.

Postwar Taxation and Economic Progress

No phase of taxation offers more opportunity for gain in both equity and nonrepressiveness than the integration of corporate and personal-income taxes.

SUMMARY OF CHAPTERS II AND III

In the early years of our income-tax history the corporate income tax was mainly a withholding levy, but gradually it developed into a full-fledged independent business tax. The theoretical support for a business levy rests upon dubious application of the benefits and ability-to-pay principles. The incidence of the tax is uncertain but in all probability it is divided among stockholders, wage earners, and consumers. Insofar as it falls on consumers, it is a haphazard consumption tax. The tax is closer and more likely to be repressive to business than direct taxes on stockholders. It creates a differential disadvantage for stock as compared with bond financing.

The biggest problem in determining the proper place for the corporate tax in the postwar tax system is that of treating undistributed earnings. The present system, which provides two taxes on distributed and one on undistributed earnings, is unsatisfactory both because it is discriminatory and because it encourages the use of the corporation by stockholders to avoid personal taxes. The undistributed-profits tax of 1936 sought to solve the problem by the imposition of an additional levy on undistributed income. This was criticized on many grounds, of which the two most valid were that it was prejudicial to new small enterprises and that it imposed further burdens on the risk-taker.

Assuming a fresh approach to the problem, three possible solutions seem worth considering. The first would treat corporations like partnerships and assess stockholders on their prorata shares of undistributed earnings. The second would allow these earnings to go untaxed until they were realized by stockholders as capital gains. And the third would use the corporate tax as a withholding levy on dividends and an

Integration and the Treatment of Undistributed Profits

advance payment on undistributed income. The last appears to be the most feasible solution and, combined with a fair application of the capital-gains tax, it would constitute a reasonably complete integration of the personal and corporate levies. Some application of the partnership and capital-gains approaches—the former in the case of unnecessary retention of earnings and the latter in the case of new small enterprises—is also desirable. A moderate business tax as such is compatible with these recommendations and is recommended for the transition period. For the permanent tax system such a levy must be given a low priority rating and is acceptable only as a lesser evil than other undesirable alternatives.

IV. EXCESS-PROFITS TAXES, MONOPOLY, AND SMALL BUSINESS

INTRODUCTION

IN THE preceding chapter, it was concluded that our federal tax system would be greatly improved by the elimination of most taxes on business, as such. It may seem a waste of time, therefore, to devote the next three chapters to problems of selecting and applying a business tax. If no business tax makes sense, how can form *A* be more sensible or less nonsensical than form *B*? Actually, the answers are not quite so black and white as that. Our recommendations call for the retention of a corporate income tax *in form* and gradual abandonment of it *in substance*. Moreover, since there is always the possibility that one's suggestions may not be followed, we need not be neutral concerning the alternative choices among business-tax procedures.

The present chapter is devoted to a discussion of business taxes as they bear on the problem of monopoly and business size. It considers the application of business taxes that aim primarily at social control.

This and the two following chapters deal mainly with federal business-tax problems, but much of the discussion applies also to the state and local situation.

EXCESS-PROFITS-TAX REPEAL[1]

The present excess-profits tax was set up as an emergency measure and its wording indicates the absence of any intent to carry it beyond the war. However, there will undoubtedly

[1] This section was written before the Revenue Act of 1945 repealed the wartime and declared-value excess-profits taxes. However, some of the issues involved in these taxes are still in debate, and, for this reason among others, the section has been retained as originally drafted.

Excess-Profits Taxes, Monopoly, and Small Business

be some demand for its retention in the peacetime tax system much like the demand following the First World War. Moreover, the timing of the repeal, if repeal is to be the outcome, involves some difficult questions of postwar fiscal policy. For these and other reasons, the future treatment of the excess-profits tax warrants a careful consideration in any postwar taxation program.

Excess-profits Tax during the War

An excess-profits tax during the Second World War was a political and economic necessity. Governmental control of the private economy has largely taken the form of freezing or attempting to freeze prewar economic relations, including the prices of finished products, raw materials, and labor. The profits tax, with its 95 per cent rate and its emphasis upon the prewar experience of each company, aimed at a near-freeze in the area of profits not very different from that applied elsewhere in the economy. Such a tax was required to satisfy the demands of those involved at other points in the freezing process. It was an answer to the natural demand for some counterpart to the sacrifices being made by persons in the armed forces. Moreover, it was a response to the feeling that the government should share in the profits (at least the extraordinary profits) created by its own extraordinary outlay. Competitive checks upon excessive earnings, which are normally operative (even though imperfectly) in times of peace, are largely suspended during a war because of the extreme urgency of much of the demand. Many risks of production normally assumed by private business are shifted to the government.

The war excess-profits tax is an example of the propensity of Congress to levy a tax at conspicuously high rates but with a relatively "easy" base. The rates are boosted to satisfy the public demand, and other terms of the tax are fitted to suit the taxpayer. The war excess-profits tax has been far less effective than one would suppose from observing the tax schedule and also less effective than the circumstances warranted.

Excess-profits Tax in Peacetime

The strongest ground for including the excess-profits tax in the peacetime tax system is that the tax affords an opportunity to recapture part of the excessive gains resulting from monopolistic business.

The monopoly problem will undoubtedly need increased attention in the postwar world. Competition is a fairly adequate policing force in the economic system when most production is carried on by numerous small units, but it is not dependable when a few large companies dominate many fields. These few concerns tend to set prices by joint action; or, with similar results, they act with conscious regard for the effect of their own price policies upon their "competitors." It is true that competition is still a very lively corpse; there are many business men who believe it was never so vigorous and effective. In addition to some competition within the same line, there is much interproduct rivalry. Thus, plastics threaten wood and steel as construction materials; electricity competes with gas; mail-order houses invade the department-store field with competitive services; and so on. Monopoly is clearly a matter of degree and some of it is acceptable as better than the alternative of either unlimited competition or direct government participation in business. It must always be remembered that the government itself deliberately creates monopoly power, as, for instance, through the granting of patents. Exactly what this adds up to is not clear, but it obviously is something less than adequate protection for the consumer.

Unfortunately for the application of the excess-profits tax as a solution to this problem, there is no clear way to isolate monopoly profits. If there were, such gains could probably be prevented from occurring in the first place. We know that, in an ideal order free from monopoly, profits would differ

Excess-Profits Taxes, Monopoly, and Small Business

among concerns because of varying degrees of risk inherent in different lines of business; because of unforeseen developments (or noneconomic factors, such as war) causing maladjustments between demand and supply; and because of differences in the efficiency of management. We know also that in the real world there are further variations in profits caused by limitations on competition resulting from monopolistic practices and also from such pervasive conditions as differentiation of product, ignorance of buyers and sellers, and the costs of communication and transportation. No doubt, there are unearned rewards in this picture, but no satisfactory technique for singling them out has yet been devised.

There are many ways, beside the taxation of profits, to attack the monopoly problem. Fewer barriers to foreign trade (lower tariffs) present one of the surest and soundest. In addition, an active and discriminating federal judicial and administrative supervision of trade practices and business combinations is needed. Cartel agreements should be subject to review and approval by the State Department as well as the Antitrust Division. A federal incorporation franchise for interstate companies has been long overdue. The development of an effective consumers' cooperative movement might help. Perhaps the tax system can be used to foster competition by supporting small or new business. Both intelligence and courage are needed to master this problem, and none of the approaches to a solution should be lightly dismissed.

More important than the recapture of monopoly gains in the postwar world will be the prevention of monopoly restriction of output. Proposals have been made that would subsidize monopoly marginal output but these have been mainly of academic interest. Probably this is a job for the legislative police power and not one for the tax system.

As previously observed, an excess-profits tax applies to the marginal segments of income (those above the credits). For this reason, among others, it discourages the incentives for risk-taking and expansion on the one hand and for efficiency and conservation on the other. No techniques in excess-profits taxation have been devised to allow for differences in the risk factor or for superior efficiency of management. It is worth noting that if a business now launches an advertising campaign, 80 per cent of the cost of such an outlay may be financed in effect by the federal government.[1] Many other outlays can be similarly financed. Thriftiness and spend-thriftiness are both shorn of meaning when a tax reduces the gain or loss to 20 cents on the dollar. Although patriotism might be relied upon to sustain the imposition of heavy taxes on profits during the war, a similar reliance in times of peace might be hazardous.

The tax may also penalize companies with irregular income. The fortunate concern that earns 8 per cent regularly may have no tax to pay, whereas the one that alternates between a 16 per cent return and no income may be taxed substantially. It is because of such effects, particularly adverse to small growing companies, that the tax is said by its critics to foster rather than discourage monopoly.

One of the chief weaknesses of an excess-profits tax lies in the technical difficulties in its application. No one can be enthusiastic about a tax measure which distributes the rewards of the economic process mainly according to luck or political (as contrasted with economic) efficiency. This is the danger that lurks in the excess-profits tax, although undoubtedly the techniques of applying this tax have improved since we last experimented with it 25 years ago. The arbitrariness and the anomalies are, however, still conspicuous. To choose a few at random: Why should the concern operating on borrowed capital have the privilege of including half such capital in the tax base (for calculating the return on invested capital), whereas a firm that rents its capital has no such privilege?[2] Why should a personal-service corporation escape the

[1] It is true that the Treasury exercises some check on advertising outlays, but this does not invalidate the illustration.

[2] The discrimination existing in some cases is alleviated but not eliminated by the fact that only half of interest paid is deductible in calculating excess profits

Excess-Profits Taxes, Monopoly, and Small Business

excess-profits tax on the ground that its income is mostly from services rather than capital, when many other taxable corporations show the same characteristic but only to a lesser degree? Why should a developing corporation be taxed on the theory that its increased profits are due to the war while a declining corporation, which may have received a lift because of the war, escapes? Most important of all, of course, are the great and thus far insurmountable difficulties in differentiating for risk. Relief provision, the carry-over and carry-back of unused excess-profits credits, and other refinements have helped to make the present law less arbitrary than that in force during the last war, but the stanchest friend of the tax would not contend that technical problems in its application are anywhere near solution.

Anyone who studies the multitudinous points of subtle distinction and classification involved in an excess-profits tax cannot fail to be impressed with the great possibilities for injustice and unfair competitive advantage inherent in its application. An exceedingly complicated law is necessary to cover the varied conditions to which it must apply and, even then, much depends upon administrative discretion. These complexities are illustrated by the provisions dealing with business reorganization, which are so involved that they are utterly incomprehensible to the layman. High compliance costs and much litigation attend such legislation. The historical approach to the measurement of capital (an element involved in one of the excess-profits-tax procedures) is probably the best that could be devised, but it involves resurrecting and recasting a multitude of records that were regarded as buried. In 1940, when the excess-profits tax was under consideration, there were cases still pending in the courts dealing with the determination of capital under the 1918 law. Annual accounting is inherently tentative, provisional, and inexact, and it is sorely pressed to give the precise answers required by an excess-profits tax.

As a levy on corporations the excess-profits tax has more

logic than the corporate net-income tax, although the latter is much simpler to administer and apply. It is said that, if an almost confiscatory excess-profits tax can be made to work in wartime, there should be no serious difficulty in making a reasonable one work in peacetime. Administrative complications of the tax are extremely difficult but perhaps not prohibitive. The economic effects are more important.

It is true that there are monopoly profits; that these profits are an economic surplus; that they are often not morally justified. To tax them, however, means that efficiency and risk profits will be singled out for special taxation at the same time. In other words, the public has the choice either of recapturing monopoly profits while penalizing efficient management and risk-taking, or of placing no special tax either on monopoly profits or on efficiency and risk-taking rewards. A further factor to be weighed in the decision is that, in the absence of price controls, we cannot be certain that the monopolist will absorb the excess-profits tax. It might be passed on, at least to some extent, in higher prices. An excess-profits tax is in no sense a regulatory and preventive measure like public-utility rate control or renegotiation of contracts. If we are sure that a monopoly exists and that it is overcharging the public, the thing to do is to restore competition or to regulate prices. If a monopoly has the power of private taxation as alleged, that power cannot be defeated by public taxation. Moreover, monopoly profits can be taxed to individuals as well as to companies. For improvement in the distribution of wealth and income, the individual tax would be far more effective. If the conclusion is against an excess-profits tax, the existence of unearned income should be recognized in setting the scale of individual rates and by closing loopholes in the personal tax system.

The point has been made that, if an excess-profits tax is good in wartime when competitive controls are especially weak, it should be good in peacetime when these controls will be only a little stronger. Waiving the question of degree, the fact

Excess-Profits Taxes, Monopoly, and Small Business

remains that a corporate tax is necessary in wartime to apply wartime rates of taxation to corporate earnings that are not distributed. Either an undistributed-profits tax or an excess-profits tax at very high rates is necessary to do this job. In peacetime, with a relatively stable tax system, personal taxes, with capital gains in the base plus a moderate levy on undistributed earnings, will constitute as effective an antimonopoly tax program as can be achieved.

In summary and conclusion, the excess-profits tax, at least in its present state of imperfection, had best be reserved for war application. Its peacetime employment might prove dangerously inimical to risky enterprise and to business efficiency. Its impact upon marginal income might make it a temptation to waste resources. As an antidote for monopoly, it would not be sufficiently discriminating to achieve its purpose, and it could do a lot of damage in the attempt. For the present, we are obliged to attack the monopoly problem with other weapons, however inadequate they may be.

Timing the Repeal of the Tax

If the excess-profits tax is to be ruled out of the peacetime tax system, the question still remains as to when the tax should be dropped. There will be strong demand for such action as soon as hostilities have ceased. This will be supported by the valid contention that a profits tax unsustained by war patriotism will lead to waste and will weaken the incentives to convert business facilities to an efficient peacetime basis. On the other hand, the problem of inflation may enter an acute phase in the postwar period, when buying power will have a long start over the production of civilian goods. Although the excess-profits tax is not in itself an effective deflationary measure, involving as it does some inflationary tendencies, it is a politically significant part of a general control program. Immediate elimination of the excess-profits tax would be the signal for a relaxation of wage and price controls. Normal competitive conditions will not be restored overnight after the war. The agricultural market will reflect a strong war influence until the important task of food relief for the war-devastated countries is accomplished. Business itself will not assume normal operation for a considerable period—material from abroad will not become available immediately, and varying periods required for conversion will create different effects upon profits.

In these circumstances the sensible procedure would be to repeal the excess-profits tax at the close of hostilities, with provision that the repeal would not take effect until positive profits resulting from war disarrangements have largely disappeared. A fair guess as to when this condition might be realized would be one year, though, with some reduction of the rates, two years might be more appropriate. This would give much the same lift to business as an immediate repeal without prematurely letting down the bars of war controls. Whenever the repeal is made effective, the administration of the law should be continued to permit the carry-back of losses and excess-profits credits until the main effects of war conversion and reconversion have been liquidated. The present law contains no commitment that this will be done, but it is in keeping with the accepted view that true war profits should be determined for the whole war period, including that in which the effects of the war are being liquidated.

Declared-value Excess-profits Tax

Mention should be made of another institution in the excess-profits-tax field, namely, the combined "declared-value" capital-stock and excess-profits taxes surviving from prewar origin in the Industrial Recovery Act of 1933. Through the connection of excess profits to net income and of "declared-value" capital stock to excess profits, these taxes, in ways that need not here be explained, amount to an additional levy on net income. They add little to the tax system but complication, extra compliance costs, and occasionally capricious results, and they are especially inimical to small companies.

Excess-Profits Taxes, Monopoly, and Small Business

Calculation for these taxes is carried on in an artificial atmosphere all but divorced from reality; they are a lawyer's plaything rather than a producer's levy; and they serve principally as a monument to the misdirected ingenuity of taxmakers. They represent the sort of complication in the tax system that ought to be avoided in the future, and they should be repealed certainly not later than the end of the war. More could be said for a genuine capital-stock tax, but it involves some of the same administrative vagaries as the excess-profits tax.

Conclusion

In conclusion, it can be asserted that an undistributed-profits tax is a far more promising candidate for a place in the permanent tax system than an excess-profits tax. Because of the unfortunate experience in 1936, the undistributed-profits tax is in disfavor with many business men, but the character of that experience was due to a badly conceived law rather than to an unsound fundamental objective. A sensible answer to the business-tax problem is more likely to be found along the road we then opened, although with inauspicious results, than on the road of excess-profits taxation we were forced to travel during the war years. Best of all, as we have indicated, would be the opening of a new road to the integration of corporate and personal taxes.

APPLICATION OF GRADUATION TO A CORPORATE NET-INCOME TAX

Considerable difference of opinion has always prevailed as to whether a business net-income tax should be flat or graduated, but the consensus among critics probably supports a flat rate. Nevertheless, in practice, business net-income taxes have often been graduated, as has been the case with the federal tax since 1936. In considering alternative forms of business taxation and the effect of taxes on monopoly and business size, attention should be given to rate structures.

Postwar Taxation and Economic Progress

Under the system of integrated business and personal taxes favored here, there would be little point (and much confusion) in graduation of rates at the corporate end of the integration. The rate scale should be graduated once only and at the personal end. The following discussion is devoted to the advisability of graduation on the assumption that a corporate tax, as such, is to remain in the federal tax system.

Often, graduated rates are initiated and defended on the invalid ground that, if a personal tax is so arranged, a business tax must be set up similarly. Graduated rates applied to the income of real persons are defended because they are related to the importance of marginal money (the extra dollar) to the individual and because they diminish inequality of personal incomes. Neither of these grounds is relevant in applying taxes to corporations. Whether a corporation can have a soul has always been a moot question. Corporations would concede (and perhaps proclaim) their own capacity to suffer. But the pleasure and pain calculus which plays such a large part in ability-to-pay analysis can hardly be dissociated from the individuals who act together to constitute the corporate entity.

Corporate net income as such tells us nothing about the rate of return on capital. A concern with a $50,000 income may have a 100 per cent return upon investment, while one with a $1,000,000 income may be earning a mere 1 per cent. That there is a necessary correlation between the size of corporate business and its profitability has not been established. What appears to be a fairer index of corporate ability to pay is the ratio of earnings to investment. This is the basis of the excess-profits tax, discussed and rejected earlier in this chapter. Moreover, the $50,000 income of a corporation owned virtually by one stockholder may represent more ability to pay per dollar of income than the $150 million income of a corporation owned by 1500 widows and orphans. This is an extreme illustration, but it is not at all established that big corporations and big stockholders are always associated. The fallacy in

Excess-Profits Taxes, Monopoly, and Small Business

the application of the ability-to-pay theory to corporations is that the theory was conceived in terms of persons and their circumstances and does not fit a situation involving inanimate entities.

Information on the correlation of large corporations and ownership by large stockholders for 1936 has been published by the Treasury. It is submitted in adapted form in Table II. This table shows some correlation between size of corporation and size of dividend recipients' net income. It shows, for instance, that, although recipients of net incomes over $1 million received 2.53 per cent of total dividends, they received 4.25 per cent of all dividends paid out by corporations with over $100 million assets. Individuals with incomes of from $5000 to $10,000 received 12.79 per cent of total dividends and 24.25 per cent of the dividends distributed by corporations with assets of less than $50,000. However, these "little" stockholders also received 13.20 per cent of income distributed by corporations with assets over $100 million. Thus the correlation is not consistent. But even if it were, it would conceal so many individual deviations from the rule that no justification for a graduated rate could be based on these facts.

Approaching the corporate income tax from the standpoint of benefits and costs, it can be argued that large corporations receive relatively more government benefits and occasion more government cost than small corporations and that therefore they should pay net-income taxes on a higher scale. But the whole benefit and cost analysis is so vague and lacking in precision that its use, to justify either a tax itself or a graduated-rate scale, is decidedly questionable.

The graduated-rate feature adds to the problem of applying the net-income tax fairly to businesses with fluctuating incomes. Corporation A, with a steady income, may always remain in the low brackets, whereas corporation B, with no greater average income but with a large fluctuation in its return, may be taxable at a much higher average effective

TABLE II

PERCENTAGE DISTRIBUTION OF DIVIDENDS PAID TO INDIVIDUALS, 1936*

Classified by size of total assets of dividend-paying corporations and by size of net income of dividend-receiving individuals,†
(per cent)

Dividend recipients. Net income classes of dividend-receiving individuals (thousands of dollars)	Total	Total assets classes of dividend-paying corporations (thousands of dollars)									
		Under 50	50–100	100–250	250–500	500–1000	1000–5000	5000–10,000	10,000–50,000	50,000–100,000	100,000 and over
Deficit.........	1.68	1.86	1 82	1.39	1 41	1 31	1.99	2 13	1.77	1.35	1.61
Under 1........	1 12	1 04	0 94	0.90	0.73	0.63	0 76	0 93	1 08	1.23	1.52
1–2...........	3.29	3 52	2 26	2.12	1.89	1.98	2 02	2 32	3 23	3 64	4.82
2–3...........	4.42	6 36	4 25	3.52	3.16	2 84	2.92	3 24	4.06	4.52	6 13
3–4...........	4 73	9 21	6 32	4.50	3 52	3.39	3 12	3 57	4.41	4.77	6 02
4–5...........	4 72	8.68	6 50	5.20	4 12	4 18	3.70	3 73	4 33	4 27	5 46
Total, under 5 .	18 28	28.81	20 27	16.24	13 42	13 02	12.52	13 79	17 11	18 43	23.95
5–10...........	12.79	24 25	24 45	17.78	13.90	11 41	10 29	9 83	11.44	11 86	13.20
10–15..........	8 60	14 07	15 35	15.12	12 15	9 86	7.58	6 62	7 14	7 37	7 75
15–20..........	6 58	8 55	11 59	11.35	10 30	8 57	6 24	5 77	5 40	5 30	5 48
20–25..........	5.18	5 47	7 78	7.97	8.63	7 19	5 33	4 34	4.49	3 89	4 28
25–30..........	4 17	3 73	4 90	6.22	6.88	7 01	4 59	3 43	3 49	3.23	3 30
30–40..........	6 57	4 04	5 09	7.81	9 99	10.29	8 42	5 91	5 96	5.36	5 14
40–50..........	4 81	2 48	2.10	4.62	6 83	7 51	7.08	5 38	4 27	3.77	3 63
50–60..........	3 80	1 70	1 68	3.02	4 73	6 17	5.53	4 21	3 80	2 93	2 87
60–70..........	3.10	1 48	1 43	1.89	2 94	3 67	4.94	3 88	3 03	2 64	2 54
70–80..........	2 33	0 43	0 54	1.03	1 36	2 76	3 30	3 00	2 94	2 45	1 94

TABLE II.—(Continued)

Dividend recipients. Net income classes of dividend-receiving individuals (thousands of dollars)	Total	Total assets classes of dividend-paying corporations (thousands of dollars)								
		Under 50	50–100	100–250	250–500	500–1000	1000–5000	5000–10,000	10,000–50,000	50,000–100,000	100,000 and over
80–90............	1.88	0.31	0.37	0.86	1.23	2.39	2.60	3.47	1.93	1.50	1.66
90–100...........	1.69	0.40	0.40	0.56	1.10	2.01	2.28	2.53	1.82	1.30	1.65
100–150..........	5.09	1.40	1.12	1.42	3.02	3.05	6.77	9.72	6.45	6.01	4.30
150–200..........	2.83	0.41	0.24	0.54	0.71	1.30	4.15	4.96	4.03	3.30	2.44
200–250..........	1.73	0.12	0.05	0.56	0.49	1.07	1.50	3.33	2.55	2.07	1.77
250–300..........	1.08	0.02	0.43	0.16	0.12	0.33	0.49	1.82	1.61	1.57	1.41
300–400..........	1.47	0.03	0.16	0.62	0.33	0.50	1.25	1.74	1.94	2.76	1.70
400–500..........	1.12	0.34	0.12	0.39	0.25	0.13	0.92	0.87	1.82	1.03	1.53
500–750..........	1.68	0.07	0.03	0.27	0.16	0.30	1.19	2.63	2.04	3.23	2.15
750–1000.........	1.01	0.02	0.03	0.18	0.04	0.05	0.30	0.11	2.20	1.53	1.45
1000 and over ...	2.53	0.01	0.05	‡	0.01	0.10	0.74	0.53	2.77	7.12	4.25
Total........	100.00	100.00	100.00	100.00	100.00	100.00	100.00	100.00	100.00	100.00	100.00

* Estimated on the basis of corporate, individual, and fiduciary tax returns for 1936
† Based upon dividend payments to individuals and taxable estates and trusts filing individual tax returns.
‡ Less than 0.005 per cent
SOURCE: *Bulletin of the Treasury Department*, U.S Treasury Department, Office of the Secretary (January, 1943), pp 4–6

rate. This may be unavoidable in the case of individuals, but it is hardly necessary in the case of corporations.

If there is any real justification for a graduated rate, it must be found in the effects on the economy. Using this approach, one can conceive several possible and plausible supports for graduation. It provides a tool for favoring smallness or penalizing size. Graduation at the bottom of the corporate scale not only favors small companies but reduces the differential burden between them and partnerships. The graduated rate also provides a means whereby (on the assumption that the large corporations are the monopolistic ones) the recapture of monopoly profits can be attempted.

It is apparent enough that the corporate family is not one homogeneous group. Many thousands of corporations are little more than converted or overgrown partnerships, usually dominated by a single family group. On the other hand, there are a few hundred "giant corporations" which, in addition to great size, are characterized by divorced management and ownership and by the tendency to dominate markets and wield monopolistic power Between the giants and the little companies is the intermediate group with mixed characteristics. A graduated rate might be justified as an adaptation of the tax system to the varied characteristics of the corporate family. It might thus serve the social interest by favoring small companies and by checking monopoly.

Specific proposals for rate graduation are usually vulnerable either because their objective is improper or because it is not achieved. To check the development of corporate size by tax measures would require heavy graduation *at the upper end* of the corporate size scale instead of at the lower end where it is now applied. Such a program, though defensible in its objective, would be painfully undiscriminating in its operation. It could take no account of the fact that much capital may be necessary and desirable in some lines but conducive to monopoly in others. The capital needed for a large laundry would be inadequate to supply the smallest con-

Excess-Profits Taxes, Monopoly, and Small Business

ceivable steel manufacturing company. Perhaps neither the taxing power nor the legislative police power can be expected to make sharp distinctions among corporations to achieve antimonopoly objectives. But the police power seems much the better "bet" for the role. Attempts to favor small business as such confront the fact that much small business is large business *in its line* and suffers from no inferior status as to its prosperity. There is no evidence that corporate taxation has made any dent in the monopoly problem either as a preventive or a recapture device.

It is true, of course, that rate-scale concessions to small corporate business might reduce the differential in tax burden between it and unincorporated business. This is as sound a reason for differentiation in rates as any. On the other hand, if corporations are allowed some immunity on undistributed earnings, they may already have an advantage over partnerships for which a moderate corporate tax would merely compensate.

On balance, the argument for graduated rates seems unconvincing. However, some support for small business from the tax system is highly desirable, and unless better means can be found, the graduated scale for corporations should be retained.

CHECKING MONOPOLY BY TAXING INTERCORPORATE HOLDINGS

Criticism of Holding Companies

Holding companies have always been criticized to some degree but, following the failure of several public-utility holding companies during the thirties, the criticism became acute. Historically, the right of corporations to invest in the common stock of other corporations was not recognized in the common law and, before 1888, it was granted by statute law only specifically and under exceptional circumstances.[1] Inter-

[1] James C. Bonbright and Gardiner C. Means, *The Holding Company*, McGraw-Hill Book Company, Inc., New York, 1932, pp. 55–57. See also Henry W.

corporate holding is now generally allowed, although it is still restricted to some extent in some states. The holding company is uniquely an American institution. Nearly all the great American consolidations, such as the United States Steel Company and the International Harvester Company, have been consummated by use of the holding-company device. The holding company lends itself readily to consolidation because it avoids the necessity of raising large amounts of cash, substituting for this procedure an exchange of stock.

The holding company is criticized as facilitating concentration of control (pyramiding) with a minimum of investment; as contributing to monopoly by making consolidations easier; as encouraging manipulation by its sheer complexity. The holding company in the public-utility field is accused of special abuses, including the "uneconomic" integration of companies, excessive service charges, overcapitalization, and undue concentration of control.

On the other hand, the holding company is defended as a legal necessity under the American system of government and as a requisite for engaging in interstate business in some lines. Some states prohibit nonresident corporations from operating within their boundaries or at least discriminate against such operation. The holding company is said to facilitate geographic decentralization and the delegation of managerial powers. In this respect, the American Telephone and Telegraph Company, with its state subsidiaries, is compared with the federal system itself. The holding company is also defended as conducive to efficiency in that it specializes functionally and provides financial and engineering services to small companies in an economical manner.

The use of the police power to control holding companies is confined largely to the public-utility field, where it was introduced into federal practice in 1935. Public-utility holding

---

Ballentine, *Ballentine on Corporations*, Callaghan & Company, Chicago, 1927, pp 230–233.

Excess-Profits Taxes, Monopoly, and Small Business

companies selling securities on an interstate scale must now be registered with the Securities and Exchange Commission, and security issues must be approved by that agency. The Commission can order the reorganization and simplification of holding-company structure in the utility field and can limit pyramiding to three tiers of companies.

The taxing power has also been used to control holding companies. Here the principal devices have been the taxation of intercorporate dividends and the prohibition of, or special tax upon, the use of a consolidated return in reporting for income and profits taxes. A consolidated income-tax return merges the income-tax accountability of a number of closely affiliated corporations.

All corporations, including financial and nonfinancial, received 34 per cent of all corporate dividends paid out in 1937.[1] It has been said that intercorporate investment is so widespread that "approximately half of corporate America is owned by the other half of corporate America."[2] Subsidiaries are most numerous in the public-utility field, but, even in manufacturing, those corporations listed with the SEC and covered in *Statistics of American Listed Corporations* had an average of six subsidiaries each. The number increased substantially with the size of corporations.[3]

History

From the beginning of the federal income tax, the general rule has been that dividends must be included in net income. In the first few acts, no distinctions were made as to the character of the dividend recipients. However, under the high income and excess-profits taxes of 1917 and 1918, steps were taken to permit consolidated returns for affiliated corpo-

---

[1] Walter A. Chudson, *The Pattern of Corporate Financial Structure*, National Bureau of Economic Research, 1945, p. 88.
[2] Hynning and Colm, *op. cit.*, p. 40.
[3] Chudson, *op. cit.*, p. 91.

rations, largely intercompany owned (1917), and for the elimination of the taxation of intercorporate dividends (1918). The guiding principle until 1935 called for an income tax to be levied at two points: on the original operating corporation in which the income was earned and on the ultimate individual stockholder as a surtax when he collected the dividend. The personal stockholder was not required to pay a "normal" tax on dividends on the theory that one "normal" tax on the same bit of income was sufficient.

In 1935, the law was amended[1] to require that dividends received by corporations be reported as a part of gross income, subject to a deduction of 90 per cent of this amount. This meant, in effect, that 10 per cent of intercorporate dividends would be subject to regular corporate income taxes. The Act of 1936[2] changed the form of allowance for intercorporate dividends from a deduction to a credit and reduced the amount to 85 per cent. In 1938,[3] a proviso was added limiting the credit to 85 per cent "of the adjusted net income." This meant that the corporation could get the full benefit of the credit only if the adjusted net income were greater than the credit. The idea was to prevent the credit from wiping out all remaining taxable income and thus to collect a minimum tax from the corporation. (A corporation receiving $1 million of dividend income would have a tax base of $150,000 even though it had an operating loss.) The credit provision of the 1938 Act has continued to the present, but the 1942 Act reinaugurated the privilege of filing consolidated returns by affiliated corporations. A large portion but by no means all of intercorporate dividends are canceled by consolidated returns.

In supporting the taxation of intercorporate dividends during the thirties, the Treasury indicated that it had other than purely fiscal objectives in mind. One objective sought

[1] Sec 102(h), 1935 Act.
[2] Sec 26(b), Revenue Act of 1936
[3] Sec. 26(b), Revenue Act of 1938.

Excess-Profits Taxes, Monopoly, and Small Business

was "simplification of corporate structures"; intercorporate dividends were regarded "as largely unnecessary transfers brought about and multiplied by complex corporate structures."[1]

During the life of the federal income tax, we have wavered between two theories. At times we have looked upon the corporation entirely as a separate legal entity—a person on a level with all other persons, to be taxed on all its income accordingly. At other times, we seem to have treated the corporation as the legal shell in which the real parties at interest are the stockholders. On the second theory, intercorporate dividends should not be taxed unless it be to "control" holding companies. The British have applied this theory of corporate entity most consistently; they do not tax intercorporate dividends.

Policy

As a social control measure, the taxation of intercorporate dividends raises several questions. Does it curb the use of the holding-company device? No convincing quantitative evidence has been found to answer this question, but it hardly seems disputable that the inclusion of 15 per cent of intercorporate distributions in the income-tax base of the recipient is enough to influence corporate financial policy.

The second question is more crucial: Granting that there are abuses and excesses in the use of the holding-company device, is the taxation of intercorporate dividends the best way to eliminate these abuses? If one were to accept the view that all holding companies are bad and that the fewer of these institutions existing, the better, he could perhaps support any curb on intercorporate holdings as a social gain. There is something to be said for this view and it would have been especially persuasive before we became so heavily committed

[1] Hearings before Senate Finance Committee on the Revenue Act of 1935 (testimony of Robert H. Jackson), 74th Congress, First Session, 1935, p 226.

to the holding-company institution. But most critics would probably agree that, under existing conditions, some holding companies perform a useful function and ought not to be penalized. If this is true, the conclusion follows that the taxation of intercorporate dividends is a crude and rough instrument for holding-company control, since it is entirely undiscriminating in its application. It curbs all holding companies and does not confine itself to those which should be eliminated or to the abusive practices of those that should be reformed. Like so many other instances in which taxation is used for control purposes, the job must be done with a cleaver instead of a scalpel, and the operation is likely to do more harm than good. The object is proper and the means, as such, are unobjectionable, but the results are usually disappointing.

Are there other available means of controlling holding companies? The answer is affirmative; the Securities and Exchange Commission is already heavily involved with the control of holding companies in the public-utility field. If other fields need policing, its powers can be extended. Moreover, it has long been recognized that further limitation on holding companies should be provided in incorporation laws. Although adequate policing at this point is probably too much to expect as long as incorporation is a state privilege, it is high time that the federal government assumed this prerogative for corporations engaged in interstate commerce.

Probably some will defend the intercorporate dividend tax on the ground that it does bring in some revenue and mainly at the expense of large corporations. There may be better ways not only of obtaining revenue but of obtaining it from large corporations.

The conclusion is that other means of controlling over-complicated corporate structure are preferable to taxation and that these, if attainable, should be substituted for the taxation of intercorporate dividends. In the meantime, the present system should be retained.

Excess-Profits Taxes, Monopoly, and Small Business

Consolidated Returns

The tax treatment of consolidated returns in the federal income-tax statute has wavered at least as much as that relating to most other features of the law.[1] With the outbreak of the Second World War and the imposition of an excess-profits tax under the Second Revenue Act of 1940, Congress made it possible to file "consolidated excess-profits tax returns." The privilege was extended in the Revenue Act of 1942 to include the regular corporate income tax. An additional tax of 2 per cent of the consolidated corporate surtax net income is charged for using the privilege.

Much of the argument previously cited against the taxation of intercorporate dividends applies also to a rule against the use of consolidated returns. In addition, the factor of convenience in administration and compliance is strongly on the side of allowing consolidated returns.

Should the privilege of filing consolidated returns call for

[1] Consolidated reporting had its inception in the experience with high wartime profits taxes of the First World War. This was by regulation, but statutory action in 1918 extended the mandate to the corporate income-tax field as well. The Federal Revenue Act of 1921 allowed the taxpayer an option of making a separate or consolidated return. It was argued that the requirement of a consolidated return, under all circumstances, was a harsh one in peacetime—one that would entail injustices and inequalities of taxation (Randolph E. Paul and Jacob Mertens, *The Law of Federal Income Taxation*, Callaghan & Company, Chicago, 1934, Vol. IV, p. 423) The Act of 1932 introduced the idea of an additional tax (0 75 per cent) for the privilege of filing consolidated returns. In 1934, the privilege of filing consolidated returns, except for railroads, was abolished. This action was taken against the advice of the Treasury, which argued that consolidated returns resulted in less expense to both itself and the taxpayer The 1934 limitation continued in effect until 1940.

One of the many problems associated with the use of consolidated returns is that of defining an affiliated group. The statute provides that an affiliated group shall include one or more chains of corporations connected, through common stock ownership, with a common parent where (1) the parent owns directly at least 95 per cent of each class of stock (voting and nonvoting) of at least one of the other corporations, and (2) at least 95 per cent of each class of stock (voting and nonvoting) is owned by one or more of the other corporations. The term "stock" used here does not include any nonvoting stock which is limited and preferred as to dividends.

the payment of an additional tax? Supporting such a special levy is the argument that a group of corporations reporting their income collectively have the advantage that the losses of one company cancel out the gains of another. It is the algebraic sum of the group's profits that is submitted for tax purposes. If all the corporations in the United States could submit a consolidated return, the tax base would be substantially reduced. At the present time, the advantage usually associated with the cancellation of gains by losses also includes offset of excess profits by unused excess-profits credit. In addition, the consolidated return wipes out much of what would otherwise be intercorporate dividends. As previously suggested, there are some compensating disadvantages; but how they balance against these gains has not, to the author's knowledge, been demonstrated. There would be less occasion for this special tax with the allowance of a generous carryover of losses and the elimination of the special tax on intercorporate dividends. If the privilege of consolidated returns is closely circumscribed and thus confined to cases where corporations in reality function as single business units and if adequate police measures are found for controlling holding-company practices, both the intercorporate dividend tax and the consolidated return levy can be abolished. Until this condition is met, they should be retained. The degree of the special levy should be based on concrete study of the net tax advantage resulting from the use of consolidated returns.

TAXATION IN ITS RELATION TO SMALL AND NEW BUSINESS

Significance of Small Business

Nearly everyone in America has a kind word for small business, though there is a widespread cynical impression that the kindness is largely confined to words. Big business itself frequently expresses confidence in its own ability "to weather the storm" but misgivings as to the survival of small business. Small business provides many with the opportunity to work

Excess-Profits Taxes, Monopoly, and Small Business

independently rather than "take orders." It is particularly prominent in small communities, which make an important contribution to American life. Small business is often new business and this involves new investment, an especially strategic factor in full and sustained employment. Small business is properly lauded as a challenger of monopoly and as the consumers' protector against the monopolistic and price-leadership tendencies of its larger competitors. Small business also provides many new ideas and innovations; it furnishes a spur that keeps the large corporation on its mettle. No one with even a casual knowledge of American business history can doubt either the tenacious will to live on the part of small business or the American people's support of it.[1]

Definition of Small, New, and Competitive Business and New Business Developing New Products

One of the knotty problems in dealing with the question of small business is defining it. The term is used in connection with family business units, including individual proprietorships such as farmers, retailers, and those in the service trades. It is also used to designate corporations having sales, assets, or net worth below a certain maximum or having less than a specified number of employees. In many instances, the matter of size is related to the nature of the business; a small steel company is one thing and a small laundry is another.

---

[1] From the standpoint of numbers, the small business unit dominates the economic scene in this country. There are 2 million businesses in the United States employing less than 100 workers each, representing 45 per cent of all workers (*Committee for Economic Development News*, April, 1944, p 8) According to data submitted by the Temporary National Economic Committee (*Problems of Small Business*, Monograph No. 17, 1941, p 248), of the total business units in 1936, more than 92.5 per cent were small (with less than $250,000 in total assets) and about 6.5 per cent were intermediate (with $250,000 to $5 million in total assets).

Small business is characterized by a very high mortality rate and also a very high birthrate. (See W. L. Thorp and W. A. Rothmann, "Business Births and Deaths," *Dun's Review*, February, 1937, p. 10; "Problems of Small Business," *op cit*, p. 66; W. Mitchell, Jr. and W Hayes, "Births and Deaths in Business," *Dun's Review*, November, 1942, p 16.)

Postwar Taxation and Economic Progress

The capital required for a successful laundry is infinitesimal compared with that needed to initiate a promising steel company. The term "small" is likely also to have different meanings according to the units in which it is defined. For instance, whether capital assets or the number of employees is chosen as the measuring stick will mean quite different relative positions for enterprises in the predominantly capital-using industries, such as public utilities, or for the predominantly labor-using enterprises such as chain stores.[1] Moreover, although small business and big business are in many respects fundamentally different, it is important to recognize that between the two there is an intermediate region.

New business is nearly as difficult to distinguish as small business. A new enterprise involves a new company and it is usually, though not necessarily, small. Not all new companies are new enterprises since some are the products of reorganization. Moreover, the term "new business" may be used to describe the expansion of old firms as they take on new products or even develop new markets. New business developing a new product is a still different category. Obviously, both the newness of the product and the exclusiveness of a firm's devotion to its development are matters of degree.[2]

Finally, competitive business is something distinct from either small or new business. Many large companies cannot be called monopolies by any stretch of the facts. On the other hand, very small businesses may exercise a considerable degree of monopoly in their particular localities, *viz.*, the barber service trade in many cities. Large enterprises may not seriously impede competition in some industries with widely scattered activities, but a small organization may be the dominant one for some individual product. Large firms

---

[1] E. B. George, "How Big is Big Business?" *Dun's Review*, March, 1939, p 19

[2] Thus Oxenfeldt distinguishes completely new business from succession in business and expansion of old business. He also presents a stimulating discussion of the conditions under which new business is socially advantageous (See A. R. Oxenfeldt, *New Firms and Free Enterprise*, American Council on Public Affairs, Washington, 1943.)

Excess-Profits Taxes, Monopoly, and Small Business

may be forced to compete with other large firms in large markets, and a small firm may conspire with other small organizations to obtain a monopoly in a small market. In most instances, monopoly or "monopolistic competition" results from the development of a few large firms in an industry—so large and so few that action by any one of them has an important effect on the market. Various forms and degrees of collaboration and conscious price manipulation grow out of these situations. However, no definite answers are available as to the number and size of small firms required in different lines to establish "effective competition."

Government Aid for Small and New Business

The social interest in giving small business all legitimate support, with solicitude both for employment and for the maintenance of effective competition, has been discussed earlier.[1] Interest in fostering competitive business is associated with a long-standing concern over the monopoly problem. However, when new small enterprises are engaged exclusively in the development of new products, the interests in economic expansion, competition, and economic innovation are all combined. It can be argued, of course, that innovation on the economic and engineering fronts can proceed too swiftly; that social adjustment is likely to lag in a period of rapid technological change, giving rise to serious problems. But this is reason for more social rather than less economic innovation. We are not likely to sanction a halt in economic progress while poverty remains so widespread. Moreover,

[1] Support for this view recently came from former Vice President Wallace as follows: "In the postwar period, if we are to create the maximum number of jobs for labor, it is apparent that rapid growing enterprises that are in the social interest should be encouraged by government policy to expand especially when they start small. Enterprising young men, eager to serve the general welfare, should not be forced to look upon the government as the only outlet for their energies. Big established concerns should not be so favored by the taxation system that they keep out new, small, growing enterprises for all time to come." ("Work, Peace, and Health," an address delivered at the American Labor Party dinner, New York, May 16, 1943)

Postwar Taxation and Economic Progress

there are hundreds of economic institutions, vested interests, and practices that protect the old against the new. Innovation deserves and needs all legitimate support, both governmental and nongovernmental.

The question of what constitutes legitimate aid is a difficult one. Some argue that business size should be determined in free competition and that any interference by the government is illegitimate. A deliberate attempt to subsidize smallness or penalize size as such would be and should be highly suspect. The proponents of small business do sometimes seek and secure passage of legislation that makes it impossible for large business to compete on the basis of efficiency. But aids may take the form of helping small business solve its own problems or of counteracting certain competitive factors that are obstructive to the free market.

The difference between giving a subsidy and correcting an unwarranted disadvantage is likely to be rather subtle. An advantage resulting from superior efficiency in economic competition is considered fair. An unearned advantage is one resulting from some factor other than superior efficiency. For instance, if chain stores can buy more cheaply than independent merchants as a result of reduced cost in handling large quantities of goods, then they have a legitimate advantage of large-scale distribution that should have the blessing of the consumer. But if they buy more cheaply than independent merchants merely because their size gives them greater bargaining power, the fairness of the advantage is questionable. The latter instance is reminiscent of the advantage that large shippers gained from railroads through the rebate system. The ability of large corporations to obtain capital through the security markets, which smaller companies find prohibitively expensive, is probably a borderline case, but on the whole it seems more of a size than an efficiency advantage. The distinction no doubt is one of degree, but it is real and important. A chain-store tax, in most instances, is clearly a penalty on size. However, as will be discussed

· 100 ·

later, there may be ways of modifying the tax system in the interest of small business without recourse to penalties or subsidies.

Obviously, much can be done for small and new business outside of the tax system. There has been a growing tendency on the part of capable and talented men to choose careers within established business. This might be checked to some extent, perhaps, by a different type of conditioning in colleges and communities. Governmental agencies and universities can provide services that will increase the efficiency of small business in many ways. For personal limitations, better training and guidance are the obvious remedies. But perhaps the most promising form of aid to small business is the development of financial institutions to serve its needs for equity capital. A possibility here is the formation of community organizations to facilitate investment of community funds in sound local undertakings. These institutions might operate like investment trusts or they might confine themselves to advisory services only. They already exist in some communities and should be studied and copied by others. Here we are principally concerned with modifications of the tax laws that will aid small business in surviving and new business in becoming successfully established.

Many of the improvements in the tax system recommended primarily for other reasons may also be supported as aids to small business. A more generous carry-over of losses would help both small and new business because such enterprises frequently operate with deficits. Simplification of the tax system would help small companies, since often they are unable to minimize their taxes to the same extent as large concerns having specialized tax personnel. The declared-value capital-stock excess-profits-tax combination has been especially inimical to small companies that have neither the time nor personnel to play the puzzle game involved in its application. Adequate and well-timed allowances for depreciation and obsolescence are especially important to companies contending with frequent losses and the inability to insure one risky venture with another. It seems highly probable that a sensible and well-balanced tax system is the best promotion government can give to business, both big and small.

As a special tax aid to small business, we suggested in an earlier report[1] that some concession be given to the reinvested earnings of new small companies. The concession might be supported for several reasons. First, this is a point in the competitive struggle where small business is especially handicapped, and the impediment is not a matter of efficiency or inefficiency but mainly an attribute of size. Companies of small size and at an early stage of their growth find the capital market prohibitively expensive. Second, tax concessions to reinvested earnings can be made temporary rather than permanent. If the company grows and flourishes, the government can claim a share in its prosperity when the owner retires. This it can do through the capital-gains feature of the income tax. (Thus, if the taxpayer invested $25,000 in the business itself and the business doubled the investment, without taxes, the basis of the investment would be $25,000. If he subsequently sold out his interest in the business for $50,000, he would then be subject to a tax on a capital gain of $25,000.) Better understanding and more general acceptance of the function of capital-gains taxation would open the road to sound methods of business promotion through the tax system. The concession would be one of time only and give no permanent advantage. Of course, a postponed tax gives the taxpayer the benefit of the doubt as to the retention of the tax provisions under which he would make his ultimate settlement. Obviously then, it is important to stabilize the tax treatment of capital gains. Certainly it would be much better for the federal government to attempt a promotional role of this character than for the states to bid for the location of new business, as many of them now do.

[1] *Production, Jobs and Taxes*, McGraw Hill Book Company, Inc., New York, 1944.

Excess-Profits Taxes, Monopoly, and Small Business

The major obstacle to overcome in such a program is again that of definition and classification. First, there is the question of whether concessions to reinvested earnings should be confined to corporations. Extending them to unincorporated companies would seriously impair the universality of the personal income tax and would further complicate the problem of definition and administration. On the other hand, restricting a promotional program to corporations would be open to serious attack on the score of discrimination. In our earlier report we suggested confining the concession to corporations in the manufacturing field, where almost all business is incorporated. However, this not only creates the difficult problem of defining the manufacturing field but greatly restricts the usefulness of the program. On further consideration, it seems probable that such concessions had better be limited only to those concerns with accounting records sufficient to determine the facts of reinvestment and withdrawal.

It would certainly be quite a task to specify what constitutes new business in the fields of farming, retailing, and the service trades. Should the determining factor be new ownership, new management, new premises, or a new line of business? If A starts his son in a store previously operated by A, or by A and his son, is this a new business? If a store acquires new ownership and management but retains the same name, location, and line of merchandise, is this new business? Probably new ownership and management and either new premises or a substantially new line of merchandise are requisite for an undertaking to qualify as "new." To these problems would be added that of defining business itself. Does it include farming and the professions? The difficulties of establishing and enforcing rules over such a wide territory are obvious enough, but they might not prove prohibitive.

The limits of a concession to reinvested earnings also require consideration. The time limit might be placed, for instance, at 5 years and the size limit at a half million dollars of assets. The privilege should be confined to independent companies owned exclusively by noncorporate stockholders. The half-million-dollar limit is well below the point at which the capital market becomes accessible, and the 5-year period should give the company ample time to acquire momentum.

The suggestion has been made that it may be possible, with the aid of the U.S. Patent Office, to determine new businesses that are devoted mainly to the development of new products If it seems desirable to limit strictly the field for concessions, they could be confined to companies of this sort. It is true that business developing new products often already has the benefit of a patent monopoly. But this contemplated classification could be somewhat broader than that which serves as the basis of patents. Moreover, the success of such new ventures is by no means assured by the patent. Since the social interest in innovations is especially high, concessions in this direction seem warranted.

Would a 5-year period in which to reinvest earnings without immediate tax be of much assistance to new businesses? Many of them start their careers with losses and, in that event, the loss carry-over might be of more consequence. But probably enough new businesses have vital need for new capital, which they themselves might supply out of earnings, to make this kind of tax concession significant.

It is recommended that new small companies be taxed only on dividends and withdrawals for the first 5 years of their development.

Some discussion of the use of graduated rates in a corporate income tax was presented in this chapter. This procedure has always been unpopular with a majority of the expert critics. Some object to graduation on the ground that the corporate tax is but an attempt to collect at the source for individuals and progressive rates only confuse the process. Graduation involves the difficulty, previously discussed, of defining small business and, in addition, is complicated by the fact that large businesses sometimes have small incomes. Graduation entails deliberate discrimination, whereas a con-

Excess-Profits Taxes, Monopoly, and Small Business

cession to reinvested income more largely counteracts an unfair advantage. Although monopoly elements in income probably have some relation to the size of a company, the correlation is much too rough to serve as a satisfactory basis of tax classification. On the other hand, it is true that very small corporations have more in common with individual proprietors than with large corporations. If the special corporate tax is retained, perhaps some graduation in the lower brackets of income is warranted. But it appears that a better device for aiding small corporate business would be to allow it the option of being taxed like a partnership. A small corporation would either be taxed exactly like an individual proprietor or it would pay a special corporate tax on reinvested income and a franchise tax on all earnings. Exercise of this option might be required to cover a longer period than one year; it might be made irrevocable for a 5-year interval.

Summary of Recommendations for Small Business

The social interest in the development of new small business is obvious, but problems of definition and of avoiding discrimination are extremely difficult. Accordingly, some special tax consideration for reinvested earnings in the case of new small companies has been recommended. These tax concessions would have the advantage of being temporary only. Such income must eventually confront the tax system through the capital-gains tax. If a corporate tax as such is retained, new small companies might be given an additional advantage in the option of being treated like partnerships, thereby paying only personal taxes on the prorata share of the company's earnings.

TAXES ON SIZE OF BUSINESS

Considerable support can always be found for the view that the tax system can and should be used to discourage business size. One such use can be observed in chain-store taxation, which finds its principal disinterested support among those who object to business institutions of great size and with far-reaching tentacles. But chain-store taxation is chiefly a matter of carrying economic competition to the legislature, where the decision is likely to be influenced not by any principle or any consideration of the public interest but by the more effective lobby. It is probably true that our business institutions are "too big"; but no criterion of excessive size is available except the test of efficiency in a market that is free, though policed to prevent monopoly.

CONCLUSION

The tax system is not a discriminating means of dealing with the monopoly problem. A more effective and courageous use of the police power would be preferable. However, pending such development, the use of the taxing power in the form of a special levy on intercorporate dividends, in spite of its admitted crudeness, is probably better than no control. And tax concessions, not involving subsidy, might well be granted small new business. The regulation of intercorporate financial practices should be squarely lodged with the federal government and should be exercised to prevent abuses and any interference with legitimate business operation and expansion. Beyond this, we need to know much more about the impact of monopoly on the economy, and we certainly need a more clearly defined policy in this field. A sounder view among business men on the suicidal effects of destroying competition and restricting output would be helpful. Where reasonably effective competition cannot be maintained, government regulation, government ownership, or competition of cooperatives are the appropriate remedies. This is an issue that needs more illumination and courageous action. When such illumination and such action are achieved, it probably will be apparent that the usefulness of taxation in the control of monopoly is extremely limited.

V. FURTHER PROBLEMS OF SELECTING AND APPLYING A BUSINESS TAX

INTRODUCTION

IN THE preceding chapter, business taxation was discussed mainly as it relates to the social control objectives of checking monopoly and recapturing monopoly profits. This chapter deals with problems of selection, particularly as between a cost tax and a net-income tax and as between a general business tax and a corporate business tax. It also discusses the application of business taxes to cooperatives and to publicly owned utilities, and finally, certain problems of business-tax administration, especially at the federal level. Certain special problems, particularly those connected with determining a business net-income base, are presented in Chap. VI.

NET VERSUS GROSS-INCOME TAXES

Possible Business Income-tax Bases

Obviously there are many degrees of "grossness" among possible business income-tax bases. Gross income is usually defined to include all receipts without any deductions. The objection to this base is that as goods move from one processor to another, values are recounted at successive transfers. The amount of tax paid on goods by the time they reach the consumer will depend on the number of transfers involved in their preparation. Some of this tax can be avoided by the integration of industry, which eliminates transfers in the processing and distribution of goods. It has been suggested that "value added" might serve as a more suitable base than gross income. Under this procedure the cost of goods sold or materials purchased would be deductible. A business pay roll tax applies to a narrower base; it focuses upon one element of business cost and ignores the others. A tax on "operating income" allows deduction of all business expense except interest paid and, perhaps, rent paid. Finally there is the net-income tax under which all business expenses, including pay roll, interest paid, rent paid, and cost of materials, are deductible.

Seeking a rational basis for a business tax, the National Tax Association Committee on Federal Taxation of Corporations[1] suggested that a net-income tax could be defended on the ground that the government is a "silent partner" of business and should share accordingly in the latter's success. As stated in an earlier chapter the government might also be conceived as a factor of production, in which case business should make a tax payment along with other cost outlays, whether or not it makes a profit. To the author, all these theoretical props for business taxation are more or less rationalizations to support a tax program chosen mainly with opportunistic motives. The business tax is acceptable at all only on the score that there are worse ways of raising revenue. In choosing among forms and bases of business taxes, principal attention should be given to their incidence and effects.

Incidence of Alternative Forms of Business Taxes

How will the incidence (final burden) of a business income tax be affected by changing the base from net to gross? What bearing does incidence have on tax policy?

One may answer the second question by posing a further question: If business taxes are shifted to the consumer, what becomes of the supposition that business should pay for the benefits of government? Of course, it can be argued that business taxes are no less defensible because they are shifted forward. It can be contended that the consumer should expect to bear a part of business taxes, since he is paying only for the true costs connected with goods and services he

[1] *Final Report of the Committee of the National Tax Association on Federal Taxation of Corporations*, 1939, p. 35.

Further Problems of Selecting a Business Tax

receives. But the uncertainties in the shifting process—the possibility that the results may be purely haphazard—are reason for avoiding indirect taxation. Especially objectionable are taxes that involve several steps of shifting; that is, taxes intended or expected to fall upon ultimate payers twice or three times removed from the original taxpayer. If we must use indirect taxes and charge the consumer for the benefits of government in accordance with his purchases, why not use a retail sales tax, which is shifted in only one step, with its incidence reasonably clear?

Some aspects of the problem of incidence in business taxation were presented in an earlier chapter. There it was observed that the corporate net-income tax is open to objection because, on the basis of analysis and according to some authority, part of the tax may be shifted forward to consumers. However, much of the tax probably "stays put" and the uncertainties are less than those entailed in the use of many other taxes. As more elements of "grossness" are introduced in the income-tax base and a larger number of costs are included, the possibilities of shifting become greater. The uncertainty of the incidence also increases.

The gross-income tax is subject to two kinds of uncertainties. One attends the duplication of values during the course of processing and distribution. As already indicated, the total accumulation of taxes will depend on the number of transactions before the commodity reaches the consumer.

To illustrate, the manufacturer sells goods to the jobber at a price of $1,000,000; the jobber sells them to a wholesaler at a price of $1,050,000; and the latter passes them on to several other middlemen, each one adding a moderate mark-up until they are ultimately sold to the final consumer at a price of $1,500,000. A gross income tax would include in its base the sum of all of these exchange values. A retail sales tax based on the final exchange avoids this overlapping and in this respect is a sounder form of business taxation.[1]

[1] Harold M. Groves, *Financing Government*, rev. ed., Henry Holt and Company, Inc., New York, 1945, p. 255.

Postwar Taxation and Economic Progress

The other kind of uncertainty is that of shifting. Gross income includes all business costs and the element of business profit in addition. Under ordinary circumstances, the bulk of a gross-income tax can probably be passed on along with the other costs of doing business. But there are important exceptions. Every business man knows that, because his costs of manufacturing are, let us say, $100 per unit, there is no assurance that $100 per unit can be recouped in the selling price. The elasticity of consumer demand, the extent of control over price (monopoly), and the business-cycle phase involved are all important elements determining the degree of shifting. No doubt, long-run adjustments to the tax will be more complete than short-run adjustments; but the latter may be of crucial importance.

Since the element of duplication in a gross-income tax is a fairly conclusive count against it, "value added" has been advocated as an alternative base. This would differ from gross income, as previously explained, in that the cost of goods sold would be a deductible expense. The "value-added" base would eliminate the duplication factor but it would not solve the problem of uncertainties of incidence. The proponents of this tax base apparently believe that much of the tax would be absorbed by industry. If the objective is to assess the consumer according to his use of the end product of American business, certainly a retail sales tax is a simpler and surer means.

As to uncertain incidence, a pay roll tax is at least as objectionable as any other gross business tax. The author has stated elsewhere:[1] "The incidence of these [pay roll] taxes cannot be predicted with any great degree of assurance. On the whole, the safe conclusion would seem to be that it is divided among employers, labor, and consumers; but in what proportion cannot definitely be said." This noncommittal judgment has been criticized as "too defeatist." But the author has seen no analysis of the problem that would warrant

[1] *Ibid.*, p. 148.

Further Problems of Selecting a Business Tax

a change in the conclusion. It is usually conceded that the pay roll tax as a support for general government would be objectionable. It is defensible as a support for social security since it correlates a discernible special benefit from government with the charge made to maintain that benefit. The desirability of some measure of personal responsibility in the social security system probably overrides, in this instance, the objection of obscure incidence in pay roll taxes.

Effects of Alternative Forms of Business Taxes

As to the effects of various forms of business taxes, the first point to consider is their impact upon business incentives and other aspects of production. Insofar as a gross tax is shifted to the consumer, it is not a penalty upon success or a deterrent to business incentives since net profits *may* not decrease as a result of the tax. The effect is the same as though the tax had been levied on retail sales. However, either a gross tax or a retail sales tax may affect profits adversely insofar as these profits depend upon the consumer's purchasing power. Also, the uncertainty and capriciousness of incidence in a gross tax may have an adverse effect on incentives. All business taxes are closer to the sphere of active business management than personal taxes and take more chances with business incentives accordingly.

A gross tax is probably more inimical to the development of "infant industries" than a net tax. During the struggling years of business infancy, the net tax presents no problem, whereas a gross tax increases costs and decreases chances of survival. Whether big business enjoys a higher rate of profit than small business has long been a matter of dispute. If it is true, as here contended, that big business is generally more profitable, the net-income tax will favor small business. Small business may also be favored by a graduated rate and, while graduation may be used with a gross tax, in practice it is more often applied to the net-income tax. Graduation of a gross tax would add confusion as to its incidence. A net-income tax is unfavorable to small business in one respect: it cuts into the main source of capital for small business—earnings available for reinvestment. A program that would confine the business tax to undistributed profits and grant small business a postponement of this levy would help solve the capital problem of small enterprises. Undoubtedly the deduction of losses does much to lift the curse from the net-income tax as far as risk-taking is concerned; and it has been argued that, under some conditions, this tax may actually increase the propensity to risk.

When any departure is made from the net-income base, there is a greater possibility that the tax may be a contributing cause of bankruptcies. In fact, a gross tax of any sort may be a direct cause of business failure. This may or may not be a bad effect. It can be argued that bankruptcies exercise a wholesome influence—that they are a good purge for the economic system. On the other hand, bankruptcies often involve painful readjustments and confusion. They may mean the loss of investment in going-concern value. Most students of business finance would probably agree that an element in the tax system which contributes to the instability of business is undesirable.

The impact of the net-income tax fluctuates with the prosperity of business. This takes no account of the immediate financial needs of government. It creates budgetary instability and leads to deficit financing. On the other hand, although opinions differ as to whether deficit financing can reduce the severity and shorten the length of depressions, the consensus probably favors the affirmative view.

As previously suggested, the net-income tax encourages financing with loan capital. In this respect, it probably contributes to the instability of business. Concerns financed with loan capital have higher fixed charges than those financed with equity capital and may, as a result, be less able to meet contingencies—either those that arise in a particular business or those due to a general economic slump.

Further Problems of Selecting a Business Tax

The National Tax Association Committee on Federal Taxation of Corporations summarized[1] the effects of cost and surplus taxes as follows:

> On the other hand, its repressive influence [that of the surplus tax] upon business enterprise would probably be considerably less, for the tax on pure economic profit would not be paid unless the gamble were a successful one and probably more businessmen would risk a venture under this arrangement than would be the case if a somewhat smaller amount were to be exacted from every venturer, irrespective of whether he won or lost. It must be recognized, however, that it is quite possible for a general business tax based on pure economic profit to be seriously depressive to enterprise if the rates are pushed to very high levels. Similarly, very heavy general business taxes based on sales or other cost factors may materially repress consumer demand.

More positive support for the surplus form of tax on the score of its effect on production was expressed by the Canadian Royal Commission on Dominion-Provincial Relations as follows:[2]

> Another unfortunate result . . . of the present distribution of financial powers is the incentive to rely on taxes on costs instead of taxes on surpluses. By taxes on costs, we may include not only direct taxes on business imposed without reference to the net income of the business owner, but also consumption taxes (including property taxes on residential and commercial buildings) which affect costs of living, wages, and eventually all costs of production. Consequently, many resources which would be used at lower production cost levels must be left idle and the tendency to increase taxes on costs during time of depression greatly weakens Canadian competitive power abroad, and increases rigidities and difficulties of adjustment at home. The effect of this pressure on marginal enterprises, on the general level of economic activity, and on the national income cannot be calculated. But now that 30 per cent of the national income is collected by governments and spent by them

---

[1] *Final Report*, pp. 36–37.
[2] *Report of the Royal Commission on Dominion-Provincial Relations*, Book II, 1940, p. 79.

(either by redistribution in the form of pensions, relief, and interest payments, or in payment of the costs of government services), any avoidable waste or inefficiency in the process is serious.

On balance, the conclusion is that if we are to have federal business taxes as such, the net-income tax is preferable. This is in accord with what is and has always been the predominant federal practice, at least in times of peace. As for the states, a presumption in favor of the net-income tax can also be recognized. State finance, however, involves special problems which will be considered later.

CAPITAL-STOCK TAXES

Thus far, the discussion has been confined to cost taxes based on income, but most of what has been said applies also to such taxes based on capital stock. Here, however, additional difficulties of administration appear. Our present federal capital-stock tax is based on declared value checked by the use of the same base for the attending excess-profits tax (of prewar origin and not to be confused with the excess-profits tax developed during the recent war). This combination has been discussed; but it should be repeated that under this levy no attempt is made to assess the actual capital or capitalization of corporations. A real capital-stock tax would require either an appraisal of each corporation's capital or reliance upon the face or par value of outstanding securities. The appraisal is an extremely difficult task, much like that of establishing "invested capital" for purposes of the war excess-profits tax. The use of par value as a base puts a premium on undercapitalization. This could be avoided by including surplus in the base, but it would encounter the obvious difficulties of appraising assets or accepting book accounts. The capital-stock taxes employed by the states usually aim only at the equity value of corporations, ignoring the value represented by indebtedness. This again puts a premium upon bond financing.

Further Problems of Selecting a Business Tax

Support for a federal capital-stock tax is based upon the theory that corporations should pay for the benefits received from government. Capital stock is a measure of corporate size, and the latter presumably has some relationship to government services received. If, as the author holds, the benefit theory is largely a vague rationalization, there seems to be no adequate reason for undertaking the heavy administrative task of applying a capital-stock tax at the federal level.

A federal capital-stock tax was imposed between 1916 and 1926. The tax aimed at the total value of a company's business, "including stock, surplus, undivided profits, tangible property, goodwill and other intangibles—in short, every element that gives it an important present or prospective value."[1] The problems involved in this ambitious program were summarized by Professor Harley Lutz[2] as follows:

> The problems of corporate valuation presented by this tax were stupendous. . . . The capital stock tax required that an appraisal be made of all the corporations doing business in the United States, covering every factor and element in the business and property of each that might contribute to its value. About 340,000 returns are handled annually by an office force of 128 persons This was manifestly an impossible task, unless a very large element of self-assessment were permitted. The returns were "audited" but this process must obviously have been the sheerest formality in the vast majority of cases. With all due credit to the ability and the good intentions of the Capital Stock Division, it seems, in view of the difficulties of accurate corporate appraisal, that if the burden of the capital stock tax were equitably distributed it was simply a miracle. The only ustification of such a tax was as an emergency war revenue measure. It was repealed by the Revenue Act of 1926.

[1] C. A. Drake, "The Federal Capital Stock Tax," *Proceedings of the National Tax Association*, 1922, p. 224.
[2] Harley L. Lutz, *Public Finance*, 2d ed., D. Appleton-Century Company, Inc., New York, 1929, p. 500.

Postwar Taxation and Economic Progress

MULTIBASE BUSINESS TAX

A proposal still to be considered is that of a multiple-base business tax. Alternative bases would be specified and the one producing the highest tax would be used. This was suggested by the Second Model Plan of the National Tax Association Committee on State and Local Taxation.[1]

Of the alternative levies suggested, the first was a flat minimum tax, something like a poll tax, to cover the cost of administration or to exact a small charge for the privilege of corporate existence. The minimum charge might also be regarded as an administrative device to avoid the difficulty of applying other taxes to small business. In the case of small and inactive businesses, this minimum charge would probably be the only business tax paid. The second alternative suggested was a tax based on net income. This levy would be especially effective in reaching the more profitable businesses. The third alternative was a tax on gross income. This would reach the large but unprofitable businesses and the nonprofit cooperatives, and it would provide needed revenue in depression years. Rates would be adjusted so that normally the average business would pay the net-income tax as the highest of the three alternative levies. The model plan recommended no distinction between incorporated and unincorporated business in the application of this tax. However, some classification, differentiation, and exemption would not be incompatible with the plan, and "value added" could be substituted for gross income if the former seemed preferable.

The Committee's proposal is attractive in some respects, especially as a plan for state business taxation, where it would surely be an improvement on the arbitrary and chaotic practices of many states. For use by the federal government, the objection is that it might be the signal for an enlargement

[1] Committee on State and Local Taxation, "Second Report on a Plan of a Model System of State and Local Taxation," *Proceedings of the National Tax Association*, 1933, pp. 353–427.

Further Problems of Selecting a Business Tax

of the business-tax field. It would add administrative complications and introduce further confusion as to the incidence of the business-tax system. If the federal government maintains an independent business tax at all, it had better continue with its time-honored plan of taxing corporate net income.[1]

CORPORATE VERSUS GENERAL BUSINESS TAX

The rational justification for a business tax—whatever it may be—would seem to require payment by partnerships and individual businesses as well as by corporations. It has been said that "taxes restricted to corporations alone and not applying to unincorporated business must find their justification in special privileges granted the corporations."[2] However, the case for the retention of business taxes on rational grounds is extremely weak at best, and proponents are more nearly convincing when they use an opportunistic approach. But the practical results of extending business taxation to individual businesses and partnerships lend little support to the argument.

Among the difficulties in applying a business tax to unincorporated business is that of defining a business. What about farming and practicing medicine and serving as an engineer for a salary? Unless everyone is to be taxed twice upon all of his income, an arbitrary line must be drawn somewhere, and probably the point between incorporated and unincorporated business is as reasonable a place as any. Some advocate drawing the line even higher and would apply a business tax to large corporations only. There is much to be said for the view that, since large and small corporations differ greatly in their characteristics, there are really two

[1] This chapter deals primarily with the federal tax system, and a different conclusion might be warranted in the case of the states The latter have many special problems, one of which is integrating a business-tax system with the general property tax. The state problem is discussed in a later chapter.
[2] *Final Report of the Committee of the National Tax Association on Federal Taxation of Corporations*, p. 31; *Proceedings*, 1939, p. 562.

species in the corporate family and this distinction should be recognized in the tax treatment.

Confining the business tax to corporations creates the danger of a differential burden for small corporations as compared to their unincorporated competitors, with the possible result of disincorporation to avoid the differential. Probably the effects of some disincorporation would not be too serious. For large businesses, the advantages of incorporation are usually conclusive, but there may often be a close choice in the case of smaller companies. Some graduation in the tax rate has been used to reduce the discrimination to a minimum, though this is a dubious remedy. Then too, small corporations often avoid corporate income by paying out profits as salaries. Corporations have an advantage over unincorporated businesses in the inapplicability of the personal tax to undistributed earnings. The continuation of this latter advantage is itself a major question discussed in an earlier chapter. However, even if a special tax on undistributed profits were imposed, small corporations might be allowed a special exemption or favorable rates. This is recommended in the case of new small business. Unless the undistributed-profits tax were imposed at a rate considerably higher than the lowest bracket individual rate, an advantage in the corporate form would still remain to justify a compensating levy on corporate income.

The reasons for usually confining business taxes to corporations were summarized by the Committee of the National Tax Association on Federal Taxation of Corporations as follows:[1]

1, The administrative difficulty and low revenue yield of taxes applying to large numbers of relatively small taxpayers; 2, the political unpopularity of the corporation based often on mere prejudice; and 3, the conscious desire, on grounds of public policy, to encourage small enterprise and discourage large concerns, or at

[1] *Final Report of Committee of the National Tax Association on Federal Taxation of Corporations*, 1939, p. 33.

Further Problems of Selecting a Business Tax

least to offset some of the competitive disadvantages of the small enterprises.

In many countries there has been experimentation with the application of a business-tax program to unincorporated business, either at the state or federal level, but the predominant practice confines the program to corporations. In our own country, New York and Connecticut have experimented with special taxes on unincorporated business. The base of the New York tax is net income and that of the Connecticut tax is gross income. Both states allow a substantial number of exemptions and New York, in addition, confines its tax to recipients of $5000 or more net income. About 8000 firms were subject to the tax in New York when the law was first passed and under prewar conditions; the number in Connecticut was about 30,000. These taxes determine taxability differently from a corporate business tax, but it is difficult to see wherein they afford an important clarification of business-tax theory.[1] Of course, many of the occupational taxes found in the states apply to unincorporated as well as incorporated business. There is little in experience with general business taxes that serves as an example of improved taxation. Most of the successful unincorporated business taxes exist only in college textbooks and tax committee reports.

APPLICATION OF THE TAX SYSTEM TO COOPERATIVES AS COMPARED WITH PRIVATE BUSINESS

Cooperatives have a definite place in "free enterprise," and they can play a significant and beneficial role in the future economy. As previously observed, they can serve as a check

---

[1] For sources see Paul Studenski, "New York State's Experience with a Tax on Unincorporated Business," *How Shall Business Be Taxed?*, Tax Policy League, New York, 1937, pp 86–87; J. J. Rauh, "The New York State Tax on Unincorporated Business," *Taxes*, Vol. 17 (June, 1939), pp. 345–347, 377; Ernest S. Goodrich, "Connecticut's Unincorporated Business and Cigarette Tax," *Bulletin of the National Tax Association*, Vol. 22, No 6 (March, 1937), pp. 168–171; State of Connecticut, *Report of the Connecticut Temporary Commission to Study the Tax Laws and to Make Recommendations concerning Their Revision*, 1934, pp. 460–469.

on monopoly. The cooperative movement offers a motivation different in many ways from that of profit business. To be sure, the monetary appeals are widely applied even here, but the service incentives are given greater stress than elsewhere and the profit motive is largely eliminated. The cooperative movement offers an avenue to those who dislike the motivation of profit business. Consumers' cooperation is based on the idea that "a business owned by its consumers, managed under their direction, and having no legitimate loyalties except to them, has a better chance to meet their needs than one owned and managed by outsiders."[1]

Whether this view has merit can and should be proved in the open market in a fair competition both of ideas and performance. But this does not imply that cooperatives should be subsidized, either directly or indirectly, by the government. From the standpoint of businesses competing with cooperatives, subsidies for the latter are demoralizing; from the standpoint of the cooperatives themselves, special favors from the government are paternalistic and contrary to the principle of independence and self-help which is a cornerstone of cooperative tradition. No doubt there are much less appropriate objects for subsidies than cooperatives, but this does not justify subsidies.

That a cooperative may have a net income, in the sense of a surplus above operating expense, is obvious. The surplus may be distributed to the stockholders in proportion to their stock (not exceeding a top rate, in some cases); or it may be retained as a reserve, to be used, perhaps, for expansion of the business; or it may be distributed to the patrons in what is called a "patronage dividend." In the latter type of distribution, the patrons, or consumers, share in proportion to their purchases. If a cooperative is a marketing association, the sellers take the place of the patrons and distribution may be according to the produce marketed.

[1] Charles Bunn, "Consumer's Cooperatives and Price Fixing Laws," 40 *Michigan Law Review* 165 (1941).

Further Problems of Selecting a Business Tax

It should be noted that the so-called cooperative movement includes a great variety of institutions and viewpoints, ranging from those of the neighborhood buying clubs to those of the California Fruit Growers' Association.

Cooperatives usually enjoy no special consideration under the general property tax, the social security tax, the sales tax, or any tax except the net-income tax and other business taxes. Flat annual license fees are frequently charged in lieu of franchise taxes and sometimes in lieu of all other state taxes. Specific exemptions from income taxes are accorded quite generally to farmers' cooperatives and sometimes to all corporations organized under general cooperative laws. Frequently, reserves are allowed as a deductible business expense.

Under the federal income-tax law, cooperatives are exempt from the corporate levy providing they are farm-marketing or farm-purchasing associations and if not more than half their business is with nonmembers. Other cooperatives are exempt only on income paid out as patronage dividends. Under some state income-tax laws (Wisconsin's, for instance), all cooperative associations are exempt provided they meet certain standards specified in the statutes. However, under both federal and state laws, corporate income distributed as dividends on cooperative stock is ordinarily subject to the corporate income tax. Administrative practice of long standing permits a deduction of patronage dividends by the cooperative, but the reporting of such receipts by producers (such as farmers or merchants) is required for the personal tax. Patronage dividends are probably not taxable to consumers though this seems not fully established. Personal exemptions have been so high and distribution has been in such small amounts to so many recipients, mostly rural, that the issue has not often troubled administrators. The present federal declared-value capital-stock excess-profits-tax combination and the war excess-profits tax follow the same rules of classification for cooperatives as the net-income tax.

Postwar Taxation and Economic Progress

Application of the income tax to cooperatives has been an issue of long standing in Great Britain. The House of Lords went so far as to hold that not only were patronage dividends not income but that earnings "held in common to advance the common purpose" (reinvestment) were in the same class. Parliament later (1933) provided that the savings effected by consumers' cooperation over and above patronage dividends should be taxed.[1]

In a recent case involving the issue of whether a consumers' cooperative engaged in buying and selling coal was cutting prices (in violation of a special statute) when it distributed a rebate, the decision was in the affirmative.[2]

In taxing cooperatives, the application of corporate and personal income taxes to patronage dividends is the point of major difficulty and confusion. A rebate (patronage dividend) to customers may be conceived as a retroactive price adjustment not representing income to the distributor. On this theory, the cooperative is an agency for increasing the bargaining power of its patrons. The cooperative charges or pays tentative or nominal prices subject to adjustment through a rebate, the latter determining the effective prices. If gains based on nominal prices, taking no account of effective prices, were subject to tax in the hands of the cooperative, the gain could be avoided by cutting the nominal to the effective price. In other words, cooperative pricing could be at cost, so that the business would have no patronage dividends to distribute. This would be inconvenient for the cooperative and contrary to its tradition opposing price wars.

In the case of the personal income tax, patronage dividends on production goods (those used in creating income) would

[1] Carr-Saunders, *et al.*, *Consumers Cooperation in Great Britain*, London, 1938, pp 464–468.

[2] *Midland Cooperative Wholesale v Ickes*, Secretary of the Interior, 125 Federal 2d 618 (CCA 8th), 1942, Certiorari denied, 316 U.S. 673, April, 1942, Rehearing denied, 316 U S. 712, June, 1942; Rehearing denied, 317 U.S. 706, October, 1942

Further Problems of Selecting a Business Tax

seem to be properly included in the tax base of customers. If a farmer buys a tractor at a bargain through a cooperative, his expenses of production will be reduced and this will augment his income from farming. Wisdom and shrewdness in buying are often a factor in income. On the other hand, patronage dividends on consumption goods (those used in the consumption of income) purchased by the final consumer would seem to be improperly included in the tax base of the customer. Thus, if a farmer buys groceries at a bargain he is merely reducing his cost of living. Cost of living expenses are not deductible, although a personal credit approximating average cost of maintenance, perhaps, is allowed. Buying at a bargain is a way open for all to beat the exemption. Income arises from selling goods dear, not from buying them cheap.

Most of those who accept the view that a patronage dividend is a retroactive price cut would concede one limitation to its application. Where a cooperative does a substantial business with nonmembers and distributes only to members, the distribution takes on the aspect of dividing profits. It is conceded also that dividends to stockholders according to investment, or the reinvestment of earnings which might later be so distributed, does not differ from similar procedures by noncooperative business. However, reinvestment may be earmarked (through stock dividends to purchasers) for ultimate distribution as patronage dividends, and in this case it does not differ substantially from a current patronage dividend.

Not everyone accepts this interpretation of the nature of a patronage dividend and the logic of its immunity from corporate income taxation. To some, the earnings or savings of a cooperative are a clear case of profits, and the disposition of such "profits" to members (usually both investors and patrons) regardless of the principle of division should make no difference in its taxability.

Even though the plausibility of exempting patronage dividends from taxation might be conceded, it could still be argued that the exemption leads to unfair competition. It is true that the exemption can be and is applied impartially. Patronage dividends distributed by noncooperative business are not uncommon. The trading stamps issued with purchases are retroactive price cuts not very different from rebates. Bonuses to employees are also given. All of these are treated as deductions and are allowed as offsets in arriving at the income tax base. But the patronage dividend is available to cooperatives in a way and to a degree not enjoyed by their rivals. It is only in the case of the former that a list of investors and one of customers corresponds and that the interests of the one and the other are so balanced that the alternatives of distribution to stockholders or rebates to patrons are not infrequently a matter of little consequence. For noncooperative business a patronage dividend must be either philanthropy or an attempt to build still greater (and taxable) profits for stockholders. For cooperative business, a patronage dividend is the normal procedure through which a successful business "squares up" with those who created and maintain it. Thus the exemption of patronage dividends is regarded by some noncooperative business as a government subsidy and a clear case of favoritism.

A program eliminating business taxes as such and integrating business and personal taxes would go a long way toward the exclusion of any present tax advantage enjoyed by cooperatives. It would extend to noncooperative business the status now enjoyed by *some* cooperative business. Certainly this is politically the most feasible move toward greater equality of competition. It would universalize the cooperatives' own view that a business association is essentially a group of individuals acting together for a common purpose. Of course, this would not eliminate the "special favor" shown patronage dividends in the hands of consumers, but it would go a long way toward making the income tax apply more equally between cooperatives and their rivals. Elimination

Further Problems of Selecting a Business Tax

of the competitive advantage of cooperatives is hardly ground for the selection of a business tax base other than net income.

Business, as well as the public, benefits by the competitive system and neither should seek to destroy it through tax exemptions. It is in the economic and not the political arena that business survival and success should be determined.

APPLICATION OF BUSINESS TAXES TO PUBLICLY OWNED UTILITIES

At present, publicly owned utilities are exempt from federal business taxes and in most cases they are also exempt from state and county business taxes, including the general property tax. They frequently pay the equivalent of local property taxes into municipal treasuries and sometimes an additional amount representing the profit on the business. The Tennessee Valley Authority pays local governments some equivalent of local taxes, but the payment is through federal legislation and is more or less gratuitous. Exemption of state and municipal utilities from federal taxes and of federal utilities from state and local taxes is a matter of time-honored legal precedent. The precedent holds that federal sovereign authority cannot tax the instrumentalities of the sovereign states, or vice versa. This means that municipally owned utilities escape federal income, profits, and capital-stock taxes. In addition, these utilities may be financed by municipal bonds, interest from which is not taxable to the recipient under the federal income tax. Acting on the grounds of policy rather than legal necessity, states often exempt publicly owned utilities from state business taxes, state and county property taxes, and sometimes even local property taxes.

It may be argued that to tax publicly owned utilities is merely taking money out of one pocket and putting it into another—a case of the public imposing taxes on itself. Since publicly owned utilities are not in competition with those that are privately owned, there can be no discrimination These propositions are plausible, but they will not stand analysis.

Let it first be said that, for purposes of this discussion, we are neither concerned with the question whether utilities should be under public or private auspices, nor with the dispute whether the results of public or of private management are better. One may favor public ownership (or oppose it) and still object to tax differentials between publicly and privately owned utilities.

Although there are good arguments for public ownership of public utilities, escaping federal or any other taxes is not one of them. It is not true that the public only taxes itself when it taxes a public utility. There are several publics involved in this issue: the consuming public, the taxpaying public, and, within the latter, the local, county, state, and federal taxpaying publics. It is not a matter of indifference in the interrelationships of these groups whether publicly owned utilities are subject to taxation. If a utility pays no taxes, the consuming public may get the equivalent in reduced rates. But the consuming public is not the taxpaying public even at the local level, and, of course, it is only a minor part of the taxpaying public at other levels.

There is no direct competition between publicly and privately owned utilities, it is true; but the ideas and performances associated with each are in constant competition, and the contest should be as fair as possible. It is obvious that, under present taxation schedules, immunity from the tax burden can be a conclusive factor in a business decision. Private utilities claim that their rates could be from 20 to 30 per cent lower if they had no federal taxes to pay.

Unfortunately, there are parties other than the federal government and the taxpayer involved in the abolition of tax privileges for publicly owned utilities. The states take the position that their independence would be destroyed were the federal government to tax the net income of their water

Further Problems of Selecting a Business Tax

and power projects. The answer is, of course, that a nondiscriminatory tax is not the power to destroy. Surely the law can define some middle course between immunity of municipal undertakings from federal taxes and a surrender of freedom to make choices vital to the independence of local government. At least in state administration, where immunities are not a matter of legal doctrine but of policy alone, the simple remedy for tax favors to municipally owned public utilities is to eliminate the favors. Of course, the discarding of business taxes as such would largely eliminate this problem along with many others.

PROBLEMS OF ADMINISTRATION

The impression prevails among many persons throughout the United States that the Bureau of Internal Revenue is more interested in raising revenue than in giving the taxpayer a fair deal under the law. Another impression widely held is that Bureau personnel are judged and promoted by the amount of revenue they "bring in" rather than by their efforts to keep the good will of the taxpayer or to administer the law equitably.[1]

---

[1] The views of some of the private accounting profession were expressed as follows at the 1941 National Tax Association Conference:

" . . I can dwell on another phase . . . that accountants are very much interested in, and that is the flavor of the administration of the corporate and personal income tax structure such as it is at the present time. Accountants and taxpayers may be wrong but I am giving it to you straight from the shoulder when I say that they almost unanimously believe that they are being dealt with increasing unfairness and lack of good faith. . . .

"Taxpayers who would not have thought of such a thing years ago are now putting what we call sleepers in their tax returns. . . A good deal like the situation of a contractor who was building roads for the State of Michigan, and he found that they always made him tear up a mile or two, or do something like that—so he got onto it, shortly, and began to leave a mile or two in bad shape. When the inspector came along and struck that, and got his note book and told him where to head in, the contractor went ahead and did it just like he expected " (Discussion of William A. Paton, *Proceedings of the National Tax Association*, 1941, pp 353–354.)

Postwar Taxation and Economic Progress

These views are especially common among accountants, but the latter are by no means unanimous on the subject. (And, outside the accounting profession, there are many who feel that it is the accountants who deserve a good spanking.) Some are convinced that the Bureau of Internal Revenue tries to be scrupulously fair and succeeds as well as can be expected, considering the size of its task.

The American theory of income-tax administration is to pit the best brains that can be recruited for the government against a "tax bar," at least equally competent and usually much better compensated, and let them fight in the hope that justice will emerge as a by-product. It is a very different procedure from that prevailing in Great Britain, where the administration takes pride in protecting the taxpayer as well as the revenue, and where public accountants are regarded as agents of the public as well as of private companies. It may not be possible to shift entirely to the British type of administration, but some of the confidence and good will that is generated by their system can be sought and achieved in our own. ·Better relations between government and business are desirable and important in many instances, but no field offers greater opportunities for improving these relations than that of taxation.

Facilities of business income-tax administration have greatly improved in recent years, much to the benefit of the taxpayer. During 1938, the Bureau of Internal Revenue adopted a progressive program of decentralization so that hearings and settlement of disputes could be conducted in regional offices. This has proved a great convenience to the taxpayer; it has reduced considerably delay in settlements; and it has saved government as well as taxpayer expense. It is judged by competent authority[1] to be the most important reform in federal tax administration in many years. Political appointment of the collectors (and until recently most of their

[1] Roswell Magill, *The Impact of Federal Taxes*, Columbia University Press, New York, 1942, p. 200.

Further Problems of Selecting a Business Tax

staffs) is still a target for criticism, but substantial progress is being made to eliminate this defect. Employees in the collectors' offices have recently been placed under civil service. However, both state and federal personnel is weakened by the continual seepage of trained men into more remunerative private practice. In the case of the states, personnel for tax administration is often recruited without the benefit of the merit system.

The judicial aspect of tax administration is very important. Tax controversies are by far the largest single category of cases heard by the Supreme Court. The Tax Court (formerly Board of Tax Appeals), with 16 judges, handles much of the appeal traffic but its jurisdiction is neither complete nor exclusive. Because of divided jurisdiction in tax cases, annoying conflicts of decision arise. It has been suggested[1] that this situation could be relieved to some extent were the Tax Court given jurisdiction in cases involving claims to refunds of income and estate taxes, as well as in cases involving deficiencies. Delay in litigation has been reduced, but the layman is shocked to learn that the average period required to carry a case to decision by the Supreme Court is still 9 years.

[1] *Ibid*, p. 210.

VI. PROBLEMS OF THE BUSINESS INCOME-TAX BASE

BUSINESS LOSSES[1]

General Considerations as to Business Losses

THE treatment of business losses is an important aspect of federal tax policy. The following considerations are especially relevant:

1. Fear of possible losses is often as important in business decisions involving large uncertainties as the hope of profits. "Businessmen are willing to continue operation of their enterprises at times when prospect of profit is small, providing they do not, by so doing, incur too great a risk of loss."[2] During the First World War a prominent critic[3] went so far as to suggest postwar government absorption of business losses in order to encourage the continuation of production at wartime levels. Business men and economists who have studied the subject agree that the importance of losses in the business calculus has been and is likely to be much underemphasized.

2. A business income tax paid on current income before the accumulated deficits of previous years have been absorbed is really paid out of capital rather than out of income.

3. Small businesses are less profitable as a group than large and established concerns, and the range of profitability and loss is much wider.[4] It is true that apparent conclusions

---

[1] The quantitative material in this section is largely the work of Oscar Litterer.
[2] David Friday, "Maintaining Productive Output," *Journal of Political Economy*, Vol. XXVII (January, 1919), pp. 117–126.
[3] *Ibid.*
[4] William Leonard Crum, *Corporate Size and Earning Power*, Harvard University Press, Cambridge, Mass., 1939; National Industrial Conference Board, *Effects of Taxes upon Corporate Policy*, 1943, p. 19.

Problems of the Business Income-tax Base

need to be qualified by the fact that small corporations often pay out profits as salaries. But it seems unlikely that this qualifying circumstance invalidates the generalization stated above. The mortality of companies in the infancy stage is evidence that losses are heavy among this group, and a mitigation of the effects of losses would help to preserve small business. The large corporation is in itself a "mutual insurance company," reducing the risk of loss from innovations. "Insurance" against loss is often a major reason for consolidation. A big company can offset losses from unsuccessful ventures against gains from successful ones, but a small company must rely on a carry-over to balance the results of unsuccessful against those of successful years.

4. The equipment industries are especially sensitive to business cycles and shifts in business confidence. On the downswing, the demand for their products (except for replacement and repair parts) can, and often does, approach zero. Therefore, they are particularly susceptible to losses in depression years. Whereas the production of consumers' goods varies directly with the demand for such goods, the production of industrial equipment is a "derived demand" that varies with the "acceleration" or "pick-up" in the demand for consumers' goods.

5. The degree and the scope of corporate losses, both in good and bad years, are rarely fully appreciated. Someone has suggested that our economic system should not be described as the "profit" system but rather as the "profit and loss" system. Had all American corporations been allowed to file a joint consolidated return with an unlimited carry-over and carry-back of losses from 1922 to 1939, their net income would have been reduced 45.7 per cent.[1]

6. Incompetence of management is sometimes responsible for losses, but market fluctuations and other impersonal factors are at least of equal importance.

[1] Calculation based on *Statistics of Income*, U.S. Treasury Department.

Postwar Taxation and Economic Progress

7. That business losses fulfill a useful economic function is evident, but it does not follow that they should be ignored by the tax system. Losses serve as a warning against a repetition of mistakes and (like positive profits) as a guide to the future allocation of resources. These functions would not be seriously impaired if the income tax were operated as a *true net-*income tax instead of as one in name only.

Losses in Capital-goods and Consumption-goods Industries

As mentioned in point 4 above, some industries are affected more than others by the fluctuations of general business activity. The capital-goods industries are subject to large cyclical losses, while the consumption-goods industries are subject to relatively smaller losses of this nature. For example, from 1922 to 1939, net losses reported by firms in the construction industry constituted 64.8 per cent of net income reported in the industry, while firms in trade reported such losses only to the extent of 20.9 per cent of net income.[1] The difference is no doubt largely due to the relative stability of demand in the two lines of business. The purchase of new durable goods, such as machinery and equipment and durable consumption products, can be deferred indefinitely. On the other hand, replacement of many kinds of consumption goods, such as food and clothing, cannot in most instances be postponed. With a highly stable demand, losses are generally due to low efficiency or errors of enterprisers.

A statistical study[2] of business losses accruing to 219 companies producing capital goods and 181 companies producing consumption goods, from 1929 to 1938 inclusive, reveals these differences strikingly (Table III). The annual net profit or

---

[1] These percentages were computed by comparing the total net statutory income and the total net deficit reported by the firms in the two respective industries, as published in *Statistics of Income*, 1922 through 1939, U S. Treasury Department.

[2] *Capital Goods Industries and the Federal Income Taxation*, Machinery and Allied Products Institute, Chicago, 1940, pp. 3–39.

Problems of the Business Income-tax Base

TABLE III
INDEX OF THE COMBINED NET PROFIT OR NET LOSS OF 219 CAPITAL-GOODS AND 181 CONSUMPTION-GOODS COMPANIES, 1929–1938

(Indices of net profit or net loss are calculated as a per cent of 1929 net profit Net loss is indicated by a minus sign)

Year	Capital-goods companies, per cent	Consumption-goods companies, per cent
1929	100 0	100.0
1930	50 1	85 1
1931	− 8 5	64 2
1932	−38 2	45 3
1933	−12 6	60 8
1934	5 9	64 2
1935	23 4	64 2
1936	51 9	77 6
1937	69 8	69 1
1938	14 2	55 3

SOURCE: *Capital Goods Industries and the Federal Income Taxation*, Machinery and Allied Products Institute, Chicago, 1940, Appendix A, p 27.

TABLE IV
PERCENTAGE OF 219 CAPITAL-GOODS AND 181 CONSUMPTION-GOODS COMPANIES REPORTING A PROFIT, 1929–1938

Year	Capital-goods companies, per cent	Consumption-goods companies, per cent
1929	96 8	93 4
1930	75.3	79 0
1931	29 2	70 7
1932	13 7	63 5
1933	30 1	90 6
1934	54 3	88 4
1935	71 2	87 8
1936	87 7	94 5
1937	95 0	90 1
1938	61 6	81 2

SOURCE *Capital Goods Industries and the Federal Income Taxation*, Machinery and Allied Products Institute, Chicago, 1940, Appendix A, p 27

Postwar Taxation and Economic Progress

net loss is expressed as a percentage of the amount realized in 1929. For three consecutive years, from 1931 through 1933, the capital-goods companies incurred net losses and in only three years during the period from 1929 through 1938 were the profits more than 30 per cent of the 1929 figure. The consumption-goods companies, on the other hand, realized a combined net profit each year, and only in one year, 1932, was it less than 50 per cent of the 1929 total.

TABLE V
CAPITAL-GOODS AND CONSUMPTION-GOODS COMPANIES CLASSIFIED BY THE NUMBER OF YEARS LOSSES* WERE INCURRED, 1929-1938

Years of net loss†	219 capital-goods companies		181 consumption-goods companies	
	Per cent in period	Per cent accumulated	Per cent in period	Per cent accumulated
0	8.2	100.0	47.5	100.0
1	9.1	91.8	13.9	52.5
2	11.4	82.7	11.0	38.6
3	15.1	71.3	11.0	27.6
4	16.9	56.2	5.5	16.6
5	15.1	39.3	3.9	11.1
6	12.3	24.2	4.4	7.2
7	6.8	11.9	1.1	2.8
8	3.2	5.1	1.1	1.7
9	1.4	1.9	0.6	0.6
10	0.5	0.5	0.0	0.0

* Federal income taxes were deducted from gross income
† The average number of years losses were incurred over the 10-year period
    Capital goods . . . . 3.8 loss-years
    Consumption goods . 1.4 loss-years
SOURCE: *Capital Goods Industries and the Federal Income Taxation*, Machinery and Allied Products Institute, Chicago, 1940, Appendix B, p 30

Contrasts are further revealed by an examination of the range in profit and loss by individual companies (Table IV). From 1929 through 1938, the percentage of capital-goods companies realizing a profit ranged from 13.7 to 96.8, while the comparable percentage for consumption-goods companies

Problems of the Business Income-tax Base

ranged from 63.5 to 94.5. Table V shows the losses by years. The majority of concerns producing capital goods incurred losses for four or more years. Nearly half of the companies producing consumption goods incurred no losses. Only 16.6 per cent of the latter group, as compared with 56.2 per cent of the former, had losses for four or more years.

Effective Rates of Tax

Companies with large nondeductible net losses pay a higher effective rate of income tax over the years than companies with an equal but regular income. This places a special burden upon risk-taking, which is precisely what an intelligent government, interested in a dynamic economy and high employment, should avoid. By assuming that all firms in an industry were allowed to make a consolidated return for the industry as a whole and by finding the ratio of taxes actually paid to the net income on a consolidated basis, effective tax rates *by industries* may be determined and compared. This was done for the period 1922 through 1939, covering a complete major business cycle. The total net income and the total net deficit in this period were computed for the various industries.[1] A rate of 13 per cent, the average legal rate for the period, was applied to the positive net incomes of particular firms to approximate actual taxes, and a limited carry-over of losses during part of the period was disregarded. The procedure shows discrimination among industries over the period but it does not show the still larger discrimination among firms.[2] The greater the losses among the companies

[1] This procedure was suggested by J Keith Butters, *Federal Taxation of Corporations*, unpublished doctoral dissertation, Harvard University, 1941. A part of this study has been published: "Discriminatory Effects of the Annual Computation of the Corporation Income Tax," *Quarterly Journal of Economics*, Vol. 54 (November, 1939), pp 51–72.

[2] This method of subtracting the annual net deficits reported by firms from the annual net income reported by other firms in the same industry is only an approximate measure of the stability of the industry. In some industries it is easier to organize corporations than in others. The newly organized firms have a greater mortality rate. Losses from such concerns are an important

making up the industry and the more frequent these losses, the greater the average effective tax rate.

The results of the study are shown in Table VI. From 1922 through 1939, agricultural and related industries paid a sizable net-income tax on an actual net deficit; and the service industry paid 149 times more in taxes than the actual net income, or a tax rate of 14,920.6 per cent.[1] Public utilities, on the contrary, paid only 18.3 per cent of their actual net income in taxes. Even though there is a much greater degree of homogeneity among manufacturing industries, there is still a wide range in the tax rate on the actual net income. The forest-products industry paid slightly over one-half, or 51.3 per cent, of the actual net income in taxes, and the food-products industry paid only 16.2 per cent.

To study the discriminatory effects of the federal income tax as a result of the variation in business losses among individual firms, the net statutory income or net deficit, from 1930 through 1942, of 60 corporations operating in Wisconsin was secured.[2] The companies were selected at random from the files of the corporation income-tax returns. The sample, however, was limited to companies incorporated prior to 1930 and having a complete record for the 13 years. It was also confined to companies with total assets of $50,000 or over; the smaller corporations of the owner-manager type tend to report compensation to their officers of an amount that will

---

part of the aggregate. In a few industries, a large proportion of the corporations are small and of the owner-manager type To avoid the income tax, these firms tend to take all the earnings in the form of salaries. Consequently, they report losses from year to year on the income-tax returns.

[1] The firms in the service group consist primarily of small corporations. The average amount of capital assets is significantly smaller than those, for example, in the retail-trade group that have a relatively stable aggregate income. This holds true for firms reporting a net income as well as those reporting a net deficit. Small corporations of the owner-manager type tend to report compensation to their officers of an amount that will result in a net operating loss in order to avoid the income tax. This fact, no doubt, accounts for a large share of the net deficits reported by firms in the service group

[2] From the files of the Wisconsin Tax Department.

Problems of the Business Income-tax Base

TABLE VI
EFFECTIVE FEDERAL INCOME-TAX RATE ON ACTUAL CORPORATE NET INCOME ACCRUING TO INDUSTRIES FROM 1922 THROUGH 1939
(Tax assessed on a strictly annual basis)

Industry	Tax Rate* 1922–1939
Agricultural and related industries	†
Construction	36.9
Finance	99.2
Manufacturing	18.7
Mining and quarrying	82.5
Trade	24.9
Transportation and other public utilities	18.3
Service	14920.6
All industries	24.4
Manufacturing industry	18.7
Chemicals and allied substances	16.5
Food products, beverages, and tobacco	16.2
Forest products	51.3
Leather and its manufactures	27.4
Metal and metal products	17.4
Paper, pulp, and products	18.0
Printing and publishing	17.7
Rubber products	26.7
Stoves, clay, and glass products	17.9
Textiles and its products	32.0

* The tax rate is the approximate federal corporate income tax paid divided by the actual net income accruing to the industry from 1922 through 1939

† The net deficit is larger than the net income

SOURCE: Calculated from *Statistics of Income*, 1922–1939, U S Treasury Department.

result in a net operating loss, thus avoiding the income tax.[1] The average legal rate of 13 per cent was used to determine the approximate federal revenue on the annual net income.

On the basis of a strictly annual assessment, 10 corporations, or 16.7 per cent, would pay a tax on an actual net deficit for the period; 15 (including these 10), or 25 per cent, would pay a tax of more than 15 per cent over (*i e.*, more than double) the average legal rate; and 19, or 31.7 per cent, would pay a tax of 10 per cent or more above the basic rate (Table VII). On the other hand, 23 corporations, or 38.3 per cent, would

---
[1] The trend of the net deficits reported in the sample approximates closely the trend for all corporations.

Postwar Taxation and Economic Progress

have been subject to about the average legal rate—less than 14.0 per cent. The average excess of the effective tax rates above the nominal legal rate for the 50 corporations with net income was 6.6 per cent.[1]

A provision for a 2-year carry-over of losses, which extends the accounting period of net income to 3 years, would reduce somewhat the divergence of effective tax rates. All

TABLE VII
Corporations Classed by Effective Income-tax Rate on Net Income from 1930 through 1942
(Tax assessed on a strictly annual basis)

Effective tax rate, per cent	Number of corporations		
	Actual	Accumulated	Accumulated, per cent
13 0–13 9	23	60	100 0
14 0–14 9	7	37	61 7
15 0–15 9	1	30	50 0
16 0–16 9	2	29	48.3
17 0–17 9	1	27	45 0
18 0–18 9	0	26	43 3
19 0–19 9	4	26	43.3
20 0–20 9	2	22	36 7
21 0–21 9	1	20	33.3
22 0–22 9	0	19	31.7
23 0–23 9	3	19	31 7
24 0–24.9	1	16	26 7
31 7	1	15	25 0
37 2	1	14	23 3
51.9	1	13	21.7
61.4	1	12	20 0
84 1	1	11	18.0
Taxes on net deficit......	10	10	16 7

Source Computations based on a sample of income-tax returns of 60 Wisconsin corporations from 1930 through 1942.

[1] Both the tax discrimination and the proportion of corporations involved were observed to be highly significant statistically.

Problems of the Business Income-tax Base

corporations subject to an effective rate above the average legal rate, when the tax is assessed on a strictly annual basis, would without exception secure some reduction with a 2-year carry-over of net losses (Table VIII). The average difference of the effective tax rate from the nominal legal rate would

TABLE VIII

CORPORATIONS CLASSED BY EFFECTIVE INCOME-TAX RATE ON NET INCOME FROM 1930 THROUGH 1942

(Tax calculated with allowance for a 2-year carry-forward of losses)

Effective tax rate, per cent	Number of corporations		
	Actual	Accumulated	Accumulated, per cent
0	3	60	100.0
13.0–13.9	30	57	95.0
14.0–14.9	2	27	45.0
15.0–15.9	2	25	41.7
16.0–16.9	1	23	38.3
17.0–17.9	3	22	36.7
18.0–18.9	3	19	31.7
19.0–19.9	1	16	26.7
20.0–20.9	1	15	25.0
21.0–21.9	0	14	23.3
22.0–22.9	2	14	23.3
23.0–23.9	1	12	20.0
32.5	1	11	18.3
35.2	1	10	16.7
59.7	1	9	15.0
70.3	1	8	13.3
Taxes on net deficit....	7	7	11.7

SOURCE: Computations based on a sample of income-tax returns of 60 Wisconsin corporations from 1930 through 1942.

be decreased from 6.6 to 4.9 per cent. According to these data, a provision for a 2-year carry-over of net losses would result in an average reduction of 25 per cent in the income-tax discrimination among corporations, caused by business losses. The combination of a 2-year carry-forward and a

2-year carry-back would reduce the average excess of effective tax rates to 4 1 per cent.

The number of years required to offset completely annual losses against net income was also calculated (Table IX).

TABLE IX
CARRY-OVER PERIOD SUFFICIENT TO OFFSET LOSSES COMPLETELY AGAINST NET INCOME

Carry-over period, years	Companies offsetting losses	
	Number *	Per cent
0	13	17.8
1	22	30 1
2	32	43 8
3	39	53 4
4	45	61 6
5	45	61 6
6	51	69 9
7	53	72 6
8	54	74 0
9	56	76 7
10	61	83 6
11	63	86.3
12	65	89 0
12+†	73	100.0

* Twelve corporations incurred losses that were offset against net income at two different times during the 13-year period Therefore, these corporations were counted twice. One of these corporations incurred losses at three different times which were offset against net income, and so it was counted three times

† The eight corporations included here could not completely offset losses against the net income over the period studied

SOURCE. Computation based on a sample of income-tax returns of 60 Wisconsin corporations from 1930 through 1942.

Thirteen corporations, or 17.8 per cent of the total number, incurred no losses during the 13-year interval and consequently would have had none to offset. Approximately one-half the companies would have offset their losses over a 3-year period or less, and slightly more than two-thirds over a 6-year period or less. The remaining one-third of the

Problems of the Business Income-tax Base

companies would have needed an extremely long period to offset their losses completely against later net income. Of course, corporations which never have a net income or have had one only in the distant past and are now in chronic trouble—"on the way out" perhaps—would not be in a position to use a carry-over of losses.

Losses in Revenue Due to a Carry-over

From the annual statutory net income or net deficit reported by the sample of 60 corporations,[1] estimates were made of the

TABLE X

REDUCTION IN REVENUE RESULTING FROM THE CARRY-OVER OF ANNUAL CORPORATE LOSSES

Carry-over Period of Losses, Years	Per Cent Reduction in Corporate Tax Revenue
2	4.1
4	7.4
6	10.8
8	13.0
10	13.4
12	13.5

SOURCE: Computations based on a sample of income-tax returns of 60 Wisconsin corporations from 1930 through 1942

loss in revenue resulting from a carry-over of losses to the two subsequent years; from a carry-back of losses to the two prior years as well as forward to the two subsequent years; from a carry-over of losses to the six subsequent years; and from a carry-over of losses for an indefinite period to prior or subsequent years. The average legal rate of 13 per cent was used to determine the approximate federal revenues. A

---

[1] Selection of the sample is described above. The total annual deficits reported by the sample were compared with the total deficits reported by all the corporations in the United States to determine the validity of the sample. The trend of the deficits for the sample deviates considerably from the trend for all corporations, particularly for the period from 1932 to 1934. There is a fairly close agreement between the sample and the universe for the other years. Since the corporations in the sample reported more losses proportionally than all corporations combined for some years, the effect of the various loss carry-overs is slightly exaggerated.

Postwar Taxation and Economic Progress

2-year carry-over would result in a revenue loss of 4.1 per cent of the total yielded on a strictly annual assessment of the tax. A 6-year carry-over of losses would increase the loss in revenue to 10.8 per cent and a carry-over for an indefinite period from 1930 through 1942 would increase the revenue loss to 13.5 per cent.[1] A combined 2-year carry-over and

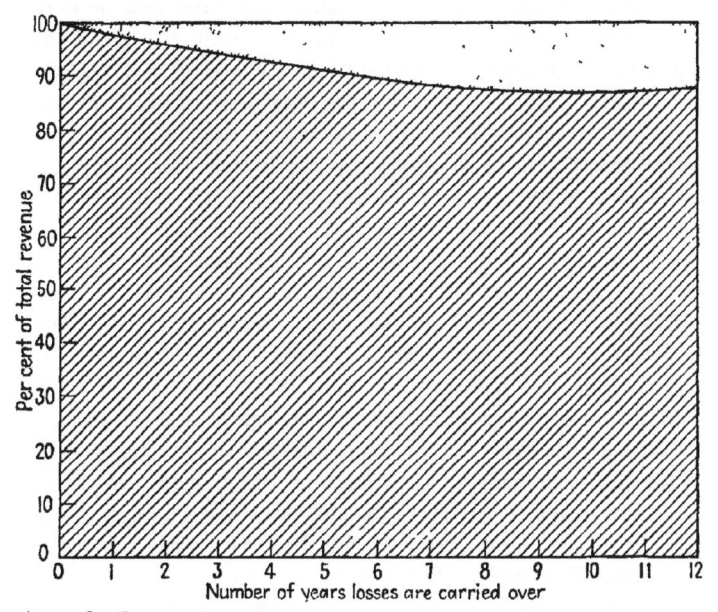

CHART I.—Decrease in corporate income-tax revenue resulting from carry-over of annual corporate losses.
SOURCE: Based on a sample of 60 Wisconsin corporations, 1930–1942.

carry-back would reduce the revenue yield by 5.1 per cent. The complete results of the study are presented in Table X and Chart I. The figures are influenced by the period selected for study. The loss would vary significantly with the nature of the period. This period was probably one of unusually heavy losses. The fact that the equipment industries are

[1] These figures are in approximate agreement with those found by Butters *Federal Taxation of Corporations*.

highly developed in Wisconsin should also be taken into account.

Tax Treatment of Losses Here and Abroad

Of course, a net-income tax allows business losses in a given year and for a given company to be offset against corresponding business gains—it would not otherwise be a *net-*income tax. The problem lies in the treatment of *net business losses* over a period of years. A carry-over of such losses for limited periods, never longer than 2 years, so they may be offset against net business gains of subsequent years, has been provided intermittently by the federal tax system. A carry-over provision was introduced in 1919 and remained in the federal revenue act until the Industrial Recovery Act of 1933. During the period of heavy losses in the thirties, businesses were without the benefit of this provision. It was reintroduced in 1939 and, in 1942, a carry-back of 2 years was added. The carry-back is based on the theory that certain postwar losses from reconversion should be taken into account in appraising the true net gains made by a business during the war years. It means that the tax calculations of the best war years may be reopened and scaled downward to take account of the effects of early postwar changes. This represents equitable treatment for those businesses that suffer losses, and it is thoroughly sound.

The British have been much more generous in their tax treatment of business losses than has the United States. The Royal Commission on the Income Tax (1920) recommended a 6-year carry-over, and this recommendation was adopted in 1926. Prior to 1926 a 3-year moving average of income had been in effect, and the British had experimented with even longer periods for reckoning business income. The shift from the averaging system to a carry-over for losses was recommended by the Royal Commission, which observed: "Hardly anyone has a good word for the average." The Act of 1932 extended the carry-over of losses beyond 6 years by permitting the deduction, without limits as to time, of either the balance of the loss or the total depreciation, set off within the 6 years in priority to such loss, whichever is less. The British are reputed to have a "tough" tax system, but in many respects it is sounder than our own.

Before the Second World War, France allowed a carry-over of business losses for 5 years, Germany for 2 years,[1] and Autsralia, in its laws of 1936–1937, for 4 years.[2]

Miscellaneous Considerations

The problem of losses is related to that of depreciation and obsolescence, discussed later in this chapter. Without a carry-over of losses, many companies in effect get less than full income-tax credit for the wear and tear upon their capital. A depreciation allowance which only adds to a loss is gone and gone forever so far as the income-tax base is concerned.

The carry-over of losses is related in some degree to the problem of integrating corporate and personal income taxes. Where the corporate tax becomes only a withholding device and a means of collecting an advance payment upon retained income, losses are important mainly in determining the retained income, although the income-tax accounting may also affect dividend policy. In any event, integration would not eliminate or greatly reduce the significance of proper allowance for losses. This is especially true when there are net deficits on the balance sheet. While this situation continues, all earnings will ordinarily be retained. The advance payment may remain indefinitely excessive because annual accounting has given an exaggerated picture of the earnings retained in the business.

From the standpoint of income tax theory and support for

[1] Gerhard Colm, in *Final Report of the Committee of the National Tax Association on Federal Taxation of Corporations*, Appendix, No. 1, Reprint, p 56.

[2] James H Gilbert, *The Tax Systems of Australasia*, University of Oregon, Eugene, 1943, p. 37.

business motivation, an indefinite carry-over of losses would be ideal. However, this would probably be unworkable administratively and would encounter problems in cases of mergers and reorganizations. Some "statute of limitations" might be required, but it should cover a carry-over period of not less than 6 years. As previously indicated, even a 6-year period would probably have been insufficient during the thirties to have allowed full credit for losses to one-third of the corporations engaged in business.

Recommendation and Supporting Argument

A carry-over of at least 6 years for net business losses should be allowed. Provisions for losses should apply to unincorporated as well as incorporated business.

There is no principle of taxation, either in terms of equity or in terms of effects on production, that warrants the discrimination resulting from the failure to carry over losses. Here again the major canons of taxation point in the same direction. Considerations of immediate adequacy of revenue may seem to argue against this change, but governments as well as individuals need to give some heed to their long-run interests. The Treasury can reduce the burden of risk-taking by assuming some risks itself. This will create problems of revenue instability but we shall have to live with these problems. There can be little doubt that an increase in income-tax rates to make up for the decrease in revenue resulting from a carry-over of losses would mean a net gain for business expansion. The correlation between losses and risk-taking, between losses and small new business, and between losses and the equipment industries is strongly indicative of the strategic importance of losses.

Much could be said for a carry-back as well as a carry-over of losses. If both were allowed without limitation, the income tax would be confined to the real earnings of a company during its life operation. In order to avoid refunds, however, and because the taxation of profits without the possibility of offset against future losses is usually regarded as less prejudicial than taxation without allowance for prior losses, the carry-back is not recommended for use beyond the first 2 years of the postwar period. It is highly important to business morale that the government maintain its present carry-forward and carry-back until the main effects of the war have been liquidated.

INVENTORY VALUATION

The Problem

Inventory valuation is one of the main factors in determining annual profits. Existing inventory valuation techniques usually seek to show annual profits including the full effect of price fluctuations. Unfortunately they do not present a true and clear picture of such profits even as so conceived. Moreover, throwing speculative gains and losses into the net income account of particular years has bad social effects. These gains and losses may cancel out over a longer span and it might be better to keep them from appearing at all in the net-income account, at least for taxation purposes.

The layman is sometimes puzzled when he is told by the business man that, while for income-tax administration a business, in some year, made a substantial book profit, actually there was no money available to pay the net-income tax. A prosperous business dislikes borrowing cash to pay taxes. Yet this is sometimes necessary. There may be more than one cause for this state of affairs, but probably the most common is inventory profits. Not only do inventory profits frequently appear in unliquid form but, in addition, they are often illusory in character. Any advantage they might give may disappear before it can be turned to useful account. Moreover, accounting procedure that recognizes speculative inventory profits annually may tend to accentuate the business cycle by amplifying the waves of optimism and pessimism attending it.[1]

[1] Inventory profits and losses may be realized or unrealized. Both are the

Problems of the Business Income-tax Base

Methods of Inventory Valuation

Cost or Market, Whichever Is Lower. The most widely used method of inventory valuation is cost or market, whichever is lower. In periods of rising prices an inventory valued at cost or market will be stated substantially at cost; in periods of falling prices, in terms of market. Critics point out that this shifting of the valuation base from one costing method to another with the turns of the business cycle will often produce highly artificial and capricious results in the statement of fiscal profits. However, space does not permit an extended discussion of this method.

Flow Theories of Cost and the Resultant Inventory Valuation. In the absence of an ideal procedure of applying specific costs to revenues (which authorities agree is impractical if not impossible in most businesses) management must select one of the "flow" theories of costing, with its subsequent valuation of inventory at the close of the fiscal period. This is based on an assumed pattern or order of flow, as follows:

1. The procession, or first-in, first-out interpretation,
2. The pool, cross section, or average interpretation,
3. The by-pass, or last-in, first-out interpretation.[1]

---

result of a rise or fall in prices while goods are being processed or stored; the realized ones have been consummated by the sale of the goods, and the unrealized ones have accrued to goods still retained by the going concern In applying the common procedure of inventory valuation—cost or market, whichever is lower—unrealized losses, but not unrealized gains, are reflected in current business income

The importance of inventories in the operation of business is rarely fully appreciated According to a recent study, the fixed assets of manufacturing and trading concerns, incorporated and unincorporated, were the equivalent of six months' output. For manufacturing, fixed capital at current valuation exceeded inventory by half, in retail trade the two were almost equal, in wholesale trade, fixed capital was one-third the size of inventory (Walter A. Chudson, *The Pattern of Corporate Financial Structure*, National Bureau of Economic Research, 1945, p. 82)

[1] William A. Paton, "The Cost Approach to Inventories," *The Journal of Accountancy*, Vol. 72 (October, 1941), p. 302.

Postwar Taxation and Economic Progress

The second of these procedures is disallowed for tax purposes, except in extremely rare instances, and need not be considered here.

First-in, First-out. The theory of first-in, first-out rests upon the assumption that costs are chargeable to revenue following the order in which they were incurred; *i.e.*, first bought, first sold. The closing inventory will be valued at approximate replacement costs by showing aggregates of the most recent purchases. It is generally agreed that this method of costing is suitable only for industries with a rapid turnover, subject to nominal price fluctuations, and showing no close relationship between raw material prices and selling prices. The "flow" is said to present historical costing, which is especially applicable to a perishable inventory condition, such as tire manufacturing. It is also said "to adhere to the balance-sheet viewpoint" in that it reflects currently changing values of the base stock.

Last-in, First-out. The last-in, first-out method of costing and evaluating inventories is based on the assumption that the cost of sales should be measured by the purchase costs of the latest additions to the inventory. The procedure attempts, insofar as possible, to match current costs with related current revenues.

Proponents of the method of last-in, first-out claim for it many advantages, among them the following: the procedure eliminates from the income report profits and losses due to price fluctuations; it provides a ceiling over temporarily enhanced earnings and, later on, a cushion against the effects of receding business; it provides better comparative data on the status of the business and thus enhances managerial efficiency; it levels profits for tax purposes, and, if adopted when prices are lowest, it also lowers taxes.[1]

[1] In the hearings held on the Revenue Act of 1938, spokesmen for certain industries requested that the law be modified to permit a new method of inventory accounting for tax purposes. The modification proposed would permit a change in the assumed order of disposition of goods so that those sold might be

Problems of the Business Income-tax Base

Critics of last-in, first-out argue that the procedure does not show inventory at approximately current purchase price for balance sheet purposes;[1] that it fails to reflect in the current income statement real economic changes (in the price level); that it levels profits where statement of profit fluctuation is

---

considered as replacing those most recently purchased—the last-in, first-ou (lifo) method A witness for the Brass Mill Products Association testified that his industry wished to use the same method of inventory accounting that it used in reporting to its stockholders and to the Securities and Exchange Commission. He contended that "the manufacturer must keep on hand an inventory which in metal content may equal several months' production The inventory must always be kept on hand, a mill could no more operate without this inventory or so-called metals in process than it could operate without its plant or any of its equipment. And its practice . . recognizes this fact. Sales are not made against this inventory, they are made against purchases of metals which occurred at approximately the same time as the sale" (Testimony of Maurice E. Peloubet, *Hearings before the Committee on Finance, Revenue Act of 1938,* U S Senate, 75th Congress, 3d Session, 1938, pp 143–167.)

The witness stated that inventory accounting was of particular importance in his industry because of the high cost of metals used, a cost amounting in some cases to 60 per cent of the final price. Moreover, the price of metal fluctuates substantially. During 1937, the price of copper rose from 12 to 17 cents and then declined to 10½ cents at the end of the year. Speculation in inventories might double the actual profit or show a loss, depending upon when the fiscal year ended. "Certainly uniform and equitable taxation cannot be predicated on such an unreal base." The problem in the brass industry was further aggravated by the long period involved in processing. In avoiding speculative risks, some industries use hedging transactions for their inventories This device had avoided inventory profits and losses for tax as well as book accounting But hedging can be used only when a futures market exists. An attempt by the brass industry to approximate the results of hedging, through a forward purchase commitment for amounts of metal about to be sold, was not recognized by the Bureau of Internal Revenue.

[1] To this the answer is made that "the inclusion of any inventory as a current asset which cannot be disposed of except on liquidation of the enterprise must necessarily confuse the picture of the current asset position, as the other components of current assets are based on the possibility of quick cash realization" One might as well alter the value of the fixed assets from year to year as to alter the figures representing a base stock On the assumption of a permanent or longtime trend in prices, such alteration for balance-sheet purposes appears desirable. But the opposite conclusion would apply for merely fluctuating prices. [Maurice E. Peloubet, "Last-in, First-out Once More," *Journal of Accountancy,* Vol. 69 (1940), p. 449.]

desirable; that it does not conform to logical physical flow of costs to revenues; and that it results in inconsistencies wherein the period of reckoning costs may influence the results obtained (charges to costs on a monthly basis will be different from those on a fiscal year basis).

The trend toward the use of "lifo" is largely explained by the desire of individual companies to report and pay taxes on their trading and processing profits and losses, leaving speculative profits and losses to cancel out over a span of time. Strong social support for this practice comes from the hope that it may apply a brake to business-cycle fluctuations. The procedure tends to discount both the excessive optimism and the excessive gloom that the business cycle develops. Earnings that are stabilized would provide capitalizations tending to prevent extreme rises and declines in the stock market.

Tax Status of Inventory Methods. Cost or market, whichever is lower, and the retail method of inventory valuation[1] have long been recognized by the Bureau of Internal Revenue. The law was modified in 1938 and 1939 to permit the use of last-in, first-out accounting under such rules as the Bureau might determine. The Bureau had not been favorable to a change in the law and the rules formulated were described as a "tight interpretation." Among other requirements was a specification that all reports to stockholders must be on a "lifo" basis and that the commodities to which the method was applied must be physically identical and the replacement identical. It was not sufficient that a given value of goods had been added and disposed of; there must be exact replace-

[1] The retail method of inventory is based on the valuation of closing inventory at selling prices that are expected to yield an experienced gross margin of profit. Closing inventories at selling prices less the computed gross margin of profit equals the approximate cost or cost-or-market figure for the valuation. The retail method has been restricted to stores selling goods in the form purchased. It is apparent that to apply the retail method effectively a complete record must be kept of actual cost outlays for merchandise, the percentage of mark-up on sales by types of merchandise, and the amounts of mark-downs

ment of the same goods. Inventories must be valued at cost rather than cost or market.[1]

Also, the Bureau does not permit, for tax purposes, the deduction of inventory reserves to cover either price declines or deterioration.

Inventory Reserves

The Canadian law provides for an inventory reserve confined to businesses subject to the 100 per cent rate on excess profits. The reserve is also limited to inventory not in excess of that on hand during the standard period. The price differential on which the reserve is based is the increase in the unit price over the unit price of the same goods in 1939. The allowable reserve is calculated in respect to each item of inventory by multiplying this price differential by the lowest of the following: the number of units on hand in the taxation period; the normal quantity in 1939; or the average quantities on hand during the base period of 1938–1939. Increases in values of the base stock are charged to current expense. This creates a reserve to be drawn upon when prices decline. The amount withdrawn from the reserve then appears as net income. The finally determined realized loss (if any) is charged against the reserve and credited to the inventory account.

A reserve similar to that employed by the Canadians could be inaugurated to provide businesses using first-in, first-out accounting with all the benefits of last-in, first-out procedure.

[1] In 1941, several large department stores in New York published reports using "lifo" for inventory accounting rather than the older retail method. It was announced, however, that this procedure was used in anticipation of retroactive legislation, extending the privilege of this method of accounting to department stores. The technique employed to apply "lifo" to a heterogeneous stock of goods involved the use of a price index. Questions arise, of course, as to the reliability of such an index and whether it is sufficiently objective and dependable to be accepted by the Bureau of Internal Revenue. Thus far such procedures have not been recognized ["The Commentator," *Journal of Accountancy*, Vol. 73 (June, 1942), p. 547.]

The difficulty in both cases is in determining the number of units in the base stock of goods. In the case of a concern with a heterogeneous stock of goods, this difficulty of counting units has been resolved by the use of a (not-too-satisfactory) price index.

The reserves discussed above deal only with *unrealized* profits or losses in the closing inventory. Inventory turnover profits and losses resulting from deviations of replacement costs from book costs are not recognized in these reserves. But an inventory reserve designed to offset speculative gains against speculative losses completely should include price fluctuations on inventory turnover. Such a reserve would go a step further than last-in, first-out accounting. Assume that an item was purchased on January 1 for $1; that no other purchases were made during January; and that the item was sold on January 31 at which time the replacement market quoted $1.25 for the item sold. Under the replacement-cost-reserve procedure, cost of sales would, in effect, be charged with $1.25, whereas under last-in, first-out, the charge would be $1. The replacement-cost-reserve method would show the 25-cent difference as a credit balance in the reserve account, representing the speculative loss on the increase in market prices over book costs. The reserve also goes further than a carry-forward of losses; it provides, in addition, a carry-back of such losses.

Conclusions

Inventory accounting is badly in need of better and more standardized practice. Perhaps it is even in order to suggest that, within a given type of industry, business, or trade, an appropriate inventory procedure should be determined and made mandatory for income-tax reporting and reports to stockholders. Determining the one best way for a given industry to evaluate its inventory and state its profits, and drafting this into an amendment to the Revenue Act, is a

Problems of the Business Income-tax Base

matter for a representative group of business men, accountants, and tax experts. A complete manual of inventory valuation procedures and the specific mandatory application of a certain method to certain businesses would go a long way toward eliminating tax discriminations and providing comparable profit-and-loss data for similar enterprises.

One of the objectives in this reform should be the elimination from the current income account of profits due to cyclical price fluctuations. That techniques can be found to accomplish this objective perfectly is extremely doubtful, to say the least. Nevertheless, the trend toward "lifo" and reserve accounting can be recognized as a hopeful one, and efforts to further the trend are very much in order.

DEPRECIATION, OBSOLESCENCE, AND DEPLETION

Introduction

Most income-tax laws accept the proposition that receipts are not considered income until an allowance has been made for impairment of capital. Impairment may occur in a number of ways: by depreciation—assets may wear out as a result of service; by obsolescence—equipment may become antiquated or out of date; by depletion—capital may be sold piece by piece, as in the case of mineral and forest resources. Maintenance and repairs are expenses incurred in avoiding impairment of capital and are sometimes and to some extent an offset against depreciation. It is logical that a deduction should be allowed for these impairments. A and B both make incomes of $5000 in a given year and these receipts are net except for the impairment of capital. A has such impairment to the extent of $1000 during the period, but B has no such impairment. It is evident that the two are not in the same class, as far as the year's operations are concerned, and that they ought not to be treated as equals by the net-income tax.

Postwar Taxation and Economic Progress

Provisions for Impairment of Capital

Stated very generally, the federal income-tax statute provides for deduction from gross income of "a reasonable allowance for the exhaustion, wear and tear of property used in the trade or business." The regulations add that the proper allowance is one which, if calculated on a reasonable plan, will, when added to the salvage value, equal the cost or "total basis" of the property. Stocks, bonds, exhaustible resources, and nondepreciable assets are not subject to depreciation, but allowances may be claimed for intangible assets such as patents, copyrights, and franchises. In principle it is not required that the rate of deduction be uniform. "Normal obsolescence" is treated as a part of depreciation. This includes impairment of capital resulting from predictable improvements or changes occurring in the art or industry generally. Another form of obsolescence, not deductible until realized, is the sudden loss of useful value due to a particular invention or a change in demand. Of course, the bulk of obsolescence is unpredictable. Anticipating an invention would be almost equivalent to conceiving it

No depreciation is allowed beyond the full value of assets. If the allowances in the early years of an asset's life prove excessive, no opportunity is provided to reopen tax returns and spread the deductions differently.[1]

---

[1] On the other hand, if the depreciation claimed proves inadequate, this is also at the taxpayer's risk and no remedy is available to add depreciation to past years' accounts. The courts have frequently held that the basis of property must be reduced by the taxpayer's usual depreciation even though no tax benefit is realized thereby. Expenses may not be "saved up" and carried over from one period to another. This means, in effect, that for tax purposes the taxpayer often does not recover his capital by the allowances for depreciation. It is a reason why the carry-over of losses is of the utmost importance to business. At present, the "basis" of depreciable property must not exceed the cost less the amount allowed or amounts allowable each year, whichever is greater. Thus if $1000 is deducted in one year when $2000 is permissible, the basis falls by $2000; and if $2000 is charged (permitted) during another year when $1000 is permissible, again the basis is reduced by $2000. A taxpayer cannot avail

Problems of the Business Income-tax Base

The "straight-line" method of depreciation accounting is favored by the Commissioner of Internal Revenue and is by far the most commonly used. It consists of an equal deduction each year over the estimated life of the asset. Time is the factor given most weight in this plan of distribution. The "units-of-production" method is permitted where it is adequately demonstrated to be more applicable. This method links the depreciation account to output and permits a uniform charge per unit produced. Owing to the difficulties of estimating the gross production expectancy of any particular plant, the unit-of-production method is rarely followed exclusively but is more often combined with some other method.[1]

Lack of Precision in Depreciation Accounting

Depreciation is, at best, a matter of estimate. Competent judges will often disagree substantially as to what the allowance should be. Allowances are often a subject of debate, and not infrequently of litigation, between the taxpayer and

---

himself, in a later year, of the fact that he may have taken, in previous years, either an obviously inadequate depreciation allowance or none at all.

[1] As to maintenance, the Bureau has ruled that "the cost of incidental repairs which neither materially add to the value of property nor appreciably prolong its life, but keep it in an ordinarily efficient operating condition, may be deducted as expense, provided the plant or property account is not increased by the amount of such expenditures Repairs in the nature of replacements, to the extent that they arrest deterioration and appreciably prolong the life of the property, should be charged against the depreciation reserve if such account is kept." [Article 23(a)-4, Regulation 94, Income Tax, Revenue Act of 1936.] The line between capital outlays, or "betterments," and maintenance is often indistinct In general, conservative accounting calls for as little capitalization of these outlays as is feasible under the tax laws. Maintenance outlays, unlike those for depreciation, tend to fluctuate substantially with the business cycle. Most businesses refrain "from making repairs when business is poor" and then make up "for lost time when the sky brightens." "That shrewd business operation should require this is interesting, since shrewd economic planning would require the reverse " (Ruth P. Mack, *The Flow of Business Funds and Consumer Purchasing Power*, Columbia University Press, New York, 1941, p. 53.)

the tax administrators. Corporate income-tax returns are probably more often changed by audit at this point than at any other.

It is also said that the estimating of income is an art as well as (or perhaps rather than) a science, and nowhere is this better illustrated than in the calculation of annual depreciation. The process involves so many variables and imponderables that it may be closer to guesswork than to estimating.

To mention a few of the difficulties, one may begin with the definition of the "useful life" of the asset. The equipment may have one useful life as an active element in production and another if its term of usefulness as "stand-by" equipment is taken into account. The value sought to be recovered may be the original investment, deflated or inflated for a price trend, or the cost of an asset which will maintain output or profit-making capacity. Depreciation may be calculated for a single asset or it may represent an average applied to a larger classification. The calculation is affected by the company's maintenance policy and it includes an allowance for "normal obsolescence," often the largest element in the estimate. "The executive must therefore also estimate the rate of invention, the promptness with which the industry will take up the new ideas available to it, product change requiring changed equipment in its production. . . ."[1] The rate of "normal obsolescence" will also depend somewhat upon future wages and the efficiency of labor. Once the time and value dimensions of depreciation are determined, there remains to be decided how it shall be spread over the years. Several alternatives are available.[2] In most cases, depreciation is set as high as the Bureau of Internal Revenue will permit, but the fact remains that significant differences are found among the estimates of firms with similar equipment.[3]

[1] *Ibid.*, p. 222.
[2] W. A Paton, *Accountants' Handbook*, 2d ed., Ronald Press, New York, 1932.
[3] Mack, *op. cit.*, pp. 224–225.

Problems of the Business Income-tax Base

Depreciation and Business-cycle Economics

Depreciation and obsolescence accounting are intimately related to business-cycle economics. It is claimed, for instance, that the "straight-line" method of calculation accentuates the cyclical fluctuations in income. The lighter wear and tear in years of partial operation is not recognized by this method. A more flexible standard would minimize both depression losses and prosperity profits. More important is the fact that the rate allowed for depreciation affects the volume of equipment replacements (and probably of additions). Purchases of new equipment during a depression are particularly needed to provide employment and to help develop currents of recovery. It is said that, in 1941, 70 per cent of machine tools on hand were 10 years of age or older, and the average age was high even in the modern factories.

Much attention has been given to the factors that determine replacement of old equipment. It is agreed that the expectation of profitable use for the new item is of paramount importance. Deciding whether the purchase of new equipment will be profitable involves a complicated estimate of expected savings through increased efficiency in production, improved quality of product, and so forth. For industry as a whole, the rate of technological change has a strong influence on equipment replacement. Maintenance of "trade position" is often a consideration. Psychological factors, especially in the case of improvements which anticipate demand, also are important.[1] Bargain prices have some influence on the decision to purchase new equipment, and the cost of capital and credit is also a factor though probably a minor one. Availability of capital is more important than its cost. Finally, the depreciation already taken on the assets to be replaced is involved. The lower the figure at which these assets are carried on the books of the company, the less the resistance to replacement.

[1] *Ibid*, Chap. VIII.

Postwar Taxation and Economic Progress

The 1934 experience with depreciation allowances is an outstanding illustration of their bearing on business-cycle economics. In 1934, a congressional committee reported[1] that depreciation allowances were amounting to about $4 billion, whereas the net income of corporations was running to only $1.5 billion. The 1930 allowances were reported to be about half again as large as those of 1924. From this slender evidence it was concluded that corporations were "padding" their depreciation returns and it was suggested that the allowances be reduced 25 per cent by legislation. This proposed action was not favored by the Treasury. It was dropped as far as legislation was concerned, but only on the assurance of the Bureau of Internal Revenue that the allowances would be substantially reduced by administrative action.. During the next 3 years, depreciation allowances were tightened accordingly. This involved a small immediate gain for the Treasury, but it was not the sort of program to accelerate industrial recovery during a depression.

Accelerated Depreciation

The contention that a generous allowance for depreciation and obsolescence is conducive to replacement and expansion investment is plausible. As to replacement, the point has been made that assets are more readily replaced when they are considerably depreciated on the books of a company. As to expansion, a company will obviously reduce its risk if a large part of the new equipment cost can be written off in the early years of its use. This was the theory underlying the privilege, given during the war, of amortizing war equipment over a 5-year period. Considerable testimony[2] indicates that this action was effective in breaking down impediments to expansion. This type of program could be used during peacetime as well as during a war.

[1] *Hearings before the Committee on Ways and Means*, Revenue Revision, 1934, pp. 367–398

[2] National Industrial Conference Board, *Effects of Taxes upon Corporate Policy*, 1943, pp. 35–36.

Problems of the Business Income-tax Base

That accelerated depreciation would be stimulating to business investment is by no means self-evident. As long as the program remained optional and some firms operated with standard depreciation accounting, it could not be presumed that sales prices would so adjust themselves as to permit a recovery of the augmented expense incurred by some through accelerated depreciation. Of course, if current tax rates are higher than those anticipated for the future, a deferment of taxable income would be an advantage. Some critics[1] have expressed the view that this anticipation of lower taxes is the only circumstance (assuming no price changes) where accelerated depreciation would have a stimulating effect. But this seems too conservative a judgment.

If a new plant could be written off against current income, this would strengthen a company's financial position very decidedly It would surely give the firm a tax advantage if it were later to encounter operating losses not subject to carry-over. It would give it the equivalent of a reserve to minimize such losses. Of course, if a concern already has present losses, it would hardly add to these deficits by seeking accelerated depreciation. But if the concern has positive income and needs cash in the business, it may well undertake to minimize present taxes even though this may involve greater liability for future taxes. The future is always an uncertain quantity, and a present opportunity to strengthen the business at the expense of the revenue (in part, at least) may well turn a business executive's decision in favor of expansion. Particularly stimulating would be the situation where net income to stockholders could be reported by standard accounting while reporting to government would recognize accelerated depreciation. This would afford a means of immediate improvement of profits at the expense

[1] See E. Cary Brown and Gardner Patterson, "Accelerated Depreciation A Neglected Chapter in War Taxation," *Quarterly Journal of Economics*, Vol. 57 (August, 1943), pp. 630–645.

of the future. Because it is at the expense of the future, it should be used sparingly and in emergencies only.

In allowing accelerated depreciation, the government in most cases would suffer a postponement rather than a loss of taxes. Perhaps the allowance would overdo the substitution (as far as annual accounting is concerned) of artificial for actual results. The postponement of taxes on income currently earned, moreover, would be at some risk to the government and would create some strain upon its current budget. However, the government may be sorely pressed to find a stimulus for an economic system in the doldrums, and this program might be held in reserve for application in extreme depression.

Less Rigidity in Depreciation Accounting

The carry-over of losses, with its diminished emphasis upon annual accounting, would facilitate greater freedom in deducting for depreciation and obsolescence. Much litigation and argument could happily be reduced by less attention to the timing of these deductions. Unfortunately, the trend is in the opposite direction. Research expense, formerly deductible on a cash basis when incurred, is required by recent ruling to be capitalized and spread over the years of usefulness of the results. This may be fiscally productive in the short run, but it seems a dubious way to encourage industrial progress. In fact, because the trend of corporate tax rates has continued upward, the government probably has lost revenue by administrative reductions in current depreciation charges. It certainly seems in order to suggest that, within a range of tolerance, business' own judgment, as indicated by its books, might well be accepted in lieu of a more precise figure laboriously calculated by the Bureau of Internal Revenue.

Obsolescence is likely to be an especially important factor for industries with a high risk factor, and a practical program to allow a broader timing of extraordinary obsolescence would

Problems of the Business Income-tax Base

facilitate such business. About the only suggestion that has been offered for accomplishing this result is that of permitting a carry-back for losses occasioned by such extraordinary obsolescence. This would involve reopening many dead accounts and some refunding by the government. Probably the administrative inconvenience involved in this proposal is prohibitive.

It has been argued that depreciation allowances tend to be excessive because of increased efficiency of capital (a less expensive new unit will, in terms of productive efficiency, take the place of the old). This is undoubtedly true in some cases, but it is not a new phenomenon nor is a quantitative measure of its net effect possible (there are cases where the opposite is true). Offset against this tendency is the fact that obsolescence is also increasing by rapid strides and is usually underallowed.

Special Problems of Depletion

As previously explained, in some lines of business such as mines, oil and gas wells, and timber reserves, impairment of capital occurs through the sale of the basic assets, piece by piece. It has been generally recognized that, unless the directors of such businesses withhold from the profits and reinvest sums equal to the value of the property exhausted in creating those profits, the dividends paid to owners will represent in part a return of the original investment. This impairment of capital is known as depletion. Thus, if an iron mine costs $1000 and contains 1000 tons of ore, each ton represents $1 of capital. If 100 tons are sold for $100 (ignoring operating costs) there is no profit.

The allowance for depletion is complicated by the fact that an accurate advance appraisal of the ore content of a particular mine, for instance, is not feasible. The case is cited of a California gold mine that began operations in 1850, is still going strong, and may continue to do so for an indefinite period.[1] The uncertainties are not only physical but include a speculation as to future prices and costs of production.

In recognition of the inherent difficulty of correctly estimating the volume of natural resources to be depleted, the present federal tax laws permit the deduction of depletion as a percentage of the annual gross income. The depletion allowed per year on gas and oil properties is 27½ per cent; sulphur mines, 23 per cent; metal mines, 15 per cent; and coal mines, 5 per cent; but the allowance may not exceed 50 per cent of the net income before depletion. Depletion is also allowable on a recovery-of-cost basis (as in the iron mine illustration above) or on a discovery-value[2] basis for mineral deposits other than those for which percentage depletion is permitted. The determination of gain or loss from the sale of assets which have been more than fully depleted is obscure and complicated. For years preceding 1932, the basis was determined as though conventional accounting (rather than percentage depletion) had been used. Since 1932, the basis for reckoning gain or loss seems to allow for full deduction of percentage depletion, though presumably not beyond a valuation of zero.

Depletion allowances, in the opinion of most disinterested persons, have not only been notoriously generous, but they are so computed that in many cases they add up to well beyond the full cost of the wasting assets.

The Treasury, at the time of the 1942 revenue revision, recommended to the Ways and Means Committee that taxpayers be permitted to obtain depletion allowances on a "cost" basis only. "Percentage depletion" was to be dis-

---

[1] Frank G. Short, "Problems of Depletion," *Journal of Accountancy*, Vol 67 (January, 1939), pp 21–22.

[2] Where a property is discovered at no cost or at a cost less than its value at the time of discovery, the question of what constitutes capital for income-tax purposes arises. The law has usually allowed discovery value rather than cost as the basis, which means that the taxpayer gets the benefit of windfalls.

Problems of the Business Income-tax Base

continued.[1] Every branch of the oil, mining, and quarrying industries appeared before the Committee in vigorous opposition to the Treasury's proposal. Arguments presented[2] by the oil industry in opposition were that there was a declining trend in the nation's known oil reserves; that there was evidence of increased abandonment of stripper or marginal wells; that percentage depletion is essential (especially in wartime) as an incentive for discovery and to extend the economic life of small wells. Similar arguments were also presented by other affected industries. Much stress was placed on the need of a maximum supply of materials for the prosecution of the war. Congress made no essential change in the depletion provisions.

The Treasury appeared a second time before the Ways and Means Committee, urging the elimination of percentage depletion.[3] It contended, among other arguments, that the present system of allowances gives a special privilege to a particular industrial group; that this cannot be justified as a stimulus to exploration and discovery (price and technical developments are more significant); that most marginal mines and wells get little if any benefit from percentage depletion because of the limitation to 50 per cent of the net income from the property; that percentage depletion involves great administrative complications.

The best ultimate solution of the depletion problem, despite the admitted difficulties, is to apply a cost basis. As a corollary to that, all developmental expenses ought to be capitalized and then depleted over the life of the assets. If the best estimates of the period during which resources will be forthcoming (or even an arbitrary period) should prove too long, depletion allowances might be redetermined on the carry-back basis,

[1] Statement of Randolph Paul, *Hearings before Ways and Means Committee*, March 3, 1942, *Revenue Revision of 1942*, Vol. 1, pp. 84, 85

[2] Report of the committee appointed by the Petroleum Industry War Council, etc, *Hearings on Revenue Revision*, Vol. 1 (March 23, 1942), pp. 1055, 1060.

[3] Statement of Randolph Paul, *Hearings before Ways and Means Committee*, April 16, 1942, Vol 3, pp. 2988–2996.

using actual experience.[1] It might be well to ease into this program with partial retention of percentage depletion for a period.

Conclusion

More latitude in the timing of deductions for depreciation and obsolescence should be granted. Less attention to the calendar year in income-tax accounting would reduce the argument and litigation over the proper amounts of depreciation and obsolescence attributable to the operation of any one period. Shortening the write-off period for these impairments of capital value promotes economic progress by reducing resistance to the purchase of improved equipment. On the other hand, depletion allowances, in the opinion of most disinterested persons, are not only notoriously generous but frequently are so computed that they total more than the full cost of the assets. The best ultimate solution in this case would seem to be the allowance of depletion on the basis of cost, with a carry-back if the period of allowance proves too short. Accelerated depreciation (as in the 5-year amortization provision for certain war capital) could be used to promote investment during a depression, and, in extreme cases, its use for such purposes is recommended.

---

[1] Thus, if a gold mine costing $100,000 were estimated to yield 10,000 units per year for 10 years, a capital value of $1 would be assigned to each unit. Now if the mine "played out" earlier than expected so that it produced only 50,000 units, the past income-tax returns would be reopened to allow depletion at $2 per unit rather than $1.

VII. ROLE OF AND CHANGES IN THE PERSONAL INCOME TAX[1]

INTRODUCTION

IF BUSINESS taxation is to be lightened after the war, some other element in the tax system must be given a more important role. The principal candidates for this role are personal taxes (personal income and death taxes) and indirect consumption (sales) taxes. Of these, the author strongly prefers personal taxation as the major source of revenue in the postwar federal tax system. The personal income tax is a logical substitute for the corporate income tax, since abandonment or deemphasis of the corporate tax is recommended on the premise that it should be integrated with the personal tax. The burden of the personal-income tax can be determined (very little shifting); the features of the tax can be readily adapted to requirements of postwar markets; and, if its graduation is not excessive and due allowance is made for investment losses, the tax should prove compatible with adequate business incentives. Regressive taxes at state and local levels are probably inevitable; but the federal government, with more adequate fiscal powers, should avoid these taxes, in the main, and confine them to special excises on nonessential consumption.

BROAD BASE

If the personal income tax is to serve as the mainstay of federal taxation in the postwar period when there will be high revenue requirements, it must be a broadly based tax. Otherwise we shall head straight for inflation or a system of heavy

[1] For the quantitative materials in this chapter, the author has relied heavily on the assistance of Oscar Litterer and Charlotte McNiesh.

Postwar Taxation and Economic Progress

indirect taxes, either of which would be much harder on the "little fellow" than the net-income tax. The income structure is like a pyramid—the volume increases rapidly as one moves down from the top. The top section contains considerable tax potential but not nearly enough for present-day requirements.

There is a widespread view that everyone should contribute something to government. At least it can be said that a majority of the citizenry should be involved in the direct tax system. A reasonably close connection between voting for budgets and paying for them is definitely in the public interest.

The number of income-tax payers was increased during the war from 4 to about 50 million. This revolutionized the tax and, although it brought some problems, the change was for the better. At any rate, the "good old days" when only one family out of 12 or 15 was ever touched by the income tax are probably gone forever. The income tax has come to the crossroads.

Relation of the Base to National Income and to Exemptions

Estimates of the postwar income-tax base, at a national-income level of $140 billion and 1944 surtax exemptions of $500 for taxpayer and each dependent, are presented in Chart II.[1] The net national-income figure of $140 billion at 1943 prices is used as the basis for estimates because careful studies by a number of independent agencies indicate that approximately this income level will be achieved if a satisfactory high level of employment is attained for the years

---

[1] The methods used in making these estimates and others included in this chapter are explained in Appendix A. It is assumed that concessions to those in the armed services are eliminated in peacetime and that there is a moderate shift back from extreme wartime concentration in the lower brackets.

National income is the net value of output as measured by the earnings paid or accruing to the factors of production It should be distinguished from the *gross national product*, which allows for no deduction for the consumption of capital equipment in the course of production. It should also be distinguished from *national income payments*, which represents distributed income received by individuals, and excludes, among other adjustments, corporate saving.

Role of and Changes in the Personal Income Tax

immediately after the war.[1] It should be emphasized that this figure represents an important goal for the postwar economy. *In no sense is it presented as a forecast.*

```
                    $57.62
              Net taxable income
          (Net income minus exemptions)

                    $90.68
                 Net income
         (Reported income minus deductions)

                   $101.84
         Income reported on taxable returns

                   $140.00
              Net national income
              (In billions of dollars)
```

Miscellaneous nonreported income	27.25%
Deductions	7.97%
Exemptions	23.62%
Net taxable income	41.16%

Per cent of national income

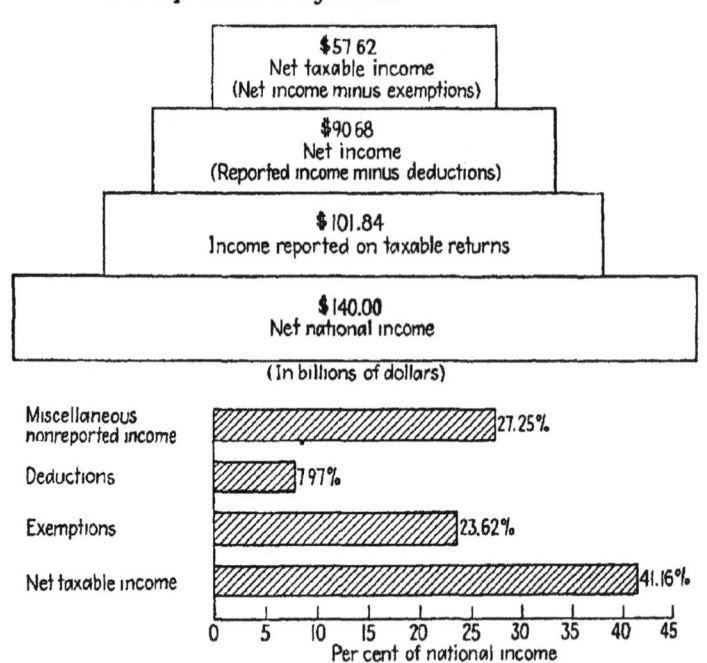

CHART II.—Estimated postwar income-tax base at $140 billion national income, 1944 surtax exemptions.

These estimates show that at $140 billion of national income, with the conditions specified, approximately 59 per cent of the national income would be exempted from, or would otherwise escape from, the application of the personal income

[1] S Morris Livingston, *Markets after the War*, U S Department of Commerce, 1943, E A. Goldenweiser and Everett E Hagen, "Jobs after the War," *Federal Reserve Bulletin,* May, 1944; "Transition to Peace: Business in A D. 194Q," *Fortune,* January, 1944 These estimates are presented in terms of gross national product rather than net national income, *Markets after the War* is presented in 1940 prices Converted into terms of net national income at 1943 prices, they group rather closely around $140 billion.

tax. As shown in the chart, this comprises deductions on taxable returns (8.0 per cent), subsistence allowance represented by the personal credits to taxpayers and dependents (23.6 per cent), and miscellaneous nonreported income (27.3 per cent). The last category includes income that avoids the tax base because it is below the personal exemption level, because it is privileged (as in the case of tax-exempt interest), because there is administrative leakage, because it is reinvested by corporations (corporate savings), and because differences occur in calculating national income and in measuring income for tax purposes.

TABLE XI
ESTIMATED INCOME-TAX BASE UNDER VARIOUS EXEMPTIONS AND INCOME LEVELS

	Tax base		Income not taxed	
	Amount, billions	Per cent of national income	Amount, billions	Per cent of national income
$140 billion national income:				
1944 surtax exemptions	$57 62	41 2	$ 82 38	58 8
1939 exemptions	29 20	20 9	110 80	79 1
1944 surtax exemptions:				
$140 billion national income	57.62	41 2	82 38	58 8
$100 billion national income	36 23	36.2	63 77	63 8
1944 surtax exemptions:				
$140 billion national income	57.62	41 2	82 38	58.8
1939 exemptions:				
$100 billion national income	17 29	17 3	82 71	82 7

Available evidence as to the proportion of income recipients who would pay taxes at 1944 surtax exemptions and a national income of $140 billion is not very reliable, but an approximate estimate indicates that probably well over one-third of income recipients would be excluded from the tax system. A tax system that protects from taxes one-third of American income recipients and between one-half and two-thirds of the income of all recipients cannot be said to err on the side of harshness or to sap unduly the purchasing power of the low-income groups.

The effect of exemptions on the tax base and the importance of a high national income in maintaining that base are shown in Table XI and Chart III. This table and chart first compare, at $140 billion national income, the tax base under 1939 exemptions with that under 1944 surtax exemptions. Exemptions in 1939 were $2500 for a married couple, $1000 for a single person, and $400 for dependents. The 1944 surtax exemptions are $500 for the taxpayer and each of his dependents. Were we to return to prewar exemptions, the tax base would be cut nearly one-half. Were the government to take

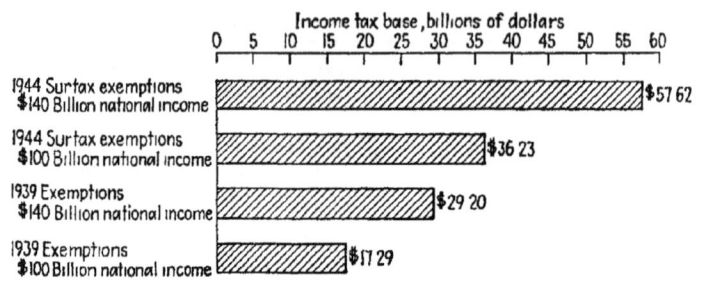

CHART III.—Estimated income-tax base under various assumed conditions

all of this base (an effective rate of 100 per cent), the yield would be less than the $30 billion frequently estimated as the postwar revenue requirements of all governments, federal, state, and local!

The table and chart also compare the tax base under 1944 surtax exemptions at two levels of national income: $140 and $100 billion. Ignoring price changes, the latter figure is substantially above prewar levels ($71 billion in 1939), and many feel that we shall be fortunate to attain even this degree of prosperity after the war. It will be observed that a reduction of about 29 per cent in national income results in a decrease of 37.1 per cent in the tax base.

The effect of higher exemptions *and* lower income can be

seen in the application of 1939 exemptions to a national income of $100 billion. Under these unfavorable conditions, the tax base would be under $18 billion which, according to several estimates, is less than the postwar tax requirements of the federal government alone. The tax base would constitute less than one-fifth of the national income.

Those who argue that present surtax exemptions are too low for peacetime application should find their answer in these figures.

Deductions

The net taxable income of taxpayers would fall considerably short of their net income even if there were no personal exemptions and credits. This is due to the deductions, which ordinarily mean a loss of 10 to 15 per cent of the tax base. In the calculation of national income, business and professional expenses have been deducted. The deductions from net income to obtain net statutory income are the personal expenses, such as interest paid on homes and on other durable goods purchased for consumption, property taxes on homes, other taxes paid (including state income and usually consumption taxes), and medical expenses (with limitations). Contributions are allowed up to 15 per cent of net income.

Several of these allowances are clearly warranted but others are of dubious propriety. Medical expenses represent important differences among individuals; their deduction results in a closer approximation of ability to pay. The allowance of state income taxes is an important element in coordinating state and federal levies and it prevents a confiscatory combination of the two taxes in the higher brackets. On the other hand, interest paid might well be limited to that paid on funds borrowed to produce income excluding debts contracted for other than business purposes. There is precedent for such limitation in the laws of other countries, as, for instance, in Australia.[1] Property taxes on owner-

[1] James H. Gilbert, *The Tax Systems of Australasia*, University of Oregon, Eugene, 1943, p. 31.

occupied homes represent a large and dubious deduction item. The allowance of this deduction and that of interest paid on home mortgages is inequitable because there is no similar allowance to tenants for rent paid. Many of the other deductions are for outlays in the nature of personal and consumption expenses for which allowance has already been made in the personal exemptions and credits. Disallowance of most of these items would save the income-tax base several billions of dollars.

The present trend toward simplified reporting permits taxpayers to make a flat presumption as to deductions. This eliminates differentials and amounts to a change in the rate schedule. It is probably the most feasible political means of eliminating deductions in effect, but it is open to serious objections. The first of these objections is that this practice results in an exaggeration of apparent as distinguished from effective rates. The second is that it tends to ignore real differences among taxpayers, which some of the specific deductions properly recognize.

Exemptions and Credits

There are several reasons for income-tax exemptions and credits for dependents: (1) they protect a subsistence standard of living; (2) they provide a basis for differentiating among taxpayers according to need; (3) they avoid the administrative inconvenience of extending a personal tax to millions of small taxpayers; (4) they help to preserve the market for consumers' goods; and (5) they afford the political advantage of applying the direct tax system to a relatively small number of persons.

These reasons may be considered briefly in turn. The first—allowance of a subsistence standard—appeals quite properly to humanitarian impulses. But subsistence is a flexible standard depending on what a country can afford, what the economy produces, and what services a government provides its poorer citizens. Then too, government is quite as much a necessity as any of the other elements of subsistence. The individual's standards are protected also by graduation in the tax rates. As previously stated, conservation of human resources is of highest importance, not only for its own sake but also for production and for national defense. But no reasonable complaint could be registered against an income-tax system that protects from tax more than one-third of American income recipients and well over half of the national income.

The second reason for exemption—differentiation—is undoubtedly valid, but it affords justification only of allowances for dependents. From this viewpoint, the victory tax was quite perverse in nature and so also was the normal tax under the 1944 Act. The normal tax allowed a flat exemption of $500 for all taxpayers with no differentiation according to number of dependents. There might be more justification for the reverse type of measure making generous allowance for dependents but none for the taxpayer himself. In evaluating credits for minor dependents, the effect on the birth rate may also warrant consideration. Recent interest in family allowances indicates a trend toward greater social responsibility for families. Raising the exemption for dependent children to that allowed adults in 1944 was a move in the right direction.

The third ground for exemption—administrative convenience—probably is sufficient basis for some allowance. Here, much depends upon the development of better techniques in administration.

As to the fourth reason, it is true that purchasing power can be protected by exemptions. However, where high exemptions lead to inadequate yields in the personal tax and the result is a shift from the personal tax to regressive substitutes, nothing is gained for purchasing power.

Finally, there is strong political opposition to low exemptions. Very frequently a congressman is more interested in

Role of and Changes in the Personal Income Tax

the number of people affected by a direct tax than in any other aspect of the tax. The citizenry must have a high level of self-discipline to finance itself mainly by direct levy.

Retention of present surtax exemptions after the war seems desirable. The normal tax, with its allowance only for the taxpayer and not for dependents, should be repealed. Surtax exemptions are still high by any criterion other than a political one, and they are actually higher than they appear because of the provision for minimum deductions. Thus, the present allowance ($500 for the taxpayer and for each of his dependents) is really $2750 for a family of five, rather than $2500. An exemption of $500 for dependent children means a $10,000 allowance per child over a 20-year period—$40,000 for a family of four children. This represents a standard above that of the average taxpayer. Quite possibly it is justified by the interest in encouraging the maintenance and gradual expansion of the population.

Nevertheless, even with exemptions popularly regarded as low, the fact that the income tax reaches only 41 per cent of income is startling and striking. It is easy to demonstrate that $1000 for a married couple is insufficient to provide them with all the necessities, let alone the amenities, of life. It is also easy to demonstrate that 41 per cent of the national income is insufficient to support, without confiscatory rates, a government that provides all the services we expect from ours. If all governments—federal, state, and local—were to be supported from our federal income-tax base alone, it would probably take a tax of over 50 per cent to do the job and require levels of productivity that some consider unlikely of postwar achievement. Following 3 or 4 years of the most expensive war in history, a return to prewar income-tax exemptions would involve heavy use of taxes much less equitable than the personal income tax or reckless chances of grave inadequacy of revenue.

Repeal of the present normal tax would in itself substantially increase exemptions. However, this would result in a reduction of some $27 billion in the present income-tax base[1] and a reduction in income-tax yield of $2.5 billion, three-fourths of which is now paid by taxpayers with less than $5000 of income. This might not be desirable except for the fact that the normal tax is decidedly inequitable.

Exemptions accomplish important objectives, and they should be as high as circumstances will allow. But if we are to work on the assumption that the personal income tax is to finance most of our postwar revenue requirements, we cannot be unrealistic as to the level of personal exemptions.

ADEQUATE STANDARD RATE

The standard rate of tax (that levied on the first bracket of income) is extremely important for the revenue. Over two-thirds of the income-tax base falls in the first bracket of taxable income (Table XII and Chart IV) to which the standard rate applies, and in addition, of course, all other rates are differentials from the standard rate. This bracket includes not only small incomes but also a portion (the lowest sector) of all incomes that exceed the bracket limit.[2] Thus the standard rate applies not only to small incomes; it cuts across the entire tax base. It is the only rate applicable to all taxable income. Obviously, then, an adequate standard

[1] In other words, $27 billion of income is now subject to the normal tax but not to the surtax.

[2] Distribution of taxable income by brackets must be distinguished from distribution of taxable income by classes of income. The former includes the first sector or sectors of all incomes (above exemptions and deductions) and the latter includes the total of income (above exemptions and deductions) of those whose total income falls within the stated class intervals. The bracket analysis is especially significant for yield calculations, the classes-of-income analysis is particularly useful in showing income distribution.

Thus if *A* has a net taxable income of $4000, a bracket analysis with bracket intervals of $2000 will include $2000 of his income in the first bracket and the remaining $2000 of his income in the second. A classes-of-income analysis will include all of his income in the class entitled "$2000 to $4000."

The term "standard rate of tax" is used to describe the rate applied to the first bracket of taxable income. The discussion does not use the term "normal tax" but only "standard rate" and "surtaxes," the latter being the rates applicable to brackets above the first.

Role of and Changes in the Personal Income Tax

rate is an important factor in the effective tax rate at all income levels. A change of 1 per cent in the standard tax

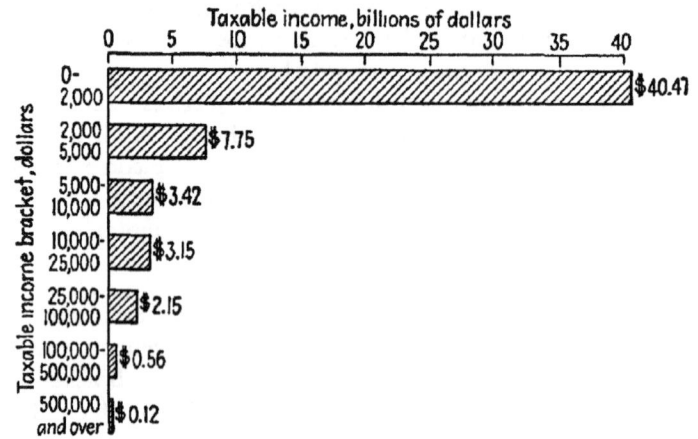

CHART IV —Estimated distribution of taxable income by brackets, $140 billion national income.

Taxable income bracket (dollars)	Amount (billions)
0–2,000	$40.47
2,000–5,000	$7.75
5,000–10,000	$3.42
10,000–25,000	$3.15
25,000–100,000	$2.15
100,000–500,000	$0.56
500,000 and over	$0.12

rate would affect the revenue as much as a change of 14 per cent in the brackets above $25,000. The low bracket is the

TABLE XII

ESTIMATED DISTRIBUTION OF NET TAXABLE INCOME BY BRACKETS, $140 BILLION NATIONAL INCOME

(Calculations based on 1944 surtax exemptions)

Taxable income bracket	Net taxable income, billions	Per cent of total taxable income
$ 0–$ 2000	$40 47	70 2
2000– 5000	7 75	13 5
5000– 10,000	3 42	5 9
10,000– 25,000	3 15	5 5
25,000–100,000	2.15	3 7
100,000–500,000	0 56	1 0
500,000 and over	0 12	0 2
Total.	$57.62	100.0

most stable element in the tax base. This is true because it is not heavily weighted with dividends and capital gains which

Postwar Taxation and Economic Progress

are subject to high fluctuations. Moreover, high incomes can fluctuate substantially and still exceed the first bracket limits. The effective average rates of taxation in the low brackets are much lower than the marginal rates because of personal exemptions (see Table XIII). Postwar reductions in the

TABLE XIII
INDIVIDUAL INCOME TAX, EFFECTIVE RATE, AND MARGINAL RATE FOR SELECTED NET INCOMES UNDER THE 1944 LAW

(Calculations for a married couple with 2 dependents. Exemption normal tax $500, surtax $2000)

Net income before personal exemption	Amount of tax	Effective tax rate, per cent	Marginal tax rate,* per cent
$ 1000	$ 15	1.5	3
1250	23	1.8	3
1500	30	2.0	3
1750	38	2.2	3
2000	45	2.3	3
2250	103	4.6	23
2500	160	6.4	23
2750	218	7.9	23
3000	275	9.2	23
4000	505	12.6	23
5000	755	15.1	25
6000	1005	16.8	25
8000	1585	19.8	29
10,000	2245	22.5	33
15,000	4265	28.4	46
20,000	6785	33.9	53
25,000	9705	38.8	62
50,000	26,865	53.7	75
75,000	46,785	62.4	84
100,000	68,565	68.6	90
500,000	442,985	88.6	94
1,000,000	900,000	90.0	94
5,000,000	4,500,000	90.0	94

* Includes 3 per cent normal tax and surtax applicable to highest bracket. Married couples with two dependents, having a net income of $2000 or less, would be subject only to normal tax of 3 per cent since the normal tax exemption is $500, surtax exemption $2000.

Role of and Changes in the Personal Income Tax

standard rate of tax can probably be substantial, but they must stop at levels far above those of prewar. The only alternative to an adequate standard rate is irrational forms of taxation, including the much less defensible sales taxes.

SURTAX LEVELS

Several factors must be considered in adjusting rates above the standard rate (for convenience here referred to as surtaxes):

1. These rates provide a substantial but by no means large share of revenue. All the income in the brackets above $25,000 is estimated (under peacetime conditions and a national income of $140 billion) to amount to some $2.8 billion, not one-sixth of what the federal government alone will probably require after the war. If the federal government were to finance itself by leveling all taxable incomes to the point where it could satisfy its postwar revenue needs (perhaps $18 billion), it would have to dip below the $2000 taxable income level. No taxpayer could retain more than about $2000 above his deductions and exemption credits. It would be necessary to go below $4000 to get $12 billion of revenue. This is shown in Chart V. A supplementary calculation indicates that if the taxpayer were allowed *no* deductions or exemption credits and $18 billion of revenue were required, a confiscatory tax would leave each taxpayer about $4000 of his earnings.

2. Present surtaxes reach a top of 91 per cent (94 per cent, including the normal tax). An 89 per cent marginal rate (92 per cent, including the normal) applies to net taxable income in excess of $100,000, and a 59 per cent marginal rate (62 per cent, including the normal) to income in excess of $25,000.

3. These rates are by no means always effective. Wealthy persons are able to avoid high rates through the use of corporations as savings banks. A large stockholder in a closely held corporation can escape the personal tax on all but a sliver of his income; the bulk of his income remains in the company. The higher the personal tax rate, the less likely

Postwar Taxation and Economic Progress

it is to touch this person at all. It is significant in this respect that, in spite of large earnings, the income in the upper brackets has increased very little during the war. Large fortunes can be, and often are, invested in government bonds on which the interest income is exempt from taxation. Capital gains (on the sale of securities) are taxed at specially

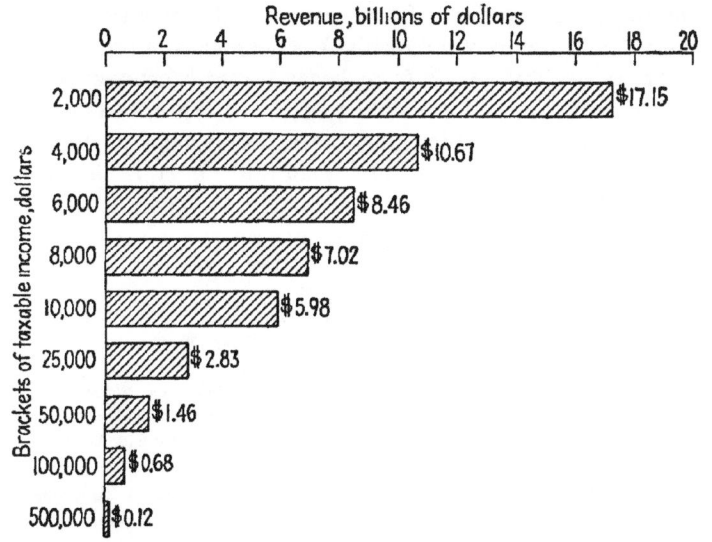

Brackets of taxable income, dollars	Revenue, billions of dollars
2,000	$17.15
4,000	$10.67
6,000	$8.46
8,000	$7.02
10,000	$5.98
25,000	$2.83
50,000	$1.46
100,000	$0.68
500,000	$0.12

CHART V.—Revenue resulting from a confiscatory income tax that levels taxable income to selected points, $140 billion national income.

NOTE: The respective yields are computed by confiscating all taxable income above the indicated brackets, i.e., taxing this income at 100 per cent.

favored rates which are often well under half the rates paid by other income. Many of these gains are "forgiven" at death and not taxed at all. It is extremely doubtful if the special favors to capital gains can be removed while surtax rates remain as high as at present.

Nominal surtax rates should not be higher than those we are willing to apply consistently and enforce effectively. From the standpoint of distribution, the total tax paid, not the rates, is most important. A persuasive case certainly can be made for a moderation of rates, conditional upon closing loopholes. If these loopholes are considered, as well as the waste attending the imposition of excessive taxes (investment in recreational farms, for instance), it is apparent that a substantial reduction of rates could be accomplished without loss of revenue or any great change in the average distribution of the tax burden. Some argue for the preservation of loopholes as the only politically feasible means of preventing taxes on wealthy people from becoming so exorbitant as to kill all incentive. This may be true, but it expresses a degree of cynicism in tax policy that the author refuses to accept. The loopholes, moreover, are notoriously unequal in their effect as moderators of the rate schedule. There is such a thing as fairness even among millionaires.

TABLE XIV
EFFECT OF THE 1944 PERSONAL TAX SYSTEM ON THE NET YIELD OF INVESTMENTS AT THE MARGIN OF A $200,000 INCOME

Equity investment yield before tax, per cent	Yield in per cent after deducting 90 per cent tax			Differential yield in per cent of equity investments as compared with bonds	
	Equity investment	2 per cent bond	Tax-exempt 2 per cent bond	2 per cent bond	Tax-exempt 2 per cent bond
2	0.2	0 2	2 0	0.0	−1.8
8	0 8	0 2	2.0	0 6	−1 2
12	1 2	0 2	2 0	1 0	−0 8
16	1.6	0.2	2 0	1.4	−0.4
20	2 0	0 2	2 0	1 8	0 0
30	3 0	0 2	2 0	2 8	1 0

4. Excessively high and steeply graduated rates may be injurious to investment incentives. Retention of only a small equity in the marginal dollar of a high income tends to dissuade the individual who can and should invest in stocks and prompts him to invest in high-grade bonds or to hoard cash.

Postwar Taxation and Economic Progress

A 20 per cent yield on stocks is reduced by a 90 per cent tax to a net yield of 2 per cent—less than the yield on many government bonds and insufficient to compensate for much risk-taking (see Table XIV). Large income recipients often retain their investment interest in stocks because of the control feature; but control itself ceases to have much monetary value when taxes on income become extremely high.

5. Substantial progression in rates is required to provide a more nearly equal distribution of income after taxes. Although it is true that a few conspicuous incomes at the top attract attention much beyond their fiscal importance, these incomes are by no means insignificant from the standpoint of inequality. Moreover the high incomes contribute heavily to our fund of savings, and a redundancy of the latter may act as a brake to economic progress. Some net stimulus to enterprise could be had by combining a considerable reduction in surtax rates with a more effective death tax.

SUGGESTED SCHEDULE OF RATES

In determining relative rates for various levels of income, the following factors must be considered:

1. Although the brackets of income that are important in the supply or the potential supply of equity capital are not known, it can be presumed from observation that the range from $5000 to $100,000 of income is very significant.

2. Tax rates below 20 per cent are probably not of great consequence in economic motivation. Within this range, the taxpayer is likely to consider his taxes a fair price for the benefits he receives from government.

3. The lower brackets of income contain the highest proportionate amounts of "earned income," which, as a rule, is much less able to contribute to government than property income.

4. Other taxes than the income tax and other features of the income tax than the rates are important. Capital gains are especially prominent in the high incomes.

Role of and Changes in the Personal Income Tax

A schedule of rates proposed for postwar application is submitted below:

Taxable income bracket	Proposed rate, per cent	Taxable income bracket	Proposed rate, per cent
0–$ 2000	18	$ 50,000–$ 75,000	47
2000– 4000	21	75,000– 100,000	50
4000– 6000	24	100,000– 125,000	53
6000– 8000	27	125,000– 150,000	56
8000– 10,000	30	150,000– 200,000	59
10,000– 12,000	33	200,000– 300,000	62
12,000– 16,000	36	300,000– 400,000	65
16,000– 20,000	39	400,000– 500,000	68
20,000– 25,000	42	500,000– 700,000	71
25,000– 50,000	45	700,000– 1,000,000	74
		Over 1,000,000	75

These proposed rates provide for a moderate reduction of burden at all levels. The reduction (from the present scale) suggested for the upper middle brackets—$20,000 to $100,000—is somewhat greater than for the remainder of the scale since income in this range is an important recruiting ground for equity capital. Rates are then graduated upward to a level of 75 per cent.

The proposed scale was devised on the premise that capital gains be taxed like other income, and the rates on the higher brackets *should be regarded as conditional upon this change.* Capital gains mount progressively as income advances. On the other hand, capital losses follow a reverse correlation and are relatively heaviest in the lower brackets. It is here recommended that capital gains be taxed at full rates with parity treatment for losses, and that gains and losses which have accrued on the capital assets held by the taxpayer at the time of his death be included in the income-tax base the last year of the deceased's life.[1] At present, such gains are

[1] Proposed treatment of capital gains and losses and its anticipated effects are considered in Chap. VIII

Postwar Taxation and Economic Progress

taxed at special low rates (not exceeding 25 per cent), and gains and losses on property transferred at death are disregarded. Losses, in the main, are deductible only against similar gains. The change would have a profound influence on distribution of the tax load.

An estimate of the effect of special treatment of capital gains and losses on the effective rates of tax, prewar and present, is presented in columns (c) and (d) of Table XV. It was assumed that income at the specified levels includes an average amount of these receipts at these levels. Based on a national income of $140 billion, an estimate was made of net capital gains that would have been reported by taxpayers. A similar estimate was made for net capital losses. From these estimates, an average net gain for each income class was derived. The tax on these receipts was computed according to the provisions of the 1944 Revenue Act as well as those of the 1939 law. Another set of estimates was made of capital gains and losses that have accrued on capital assets held by taxpayers at the time of their death. These average net gains were assumed to be a part of the taxpayer's total income.

Since gains exceed losses by a significant amount during prosperous periods and losses exceed gains during depression periods, estimates of the average net gain may be subject to a rather wide margin of error. In the computation a moderately prosperous period was assumed. On this assumption, the estimates are extremely conservative.[1]

It will be observed that special treatment of capital gains and losses, during the prewar period and at present, results in a wide difference between apparently effective and actually effective rates. Compare the apparent top effective rate of 90 per cent, which seems to apply to present income of $5 million with the actual effective rate, conservatively calculated, of only 71.5 per cent. The suggested scale, with capi-

[1] For a fuller explanation of methods used to make these estimates, see Appendix B

Role of and Changes in the Personal Income Tax

tal gains and losses fully included in the base, is not lower at this level of income but actually higher than the present scale.

A comparison of 1944, prewar, and proposed effective rates, with allowance for different treatment of capital gains and losses, is presented graphically in Chart VI. The increased burden introduced by the suggested scale over that of prewar is quite uniform. Reductions from the present scale are considerably greater in the upper middle brackets than at either end of the scale.

TABLE XV
COMPARISON OF PREWAR,* 1944, AND PROPOSED EFFECTIVE TAX RATES FOR SELECTED NET INCOMES WITH AND WITHOUT ALLOWANCE FOR CAPITAL GAINS AND LOSSES

(Tax rates for a married couple with two dependents)

Net income before exemption	No allowance for capital gains and losses, per cent		With allowance for average capital gains and losses, per cent		Proposed, per cent	Per cent reduction $(d) - (e)$
	Prewar	1944	Prewar	1944		(d)
	(a)	(b)	(c)	(d)	(e)	(f)
$ 2000	0.0	2.2	0.0	2.2	0.0	100.0
4000	0.7	12.6	0.6	12.2	9.0	26.2
6000	1.8	16.8	1.7	16.3	13.0	20.2
8000	2.7	19.8	2.6	19.3	15.8	18.1
10,000	3.8	22.4	3.7	21.6	18.0	16.7
16,000	6.3	29.5	6.0	28.1	23.6	16.0
25,000	9.5	38.8	9.0	35.9	29.3	18.4
50,000	17.4	53.7	16.0	47.8	37.0	22.6
75,000	24.6	62.4	21.4	55.4	40.3	27.3
100,000	32.1	68.6	26.8	59.8	42.7	28.6
500,000	60.7	88.6	45.5	68.8	58.8	14.5
1,000,000	67.8	90.0	50.9	70.9	65.8	7.2
5,000,000	75.8	90.0	56.7	71.5	73.2	+2.4†

* The provisions prevailing in 1939 were used for prewar calculations
† The proposed schedule (compared to the 1944) would increase the effective rate of tax 2.4 per cent for a $5 million annual income

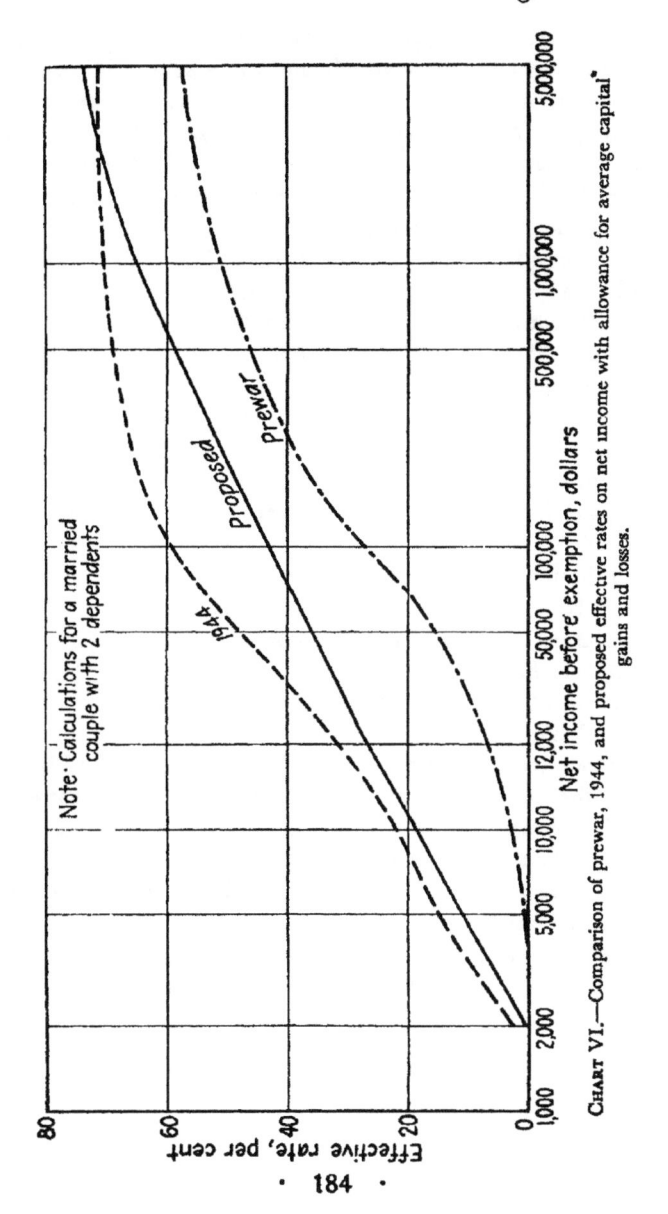

CHART VI.—Comparison of prewar, 1944, and proposed effective rates on net income with allowance for average capital gains and losses.

Note: Calculations for a married couple with 2 dependents

Role of and Changes in the Personal Income Tax

Comparisons of a suggested scale of rates with both present and prewar scales are inevitable and valuable, but it is important to point out that such comparisons have limited significance. The goal sought is a reasonable rate schedule, and, to attain this objective, a new deal might serve more efficiently than modification of existing or prewar practices. One recalls, in this connection, the story of the traveler who sought directions to the Park Hotel. His guide tried to supply the necessary information but this proved to be extremely complicated. Finally the guide gave up in desperation with: "Well, sir, if I were going to the Park Hotel, I don't believe I'd start from here!"

The rate scale suggested must be interpreted with regard for the other tax changes here recommended, among them the following:

1. Taxation of interest from government bonds, hitherto exempt.[1]

2. Elimination of tax avoidance through separate reporting of income by members of the taxpayer's family.[1]

3. Elimination or reduction of sales taxes.

4. More effective death taxation.

5. Integration of corporate and personal income taxes and repeal of the excess profits tax

Whether the total effect of the above changes would be a shift in the tax load from rich to poor, or vice versa, cannot be definitely ascertained. Much depends on assumptions as to the incidence of the corporate tax. On the theory that this tax is borne largely by stockholders, the recommendations might mean some shift of relative tax burdens from the top to lower levels of income. If the corporate tax falls heaviest on consumers and wage earners, the opposite conclusion would seem more plausible. On the former assumption, the retention of a moderate independent business levy would make a net downward shift less likely. For political and fiscal reasons such a tax is very likely to be retained.

[1] See Chap. VIII.

Postwar Taxation and Economic Progress

The proposed schedule is somewhat higher for the brackets above $75,000 than that suggested in the policy statement of the Committee for Economic Development. It is believed that, with due allowance for losses and the adoption of some technique for mitigating the impact of the progressive rates on fluctuating income, the proposed scale will not interfere greatly with the effectiveness of incentives. On the other hand, universality of coverage is far more important than the nominal rate scale and, if it is necessary to give ground on one or the other, the rate scale should be the choice.

YIELD OF THE RATE SCALE AT VARIOUS LEVELS OF INCOME

Table XVI presents the yield of the proposed rate scale at various levels of the national income.[1] It will be observed that, as the national income rises (within the range here covered), approximately 50 per cent of the increase goes into the tax base. Thus a rise of $70 billion in national income is accompanied by an increase of $35.3 billion in the tax base. As more persons and more money are drawn into the base and more income moves into higher brackets at higher national-income levels, the effective rate of tax also steadily increases. Doubling the national income results in more than two and one-half times the original income-tax yield. Maintaining a high national income is an extremely effective tax policy.

Several questions may occur to the reader upon a close examination of Table XVI. As the national income increases, why does the tax base take on only half the increase? The answer probably is that the tax base at the assumed levels of income and assumed exemptions is well under half of the national income. Corporate savings, deductions, administrative leakage, and other elements of income not taxed, take

[1] Methods of computation are explained in Appendix A. Exemptions and other provisions of the 1944 Act are assumed, except for the normal tax, which is eliminated. An allowance of 3 per cent for averaging credits and refunds is deducted.

up some of the expansion. Exempt income must eventually reach a saturation point, but even it may increase over a considerable range, at least in proportion to the increase in national income.

TABLE XVI
ESTIMATED TAX BASE, YIELD OF TAX, AND EFFECTIVE RATE OF PROPOSED PERSONAL INCOME TAX AT VARIOUS LEVELS OF INCOME

Level of national income, billions	Tax base, billions	Yield of proposed tax,* billions	Effective rate,† per cent	Indices ‡ National Income	Tax base	Yield of proposed tax
$ 70	$22.34	$ 4.76	6.8	100	100	100
100	36.23	7.66	7.7	143	162	161
120	46.00	9.72	8.1	171	206	204
140	57.62	12.08	8.6	200	258	254
160	67.51	14.20	8.9	229	302	298

* Yield estimates have been decreased 3 per cent to allow for revenue loss due to averaging irregular incomes
† The effective rate is here defined as the effective rate on national income, i.e., tax yield divided by national income
‡ All indices computed on the basis of a $70 billion national income

Why does the index yield consistently show a lesser increase than the index base? The answer is that (for the income levels in Table XVI) the increases add more weight to the lower than to the higher brackets.[1]

[1] Estimates of income-tax statistics are subject to a substantial margin of error, especially when covering such a wide range in income levels. Estimates of distribution of income above $5000 are based on extrapolation of the patterns prevailing in the thirties, distribution below $5000 is based on inflation or deflation of the pattern in 1941 (See Appendix A for complete discussion.) The margin of error will probably increase as the assumed income levels rise or fall considerably beyond those prevailing in the thirties and in 1941 Furthermore, these distributions to some extent depend upon the economic institutions existing at the time the income is produced An increase in income level may mean primarily that more individuals are earning money or it may mean that those previously employed are adding to their earnings. An increase due to cyclical fluctuation might result in relationships quite different from increases due to technological progress. It is extremely difficult to weight all these variables mathematically, and no claim is made for more than reasonably probable approximations.

Postwar Taxation and Economic Progress

The table presents a dilemma: The budget *might* be balanced in bad years by the enactment of regressive (sales) taxes, but such taxes might only deepen the depression. Relying mainly on progressive taxes with stable rates, we might accept a budgetary deficit in bad years, but this too is alleged to check recovery. This problem is considered further in Chap. XII, where the second horn of the dilemma is given preference as more conducive to economic progress and more compatible with other objectives than the first.

RELATION OF EXEMPTIONS, STANDARD RATE,
AND SURTAXES

The relationship between personal exemptions and credit for dependents, the standard rate, and surtax rates is revealed by a series of calculations. An approximately constant amount of revenue is derived from the personal-income tax by each of the following manipulations of these three variables: (yield is the same as though no manipulations were made; that is, with personal exemptions of $500, standard rate at 18 per cent, and surtaxes ranging upward to 75 per cent as in proposed scale, page 181.)

1. Maintain the present $500 exemption per capita; reduce the standard rate by 2 per cent (from 18 to 16 per cent); raise the surtaxes on all brackets above $40,000 to 100 per cent, leaving surtaxes on brackets from $2000 to $40,000 unchanged.

2. Increase personal exemptions and credit for dependents 20 per cent (from $500 to $600) and

    a. Increase the standard rate by 3 per cent (from 18 to 21 per cent) and all surtaxes by 2 per cent (*e.g.*, from 21, 24, 27 . . . 75 to 23, 26, 29 . . . 77 per cent), or

    b. Increase standard rate 2 per cent (from 18 to 20 per cent) and all surtaxes 4 per cent (*e.g.*, from 21, 24, 27 . . . 75 to 25, 28, 31 . . . 79 per cent).

Role of and Changes in the Personal Income Tax

3. Decrease personal exemptions and credit for dependents 20 per cent (from $500 to $400) and
   a. Decrease standard rate by 2 per cent (from 18 to 16 per cent), or
   b. Decrease standard rate by 1 per cent (from 18 to 17 per cent) and decrease all surtaxes from 2 to 3 per cent (*e.g.*, from 21, 24, 27 . . . 75 to 19, 21, 25 . . . 72 per cent).

4. Maintain the present personal exemptions and credits for dependents and the standard rate; change the progression in the surtax brackets from $2000 to $10,000 so that each succeeding bracket bears a rate of 2 instead of 3 per cent higher than the preceding one; change the progression in the surtax brackets above $10,000 so that each succeeding bracket bears a rate of 4 instead of 3 per cent higher than the preceding one, ending with a top rate of 90 per cent (the yield would be $150 million short of that of the proposed scale).

These comparisons show the great importance for the revenue of moderate exemptions, an adequate standard rate, and substantial progression in the lower surtax brackets.

The estimates disclose the further interesting fact that raising exemptions from $500 to $600 would decrease the income-tax base $7.79 billion or 13.5 per cent; lowering these exemptions to $400 would increase the base $4.64 billion or 8.0 per cent.

INSTABILITY OF YIELD

It is often said that the net-income tax is a "fair weather" source of revenue and that heavy reliance upon this source will mean alternating feast and famine for the Treasury. The record of federal income-tax receipts seems to bear out this indictment. Net personal income-tax revenues over the 18-year period from 1922 to 1939 ranged from a high of $1,214 million in 1936 to a low of $246 million in 1931. The corporate tax showed a range from $1,233 million in 1937 to a low of $286 million in 1932.[1] These ratios of about 5 to

[1] The tax figures are taken from *Statistics of Income*, U.S. Treasury Department

Postwar Taxation and Economic Progress

1 are significantly greater than those of any other major element in the revenue system. During the depression phase of this period, the changes in exemption provisions, treatment of dividends, capital gains, and rate scales were directed toward broadening the personal tax base and increasing the rates. Had these provisions remained constant during the

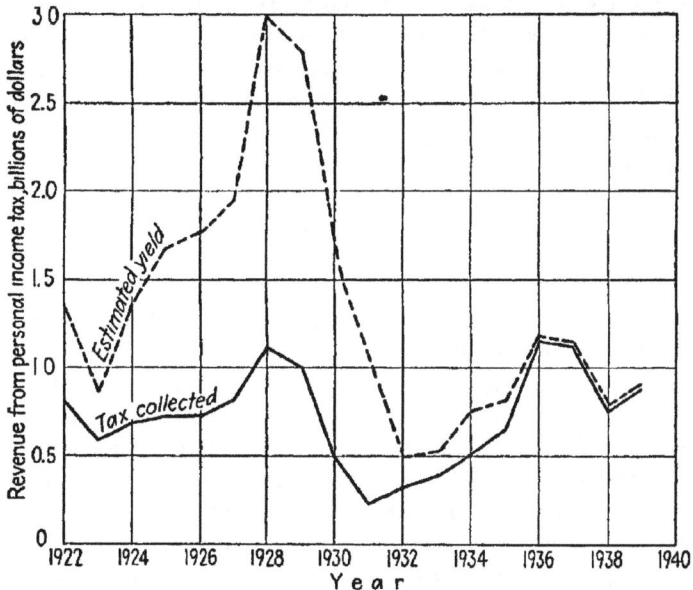

CHART VII.—Comparison of actual tax collected with estimated yield, assuming constant 1939 provisions,* 1922–1939

*1939 rates and provisions applied to 1922–1939.

18-year cycle, the instability would have been even more pronounced. Chart VII compares the actual personal income tax collected with the estimated yield, assuming 1939 provisions prevailed throughout the cycle.[1] The chart indicates that the range in taxes would have increased from less than 5 to 1 to about 6 to 1. These fluctuations are much

[1] The method used in estimating these yields was developed by Susan Burr and William Vickrey in *Studies in Current Tax Problems*, The Twentieth Century Fund, New York, 1937, pp. 141–231.

Role of and Changes in the Personal Income Tax

greater than those of the British income tax, which showed a range of 1.35 to 1 from 1923 to 1933 inclusively.[1]

The instability in the yield of the net-income tax has been due, in large part, to the way in which the tax was levied rather than to its inherent character. Much of the trouble has arisen from the fact that the net-income tax as applied in the United States has had too narrow a base and too low a standard rate. Too great reliance has been placed on the upper brackets of income. These are less stable than the lower brackets, (1) because they are so largely composed of dividends and capital gains, which are notoriously unstable elements of income, and (2) because the lower brackets include portions of higher incomes that are constant from year to year unless these incomes fluctuate extremely and, in the case of the lowest bracket, unless they turn to losses. To take one example, it has been calculated that in Wisconsin, from 1929 to 1934, total income in the bracket from $1000 to $2000 fell 28.54 per cent, while total income in the bracket from $9000 to $10,000 fell 67.99 per cent.[2] Of course it could be argued that, because of their tendency to aggravate instability of yield, capital gains should be excluded from the tax base and that capital and other losses should be disregarded. But stability, like some other good features of an income tax, can be bought at too high a price.

It might be argued, too, that instability in a tax is a virtue rather than a vice, that it is desirable for tax yields to fluctuate with the business cycle, and that such fluctuation gives the tax system a countercyclical fiscal effect. If it is assumed that Congress is "up to" the politically difficult discipline of balancing budgets over the business cycle and maintaining taxes which produce substantial surpluses in some years to offset substantial deficits in others, this conclusion is

[1] *Prevention of Tax Avoidance*, Preliminary Report of a Subcommittee on Ways and Means, 73d Congress, 2d Session, 1933, p. 32.
[2] Computed from data in Wisconsin Tax Commission, *Wisconsin Individual Income Tax Statistics* 1929 *Income*, Vol. 1, Table 2, p. A-8; 1934 *Income*, Vol 1, Table 1, p. A-2, Madison, Wis, 1939

Postwar Taxation and Economic Progress

valid. At least, it seems that we might learn to "live with" some instability of revenue for the sake of its desirable fiscal effects. But such a program creates a strain in the political processes of democratic government, and this strain ought to be kept within reasonable bounds. It can be done by placing the emphasis in income taxation upon a broad base and an adequate standard rate. Some reliance upon taxes other than the income tax also appears necessary.

CONCENTRATION OF THE INCOME TAX AMONG CLASSES OF INCOME, SOURCES OF INCOME, AND GEOGRAPHIC REGIONS

The net-income tax, as usually applied, involves a high degree of concentration of tax burden among incomes classi-

TABLE XVII
Estimated Postwar Distribution of Net Income,* Tax Base, and Proposed Tax by Net-income Classes, $140 Billion National Income
(Estimates based on 1944 surtax exemptions)

Net-income classes	Net income,* billions	Net taxable income, billions	Proposed tax, billions	Percentage distribution Net income	Percentage distribution Proposed tax
$ 0-$ 2000	$ 36 03	$11 79	$ 2 06	34 0	17 1
2000- 5000	50 15	28 43	5.06	47 3	41 9
5000- 10,000	7 55	5 86	1 18	7 1	9 8
10,000- 25,000	6 80	6 13	1 60	6 4	13 2
25,000- 100,000	4 08	3 95	1 45	3 8	12 0
100,000- 500,000	1 20	1.19	0 56	1 1	4 6
500,000 and over	0 27	0 27	0 17	0 3	1 4
Total	$106 09†	$57 62	$12 08	100 0	100 0

* Net income is defined as total gross income minus business expenses, taxes, contributions, and other allowable deductions These figures include the estimated net income of *all* income recipients
† Not additive due to rounding

fied according to size, among sources of income, and among regions. Much depends, however, on the nature of the rates and exemptions applied.

Table XVII and Chart VIII show the estimated amounts of net income, net taxable income, and taxes (under proposed rates and exemptions) by income size groups. It will be observed that those with net incomes of $5000 and over would receive 19 per cent of total net income, 30 per cent of total taxable income, and would pay 41 per cent

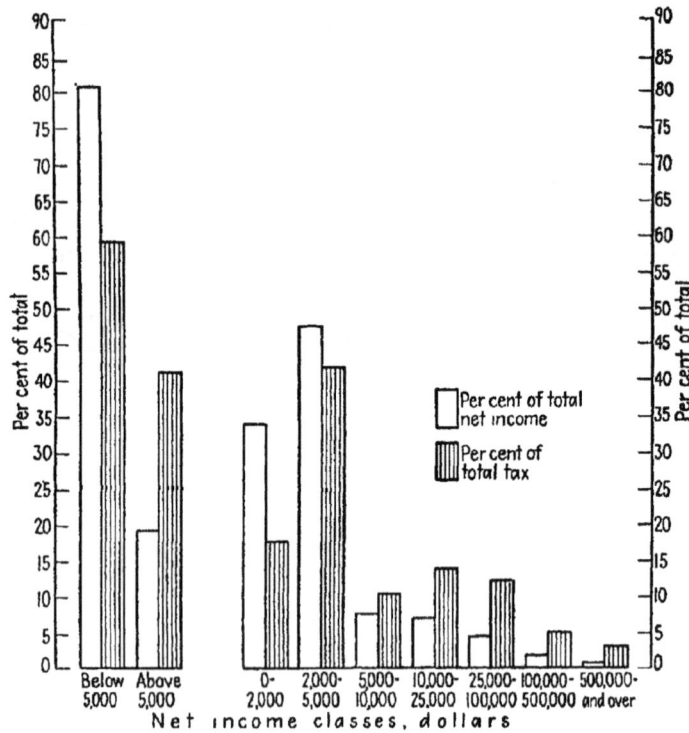

CHART VIII.—Percentage distribution of net income and proposed tax by net income classes, $140 billion national income.
SOURCE. Data from Table XVII, columns 4-5, page 192.

of total income taxes. Twenty-five per cent of their net income would be paid in income taxes. Those with net incomes below $5000 would receive 81 per cent of net income, 70 per cent of taxable income, and would pay 59 per cent of total taxes. No attempt is made here to compare the concentration of tax burden on the upper income brackets under the proposed rates with that which prevailed before the war. The difference in treatment of capital gains and other privileged income would make a fair comparison extremely difficult.

TABLE XVIII
ESTIMATED PORTIONS OF TOTAL REPORTED INCOME DERIVED FROM THREE MAJOR SOURCES, BY NET-INCOME CLASSES, $140 BILLION NATIONAL INCOME

Net-income classes for those reporting net income*	Per Cent of total reported income derived from:			
	Wages and salaries	Dividends	Net capital gains	Other
$ 0–$ 5000	82 9	2 9	0 3	13 9
5000– 10,000	43 4	8 4	3 2	45 0
10,000– 25,000	34 8	12 8	5 2	47 2
25,000 - 100,000	30 3	24 8	9 4	35 5
100,000– 500,000	16 8	36 1	15 6	31 5
500,000 and over	3 0	58 9	33 7	4 4

* Net income is defined as gross income minus business expenses, contributions, and other allowable deductions

As to income by source, it is a well-known fact that the higher brackets of income are composed, to a large extent, of dividends and capital gains and that the lower brackets are heavily weighted with wage and salary income. A graduated rate thus means a higher effective rate of tax on dividends and capital gains than on wages and salaries. This may seem objectionable since the latter types of income are associated with risk-taking investment. However, wages and salaries are earned or unfunded income, with less permanence and security than property income. Moreover, property income would be substantially relieved from present burdens by the elimination of double taxation (corporate and personal).

Estimated portions of total income derived from wages and salaries, dividends, and capital gains are shown in Table XVIII. Chart IX compares the distribution of three major sources of income by means of Lorenz curves. The chart is

Role of and Changes in the Personal Income Tax

based on Wisconsin income-tax returns for 1936.[1] It is apparent from the graph that dividends have the greatest inequality of distribution, with capital gains not far behind.

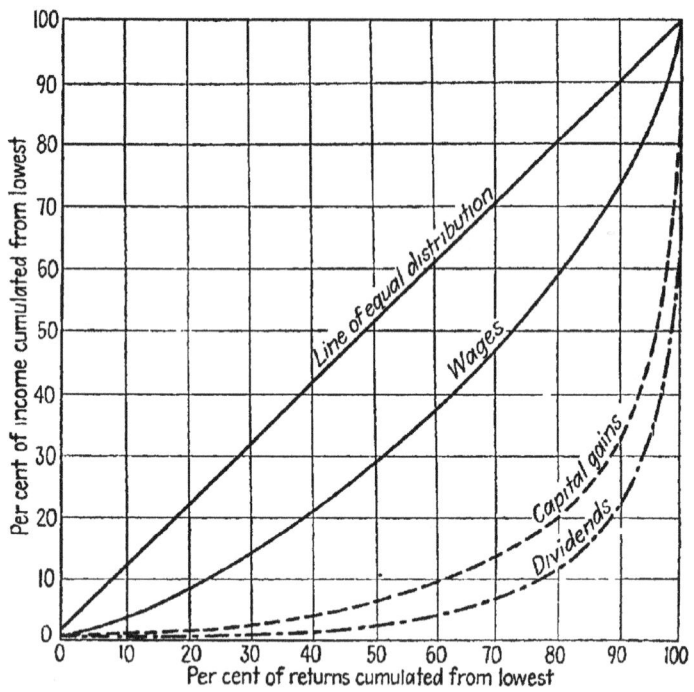

CHART IX.—Lorenz curves comparing the distribution of three major sources of income reported on Wisconsin tax returns, 1936.
SOURCE: Frank A. Hanna, *Wisconsin Individual Income Tax Statistics: 1936 Income*, Vol IV A, Wisconsin Tax Commission, 1939, Table E, pp. 17–18

Dividends from corporations operating within Wisconsin are not taxable according to state income-tax provisions but they must be reported on the return. Statistics used in preparing Chart IX include all dividends reported.

[1] Frank A. Hanna, *A Critical Analysis of Wisconsin Individual Income Tax Statistics*, Wisconsin Tax Commission, Madison, Wis, 1939, p. 78.

Postwar Taxation and Economic Progress

The personal income-tax base is also characterized by a high degree of geographical concentration. The distribution of per capita income varies widely throughout the United States and is particularly concentrated in urban areas, especially those specializing in financial functions. Business income and wealth are also concentrated, but the incidence of business taxes is not so clearly upon the areas which bear their impact.

Studies of the territorial distribution of income show sharp differences among states. One such study[1] observes that "variations are so great that the average income in one State is not even an acceptable relief standard in another. To illustrate, the average old-age pension in California in 1939 was $345. This exceeded the per capita income in 10 States in this year; it exceeded the per capita income of the poorest State by 70 per cent."

The proportion of the 1940 personal-income tax collected from selected states is presented in Table XIX. This is compared in the table with the estimated proportion of taxes other than income taxes borne by the residents of these states. The estimate used is that prepared for the Committee on Intergovernmental Fiscal Relations by Mabel Newcomer.[2] The incidence of the corporate tax was assumed by Miss Newcomer to follow the stockholders of the corporation. The incidence of other taxes is based on various factors, chiefly statistics of consumption.

It will be noted that the share of the poorer states in the personal income-tax dollar collections is considerably less than their share in all other taxes. Broadening the base of the income tax has probably increased the poorer states' share in income-tax payments to some extent. Nevertheless, a federal tax system featuring the personal-income tax will

[1] Committee on Intergovernmental Fiscal Relations, U.S. Treasury Department, *Federal, State and Local Government Fiscal Relations*, Senate Document No. 69, 78th Congress, 1st Session, 1943, p. 37. This part of the study was made by Mabel Newcomer.

[2] *Ibid*, pp. 213–219.

Role of and Changes in the Personal Income Tax

TABLE XIX
COMPARISON OF THE PERSONAL-INCOME-TAX BURDEN WITH THE INCIDENCE OF OTHER TAXES FOR SELECTED STATES, 1940

State	Per Cent of total		
	Personal-income tax collections	Incidence of corporate income tax	Incidence of all other taxes
Arkansas	0.21	0.37	0.55
California	7.23	8.66	7.18
Delaware	2.53	0.59	0.39
Michigan	4.35	3.04	4.70
Nevada	0.21	0.13	0.15
New York	25.13	21.55	16.89
Washington	0.67	0.96	1.43
Wisconsin	1.21	1.70	2.48

SOURCE *Federal, State and Local Government Fiscal Relations*, Senate Document No 69, 78th Congress, 1st Session, 1943

show a considerable degree of territorial concentration. This has its disadvantages but it does tend to mitigate territorial inequalities.

EFFECT OF PROPOSED CHANGES ON THE TAX SYSTEM

It is evident that the proposed modifications would create a tax system more consistently progressive[1] than that which prevailed before the war. (The proposed modifications include those offered in subsequent chapters.) In 1938, at least 55 per cent of federal income came from regressive sources (assuming that the corporate tax is half progressive and half regressive). Had these modifications been in effect, not more than one-third of the revenue (and probably con-

---

[1] The term "progressive" is used to describe a scale of relative burdens in which higher proportions of income are paid in taxes as income advances. The term "regressive" is used to describe an opposite set of relationships, in which lower proportions of income are paid in taxes as income advances Thus, the income tax is progressive because the ratio of tax to income increases as income increases. The cigarette tax is regressive because the ratio of tax to income decreases as income increases.

siderably less) would have come from regressive sources. (Yield calculations are presented in Appendix A.)

A Temporary National Economic Committee study of the incidence of the federal tax system[1] concluded that the federal tax system for 1938-1939 was mildly regressive for incomes up to $3000 and not markedly progressive until incomes of over $5000 were reached. With the proposed broader base and the more prominent role of the personal-income tax, progression would probably begin as low as the $1000 incomes and might become characteristic of the entire income range. The obvious and certain way to make a tax system generally and consistently progressive is by raising most of the revenue with a broadly based personal income tax after allowing reasonable personal exemptions.

IMPROVED ADMINISTRATION

If the personal income tax is to play the major role in postwar financing, more investment must be made in improving its administration. No doubt a high percentage of persons will report honestly and pay without compulsion what they deem to be a fair tax. Unhappily, however, experience has shown that reliance upon respect for the obligations of citizenship is not enough for the administration of any tax. This is particularly true when taxes reach the levels that postwar exigencies will require. A large proportion of income can be checked adequately through information furnished at the source and through auditing, but the considerable income of professional persons, independent business men, and farmers cannot be satisfactorily verified in this manner. Much of such income is known only to the recipient, his secretary, and God; and two of these parties are sometimes corruptible.

There are devices for checking these incomes with tolerable adequacy, some of which are more highly developed in the best state income-tax administrations than in that of the

[1] Gerhard Colm and Helen Tarasov, *Who Pays the Taxes?* Temporary National Economic Committee, Monograph No. 3, 1940, p 6

federal government. An impressive array of secondary information sources is available to administrators. For example, warehousers and distributors of farm products are potentially productive sources of information concerning farm income. Death-tax and property-tax information can be used as well as many additional governmental and nongovernmental data. We are certainly a long way from the happy state where it can be said: "Nothing is overlooked and no source neglected." Whether a peacetime personal income tax with a broad base and an adequate standard rate can be administered with a reasonable degree of equity is not yet established, but it is certainly worth attempting.

Federal administration has operated on the misguided principle that income-tax policing should be largely confined to spots where it yields large returns for the outlay. The fact that the cost of collecting $100 of revenue in 1944 was only 32 cents[1] may be reason for circumspection rather than complacency. Adequate income-tax policing is essential for the broader objectives of fairness and maintenance of taxpayers' morale. Even in the interest of total revenue we should spend substantially more on direct enforcement. Enforcement activities serve to increase payments from taxpayers other than those "brought to book." The income tax without adequate administration will degenerate into an unfair tax largely on wages and dividends. Administration should be recognized as the most important limiting factor in the application of a rational tax system. Unless this function is materially strengthened, we shall be obliged to utilize revenue sources that are inequitable and economically unsound.

[1] U S Treasury Department, *Annual Report of the Commissioner of Internal Revenue, Fiscal Year Ended June* 30, 1944, p. 4.

VIII. PERSONAL INCOME TAX (*Continued*)

TAX-EXEMPT SECURITIES

CRITICS have often referred to tax exemption of interest on government bonds as the crowning arch in the perverseness of the federal tax system.[1]

[1] The historical background of the tax-exempt security problem may be summarized as follows:

The tax-exempt security issue is by no means a new element in American tax conflict. The attempt by the federal government to tax the interest on state and local bonds was one of the issues at stake in the Pollock decision, which overruled the early income-tax statute of 1894. Passage of the Sixteenth Amendment, authorizing the federal taxation of income without apportionment according to population, involved a discussion of the question, and some assurances from the proponents of the amendment that it did not contemplate federal power to tax the income from state and local securities. As the graduation of rates increased, the exemption feature drew more and more criticism. Presidents Harding, Coolidge, and Roosevelt, and all the Secretaries of Treasury since 1919, have opposed tax exemption and advocated its elimination at least as to future issues. The power of the federal government to tax its own securities is conceded, but, as a matter of policy, many fully or partly tax-exempt federal bonds have been issued, and the policy was not definitely discontinued as to new issues until 1941. In the case of outstanding federal issues, the government is bound by contract, and only by the gradual process of refunding and reissue can these obligations be made fully taxable. Fortunately, the volume of such fully tax-exempt securities is not very large. The immunity of state and local bonds from federal taxation is protected by a long line of legal precedent. Recently the legal doctrine protecting state and local instrumentalities was revised by the Supreme Court to permit the taxation of salaries of public officials. This raised the hope of proponents of exemption elimination that the effort to tax the interest on state and local bonds would also be sustained. The taxation by states of federal bonds (through state income taxes and intangible property taxes) is also at stake and would probably follow the same rule as that accepted for federal taxation. During the twenties and middle thirties, attempts were made to secure Congressional authorization of constitutional amendments to clear away legal impediments to the elimination of exemptions. These attempts were unsuccessful and recent interest has centered about efforts to get action by Congress that would present the issue squarely to the Supreme Court. Early proposals covered future issues only, but in 1942 the Treasury advocated the taxation

Role of and Changes in the Personal Income Tax

A Few Facts Concerning Tax-exempt Securities

Facts disclosed at the last hearing on the tax-exempt security issue[1] indicated that, under rates then being proposed by the Treasury, a tax-exempt security yielding 2½ per cent would afford as much net income after taxes to a holder with a $100,000 income as a taxable security with a yield before taxes of 20.8 per cent. More than half of the tax-exempt bonds had been outstanding 10 years or more. A taxpayer with a $100,000 income from other sources, who purchased a 4 per cent tax-exempt bond in 1929, could expect a return on this bond equivalent, after taxes, to that of a 5.26 per cent taxable security under 1929 rates; under 1942 income-tax rates, the equivalent return would be that of a taxable security yielding 33⅓ per cent. At 1942 levels of holdings and federal rates, the estimated loss of revenue from exemption was $275 million. Available data indicate some tendency (though less than would be supposed) for large estates to increase their proportionate holdings of tax-exempt securities. For estates with net assets of $1.1 million, this proportion increased from 6.2 per cent in 1928 to 15.1 per cent in 1940.[2]

On June 30, 1941, there were $20 billion worth of state and local securities outstanding, interest from which was wholly tax-exempt. About $4.8 billion of these securities were held by federal, state, and local government trust and investment funds. Of the federal public debt outstanding on June 30, 1941, only $4.07 billion was wholly exempt from

---

of all interest on all government bonds, except in the case of such bonds of its own as were barred by contract from such action (Adapted from *Federal, State, and Local Government Fiscal Relations*, p. 302.)

Corporate holders of partly tax-exempt securities do not pay the corporate normal tax, now 24 per cent, on the interest they receive therefrom, but they do pay surtaxes and profits taxes upon this income.

[1] *Hearings on Revenue Revision of* 1942, statement of Randolph E. Paul, tax advisor to the Secretary of Treasury, before the Ways and Means Committee of the House of Representatives, on Tax-exempt Securities, April 16, 1942, Vol. 3, p. 3079, *et seq.* p 3087

[2] *Ibid*, Table 2.

both normal and surtaxes. Some $26.6 billion of securities in private hands were exempt from the normal tax only, and an additional $1.1 billion of wholly tax-exempt Federal Land Bank and Joint Stock Land Bank bonds were outstanding.[1]

Arguments Concerning Tax Exemption

Without reviewing extensively the pros and cons regarding tax exemption, we may state the two main affirmative arguments for elimination of the existing exemption privilege:

1. Considerations of equity require uniformity in the application of the income tax to income from all sources.

2. Considerations of economic expansion forbid tax favors to the rentier as compared with investors who assume risks.

The second argument is of special interest here and may be somewhat developed accordingly. Good municipal bonds now command an interest rate of from 1 to 1¾ per cent. "It is evident . . . that only investors with income in the high brackets can afford to buy high-grade tax-exempt bonds, and that those in the highest brackets obtain a degree of tax shelter that they do not begin to pay for."[2] Obviously, this situation has a perverse effect on investment at both ends of the income scale. Small investors are denied a desirable outlet for their funds because of the low interest yield of state and local issues; large investors are attracted to this field although they are particularly qualified to assume risk-bearing investments. Not only can they afford to take risks, but they can reduce these risks by diversifying their investments and by availing themselves of facilities to investigate their purchases. "On all these scores, exemption does things which would seem preposterous if done straight-forwardly."[3]

---

[1] *Annual Report of the Secretary of Treasury, Fiscal Year Ended June 30, 1941*, p. 629.

[2] John F. Thompson, "The Problem of Tax-Exempt Bonds," *The Journal of Politics*, Vol 4 (August, 1942), p 345

[3] Henry C Simons, *Personal Income Taxation*, University of Chicago Press, Chicago, 1938, pp. 178–179.

Role of and Changes in the Personal Income Tax

President Roosevelt, in his message to Congress, April 25, 1938, struck at the unsoundness of tax exemption as follows:

For more than 20 years Secretaries of the Treasury have reported to Congress the growing evil of these tax exemptions. Economists generally have regarded them as wholly inconsistent with any rational system of progressive taxation.

Therefore, I lay before the Congress the statement that a fair and progressive income tax and a huge perpetual reserve of tax-exempt bonds cannot exist side by side.[1]

The arguments against the elimination of tax exemption are largely rationalizations of well-established vested interests. Rights of security holders to present prerogatives are defended on the ground that these investors paid for the privileges when they bought their bonds and that to change the rules now by retroactive legislation would be a breaking of faith and would inflict an unwarranted hardship upon them. This argument has some validity, but the case is greatly weakened if conditions now prevailing are contrasted with those under which many securities were purchased. Generally speaking, retroactive legislation runs extraordinary chances of injury to morale and confidence.

To meet the claims of this vested interest, it has been suggested that any action on eliminating tax exemption be confined to future issues of securities. However, since it will be 1970 before 90 per cent and 1955 before 58 per cent of existing issues expire, this solution would perpetuate a reservoir of nontaxable securities. Many are now held by institutions and individuals not liable to tax or whose income is largely exempt. These outstanding securities can be purchased by others in a position to use them much more effectively for tax avoidance. Some payment for the surrender of this immunity would be well worth its cost if any fair plan of compensation could be devised. Perhaps the payment of

[1] President's Message to Congress, April 25, 1938, *Congressional Record*, Vol. 83, Part 5, 75th Congress, 3d Session, p. 5683.

the difference in interest that a bond carries because of tax exemption might be distributed to all owners of such bonds until their maturity. Although the differential would not be easy to calculate and would vary with the year of issue to some extent, the task should not prove impossible.

Another vested interest, and perhaps the most powerful, is that of the states and their subdivisions. It is apparent that ability to borrow at interest rates properly described as almost negligible is advantageous to these state and local governments. It is natural that they should defend this advantage. The municipalities found the decade before the war "tough going" financially, and any claim on their part that the inclusion of tax-exempt interest in the income-tax base would add to the load of the already overburdened general property taxpayer will meet with a ready response. But the case of the states and local governments is not at all convincing. First, there is the fact that municipalities in other federal systems (the exemption phenomenon is largely if not entirely confined to the United States) manage without this privilege, as did the municipalities of this country before the income tax appeared. Such ease of borrowing as now prevails at the local level threatens to undermine the disciplines that should attend the contraction and management of debt and thus tends to promote refunding, the funding of current costs, and even unwise expenditures. The hidden subsidy involved in tax exemption gives an unfair advantage to publicly owned projects.

Neither are legalistic arguments by which the states and municipalities defend their present subsidy convincing. It is said, for instance, that elimination of present immunities would foster a dangerous shift of power to the federal government. This is not the intent of those who seek to close this loophole in the federal income-tax law nor need it be the result of such a change. No power to levy a discriminatory tax is at issue, and equal powers of nondiscriminatory levies on federal obligations can be given the states. But it is said that if Congress has the power to tax state and local securities, it could tax some and not others. Of course, Congress already has the power to subsidize some local functions and not others through its subvention system. But the privilege of classification and special treatment need not be included in the power to levy a nondiscriminatory tax. It is also alleged that, if the door is opened to tax the interest on state and local securities, municipalities will be liable to taxation on their public undertakings. A nondiscriminatory tax on such undertakings would be entirely proper, but it is not a necessary concomitant of the elimination of tax-exempt securities. There is a wide difference between taxation of private individuals who own government securities and the taxation of government enterprises where no private parties are directly involved.

Compensation for the vested interest of municipalities and states would apply to future issues and not, as in the case of security holders, to bonds already issued. During recent years, state and local bond issues have amounted to $1 billion per year and, if this volume should continue, extra interest payments might amount to $5 to $10 million in the first year and eventually to as much, perhaps, as $100 million per year. This loss would be partly offset by any gains the states might realize were they and their municipalities allowed to tax federal bonds. A direct subsidy to the borrowing units to cover this loss would be objectionable in many respects but it might be a lesser evil than continuation of the present immunities.

Recommendation

If some compensation to the vested interests described above is necessary to rid us of tax-exempt bonds, the outlay would be well warranted. It could be regarded as an investment directly supporting important economic incentives. Ending tax exemption on new issues would be a step forward and would result in a progressive reduction of the problem at a fairly rapid pace. It is probably the most feasible solution. But complete elimination of the exemption privilege is highly desirable.

CAPITAL GAINS AND LOSSES

Past and Present Treatment

The treatment of capital gains and losses (usually gains or losses incidental to the sale of securities or real estate) is one of the most difficult issues in personal income taxation. The canons of simplicity and stability have been violated frequently, and often severely, in laws covering capital gains and losses. The main methods for the taxation of capital gains have included treatment of such gains like other income with no deduction for losses, taxation with full allowance for losses, and classified taxation of gains with losses deductible only against gains of a similar class. The reduction of gains and losses by percentages dependent upon the length of time the assets have been held by the taxpayer, the application of maximum rates, and various provisions for the carry-over of losses not currently usable to offset gains, have provided additional refinements. These features have been used in various combinations during the past 20 years. The present tax treatment classifies gains and losses as short-term when the assets to which they pertain have been held 6 months or less. Short-term gains are taxed like other income. Long-term gains may either be reduced to 50 per cent of their amount in reckoning income subject to the regular tax, or they may be taxed separately at a maximum rate of 25 per cent. The treatment of losses is parallel except that they (whether long-term or short-term) can be deducted from capital gains in full and from other income up to a maximum of $1,000. Moreover, a 5-year carry-over of unused losses is permitted. The treatment of capital gains and losses for corporations is generally similar (including the provision of a 25 per cent maximum rate on long-term gains) but there are some differences, such as the absence of the percentage reduction.[1]

[1] The definition of capital assets for purposes of reckoning gains and losses

Role of and Changes in the Personal Income Tax

British Experience

For over a century, the British income-tax law has specified that the tax was imposed "upon the annual profits or gains arising or accruing"[1] from any property or service. At least before the First World War, it was through the word "annual" that the distinction between taxable and nontaxable income was drawn. According to the summary of court decisions made by the Royal Commission on the Income Tax in 1920,[2] the word "annual" was interpreted in general to exclude all income not likely to recur each year. Since capital gains are an irregular source of income for the majority of those who realize such receipts, most of them were not taxable under the British law. This distinction between taxable and nontax-

---

has differed substantially at times from that applied in accounting. In accounting, capital assets constitute one of several classes of assets. They are more or less permanent in their nature and consequently are frequently referred to as "fixed assets." The function served by these assets in a business is aptly described by Kohler and Morrison (E L Kohler and P L Morrison, *Principles of Accounting*, McGraw-Hill Book Company, Inc., New York, 1931, p 351) when they write that "capital assets are assets which are employed indirectly in the manufacture and sale of the stock-in-trade, they are the tools of production and distribution." For most purposes, capital assets are subdivided into tangible and intangible. The items generally listed under tangible are land, machinery, tools, furniture, fixtures, and delivery equipment; and those under intangible are patents, copyrights, trade-marks, and good will

A formal definition of capital assets was incorporated in the revenue act for the first time in the Act of 1921 Capital assets were defined to include "property acquired and held by the taxpayer for profit or investment for more than two years (whether or not connected with his trade or business), but does not include property held for the personal use of the taxpayer or other property of a kind which would properly be included in the inventory of the taxpayer if on hand at the close of the taxable year." [Revenue Act of 1921, Sec 206(a) (6).] The 1934 Act defined "capital assets" to include "property held by the taxpayer (whether or not connected with his trade or business), but does not include stock-in-trade of the taxpayer or other property of a kind which would properly be included in the inventory of the taxpayer if on hand at the close of the taxable year, or property held by the taxpayer

[1] 55 Public General Statutes
[2] Robert Murray Haig, "Taxation of Capital Gains," *The Wall Street Journal*, March 25, 1937, p. 6

able income also excluded other casual gains from the tax base. Speculative profits, those from isolated or infrequent trading operations and those realized by investment trusts from the sale of securities, were exempt.

During the war economy of the First World War and immediately thereafter, there were opportunities for individuals to reap exceptionally large profits that escaped taxation at a time when the need for revenue was urgent. This aroused such public indignation that it resulted in an investigation of the income tax by the Royal Commission. Among other observations the Commission stated:[1]

> In general we consider that such powers should be given by law as would enable the taxing authorities to deal with any case of casual or nonrecurring profits arising from a transaction that is prima facie a profit-seeking business transaction, since on the score of equity practically nothing can be said for the present exemption of these profits. Profits which arise from ordinary changes of investments should normally remain outside the scope of the tax, but they should nevertheless be charged if and when they constitute a regular source of profit.

---

primarily for sale to customers in the ordinary course of his trade or business." [Revenue Act of 1934, Sec. 117(b)] In 1938, "property, used in the trade or business, of a character which is subject to allowance for depreciation" was excluded from the definition of capital assets [Revenue Act of 1938, Sec. 117(a) (1)] This provision excluded such important items as business buildings, machinery and equipment, and patents, from the classification of capital assets and limited it primarily to stocks and bonds, land, and transactions carried on with the intent of speculating.

The scope of the definition was restricted still more in 1942 when real property used in the trade or business was excluded from the concept. However, the 1943 law excludes from the category of capital gains and losses the profit and loss from a sale of real estate used in the taxpayer's business only if the real estate has been held less than 6 months. Since 1934, gains on assets held for consumption purposes (such as residences) are taxable but losses on such property are not recognized. This is one of those "one-way" provisions which creep into the statutes and play havoc with the good will of the taxpayer.

Thus, while the treatment of capital gains and losses has developed usually to favor the recipient, the definition of capital assets, at least until the 1943 law, tended to become increasingly restricted.

[1] *Report of the Royal Commission on the Income Tax*, 1920, p. 20.

Role of and Changes in the Personal Income Tax

From a careful reading of this and other paragraphs of the Commission's report, one arrives at the conclusion that the Commission advocated the inclusion in the income-tax base of profits arising from operations of a trading nature which were neither recurrent nor could be described as "annual" in the court's interpretation of the term. Furthermore, it appears that the Commission contemplated taxing profits from speculative transactions. On the other hand, it was explicitly stated that profits arising from ordinary changes in investments should remain outside the scope of the tax unless they constituted a regular source of income.

Although the recommendations of the Royal Commission were not incorporated in the statutes, the report stimulated a vigorous effort to tax the profits realized from certain transactions which the Board of Inland Revenue had regarded as outside the scope of the existing law.[1] The word "annual" as it was used in the statute was reexamined, and profits accruing from two types of transactions were reconsidered: (1) profits arising from a series of transactions, each separately not constituting the carrying-on of a trade; and (2) those accruing from a single transaction that was obviously in the nature of a trade.

The British courts have adapted their interpretation of statutes to this new trend. It is now a well-established principle that any profit from a sale or resale is generally taxable if the transaction can be regarded as an incident of a trade or business.[2] The courts have also sought to restrict the scope of "casual profits" by excluding a series of transactions, even though each individually would not constitute the carrying-on of a trade or business.[3]

Many critics who have studied the English method of deal-

---

[1] George O. May, "The British Treatment of Capital Gains," *Journal of Accountancy*, Vol. 73, p 505.

[2] "Accretions of Capital or Income Receipts," *The Law Times*, Vol. 176 (July 29, 1933), p. 85.

[3] *Pickford v Quirke Case*, 139 L. P. Rep. 500, 1927, Roswell Magill, *Taxable Income*, The Ronald Press Company, New York, 1936, p. 76.

ing with capital gains emphasize the arbitrariness and the practical difficulties encountered in drawing a line between taxable and nontaxable income.[1] Haig cites an example to illustrate the uncertainty that confronts the English taxpayer in regard to taxable and tax-free capital gains. From a chance caller, a prominent barrister learned that the owner of a certain building in the London business district desired to sell the property. The barrister knew of a prospective buyer and arranged for a meeting of the two individuals, which resulted in a £300,000 real-estate transaction and the payment of £10,000 to the barrister. Inasmuch as the payment could not be termed a legal fee or, in other words, a profit from a transaction in the nature of a trade or business, the barrister was uncertain of his tax status and disclosed the transaction to the Board of Inland Revenue. The result was a dispute finally compromised by the payment of one-half of the tax. Close cases can be cited of transactions that have been judged as being either in or not in the course of a trade or business, and the hair-splitting distinctions are both unconvincing and extremely difficult to follow.

A principal disadvantage in the British system of exempting specific capital gains from the income tax is found in the opportunities for tax evasion.[2] For most taxpayers, a number of devices are available whereby dividends and interest may be converted into tax-free capital gains, and, in some circumstances, rents, wages, and salaries can likewise be converted into tax-free receipts. Corporation stocks are often purchased for the anticipated rise in the market value rather than for the annual yield. Interest-bearing securities are purchased at a discount below par and sold at or near par just before the maturity date. Other more involved devices are also employed to the same end. A taxpayer in a high-income bracket, subject to the surtax, will sell securities just before

[1] Haig, *op cit*, p 6; Randolph E Paul, *Statement before the Ways and Means Committee of the House of Representatives on the H. R. 6358*, March 30, 1942, Exhibit 6, Magill, *op cit*, pp 88, 89

[2] Haig, *op. cit.*, p 4.

Role of and Changes in the Personal Income Tax

the dividend date to a purchaser in a low-income bracket and then buy them back shortly afterward. The temporary owner of the securities collects the dividends, which in his case are not subject to the surtax, and the owner of the securities reaps a tax-free capital gain equivalent to the dividends. A peculiarity of the British law provides such taxpayers with customers. Certain corporations are in a position to reduce their tax liability through the technique of buying securities with accumulated potential dividends and selling them without the dividends. Since the tax is collected at the source, the corporation is in a position to offset the tax on dividends with the capital losses incurred on the transactions. In other words, a corporation receives a certificate for taxes paid without paying any and thus reduces its own tax liability. Legislation passed in 1927[1] seeks to prevent a taxpayer in a high-income bracket from selling his securities before the date of dividend distribution to a taxpayer in a low-income bracket. If a taxpayer by this method avoids more than 10 per cent of his surtax, he can be assessed on the assumption that the dividends accrued daily and that the sale had not occurred. An inquiry into the loss of revenue traceable to such devices shows the loss to be much less than might be anticipated. However, Professor Haig is of the opinion that this is a high tribute to British tax administration and to the taxpaying morale of British taxpayers rather than to the British method of dealing with capital gains.[2]

Kinds and Forms of Capital Gains

Capital gains are a complex phenomenon. In the case of common stocks, such gains may be due, in whole or in part, to reinvested corporate income. Such reinvestment, if uncapitalized by the issuance of new securities, will tend to increase the value of stocks. This increase will be realized

---
[1] Finance Act, 1927, Sec 33.
[2] Haig, *op. cit.*, p. 4.

by the stockholder at the time of sale. (It is true that stock prices reflect the prospects for future earnings rather than invested capital, but investment helps to create the future earnings.) If reinvested earnings were taxed in full at the time of reinvestment, full taxation of the increment to stock values resulting therefrom would be a clear case of double taxation. Double taxation could be avoided only by crediting the taxpayer with taxes paid by the corporation on gains attributable to reinvestment. Applying a credit mechanism would be a difficult administrative task.

Some capital gains are due to changes in the general price level (inflation). It is often claimed that these are illusory increases in value and should not be taxed, but this argument loses weight when the distribution of benefits and injuries from a rise in the price level (benefiting in general those holding stocks and real estate) is taken into account. Gains due to improvement in the prospects of particular investments are sometimes the result of shrewd investment and sometimes merely a windfall. Gains may be obtained from short-term stock-market operations or may accrue gradually because of of the plowing back of profits in a long-term investment. Unfortunately, quantitative data showing the importance of these various classes are limited and unsatisfactory. Capital losses parallel capital gains and, as is usually the case with losses, their importance is rarely fully appreciated.

Characteristics of Capital Gains as Indicated by Quantitative Evidence

Available quantitative evidence concerning capital gains and their taxation supports the following conclusions:

1. Capital gains provide a minor source of income in the economy, and they are received by relatively few taxpayers. On the other hand, they are often a major source of income for particular individuals, and the total income derived from them is by no means negligible. Data on sources of income, taken from returns filed in compliance with federal and

Role of and Changes in the Personal Income Tax

Wisconsin state income-tax statutes, are available.[1] In the Wisconsin data, the percentage of taxpayers reporting gains ranges from 3.9 in 1929 to 1.8 in 1934. On the federal returns, a larger proportion of the taxpayers reported capital gains: 3.1 per cent in 1934 and 11.5 per cent in 1936. The differences may be due largely to the higher personal exemptions prevailing in the federal law during these years. (It is well known that capital gains are most common among the recipients of large incomes.) In 1929, 2.5 per cent and, in 1935, 1.5 per cent of Wisconsin taxpayers reported capital gains as their only income or as one of the two largest sources. On the 1936 federal returns, capital gains constituted 26.2 per cent, or approximately one-fourth, of the total net income of those who reported them.

2. For most taxpayers, capital gains are an irregular source of income. The occurrence of capital losses is also irregular, but the correlation of the latter with gains is very low. The Wisconsin study included a special analysis of the returns of 13,184 families, selected as a sample of those who filed income-tax returns annually from 1929 to 1935, inclusively. The families realizing gains (1,479) were tabulated by the number of years these receipts were reported. Nine hundred and seventeen families, or 62 per cent, reported them for only 1 year; 70 families, or 4.7 per cent, reported them for 4 years; and 15 families, or 1 per cent, reported them for each of the 7 years. Of the families who reported capital losses (1,865) less than one-half, or 42½ per cent, also reported gains during the 7-year period. The majority of the families, or 60 per

[1] A study of incomes was undertaken by the Wisconsin Tax Commission under the direction of Frank A. Hanna with funds granted by the WPA. The project provides complete coverage of the income reported by Wisconsin taxpayers for 1929, 1935, and 1936, a sample for 1934, and data on the changes in the individual incomes of 13,184 identical taxpayers from 1929 to 1935 inclusive. (*Patterns of Income*, 1939.)

The tabulations from the Wisconsin returns were made as a part of the Wisconsin income-tax study. The tabulations from the federal returns were made by the Division of Tax Research of the Treasury Department in cooperation with the WPA.

cent, who reported capital gains for only 1 year, reported no losses. On the other hand, 87 per cent of those who reported gains for 4 years also reported losses, and 80 per cent of those who reported gains for each of the 7 years likewise reported losses.

3. A sizable proportion (about one-third) of realized capital gains are on assets that have been held a year or less, but the majority are on assets which have been held for longer periods—in some cases, beginning before the enactment of the income-tax laws. Contrary to what might be supposed, more than a proportionate share of long accruals are associated with the larger incomes. Taxpayers with net incomes of $25,000 and less report the largest percentage of gains from assets held 1 year or less, while those taxpayers with net incomes of $50,000 and over report the largest percentage of gains from assets held over 10 years.

4. Capital gains provide a substantial but unstable portion of income-tax revenues. An estimate of the yield from 1926 to 1940 is presented in Table XX. In 1928, almost half of the revenue came from this source and, in the last 4 years of the twenties, over 30 per cent. On the other hand, in 1931 net losses decreased the revenue by more than one-fourth of the total collected, and net losses were also registered in 1930 and 1932. Over the 15-year period, the estimated net revenue from capital gains constituted 15.2 per cent of the individual income-tax revenue. It is impossible to say what the proportion might have been had not capital gains and losses been subject to special treatment. Among the unknown variables in such a calculation are the degree to which realization itself is affected by the tax rate and the effect of restrictions on the deductibility of losses.

The Joint Committee of Internal Revenue has studied the relative fluctuations of the British and United States federal income-tax revenues from 1923 to 1933, inclusively. The maximum annual revenue from the British income tax was only 35 per cent above the minimum amount, while the

Role of and Changes in the Personal Income Tax

maximum annual revenue from our federal income tax was 280 per cent above the minimum amount. This striking difference cannot be explained in simple and single terms. Cyclical fluctuations in Great Britain were less severe. The British relied much more heavily on their standard rate of tax than we did. Finally, there is the capital-gains feature of our law, which undoubtedly contributed substantially to the fluctuation.

TABLE XX
REVENUE FROM INDIVIDUAL INCOME-TAX RETURNS AND ESTIMATED NET REVENUE FROM CAPITAL GAINS AND LOSSES,* 1926–1940

Calendar year	Estimated net revenue from capital gains and losses, thousands of dollars	Total revenue from individual income-tax returns, thousands of dollars	Per cent of total revenue derived from capital gains and losses
1926	$ 225,485	$ 732,475	30 8
1927	296,879	830,639	35 7
1928	576,001	1,164,254	49 5
1929	420,971	1,001,938	42 0
1930	−15,226	476,715	− 3.1
1931	−89,001	246,127	−26 6
1932	−79,917	329,962	−19 5
1933	16,167	374,120	4 3
1934	17,197	511,400	3 4
1935	85,257	657,439	13 0
1936	201,941	1,214,017	16 6
1937	58,188	1,141,569	5 1
1938	52,873	765,833	6 9
1939	26,995	928,694	2 9
1940	12,868	1,494,139	0 9
Total	$1,806,678	$11,869,321	15 2

* Taxes computed on basis of statutory provisions in the given year
SOURCE Computed from figures presented by Randolph E Paul, tax advisor to the Secretary of the Treasury, before the Ways and Means Committee of the House of Representatives on H R 6358, March 30, 1942, Division of Tax Research, U S Treasury Department, Exhibit 3

The variation in the revenue in the United States from net taxable income with the exclusion of capital gains and losses is 45.7 per cent as large as the average annual revenue from

Postwar Taxation and Economic Progress

1926 to 1940, inclusively. A similar measure of the revenue yield of net capital gains discloses a variation of 151.7 per cent as large as the average annual revenue from these receipts.

5. The significance of capital losses (like that of other losses) is often not fully appreciated. The policy of segregating losses (allowing their deduction only against capital gains) has eliminated a considerable proportion of these losses from federal income-tax returns, and statistical evidence as to the total of such negative income is thus unavailable. However, since capital losses were deductible in full under the Wisconsin income tax, the total amount of losses realized by Wisconsin

TABLE XXI
CAPITAL GAINS AND LOSSES REPORTED BY WISCONSIN TAXPAYERS IN 1929, 1934, 1935, AND 1936

Year	Capital gain	Capital loss	Net gain or loss
1929	$58,001,035	$37,428,289	+$20,572,726
1934	6,810,274	30,171,039	− 23,360,765
1935	13,565,513	29,124,200	− 15,558,687
1936	22,279,560	26,181,050	− 3,901,490

SOURCE Compiled from Wisconsin Tax Commission, *Wisconsin Individual Income Tax Statistics* 1929 *Income*, Vol I, Table I, 1934 *Income*, Vol I, Table I, 1935 *Income*, Vol I, Table I, and 1936 *Income*, Vol I, Table IX

taxpayers can be determined from the returns. A compilation of these losses, together with the capital gains, has been made for the years of 1929, 1934, 1935, and 1936, and is submitted in Table XXI. Although gains substantially exceeded losses in 1929, the other 3 years showed losses in excess of gains. The proportion between capital gains and losses reported on the Wisconsin returns suggests that a large part of the revenue secured from net capital gains on the federal returns may be due to limitations placed on the deduction of capital losses.

6. Capital gains tend to be concentrated in the upper brackets of income and capital losses in the lower brackets. Based upon somewhat fragmentary data, a calculation was made of the difference by brackets between 1944 effective

Role of and Changes in the Personal Income Tax

rates of tax and what these rates would be were capital gains included in the base. The 1944 rate on a $500,000 income was not really 88.6 per cent. In actuality it was around 68.8 per cent. The rate on a million-dollar income, well over a third of which is capital gains, was not really 90 per cent; it was around 70.9 per cent.[1]

Issues in the Taxation of Capital Gains

Several outstanding issues in the taxation of capital gains and losses may now be discussed.

Are Capital Gains Income? Were it not for the practice of the British and the support of their procedure by many Americans, one might, perhaps, pass over this question with the assurance that an affirmative answer is obvious. Certainly, presumption favors an affirmative view and the burden of proof should rest with the dissent.

Capital gains result from a sale of real estate or securities and are not unlike, in many respects, the trading profit that results from the sale of fish or potatoes. They are an important element in the distribution of economic power. They are closely related to other forms of income. Corporate saving, as previously noted, may be realized by the stockholder in the form of a capital gain. Recognition of the latter as income is an essential step to the eventual inclusion in the stockholder's tax base of what he gains through corporate investment. A discount on a bond is a substitute for interest to be paid. In the case of a corporation, the buying and selling of securities are often closely integrated with other business of the concern; and, even in the case of individuals, the difference between buying and selling as a business and doing so as an investment avocation is rather artificial. If the depreciation and obsolescence of physical capital are (negative) income, the depreciation and appreciation of investment assets seem entitled to the same status. It may seem that a line should be drawn between short-term (specu-

[1] See Chap. VII, Table XV.

lative) and long-term (investment) gains, labeling the former "income" and the latter something else, but the distinction is not convincing.

Equity and the Taxation of Capital Gains. Is it equitable to tax capital gains like other income? The answer to this question is rather clearly and all but unanimously affirmative. Capital gains, like other income, represent taxpaying ability. If net income is used as a measure of taxpaying ability, it is essential to include all items of personal income in the tax base. One-third of the tax base for individuals who realize capital gains is made up of such receipts. The prime objective of any tax is the collection of revenue. Not only does the taxation of capital gains add to the revenue, but it prevents evasion of taxes by other types of income.

To be sure, capital gains are often, as the British would say, "casual income." This means that they are often quite irregular in their realization. But most income is casual to some degree. The main objection to taxing casual income is that, since it occurs irregularly, it is punished by the application of the higher rates in a progressive scale. We need some new techniques in our income tax to permit refunds or credits where the tax on annual income over a period of years greatly exceeds what the tax would have been on average income.[1] The development and adoption of such techniques are primary prerequisites for any reasonable and satisfactory solution to the problem of taxing capital gains.

The taxation of capital gains is a necessary feature of a program with the objective of applying the personal income tax to all the income accruing to the individual, including that which he saves through the medium of a corporation. Of course, the corporate saving may have been subject to a corporate income tax or an undistributed earnings tax at the time the corporation earned the income. As previously stated, logically it ought not to be taxed a second time without a credit for the taxes previously paid. But the credit would

[1] Discussed in detail later in this chapter.

be difficult to administer and might be ignored in the name of rough justice if the corporate or undistributed earnings tax were relatively low. The element of duplication might be accepted as a rough equivalent of the concession as to time granted the taxpayer before making a full personal tax settlement. The corporate tax would not approach the tax levels of most surtaxpayers. Should this be regarded as unfair to the taxpayers (particularly the smaller ones), some concession might be considered in the application of the normal tax to gains derived from common stock.

If capital gains are to be taxed, the present system of permitting them to be wiped out by the taxpayer's death is unjustifiable. Transfers at death and by gift should be treated as realizations by decedents and donors at market values current at the time of transfer. (At present, the "basis" of assets received by an heir is their value as of the date of death and not their cost to the donor.) This proposal is important for equity and for a generally satisfactory solution of many tax problems outside the field of capital gains. It ensures that all corporate income will eventually be taxed at the personal level. A principal argument for eliminating the corporate tax, as such, is that the levy constitutes double taxation of the risk-taker. But we cannot consistently argue thus and at the same time provide a loophole through which much corporate income escapes the personal tax entirely. The logical alternative to the taxation of capital gains at death appears to be a very high undistributed profits tax.

At the present time, many capital gains are never realized. Stock may remain in the hands of one family for generations and the values that accumulate as a result of corporate reinvestment may never appear in the personal-income-tax base. The same is not equally true of losses, for in their case the taxpayer stands to gain by an early realization.

There are some difficulties in the proposal to make a death transfer the occasion for the realization of a gain or loss for purposes of income taxation. The principal ones concern the concurrence of the capital-gains tax and the death tax at the same point of time. Of course, the tax on capital gains would reduce the base of the estate tax and would not itself be subject to a second tax. As to the timing problem, death taxes can be anticipated by gifts before death and they can be paid on the installment plan over a 10-year period after the taxpayer's decease. Provision might also be made for anticipating the capital-gains tax. The taxpayer might (within limits) be allowed to write up the basis of his assets while he still lived.

Many accept the view that loopholes in our tax laws are easier to obtain and retain than reduced rates of tax and that it is sound strategy to defend the loopholes rather than attack the rates. This represents a cynicism which the author is unable to share. It is unsound to advocate income-tax rates that Congress is unwilling to apply universally and enforce effectively.

Discouragement of Exchanges. Would the taxation of capital gains at full personal-income-tax rates greatly reduce the exchanges of investment capital and destroy the liquidity of such capital? Many answer this question in the affirmative and base thereon the conclusion that capital gains should be treated with care by the tax system. Why should a taxpayer exchange investments if by so doing he must forfeit a substantial part of his income-earning assets to the government?

This appears to be a valid argument for low-rate taxation of capital gains. But it is by no means conclusive. Account must be taken of the fact that at present it is not so much the tax on capital gains which discourages exchanges as it is the loopholes in the tax (gains wiped out at time of death). If one were to be taxed on his gains eventually anyhow and a favorable opportunity for an exchange now presents itself, the transaction may appear desirable in spite of a tax on the capital gain. It is true that postponement would leave more capital in the hands of the taxpayer. But he might also consider the embarrassment attending the combination of taxes at time of death and the higher-bracket rates (in spite of averaging) that might then apply.

As to the willingness to make exchanges, something will depend upon the rate schedule of the personal tax. If the income tax were applied universally to all incomes, rates could and should be substantially lowered from their present levels. A scale that did not exceed 50 per cent on personal income up to $100,000 might be one that could be applied to a tax base including capital gains.

There is a question as to how much the social interest is involved in the matter of liquidity of investments. It has not been demonstrated that some restraint upon the willingness to exchange securities would be disastrous.

Capital-gains Taxation and Enterprise Incentives. Capital gains, along with dividends, are the principal form of return for risk-taking, and the latter is of great strategic importance in a dynamic economy. Moreover, new enterprises might suffer a lack of new capital if investors in established enterprises were unwilling to exchange investments and thus realize taxable capital gains.

On the other hand, it can be answered that if entrepreneurial income is overtaxed, rates should be reduced and the double taxation of such income should be eliminated. There is no real distinction between capital gains and dividends as incentives that would justify a special classification and especially favorable treatment for the former. It is true, of course, that special favors for capital gains constitute the income-tax loophole easiest to obtain politically and that, if changes in the tax system were confined to plugging this loophole, some discouragement to enterprise would result.

Losses are undoubtedly an extremely important element in the psychology of incentives. A taxpayer's willingness to take risks will withstand high tax rates on his gains if he is assured parity treatment for his losses.

If in "incentive taxation" it is reasonable to draw a distinction between business and wealth, principal concern should be for the former. The capital-gains tax is more a levy on wealth than one on business. Like the death tax, it says in effect to the active business man: "We will spare you to some extent while you are developing your business and employing your funds actively in the interest of society, but when you retire we shall have to insist on a settlement with the tax system."

Parity Treatment for Capital Losses. Should capital losses be given a status in full parity with that of capital gains? The feature of our present practice especially resented by investors is the segregation of losses with the provision that they may be offset only against similar gains. Under the present law, many taxpayers feel that the government is guilty of sharp practice in taxing their gains and ignoring their losses. Emil Schram, president of the New York Stock Exchange, relates the reaction of many investors as follows: "I know that this is a sound venture and I know that it needs equity money, but I won't go into it because if it succeeds, I will have to give most of my gain to the Government, while if it fails, I will have to bear all the losses myself."[1] One-way rules usually cause resentment and there is a strong presumption against them. (Another case of this kind is the rule that gain on the sale of a residence is taxable whereas loss on the same type of transaction is not deductible.) This criticism is strengthened by the fact that gains and losses are likely to be realized in different years and that available evidence shows a low correlation in the realization of gains and losses. Consequently, the possibility of offsetting one against the other is slight in many cases, a contingency only partly relieved by the more generous carry-over of losses now allowed.

Segregation and limited deduction privileges for losses are a logical defense against the propensity of taxpayers to manipulate the realization of gains and losses. But taxation of gains

[1] Testimony of Emil Schram, *Hearings, Revenue Revision of* 1942, Ways and Means Committee, House of Representatives, 77th Congress, 2d Session, p. 923.

Role of and Changes in the Personal Income Tax

and the allowance of losses "realized" at death, plus the development and application of averaging, would make such manipulation much less attractive and feasible.

As previously stated, losses are an extremely important factor in incentives, and favorable treatment for these investment failures may be as important in motivation as favorable treatment for gains.

Conclusion

The problem of capital-gains taxation can be solved by treating capital gains like other income. This is conditioned with the corollaries that tax rates on all income can and should be moderated; that provision be made for averaging fluctuating income; that losses be granted parity treatment; and that gains and losses "realized" at death be taxed. Finally, this whole program should be part of a tax reorganization that is more, not less, favorable to enterprise.

MITIGATION OF DISCRIMINATION AGAINST IRREGULAR INCOME

Cause for Action

An attempt should be made to eliminate or at least to mitigate the present tax discrimination against fluctuating personal income. Under the tax system as it now operates, a married person with two dependents whose net income alternates between nothing and $10,000 will pay about 50 per cent more in taxes over the years than a person with the same number of dependents whose net income remains constant at $5000. This is obviously undesirable, both from the standpoint of equity and from the standpoint of incentive for risky enterprise. "Moreover, annual income tax accounting makes crucially important for Treasury and taxpayer many hard (or impossible) questions as to the precise allocation of income between years—questions which lead to interminable disputes, hearings, and litigation and which, under a

Postwar Taxation and Economic Progress

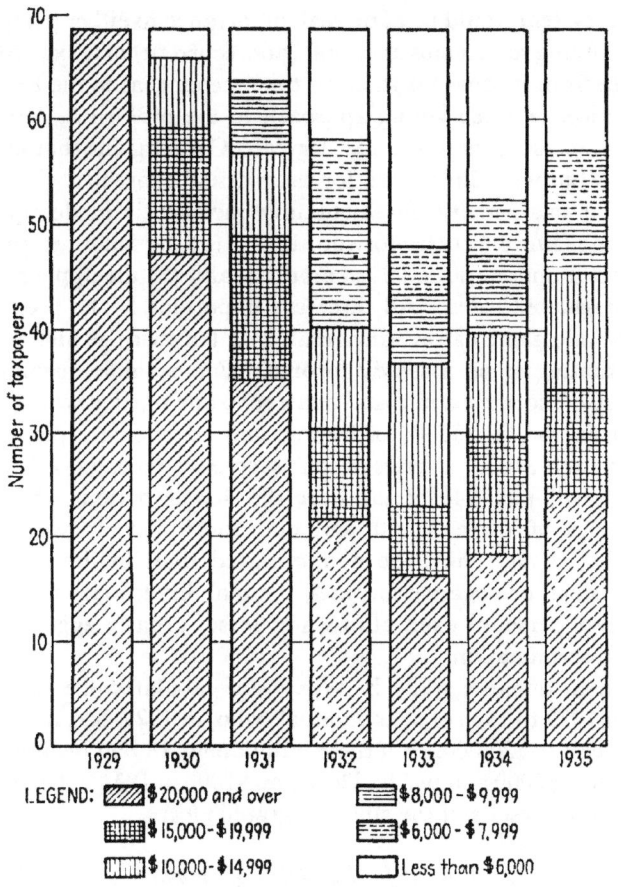

CHART X.—Fluctuation of the income of 69 taxpayers with incomes above $20,000 in 1929.
SOURCE: Frank A. Hanna, *A Critical Analysis of Wisconsin Individual Income Tax Statistics*, Wisconsin Tax Commission, 1939, Chart XVIII, p. 80.

good system would be of no real importance to either party."[1] Classifying some gains as casual (nonrecurrent) and excluding them from income taxation on that account, as in the British practice, take the wrong approach to the problem. Almost all gains are casual in some degree. Casual gains should be taxed but with due regard for their casual character.

The tax penalty on fluctuating incomes is made up of (1) the failure to carry forward losses, (2) the failure to carry forward unused personal exemptions, and (3) the application of graduated rates. All three are important. The progressive scale alone can readily result in a tax twice as high on a fluctuating as on a steady income. For example, assuming $1000 of income exempt and a rate schedule starting with 1 per cent on the first $1000 of income and advancing 1 per cent with each $1000, a series of four successive incomes of $2000 each will pay $40 of tax over the 4-year period, whereas a series of three $1000 and one $5000 income will pay $100. It can easily be demonstrated that, in the case of very small or negative incomes, the inability to carry forward unused personal exemptions and losses greatly aggravates the discrimination.

An income-tax study in Wisconsin[2] tabulated the returns from 1929 to 1935 of 69 individuals who, in 1929, had incomes in excess of $20,000. Of these individuals, 18 had incomes of less than $6000 and two had less than $1000 in 1934. Chart X shows the results of the study in graphic form.

Reasons for Instability of Income

Instability of income results from many causes. Some of it is institutional in character and evolves from the shifting policies in the distribution of income earned by corporations

---

[1] Henry C Simons, monograph submitted to the author
[2] Wisconsin Tax Commission, *Changes in Income of Identical Taxpayers*, 1929 1935, unpublished manuscript, Madison, 1940, Frank A. Hanna, *A Critical Analysis of Wisconsin Individual Income Tax Statistics*, Wisconsin Tax Commission, 1939, p. 80.

and trusts. Some of it is due to irregular periodicity (or absence of periodicity) for some kinds of income, such as capital gains. Some of it originates in the irregular fortunes of business ventures, appearing especially in the shares of those whose claims are residual, noncontractual, and contingent. Some of it is a cyclical phenomenon. Some of it is due to personal causes (such as the decline of an athlete's physical powers). And some of it is casual in character (as winning a prize). Presumably the more dynamic a society becomes, the greater the fluctuations are likely to be. The greater the severity of the tax system on fluctuating income, the more repressive its effect on the dynamic character of the economy.

Experience with Averaging

Unfortunately, experience with various schemes of averaging has not been encouraging. That of the British, who finally abandoned averaging in favor of a carry-over system, has been mentioned. Much the same thing occurred in Wisconsin, where a system of averaging was applied from 1927 to 1934 and was then abandoned in favor of a carry-over for business losses.

In both instances, the main objection to averaging was that it frequently required the taxpayer to pay taxes on a base (or with a measure) which was several years "cold." This proved especially burdensome during depression periods when many incomes were low. Other objections were made to the administrative inconvenience of securing a back file of income-tax returns when an individual moved from one reporting district to another and of obtaining a basis for averaging when his income in some years fell below the level required for reporting. Embarrassment also arose in determining how to weigh the years before or after the taxpayer's income-creating activity—before he got a job or after he retired, withdrew from the country, or died.[1]

[1] In a case that went to the State Supreme Court, the Wisconsin income-tax authorities attempted to tax the untaxed remnants of income to a person

Role of and Changes in the Personal Income Tax

One Possible Solution

The objective of the solution should be to give the taxpayer with fluctuating income some refuge from graduated rates applicable to the years when he has a high income and yet not fall into the error of simply shifting the payment of the tax to his low-income years. This could be done readily by permitting the taxpayer to sum his taxes over a period of years, calculate what his tax bill would have been if his income had been distributed evenly among these years, determine the difference between the two, and claim the difference as a refund or tax credit. To prevent minor refunds, the refund or credit might be limited to cases where the actual taxes exceeded the calculated taxes by 5 or 10 per cent.[1] The taxpayer might be permitted thus to average the income of any 5 or 10 successive years at his option, subject to the limitation that no year could appear in more than one averaging computation. The 5 or 10 per cent margin would exclude a large number of small transactions and is suggested for administrative convenience. The higher figure might be used in the case of 10-year averaging and the lower when the 5-year period is chosen. Some administrative difficulties in this procedure could be reduced by establishing rules that income prior to the first year of filing, or after the death of the taxpayer, be disregarded and that claims for a refund or offset be contingent upon provision by the taxpayer of information necessary to establish his case. Changes in exemption status

---

deceased; that is, they attempted in effect to average the last income of the deceased not only for the 3 years prior to his death but also for the 2 years after his death, as though he were living but had no income (⅓ of last year's income + ⅓ of previous year's income + zero, and ⅓ of last year's income + zero + zero). The Supreme Court decided that only the combination giving a base for the year of the decease could be taxed. [*Fitch v. Tax Commission*, 201 Wis. 383 (1930).] Since the taxpayer enjoyed the benefit of 2 years of no income when he first entered the income-tax system, he received the advantage of a rule which worked only one way—in favor of the taxpayer

[1] The major features of this proposal were suggested by Henry C Simons.

and tax rates would add a complication but not a prohibitive one.

A simplified procedure to reduce administrative complication might be considered, especially if the broadened income-tax base of the war period were retained. This would allow a carry-over of unused personal exemptions and losses for all taxpayers for a limited period. No refunds need be involved. For the lower brackets, this procedure would afford most of the advantages of averaging, even without refunds. Averaging itself might then be confined to incomes above $5000 and refunds limited to cases of substantial fluctuation (where the tax differential amounted to more than 5 per cent). Thus, low-income recipients would be protected against fluctuation due to unemployment, and taxpayers in the higher brackets would be protected from the application of graduated rates to irregular income. The administration would be spared excessive auditing and refunding.

In the case of corporations, the injustices arising from irregularity can be alleviated quite effectively by a system of carrying losses forward and backward. This would be especially true if no attempt were made to apply a graduated rate to corporate income and no specific exemption were allowed.

Quantitative Significance of Income Fluctuations and of Proposed Rebates

A study of Wisconsin incomes, sponsored by the Wisconsin Tax Commission and conducted under the auspices of the WPA, tabulated data for a sample of identical returns over the period 1929–1935, affording an opportunity to test the results of a system similar to that first outlined above. Calculations were made in terms of state rather than federal taxes. The state scale was graduated conservatively up to the $12,000 income level. Calculations were made for two sets of individuals: the first included 60 persons whose reported incomes exceeded $20,000 in at least 1 year of the 7 between

Role of and Changes in the Personal Income Tax

1929 and 1935; the second, 158 persons whose reported incomes exceeded $10,000 at least once during this period, but never exceeded $20,000. Roughly 60 per cent of the first group would have received a refund during each of three 5-year averaging periods covered. (The refunds were calculated on the basis of a 10 per cent margin of tolerance.) For the 5-year period, 1929–1933, 23.3 per cent would have received a refund of 40 per cent or more under the plan; for the 1931–1935 period, only 6.7 per cent would have received so large a refund.

Other conclusions of this investigation were: a smaller proportion of the first group (larger incomes) would have received refunds than of the second, but a larger proportion would have received large percentage refunds. These results are probably due to conflicting factors; the large incomes fluctuate more, but the small incomes fluctuate within the range of graduation. Substantial differences were found in the results, depending upon which 5-year period was chosen. Losses in revenue ranged from a possible 6.90 to 17.69 per cent, the larger figure applying to the second group and the period 1929–1933.

This study included a sample of highly fluctuating incomes over a period of maximum instability, related to a tax structure with narrow brackets and a low first-bracket rate. Very different results are shown by other data.

For purposes of the present study, a sample of Wisconsin returns over the 5-year period, 1937 to 1941, were tabulated.[1] The sample included 100 persons, 50 of whom had incomes below $5000 in 1941 and 50 of whom had incomes above $5000 in that same year. These returns were selected at random among persons who filed consistently over the 5-year period. The sample was tested for adequacy by the addition of 20 returns to each group. This addition did not materially affect the results. Still, the sample is probably not entirely representative in several respects. All the returns were from

[1] This study was the work of Edith Green.

persons living in Dane County and a few adjacent counties. (The sample does not include Milwaukee and several other industrial cities of the state.) Dane County has a considerable industrial and commercial population, but its economic life is influenced by the location within its borders of both the state capital and the state university. Most of the incomes above $5000 would be classed as intermediate in size and only one exceeded $100,000 in any one year. There was considerable fluctuation during the years studied but it was not compar-

TABLE XXII
NUMBER OF TAXPAYERS AFFECTED BY AVERAGING PLAN* FOR SAMPLE OF WISCONSIN TAXPAYERS, 1937–1941
(1943 personal exemptions used with all rate schedules)

	Taxpayers with net income:			
Item	Below $5000		$5000 and over	
	Number	Per cent	Number	Per cent
Total taxpayers in sample	50	100	50	100
Taxpayers with potential refunds due to averaging †				
1. 1943 federal rate schedule	27	54	46	92
2. Schedule A. rates of 1–25 per cent rising 1 per cent per $1000	36	72	46	92
3. Schedule B. rates of 10–35 per cent rising 1 per cent per $1000	36	72	47	94
4. Schedule C. rates of 2–26 per cent rising 2 per cent per $2000	27	54	43	90
Taxpayers with actual refunds under averaging plan				
1. 1943 federal rates	15	30	8	16
2. Schedule A	25	50	28	56
3. Schedule B	16	32	14	28
4. Schedule C	18	38	24	48

* Averaging plan provides for refunding or crediting the difference between taxes on annual basis and those that would be levied on average income over a 5-year period. Refund or credit granted *only* to the extent that such difference exceeds 5 per cent of the total taxes on annual income over the 5-year period

† This includes all taxpayers showing a tax differential due to averaging, including those with differential of less than 5 per cent of total taxes on annual income

SOURCE: Random sample of 100 Wisconsin taxpayers, 50 of whom had net incomes below $5000 and 50 with net incomes of $5000 and over

able to that of the period 1929–1933. In making tax calculations, the exemption status as of 1941 was assumed to prevail throughout the period.

The average deviation[1] of annual income from average income for the group with incomes below $5000 was found to be 13.53 per cent and that for incomes above $5000, 20.29 per cent.

TABLE XXIII
Per Cent of Total Federal Income Taxes Credited or Refunded under Averaging Plan* for Sample of Wisconsin Taxpayers, 1937–1941
(1943 personal exemptions used with all rate schedules)

Assumed rate schedule	Per cent of credit or refund to taxpayers with net income	
	Below $5000	$5000 and over
1943 federal rates..	3.73	0.25
Schedule A: rates of 1–25 per cent rising 1 per cent per $1000.......	4.73	1.16
Schedule B: rates of 10–35 per cent rising 1 per cent per $1000	3.70	0.83
Schedule C: rates of 2–26 per cent rising 2 per cent per $2000......	3.76	0.93

* Averaging plan explained in first footnote of Table XXII
Source: Random sample of Wisconsin taxpayers, 50 of whom reported net incomes below $5000 and 50 net incomes of $5000 and over

These substantial fluctuations suggest that refunds for excess taxes paid, based on the comparison of annual with average income, might be large and that they would be proportionately greater for the higher income group. However, neither conclusion is supported when the data are analyzed and tested. In Tables XXII to XXV, the results of refunding according to the plan first outlined (limiting the allowance

[1] The sum of the deviations from average income, divided by the number of years, gives the average deviation for each taxpayer. Adding these average deviations, and dividing by the sum of the average incomes, yields 13.53 and 20.29 per cent for the respective groups.

TABLE XXIV
DISTRIBUTION OF ACTUAL REFUNDS OR CREDITS UNDER AVERAGING PLAN* SHOWN AS PERCENTAGES OF TOTAL TAXES FOR SAMPLE OF WISCONSIN TAXPAYERS, 1937–1941

Per cent of total taxes actually refunded or credited †	1943 federal rate schedule ‡		Schedule A		Schedule B		Schedule C	
	Taxpayers with net income:		Taxpayers with net income:		Taxpayers with net income:		Taxpayers with net income:	
	Below $5000	$5000 and over	Below $5000	$5000 and over	Below $5000	$5000 and over	Below $5000	$5000 and over
0– 5	2	6	8	11	3	7	5	8
5–10	1	1	1	11	1	3	1	11
10–15	1	.	3	1	1	2	1	1
15–20	..	1	2	3		2	.	3
20–25	..			1				
25–30								
30–35	1			.			1	1
35–40	.	.		1	1			
40–45					.		1	
45–50	3	..	4	.	3		3	
50–55	1	.	1		1			
55–75								
75 and over	6	.	6		6		6	

* Averaging plan explained in first footnote of Table XXII
† Percentage refunded includes refund only to the extent that it exceeds 5 per cent of the total taxes on annual income
‡ 1943 personal exemptions used with all rate schedules: 1943 rates (including victory tax), Schedule A, rates of 1–25 per cent, rising 1 per cent per $1000, Schedule B, rates of 10–35 per cent, rising 1 per cent per $1000, Schedule C, rates of 2–26 per cent, rising 2 per cent per $2000
SOURCE Random sample of Wisconsin taxpayers, 50 of whom reported net incomes of below $5000 and 50 with net incomes of $5000 and over.

to differences in excess of 5 per cent) are analyzed. The tables show that, under 1943 federal rates and exemptions,[1] refunds would be more numerous and relatively larger (as a percentage of taxes) for the group with incomes below $5000 than for the group with incomes above $5000. The per-

[1] Capital gains and losses were included in the base and in the calculation of tax, like other income. Dividends were included without the deduction allowed under the Wisconsin law.

Role of and Changes in the Personal Income Tax

TABLE XXV
Distribution of Actual Refunds or Credits under Averaging Plan* for Sample of Wisconsin Taxpayers, 1937–1941

	1943 federal rate schedule†		Schedule A		Schedule B		Schedule C	
Amount of refund or credit	Taxpayers with net income.		Taxpayers with net income:		Taxpayers with net income.		Taxpayers with net income.	
	Below $5000	$5000 and over	Below $5000	$5000 and over	Below $5000	$5000 and over	Below $5000	$5000 and over
$ 0–10	1	.	20	3	6	1	12	.
10–20	3	.	5	1	1	.	3	2
20–30	.	.	.	3	1	.	3	1
30–40	1	.	.	2	.	.	.	3
40–50	1	.	.	.	2	1	.	1
50–75	1	.	.	2	2	.	.	1
75–100	2	1	.	1	1	.	.	1
100–125	1	.	.	2	3	.	.	4
125–150	1	1	.	2	.	.	.	2
150–200	1	.	.	3	.	3	.	1
200–500	3	2	.	4	.	2	.	4
500–1000	.	2	.	3	.	4	.	3
1000–2000	.	2	.	2	.	3	.	1

* Averaging plan explained in first footnote, Table XXII.
† 1943 personal exemptions used with all rate schedules. 1943 rates (including victory tax), Schedule *A*, rates of 1–25 per cent, rising 1 per cent per $1000; Schedule *B*, rates of 10–35 per cent, rising 1 per cent per $1000; Schedule *C*, rates of 2–26 per cent, rising 2 per cent per $2000.

Source. Random sample of Wisconsin taxpayers, 50 of whom reported net incomes below $5000 and 50 with net incomes of $5000 and over.

centage of tax refunded in the former case would be 3.73 per cent and in the latter, 0.25 per cent. The carry-over of unused personal credits would be highly significant in the case of low incomes. The high standard rate of the federal tax and the relatively broad brackets used in the federal scale contribute to make the allowances for the large incomes very small.

In the case of the smaller incomes, practically all the benefit of averaging seems to be attached to the carry-over of personal exemptions. If no refunding were allowed but a carry-over were permitted, the reduction of tax for this group would be slightly larger than the above figures indicate. This would result because the carry-over would not be limited by a 5 per cent differential. Only one taxpayer, with income larger in the earlier than in the later years of the series, would lose the benefit of the carry-over. On the other hand, in a prolonged period of falling incomes, the carry-over might be substantially less beneficial to low-income groups than a refunding provision.

The effect of rate structure and bracket width upon fluctuating as compared with regular incomes is shown in the tables by the use of hypothetical rate schedules A, B, and C. Schedule A, with a low standard rate, relatively steep progression, and narrow brackets, shows the largest effect of averaging and refunding. Schedule B, with a higher standard rate but small bracket intervals, shows the least effect next to the 1943 federal scale. Schedule C, with broader brackets but a low standard rate, shows an effect greater than that of B or the federal scale but less than that of A.

One might conclude from this evidence that averaging and rebates for fluctuating income are of minor importance. But that conclusion would ignore the significance of averaging and rebates for specific cases. To find such special cases, a search was made through a considerable portion of the Wisconsin returns. One case discovered was that of a contractor whose income consisted mainly of the profits of his business. His net taxable income for the 5-year period was $30,039 in 1937, $9859 in 1938, $3125 in 1939, $18,180 in 1940, and $46,845 in 1941. His taxes under 1943 tax rates would have fluctuated from $721 in 1939 to $25,468 in 1941. The total taxes for the period would amount to $49,761. Under an averaging system, this taxpayer would receive a refund of $3,806, amounting to 7.65 per cent of his total annual taxes.

Another case was that of a taxpayer who received a salary from a machine company and who also had large investments. This individual's net taxable income was less than nothing (−$66,793) in 1937, $7609 in 1938, $28,502 in 1939, $28,301 in 1940, and $32,433 in 1941. Under an averaging plan, his losses of 1937 would be carried forward to his more prosperous years and he could have claimed a refund of $33,901 or 78 per cent of his actual taxes. (The calculation is based on the assumption that no carry-over had previously been allowed for annual losses.) A third case, that of an executive of a manufacturing concern, would have involved a refund of 19.74 per cent.

In only one of these cases was realization of capital gains and losses sufficient to dominate the income pattern. Undoubtedly there are quite a number of such cases. A major reason for introducing some averaging system is that it would be the most feasible means of mitigating the injustice arising from the inclusion in a single year's income of the gains and losses accrued over long periods of time.

Were tax conditions (rates and other terms of the tax law) constant, there would be no instances where income fluctuations benefit the taxpayer and where the application of an averaging device, as outlined, would favor the government rather than the taxpayer. A requirement that the terms of tax prevailing in any one year of the series be used in applying the average would entirely eliminate cases where the average would mean more tax rather than less.

A taxpayer would be as likely to claim a refund based on averaging in a good as in a bad year. However, the carry-over of exemptions might create a lag in revenue yields as taxpayers moved from depression into prosperity, and the lag might continue even beyond the peak of a short cycle. This would be unfortunate. But the volume of the lag would probably not be of great importance and could be offset by other changes in the tax.

Conclusion

Probably the most feasible solution to the problem of fluctuating incomes is to allow a carry-over of losses and personal exemptions generally, and to provide an averaging and rebate system for incomes above $5000. This problem demands attention both in the interest of equity for all taxpayers and to lay the foundation for sound taxation of capital gains and losses. Admitting the difficulties in any scheme of averaging, one may nevertheless conclude that an attempted refinement of income-tax procedure as suggested' above is definitely worth a trial. Even a crude beginning should produce the needed experience upon which further refinements could be based.

PROBLEM OF SIMPLIFICATION

A common observation concerning the income tax is that this levy can and should be drastically simplified. It is said, and rightly, that it is hardly befitting a democracy to have tax laws intelligible only to (some) tax specialists. The writer shares this view and yet he realizes that he has made suggestions which would add complications to the tax laws. Simplicity, like other features of taxation, can be bought at too high a price. Fortunately there are many points in the tax system where greater simplicity can be had at a reasonable cost or at no cost whatever. It is, for example, quite clear that the division between normal taxes and surtaxes is an anachronism that serves no useful purpose. (It is retained largely because of interest on outstanding bonds, some of which is exempt from normal but not from surtaxes. Even before these bonds are refunded and replaced by fully taxable issues, the anachronism can and should be eliminated by making the interest subject to only part of a single tax schedule.) The former weird combination of victory, normal, and surtax has now happily been reduced to simpler and fewer elements by elimination of the victory tax (although some features of the latter have been carried over into the new normal tax). Progress in simplified reporting is now being made and can be further developed. A trend toward a sound structural basis would in itself be a move toward simplicity and stability in the income tax. It is a bad theory that identifies increasing complication with progress.

MISCELLANEOUS CONSIDERATIONS

Several problems of personal income taxation can be given only passing attention here. One is the taxation of imputed income and another is that of community property. These problems have to do with the equity of the income tax and have no special relation to the problem of employment, production, and expansion with which we are concerned. They would not be relevant at all were it not for the fact that we are recommending an expanded role for the income tax. If the personal income tax is to occupy the major place in the federal tax system, as here suggested, the universality of its application to all income on a fair basis takes on new significance.

Imputed income has been defined as "a flow of satisfactions from durable goods owned and used by the taxpayer, or from goods and services arising out of the personal exertions of the taxpayer on his own behalf."[1] Familiar examples are the rental value of owner-occupied homes, the services of housewives, and the wages and profits of subsistence farming. A complete catalogue would include such items as self-service shaving, and the enjoyment of one's leisure time.

There is little, if any, advocacy of an attempt to tax all imputed income, and probably no serious inequity arises from the practice of ignoring much of it. That many people will seek to avoid the income tax by shunning the market and going in for self-subsistence living is quite doubtful. In the case of most individuals, it can simply be assumed that the imputed income is equally or proportionately distributed and thus can be disregarded, or, at any rate, that this income cannot be measured for income-tax purposes and thus must be ignored.

[1] Donald B. Marsh, "The Taxation of Imputed Income," *Political Science Quarterly*, Vol. LVIII (December, 1943), p 514.

Postwar Taxation and Economic Progress

Serious inequities may result, however, from failure to include certain items of imputed income in the tax base, and precedents for their successful inclusion do exist. The most notable of these exceptions are the imputed rent of owner-occupied residential premises and the imputed value of farm products used to supply the farm household. It may easily be demonstrated that investment in a home substantially decreases the owner's income-tax liability. Rent saved is not taxable and interest paid is a deductible item. On the other hand, rent paid is not a deductible item for the tenant. Similarly, fuel and groceries saved by a farmer are not taxable income, but these living expenses are not deductible for those who must acquire them in the market.

Precedent for taxing as income the annual value of owner-occupied residential premises can be found in the British practice; and some states, for example, Wisconsin, attempt to include in their income-tax base the value of farm-consumed farm products.[1]

It has been estimated that in 1940 the net imputed rental value of owner-occupied homes was over $1,898 million.[2] This is a net figure with deductions made for repairs, depreciation, insurance, interest, and real-estate taxes. The gross rental was estimated at about $4,747 million.

Rough equity between tenant and homeowner could be achieved by allowing a deduction of rent paid for residential quarters, but this would violate the rule that living expenses shall not be deductible. Moreover, the equivalent of rent saved by owner-occupants would be a net and not a gross rent figure. As a matter of practical administration, an arbitrary percentage of gross would probably be the expedient allowance. On the other hand, extension of the income-tax base to include imputed rent would add new complexities

[1] Either the actual value of goods consumed or (if no account is kept) a presumed figure of $90 for each adult and $60 for each minor living on the farm

[2] Marsh, *op cit*, p. 522. The estimate was based on census data, it included the value of owned farm homes but not the land on which the farmhouse stands It did include the land on which nonfarm homes stand.

both for the homeowner in calculating his deductions and for the administration in checking them.

. As justification for the present policy of ignoring imputed rent, it is pointed out that the homeowner has a heavy local property-tax obligation and that homeownership should be encouraged. Of course, the homeowner can already deduct his property taxes for federal income-tax purposes, but this is not equivalent to paying no local tax. The tenant, too, may bear some property taxes, depending upon the incidence of the levy borne directly by the landlord. At the very least, it would seem that the owner-occupant might be denied the property-tax deduction. Whether the government should go the full way and make imputed rent taxable is a close question. The greater degree of equity resulting from such action may well be worth its cost in administrative inconvenience.

The assessment of imputed income in the form of consumed farm products can also be justified. When exemptions were high and bottom effective rates were low, the neglect of this imputed income was not important. On the assumption that the wartime range of taxation will remain in the postwar period, with only slight mitigation, this lack of significance disappears. It is also apparent that, under the personal income tax, rural taxpayers have a considerable advantage since more stringent administration can be applied to most incomes of urban residents. Some provision for reporting imputed farm income, even though arbitrary in its application, would contribute substantially to the equity of the income tax.

The problem of community property presents a unique phase in intergovernmental fiscal relations. The income tax and, until recently, the estate tax have utilized definitions of property found in the laws of the states. This precludes the uniform application of federal tax laws. The situation is somewhat analogous to the varying rules that are applicable in the case of voting for federal officials. Community property laws differ among the states but their essential feature is that income and profits from community property and earnings from the economic activities of husband and wife are jointly held. This joint ownership does not prevent granting the husband certain special prerogatives of management and control. In income-tax procedure, however, half of the community income may be separately reported by the wife. This means a quite different tax on a large salary earned by the breadwinner of the family, depending upon the state in which the salary happens to be earned.

Community property laws exist in eight states: Arizona, California, Idaho, Louisiana, New Mexico, Texas, Wyoming, and Washington. The deplorable discrimination involved is illustrated by the recent action of Oklahoma in amending its statutes with the avowed purpose of enabling its citizens to avoid the federal tax.[1] Discussion of the Oklahoma measure brought out the fact that $11,380 could be saved by those who might, by means of the new law, divide an income of $100,000. The Bureau of Internal Revenue has refused to recognize the amendment for federal income-tax purposes and the Supreme Court sustained the Bureau. The Oklahoma law offered the taxpayer an election to report on a community property basis. Most other states with community property provisions do not allow the taxpayer an election and their systems were undisturbed by the decision.[2]

The territorial discrimination involved in the community property institution could be removed were Congress to disregard state concepts of property and insist on the use of its own definition for the application of its own tax laws. To this Senator Connally has offered the objection: ". . . to treat the rights of the wife under the constitutions and statutes of eight great states as non-existent flies in the very face of the heretofore well-recognized principle that the states control the

---

[1] Harry A. Campbell, "Developments Relating to the Oklahoma Community Property Act," *The Journal of the Oklahoma Bar Association*, February 28, 1942, pp. 49–57.

[2] *The New York Times*, November 20, 1944.

Role of and Changes in the Personal Income Tax

ownership of property and income."[1] But the convincing reply is offered that the issue "is a question of taxation, not of states' rights or morals. . . . The issue basically is that of treating persons in similar circumstances alike."[2] Constitutional barriers might be confronted but it seems probable that the necessary action would not go beyond Congressional powers. In 1942, Congress took such action with respect to the estate tax, where the problem was similar. The income-tax discrimination has been before Congress on several occasions but no action has resulted.

Although the uniform application of federal tax laws with respect to the concept of property would remove territorial discrimination from the federal income tax, it would not remove all discrimination among taxpayers. The latter discrimination results from the privilege of filing separate returns by different members of a single family. The remedies suggested have been either the compulsory joint return (used in Great Britain) or the universal separation of tax liability under which all members of a family would sum their incomes, divide by the number of members, compute the tax, and multiply by the number of members. Neither of these remedies is entirely satisfactory. The first requires a combination of incomes that are, in some cases, mainly independent, and it allows the (fiscally) unimportant factor of marriage to affect tax liability; the second gives undue advantage to the person with dependents. Ability to pay in the upper brackets is mainly a matter of economic power and this is not a "per capita" proposition. A taxpayer with a net income of $100,000 and with a wife and child is not in the same ability-to-pay class as a single taxpayer with $33,333 income. The proposal could be modified to allow freedom of division between husband and wife only. This would

---

[1] William Leonard Crum, John F. Fennelly, and Lawrence Howard Seltzer, *Fiscal Planning for Total War*, National Bureau of Economic Research, New York, 1942, p. 270.
[2] *Ibid.*, p. 269.

substitute a premium for a penalty upon marriage. There is no perfect solution to this problem. However, either the per capita basis (confined to husband and wife) or compulsory joint returns would be a great improvement over present practices. Either change could be made without altering revenue yields or relative tax burdens except for specific individuals. Considering political factors and the social desirability of supporting the institution of marriage, the per capita system of reporting family income is recommended.

IX. DEATH TAXATION[1]

GENERAL CONSIDERATIONS

Introduction: The Case for Death Taxes

THE question has been raised as to whether the effectiveness of the death tax might not be increased to compensate for some loss of revenue and distributive equality resulting from a reduction of middle- and top-bracket income-tax rates. This substitution is recommended on the ground that the death tax affects business incentives less than the surtax. Most of the interests in accumulating a fortune, except certain acquisitive ambitions for one's family, are undisturbed by the death tax. Although death taxes cut heavily into the supply of available capital, no shortage in savings, as such, is anticipated at present. The shortage, if any, is in risk-seeking capital, and though inherited funds may be employed in this role, the likelihood is less than when such funds are in the hands of the founder of the fortune.

For many years, economists have proclaimed strong social and economic grounds for death taxation. A classic summary of this view by John Stuart Mill reads:[2]

> The inequalities of property which arise from unequal industry, frugality, perseverance, talents, and to a certain extent even opportunities, are inseparable from the principle of private property, and if we accept the principle, we must bear with these consequences of it, but I see nothing objectionable in fixing a limit to what anyone may acquire by the mere favor of others, without any exercise of his faculties, and in requiring that if he desires any further accession of fortune he shall work for it.

---

[1] Prepared with the assistance of William H Anderson
[2] John Stuart Mill, *Principles of Political Economy*, Longmans, Green and Company, New York, 1909 (Ashley ed.), Book II, Chap. II, p 232.

Postwar Taxation and Economic Progress

It is wholesome for society to regard the builder of a fortune as a trustee who administers a sector of the country's wealth in the interest of the economy. He has demonstrated his capacity for this role by his success in the ordeal of competition. But it does not follow that the virtues of the fortune builder are passed on to his heirs or that the corresponding responsibilities should be lodged with them. Many who have founded fortunes have been the first to recognize the soundness of this view. Equality of opportunity, which means more widely spread opportunity and incentive for enterprise, is promoted by death taxation.

As to the social interest in a wide diffusion of wealth and ownership, the following[1] from Herbert Hoover may be selected as typical of widely held views:

> I am convinced that one of the continuous and underlying problems of sustained democracy is the constant and wider diffusion of property ownership Indeed I would become fatalistic of the ultimate destruction of democracy itself, if I believed that the result of all our invention, all our discovery, all our increased economic efficiency, and all our growing wealth would be toward further concentration of ownership. We are all fundamentally interested that our economic forces, our public and private policies, should be so directed that with our increasing wealth, the tendencies of diffusion of ownership shall be greater than the tendencies of concentration.

The Case against Death Taxes

Summary of the Argument

Those opposing high death taxes claim that family interest is an incentive not to be underrated. Moreover, provision for dependent relatives is important from both the personal and the social point of view. Death taxes have always been questioned on the score that they are especially inimical to

[1] Herbert Hoover in the *Proceedings of the Academy of Political Science*, April, 1925 Quoted by A. Phillip Woolfson, "Inheritance Taxation and Maladjustment of National Income Taxes," *Tax Magazine*, August, 1937, pp. 459–460.

Death Taxation

saving and to the maintenance of an existing capital fund. It is argued also that the death tax is a deterrent to investment in risk-bearing securities because it induces estate owners to shift their investments to liquid assets (such as bonds, insurance, or cash). The shift is made in anticipation of the need for cash to pay death taxes without a hasty, forced, and losing liquidation of holdings. From the standpoint of the social interest, it is desirable that this situation be avoided since owners of large estates are particularly qualified to assume the risk-bearing functions in society. Furthermore, in closely held corporations, a forced liquidation of stock following the death of a controlling stockholder may cause considerable disruption and may result in the sale of small independent concerns to large and well-established competitors. Finally, donations are the basis of philanthropy, much of which contributes to economic progress by providing funds for research.

Arguments against Death Taxation Considered

The Effect of Death Taxation on Incentives to Work, to Save, and to Risk. As previously stated, the most frequent criticism of death taxes has been that they undermine the capital fund of society. A recent champion of this view was Andrew W. Mellon, former Secretary of the Treasury. Speaking of the federal estate tax as it stood in the middle twenties, he said:

> This excessively high taxation should be considered from two standpoints. First, its effect upon existing capital, or its static effect; and second, its effect on the production of future capital, or its dynamic effect. Death taxes are taxes upon capital. It is obvious that if the government, to maintain itself, were to take 50% of every estate large or small and if on the average a man could not double his inheritance, there would be an actual depletion of capital within the country and ultimately there would be nothing left to tax.[1]

[1] Andrew W. Mellon, "Economic Aspects of Estates and Inheritance Taxation," *Trust Companies*, Sec. 1924, Vol. 39, p. 708.

Postwar Taxation and Economic Progress

As suggested in this statement, there are several approaches to the problem of the relation of death taxes to saving. One may consider (1) the effect of these taxes on the incentives to work, to save, and to risk; and (2) the effect on the ability to supply and maintain adequate savings. The economic incentives involved are those both of the estate builder and of the heirs.

The effect of the death tax on the incentive of the estate builder to save is an intangible factor not subject to measurement, but the remoteness of the tax lessens the probability of a decisive influence. Some saving occurs during the early and middle years of life, when the desire to save for heirs is not a strongly motivating factor. As individuals grow older, they become much more interested in the size of their estates as such. However, some saving is continued as a matter of habit and much saving is also automatic, consisting of income in excess of the recipient's capacity to spend

It is probably true that the nonpecuniary motives to work and save are often strongest among persons with estates large enough to be subject to death taxes. Both Andrew Carnegie and Charles Schwab have testified that the love of power motivates many wealthy enterprisers long after they have ceased to desire money. As long as individuals can have full use, enjoyment, and control of property during their own lifetimes, they are not likely to "slow down" because of death taxes. It is important, however, to keep the level of production high so that, even after death taxes, there will be a goodly portion left to distribute and adequate capital will be forthcoming from the saving of active enterprisers.

At first sight, the inheritance tax seems to come wholly from income set aside for reinvestment. But this is not necessarily true. If the death tax were not imposed, part of what goes for taxes would be spent by the beneficiaries (perhaps none too wisely). What was principal in the hands of the predecessor is often fortuitous income to the distributees and, like all other income, will be saved and reinvested only in part.

. The privilege of inheritance and unearned income may have particularly unwholesome effects upon the heir. It may contribute to his demoralization and rob the community of his social usefulness. Unearned income often acts as a direct deterrent to the desire to work as well as to personal economy and saving. "Easy come, easy go" is the vernacular expression. On the other hand, in the case of the thousands of heirs who are not spendthrifts, the use of inherited property in a risk-taking role is not common. Too many look upon inherited wealth as something "to have and to hold." Whereas the builder of the estate "worked" with his capital actively and in an enterprising manner, the heirs (many sons and most daughters and wives) prefer to let the capital "work" for them. No one who understands the functioning of modern business enterprise would deny that there is a world of difference between $1 million in the hands of, say, Henry Kaiser and $1 million in the hands of, say, Doris Duke.

Concerning the effects of death taxes on the incentive to risk, the point has been made that, anticipating these taxes, estate owners in their later years tend to shift into liquid investments. The validity of this criticism is conceded, but the adverse effects are due mostly to unfortunate valuation procedures that could be corrected. This problem is discussed in a later section of this chapter.

Effect of Death Taxes on Ability to Save; the Adequacy of Saving. The prevailing view today is that our present rate of saving is at least sufficient and that oversaving is or may become a chronic economic problem. There is no evidence that death taxes in the United States have depleted the supply of capital or in any way imperiled the prospects for future accumulation of capital.

There may have been a time when it was necessary to maintain a class possessing large holdings, who could be relied upon to supply the capital needed for adequate expansion and production. But during the past 50 years the savings of all classes have increased substantially. The modern corporation has facilitated the mobilization of these savings. Corporations themselves are effective savings institutions; through their surpluses and reserves (as for depreciation) they can often supply the requirements for industrial replacement or expansion.

It must be remembered that the state also makes capital investments each year from the taxes collected. It often makes heavy investments in what may be called public producers' goods—such as dams, roads, bridges, harbors, buildings—all of which are productive in the broad sense and some of which are self-liquidating. The investment of part of the savings of an estate in such assets means that some of these savings remain in the capital fund.

Although the income tax is probably a lesser deterrent to the maintenance of existing capital, dollar for dollar, than the death tax, the former has a greater deterring effect on the strategic employment of capital. The income tax strikes at the available funds of the most dynamic producers. Then too, the effect of the income tax is registered on the consciousness of the taxpayer each year; it is immediate, not remote. It is more likely to affect the next year's effort than the death tax, which is far removed from the day-to-day, year-to-year economic calculations of the active enterpriser. To achieve the maximum return, capital should be in the hands of those who will make the best use of it.

Maintenance of Dynastic Enterprises. It is argued against the death tax that it breaks up closely held family concerns and fosters monopoly by forcing the owners of these concerns to sell out to large and well-established competitors. This tendency would be aggravated if capital gains realized at death were taxable under the net-income tax[1] as here recommended.

---

[1] The fact that income taxes would have been paid on the capital gains would,

Death Taxation

The argument is plausible and has some validity. Undoubtedly there are cases where, as a result of the death tax, an interference with family succession to business leadership would occur and where it would have unfortunate social consequences.

In general, however, the death tax would probably interfere less with the perpetuation of closely held family businesses than might be expected. The estate tax need not be settled in a moment of time. It can be anticipated by gifts and can be paid on the installment plan over a period of 10 years after death. This permits the payment of sizable estate taxes out of income without resort to a sale of stock. The son or business associate who is expected to follow in the dynastic control will have many advantages that will enable him to acquire a strong hold upon the business before the founder passes on.

Not infrequently the social interest would be best served were the heir to start a business of his own as his father did. The environment for such initiative should be made as favorable as possible. If the heir chooses to stay in his father's business, he can be given a long start in spite of the death tax. It is not recommended that the tax should be confiscatory in degree.

Dynastic enterprises may be as often opposed to the social interest as not. It is by no means certain that either the ability or the inspiration of the deceased will be passed on with his fortune. In 1930 John T. Flynn made a study of the outstanding business leaders living in the United States in 1840. He found that 90 years later not a single descendant of the men on the 1840 list would qualify among the nation's outstanding business leaders.[1]

Philanthrophy. It is true that the freedom to bequeath

---

of course, reduce the base of the estate tax. But the combination of the two taxes would, in most instances, be greater than if the estate tax alone were to apply.

[1] John T. Flynn, "Dwindling Dynasties," *North American Review*, December, 1930, pp. 645–649.

enables the wealthy to endow foundations for scientific research and that this makes available, to capable men without financial means, the opportunity to pursue studies which might contribute to the welfare of mankind. But even here much progress can be anticipated from the research activities of universities, governments, and especially the laboratories of business corporations. It is hardly necessary, in the interest of research and progress in science and art, to create a leisure class.

Conclusion. Consideration of incentives for risk-taking and enterprise would support a reduction in income surtaxes and an increase in death taxes. It is not necessary, however, to raise federal estate-tax rates (already among the highest in the world) in order to increase the effectiveness of the levy. Broadening the base and checking avoidance would revolutionize the tax.

The changes needed to make death taxes more effective will be discussed later in this chapter.

PROBLEM OF EVALUATING ASSETS

This section considers the effect of the death tax on patterns of investment. As previously stated, it is argued that the death tax discourages risk-taking as contemplation of death becomes a more powerful motive. This is a problem of evaluating an estate's assets and of timing such evaluation.

The quantitative evidence available concerning the investment pattern of large estates[1] indicates that there was a marked trend during the thirties from stock toward bond investment and that the trend was considerably more pronounced for large than for small estates. However, there is no indication that the trend was greater among estate owners who died during their inactive years (sixties and seventies) than among those who died during their forties and

[1] From a sample study of estates filed in the period 1928–1929 and 1938–1939, directed by the Treasury Department, Division of Tax Research, and financed by the WPA. Photostatic copy provided by Division of Tax Research

Death Taxation

fifties. Nor is there any evidence that the estates of those who died young or middle-aged were more predominantly invested in stocks than the estates of those who died at a more advanced age. Undoubtedly many factors other than the death tax affect the pattern of investment. On the other hand, if the death tax can be administered so as to avoid a bias in favor of liquidity, social interest warrants the development of such techniques. This raises the problem of how the assets of estates are valued for death-tax purposes and how the process might be improved.

Current Procedures of Evaluation

The federal estate-tax law provides only the most general guide for evaluation procedure, stating simply that:

The value of the gross estate of the decedent shall be determined by including the value at the time of death of all property, real or personal, tangible or intangible, wherever situated, except real property situated outside the United States. . . . [1]

Treasury regulations are somewhat more specific. They state:

The value of every item of property includable in the gross estate is the fair market value thereof at the time of the decedent's death; . . . The fair market value is the price at which the property would change hands between a willing buyer and a willing seller, neither being under any compulsion to buy or sell. The fair market value of a particular kind of property is not to be determined by a forced sale price. Such value is to be determined by ascertaining as a basis the fair market value as of the applicable valuation date of each unit of property. For example, in the case of shares of stock or bonds, such unit of property is a share or a bond. All relevant facts and elements of value as of the applicable valuation date should be considered in every case.[2]

---

[1] *Internal Revenue Code*, Chap 3, Sec. 811, as amended by the Revenue Act of 1942

[2] *Treasury Regulations* 105, Sec 81.10(a) as amended after the Act of 1942.

Postwar Taxation and Economic Progress

This section defines the basic standards and philosophy underlying the departmental regulations; they put emphasis upon (1) "fair market value," (2) the concept of a free exchange between "a willing buyer and a willing seller," (3) the warning that "fair market value is not to be determined by a forced sale price," (4) the significance of "each unit" of property, and (5) the instruction that "all relevant facts and elements of value" should be given due weight and consideration. The latter definitely implies that the valuation process is not carried on under some cut-and-dried formula. The Treasury Regulations have reached their present state of development only after over 20 years of administrative and judicial experience with valuation. At times they have contained quite arbitrary requirements. However, as the courts have reviewed these requirements, the Treasury has endeavored to adjust its regulations accordingly.[1]

Loss in Value during the Settlement of Estates
Due to Rapidly Declining Values

When trading in a stock that is part of an estate is reasonably active, the current price quotations tend to amount to not just *evidence of value* but to *the value itself*.[2] No serious problems arise in the administration of this standard, but there are problems which arise from the use of it. Following

---

[1] The regulations give specific attention also to the different treatment required for "listed" and "non-listed" securities. In the case of listed securities, the rules have to do with the averaging of selling prices on the security exchanges or the use of bid and asked prices in the absence of sales If actual sales or bona fide bid and asked prices are not available, then, in the case of bonds, value is determined by giving consideration to the soundness of the security, the interest yield, the maturity date, and other relevant factors; in the case of stocks, to the company's net worth, earning power, dividend-paying capacity, and all other relevant factors having a bearing upon the value of the stock If it is established that the value per bond or share on the basis of selling or bid and asked prices does not reflect the fair market value of the security, some reasonable modification of such basis or other relevant facts and elements of value are to be weighed in arriving at fair market value. [*Ibid.*, Sec. 81.10(c)]

[2] James C. Bonbright, *The Valuation of Property*, McGraw-Hill Book Company, Inc., New York, 1937, Vol. II, p. 713.

Death Taxation

1929, many hardships resulted from extreme declines in stock prices. There have been cases where the amount realized from securities has been less than the tax imposed with respect to them. Such circumstances exert pressure upon elderly owners of estates to convert their holdings. This means unloading stocks and investing in the more passive type of assets—cash, bank deposits, insurance, annuities, government and other high-grade bonds.

Due to the Rapid Disposal of Large Blocks of Stock

In death-tax cases, the common practice of valuing active securities at their quoted market prices on the day of death also runs into the problem of appraising large blocks of stock that can be sold only at a substantial discount, at least when sold en bloc and over a short period of time. Federal estate-tax administrative rulings and practices have wavered in dealing with these situations. As early as 1919, Regulation 37 contained a clause definitely forbidding any discount for blockage. For a number of years, down to 1934, subsequent regulations were silent on this issue. Administrative practice vacillated, with some tendency in the period just before 1934 to grant concessions for blockage upon the demand of the executor.[1] The estate-tax regulations were modified in 1934, and gift-tax regulations shortly thereafter. They expressly excluded a discount. The new regulation added the following to Art. 19 (1), dealing with the general valuation of property:

> The value of a particular kind of property is not to be determined by a forced sale or by an estimate of what a large block or aggregate would fetch at one and the same time. Such value is to be determined by ascertaining as a basis the fair market value at the time of the gift of each unit of property. For example, in the case of shares of stock or bonds, each unit of property is a *share* or a bond.[2]

[1] *Ibid*, p. 717.
[2] *Regulations* 80, Art. 19 (1), (1934 ed.).

Postwar Taxation and Economic Progress

Another clause in the same regulations went even further by saying that the size of the holding was not even a "relevant factor" and was not to be considered in such determination.[1] The same clause appeared in about the same language in both the 1936 and 1937 regulations.

In the case of *Bingham's Administrator v. Commonwealth*,[2] an early state court decision refused to recognize the blockage doctrine and described it as "one method applicable to the rich and another to the poor for valuing the same kind of property on the same day."

A few early state and some federal decisions gave limited recognition to the fact that dumping a large block of stock on the market at any given moment would depress the price of such stock, but none of them can be cited as clear recognition of the blockage theory.

One attorney illustrated the blockage problem as follows:

To illustrate the "Blockage rule" let us say that Smith dies in possession of a painting by an old master on which a valuation of $100,000 is placed. His neighbor Jones also dies, but has ten paintings by the same master. If the court should decide that the paintings belonging to the late Jones were worth only $90,000 each because offered as a group they would momentarily glut the market and weaken the price structure, it would be employing the "Blockage rule."[3]

The courts have not usually accepted this valuation principle.

In a leading case, *Safe Deposit and Trust Company of Baltimore, Executor v. Commissioner*,[4] the Board of Tax Appeals refused to consider the price to be realized by dumping a large block of stock, explaining its action as follows:

[1] *Regulations* 80, Art 13 (3), (1934 ed)
[2] 196 Ky. 318, 244 S. W. 781 (1922).
[3] Harvey W Peters, "The Fair Value of Blocks of Stock," *Taxes*, Vol 17 (January, 1939), p. 18
[4] 35 B.T.A. 259 (January 15, 1937)

Death Taxation

This conclusion has not been arrived at by any dogmatic recognition or non-recognition of any so-called "blockage rule." . . . Blockage is not a law of economics, a principle of law or a rule of evidence. If the value of a given number of shares is influenced by the size of the block, this is a matter of evidence and not a doctrinaire assumption.

The Circuit Court of Appeals upheld the Board in the following statement:

. . . in our opinion, the Board was right in basing its conclusions upon the realities as it found them, rather than upon considerations of abstract logic. It could not ignore the pregnant fact, having found it to exist, that a large block of stock cannot be marketed and turned into money as readily as a few shares. The opposite condition might possibly have prevailed, for the influence of the ownership of a large number of shares upon corporate control might give them a value in excess of prevailing market quotations; in which event the application of the administrative rule would be unfair to the government It would have been improper, of course, to have adopted as the true value of the stock, the price obtainable by forcing or dumping the whole block on the market at one time, and likewise improper to have based the finding on the value as of an earlier or later date. But the Board did none of these things. It took into consideration the difficulty inherent in disposing of so large a quantity of stock, the market price for a few hundred shares on the day of death, the downward trend of the market, as indicated by sales before and after death, and it made an estimate of the market value of the whole, as required by statute. In doing so it was required to use its best judgment rather than a cut and dried formula, but this was only the employment of a familiar process which on numerous occasions has been defended by the Commissioners and approved by the Courts [1]

The Treasury changed its regulations to avoid a positive prohibition against introducing evidence of the influence of the size of holdings upon valuation for estate and gift tax

---

[1] *Helvering v Safe Deposit and Trust Co.* 95 Fed. (2nd) 806, 812 (C.C.A. 4th 1938), see also *Helvering v. Maytag* 125 Fed. (2nd) 55, 63 (C.C.A 8th 1942).

Postwar Taxation and Economic Progress

purposes.[1] Since the changes, several court decisions have supported the taxpayer's claims to allowance for blockage,[2] but these concessions have been qualified either in the cases referred to or in later ones. The Circuit Court of Appeals for the 2d District has suggested that the rule has no application where a skillful broker could, within a reasonable time, realize the amount of the value set by the Commissioner.[3] The courts and the Board have refused to accept blindly the idea that a large block of securities is worth relatively less than a small block. The need for the application of the rule must be substantiated by the circumstances in each particular case and the burden of proving the need is clearly upon the taxpayer.[4] Each case must be decided on the evidence. As previously suggested, it is conceivable that blockage may enhance rather than reduce values. In some cases, no sale of the block in fact takes place; or the beneficiary may retain his stock for several years and sell it in small lots over the period. In this case no hardship occurs from disallowance of blockage. Under the gift tax, where spreading the disposition is always an available alternative, no special allowance for blockage has been authorized nor is it justified.

The basic reason for recognizing blockage is the fixed time of valuation. Adhering too strictly to "fair market value" as of a "single day" throws the entire burden of risk of loss upon the estate—a contingency which the decedent, during his lifetime, might seek to avoid by putting his assets into liquid and more stable forms of wealth.

The truth seems to be that the underlying inequity in the valuation process arises less from blockage or nonblockage

[1] *Tax Decisions* 4902, C. B. 1939-1, p. 325.

[2] Randolph Paul, *Federal Estate and Gift Taxation*, Little, Brown & Company, Boston, 1942, Vol. II, p. 1283; *Augustus v Comm.*, 118 Fed. (2nd) 38 (C C A. 6th 1941), Certiorari Denied 313 U.S. 585 (1941); *Goff v. Smith*, 34 Fed. Supp. 319 (1940); *Helvering v. Maytag*, 125 Fed. (2nd) 55 (C.C A. 8th 1942).

[3] *Bull v. Smith*, 119 Fed. (2nd) 490 (C.C.A 2nd 1941).

[4] *Estate of Leonard B. McKitterick*, 42 B.T.A. 130; Frederick S. Squier, Jr. B.T.A. memo. op April 26, 1939, C.C.H. December 10, 679-k, Joseph Soss, B.T.A. memo op. October 25, 1940, C.C.H. December 11, 371-B.

Death Taxation

than from the fundamental arbitrariness of the "date-of-death" rule of valuation. If this broader problem could be properly solved, the demand for blockage would lose most, if not all, of its validity.

Present Federal Provisions to Avoid Hardship in Case of Depreciating Assets

Mention has been made of the fact that valuation as of a particular day may create hardships in estate-tax cases. This was especially true and especially recognized during the depression of the thirties. Congress attempted to alleviate these hardships by permitting optional valuation. It provided that, if the executor so elects, he may value all property in the estate "as of one year after the decedent's death."[1] The Internal Revenue Code further provides that property "sold, exchanged, or otherwise disposed of shall be included at its value as of the time of such distribution, sale, exchange, or other disposition whichever first occurs, instead of its value as of the date one year after decedent's death." These provisions give an executor some choice and some protection on a falling market. If the property is disposed of between the date of death and one year thereafter, the property may be valued (if the executor so elects) as of the time of such disposition. This does not allow "disposition value" but comes close to it.

Another fact which helps to alleviate valuation-date hardships is that executors now have 15 months after death to decide whether to submit values as of the day of death or as of one year later. There is no necessity to make such election shortly after the date of death. There is, therefore, no risk involved in the exercise of the option. Still another advantage accruing to estates that are a long time in liquidation and whose assets cannot quickly be turned into cash to meet heavy estate taxes, is that they are permitted to pay such

[1] Sec. 811 (j) Internal Revenue Code (as amended to February 15, 1943). SOURCE. Sec. 312 (j) Revenue Act of 1926 as amended by Sec 202(a) Revenue Act of 1935.

taxes on the installment plan over a period of up to 10 years. Interest at 4 per cent is charged beginning 3 months after due date. Desirable as these provisions may be, they have not removed the psychological effects of valuation as of a single day. Quite probably many risk-takers sell their stocks to get their estates in liquid condition before there is sound justification for this action.

Recommendations

To encourage participation in risk-taking on the part of older enterprisers and large fortunes, it is suggested that property for estate-tax purposes be valued at the time of liquidation and that the time during which such liquidation could take place be extended to 3 years.

In strict legal theory, the property of the decedent passes to the beneficiaries at the moment of death. However, as a practical matter, it is months and even years before the respective shares in the estate come to the heirs in full possession, enjoyment, and control. Value does not accrue to the beneficiaries, in any real sense, until property is distributed to them. Estate-tax valuation should take into consideration what the beneficiaries receive as well as what the decedent leaves. Given the passage of time between death and distribution, these two values may be quite different.

A realistic and yet equitable standard and method of estate-tax valuation should contain these elements:

1. A general objective of attempting to value the property "received" by the beneficiary.

2. The standard of value for property sold to pay the expenses of administration should be the "fair market value" as of the time of such sale or disposition. Disposition value itself cannot be a standard; but it may be and should be important evidence of fair market value.

3. The standard value for property actually distributed to the beneficiaries should be the "fair market value" of said property as of the time of such distribution.

Death Taxation

4. The time of valuation should not be as of any single day but rather valuation should take place within a given period, such as 3 years, and as of any time within that period, but valuation must be arrived at before the expiration of 3 years from the date of the decedent's death.

These suggestions could, perhaps, run into constitutional difficulties, especially where a tax is on a valuation higher than that prevailing on the day of death. The tax might be interpreted, because of the modification, as a direct levy rather than an excise. Direct levies require apportionment not suitable to a death tax. It has been suggested that Congress take the risk of an adverse decision by the Supreme Court, providing that an option of a date-of-death valuation shall be operative only if it is found necessary in order to validate the tax.[1]

5. With the disappearance of the single-day concept of time of valuation, there would be no need for consideration of "blockage" because the necessity of rapid liquidation would be clearly removed.

6. The more liberal time period and standard of valuation should not be extended to gifts under the gift tax, for, in this case, all the choices and options are as a practical matter already within the control and discretion of the donor.

FORMS OF DEATH TAXES AND EXEMPTIONS

Death taxes in the United States have taken two basic forms —the "estate" tax and the "inheritance" tax. The estate tax is based on the undivided whole of the decedent's net estate and the inheritance tax is based upon the shares passed to specific heirs. As the estate tax is now used by the federal government, no consideration is given to the number of heirs, the degree of relationship, or the size of the bounty granted to the individual beneficiaries. The inheritance tax takes account of all these factors. This form of levy is predominant among the states, although some of them join with

[1] Bonbright, *op cit.*, p 745.

the federal government in use of the estate tax. Various combinations of the two levies are possible, either by the levy of two taxes, as in England, or by adding special features to one or the other. For instance, the levy might be on the estate as a whole after the allowance of specific exemptions for specific heirs.

Advantages of the Estate Tax

The advantages of the estate tax are "practical" or "opportunistic"; *i.e.*, easier to understand, to calculate, and to administer. Since it falls upon the entire net estate, there are no problems involving the degree of relationship of the beneficiaries to the deceased, the size of specific bequests, and rates and exemptions adjusted to a large number of classifications. Avoided also is the complicated task of determining the value of shares where the transfer takes the form of life estates, contingent remainders, vested remainders, and reverters. The size of the net estate is not affected by the whims of the will makers.

The estate tax also excels in its revenue-producing ability. It would take a legislature with immense courage to fix rates on individual heirs at anything even approximating the effective rates that are applied in estate duties, where relationship classification is not relevant. This is due mainly to the fact that most property goes to direct heirs who are usually at the bottom of the inheritance-tax classified scale Inheritance-tax rates are almost universally deceptive. They look high in the upper brackets of bequests to certain classes of heirs, but the average or effective rate of the levy is usually very low.

Advantages of the Inheritance Tax

The advantages of the inheritance tax are in the refinement it provides for taking account of the ability to pay of the heir as well as that of the deceased. Leaving $1 million to a widow is an entirely different situation from bequeathing

Death Taxation

the same sum to a distant cousin. The widow may have had a considerable part in creating the estate which she now inherits. Almost certainly she is deprived, by the death of her husband, of a major source of support. The period between her husband's death and her own may be short as compared to that which would elapse between death transfers if the property were bequeathed to younger heirs. On the other hand, a minor son has much more claim upon the state's indulgence than an older son, a fact that even inheritance taxes have failed to recognize.

Conclusion

Except for administrative difficulties and yield limitations in its conventional application, the inheritance tax as a fiscal instrument is clearly superior to the estate tax. Particularly if capital gains were taxed at death, as recommended, the inheritance tax would be more acceptable to the taxpayer. At the very least, estate-tax exemptions should be differentiated and moderated, thus enlarging the base. If an inheritance-tax schedule could be devised that would produce a yield approaching that contemplated by a revised estate tax, the inheritance tax would be preferable. In the meantime, the federal government should retain and seek to improve its estate tax.

If the estate tax is less defensible on theoretical grounds than the inheritance tax, it nevertheless is not without adequate justification. A tax on an accumulated fortune, timed to the liquidation of the fortune or its transfer to new owners, can be supported on many grounds, one of which is that it is a substitute for the income tax that might otherwise have been levied in earlier years.

In analyzing the efficiency of particular kinds of taxes to accomplish particular objectives, one eye must be kept on the tax system as a whole. When the estate tax is made broad and deep enough, it can definitely take a substantial load off the income tax.

Postwar Taxation and Economic Progress

There is much to be said for integrating death and income taxes, a move that would eliminate a form of double taxation in the tax system. On the other hand, the circumstances of death and of gift provide a special occasion that probably warrants a special tax. In any event, the degree and effectiveness of this tax may be properly considered in the determination of income-tax rates. Further integration might be reconsidered when gift and estate taxes are integrated and when averaging is an established feature of income-tax procedure.

EVASION AND AVOIDANCE OF ESTATE AND GIFT TAXES

Disappointing Yield of Death Taxes

Until 1936, Great Britain collected more death taxes than the United States (including federal and state) in spite of the fact that her population and wealth are less than a third of ours. Although the receipts in this country now exceed those in Britain, the yield is still relatively much higher there than here. In 1936, these taxes brought 9.7 per cent of total British receipts.[1] The corresponding figure in the United States was 4.6 per cent.[2] In 1939–1940, Great Britain collected £78,531,626[3] while our federal government collected $360,071,000 and our state governments $116,421,913.[4] Under present American law, $60,000 is exempt from the tax. The British begin taxing estates of £100 ($400). Of at least equal importance in both the absolute and the relative yields of the two taxes is their success in dealing with the multitudinous forms of tax avoidance. Nowhere in our entire tax system has tax avoidance been so extensive and so successful as in connection with our federal estate tax.

[1] *Tax Systems of the World*, Tax Research Foundation, Chicago, 1938, pp. 376, 377.
[2] *Ibid.*, p. 391
[3] *Finance Acts of the United Kingdom*, Fiscal Year 1939–1940, Treasury Chambers, Whitehall, p. 12.
[4] *Tax Yields:* 1940, pp. 36, 44.

Death Taxation

Rules of Property Law Prevent Successful Administration

· In dealing with these loopholes, both Congress and the courts have often been confronted with the special difficulties inherent in property law and the myriad types of transfer that it allows. Our property law developed in medieval England and its foundations go back to the eleventh and twelfth centuries. The rules of modern private property have their roots in the feudal system and its complicated scheme of land tenure. The different types of property interests crystallized during a period when land was the predominant form of wealth. Subsequently the principles and techniques multiplied and became more refined, until they constituted a complex and technical scheme of rules, rights, interests, procedures, and so forth. Conveyancing devices, first invoked to uphold and later to circumvent the prerogatives of the feudal barons, were drawn upon to avoid the transfer tax levied by a modern state. To make matters worse, property laws have evolved quite differently in our 48 states and often these various state laws determine how death taxes shall be applied. It seems certain that the federal power to tax is broad enough and deep enough to allow Congress to establish its own rules of property ownership for purposes of taxation. The 1942 Act took a long step in this direction when it wiped out the advantages accruing to husband and wife under the estate tax in community property states.[1]

Sources of Avoidance

Inter Vivos Gifts and Gifts in Contemplation of Death

When the estate tax was first provided, a favorite method of avoidance was to hold one's property until shortly before death and then give it outright to the beneficiaries, thus reducing the estate to be distributed. Congress passed the

[1] See Chap. VIII, p. 241.

gift tax in the hope that it could reach *inter vivos* gifts[1] at lower rates than those imposed on death transfers. But the gift tax became an invitation to dodge the estate tax. Under the 1942 law, annual gifts of $3000 to any one person, in addition to $30,000 further gifts, are exempt from gift taxation. This encourages the estate owner to give away the greater part of his holdings during life. If he does not, he practically throws away the benefit of the $30,000 cumulative gift-tax exemption in addition to the $3000 annual exemption for individual gifts. If he fails to take advantage of this "out," through which he may transfer $33,000 or more entirely tax-free, he transfers it subject to the highest bracket of the estate tax applicable to his estate. If he does take advantage of *inter vivos* gifts, he gets the benefit of the exemptions in addition to the lower brackets of the progressive rate schedules of both the estate tax and the gift tax, to say nothing of the lower "level" of rates on all gifts above the gift-tax exemption. But this is not all—there is also the opportunity to reduce income taxes materially by reporting income through the various members of the family.

Gift-tax rates are nominally about three-fourths of the estate-tax rates, but the effective differential is definitely greater. This is true partly because estate-tax rates apply to the total estate before taxes and estate taxes must be paid out of the property of the estate taxed. Gift-tax rates, however, apply to net gifts; that is, the amount of the tax is not included in the sum taxed. Thus, for two estates of $5 million each, one given away *inter vivos* and the other bequeathed at death, the taxes on the former would amount to only 51.5 per cent of those on the latter.[2]

Congress provided that "gifts in contemplation of death" were to be included in taxable estates, but making this provision effective presents a baffling administrative problem.

---

[1] Gifts between the living.
[2] Robert H. Montgomery, *Federal Taxes on Estates, Trusts and Gifts*, The Ronald Press Company, New York, 1943, pp. 9–10.

Death Taxation

The real difficulty lies in proving that a particular gift was "in contemplation of death." Congress has never amplified that phrase and interpretation has been left to the courts. The judiciary has interpreted "contemplation" as a state of mind—a motive. In a leading decision,[1] the Court recognized that mixed motives may prompt a gift and it therefore declared that the dominant motive was controlling. But motives are intangible and not susceptible to measurement. Proof may include a need to penetrate the recesses of dead men's minds by exploring the impressions they made upon the minds of others. Congress attempted to aid at this point by declaring that any transfer of property within 2 years preceding death should be conclusively presumed to be in contemplation of death. But this was held unconstitutional by the Court.[2] Justice Stone, in his dissenting opinion, pointed out that up to 1932 the Courts had decided 102 federal cases dealing with whether or not gifts had been in contemplation of death. In only 20 cases, involving $4,250,000, was the government successful in its efforts. In 78 cases, involving gifts of $120 million, it was unsuccessful, and there is no evidence that it has done much better since. The major difference is that, since 1932, gifts pay at least a gift tax But, as previously observed, the gift tax is by no means the equivalent of the estate tax. To remedy the situation fundamentally, it will be necessary to work out a complete integration of the two taxes with one base, one schedule of exemptions, and one scale of rates.

Transfers to Take Effect upon Death

Nature of Trusts. Since the initial enactment of estate and income-tax laws, the trust has been a favorite means of tax avoidance. "The trust is a device by which a person or corporation is vested with title to certain property that he

---
[1] *U.S. v. Wells,* 283 U.S. 102 (1931).
[2] *Heiner v. Donnan,* 285 U.S. 312 (1932); 1926 Act Sec. 302 (*c*).

or it is to manage for the benefit of another person. Usually there are at least three parties to a trust: the settlor, or the one who creates the trust; the trustee, or the one who administers it; and the beneficiary, the one for whose benefit it is created."[1] The settlor, unless he reserves specific rights to himself, surrenders all legal interest in the trust *corpus* (principal) and trust income; the equitable interest or title passes to the beneficiary and the legal title moves to the trustee.

Trusts may be revocable or irrevocable; that is, the settlor may or may not reserve the right to change his mind and take back the property from the trustee or change beneficiaries. "Trusts may be created in such a way that the benefit, or the income therefrom, goes immediately to the beneficiary, or they may be created so that the benefit or income goes immediately to the settlor, and to the beneficiary only at the settlor's death."[2] In the latter case, the settlor is said to have a "life estate" in the trust, with "remainder" to the beneficiary.

Irrevocable Trust with Benefit Reserved to the Settlor, Now Taxable. Each of the federal estate-tax laws since 1916 has contained a provision calling for the taxation of transfers "intended to take effect in possession or enjoyment at or after death," and this clause has a prior history in state inheritance-tax legislation. Contrary to the seemingly natural interpretation of the clause, the Supreme Court held in 1930[3] that property conveyed by an irrevocable trust deed, despite the reservation to the settlor of the income for life, is not a transfer intended to take effect in possession or enjoyment at or after death. Emphasis was placed on a shift in the title rather than on possession and enjoyment. Equitable title passed at once to the beneficiary, but possession and enjoyment remained with the settlor until his death. It took legislation by Congress

---

[1] Harold M. Groves, *Financing Government*, rev. ed., Henry Holt and Company, Inc., New York, 1945, p. 244.
[2] *Ibid.*
[3] *May v. Heiner*, 281 U.S. 238 (1930).

to bring this type of transfer within the scope of the taxing power.[1]

Revocable Trusts Taxable; Borderline Cases Doubtful—The Problem. As the statute now stands, it requires the inclusion of property in the gross estate where there is power to alter, amend, revoke, or terminate in the decedent "alone or by the decedent in conjunction with any person." It does not specifically get at trusts where such powers are vested solely in others, as distinguished from depending on the consent of others. There is really no difference between the two cases, and the statute should be modified to require the inclusion of trusts which may be altered, amended, etc., by a trustee who does not have an adverse interest.[2]

Through *inter vivos* trusts, the settlor surrenders legal title to the property, but there is always a strong desire on his part to retain some measure of control over the property. He will divest himself of title to avoid the death tax, but he cannot resist the temptation to keep his "finger in the pie" while he lives. One device to accomplish this is the revocable trust. As previously stated, revocable trusts have been generally taxable, but the issue of whether a given trust is revocable does not always present itself as a clear-cut matter. An almost limitless variety of trust deeds have been devised by fertile legal minds. This ingenuity is summoned sometimes to get around the estate tax and sometimes to deal with complex family situations. The many cases where the settlor irrevocably passes title and some but not all of the incidents of ownership are particularly troublesome to Congress and the courts. It is true that the courts have tried to bring about a "correspondence between the legal concept of ownership and the economic realities of enjoyment and fruition."[3] But the whole process has become one of judicial and administrative hide-and-seek, with taxpayers always able to find new hiding places.

[1] Joint Resolution, March 3, 1931.
[2] Paul, *op. cit.*, Vol. 1, p. 393.
[3] *Burnet v. Wells*, 289 U.S. 670, 677 (1933).

A trust that can be revoked only with the consent of the beneficiary seems like an outright gift. The 1924 Act, however, provided that trusts were to be taxable under the estate tax, not only where the trust may be revoked by the settlor alone but also where it may be revoked by the settlor "in conjunction with any other person." The constitutionality of this provision was in doubt for some time but the Court sustained it[1] on the ground that it was a reasonable method of preventing tax avoidance. The settlor could choose a complacent beneficiary, in conjunction with whom he could revoke the trust and thus escape liability for the tax. But in another case[2] where the trustees were given power to terminate the trust and the settlor had herself appointed one of the trustees, the Court held that this was not a revocable trust, taxable as a part of the settlor's estate. The power to revoke was acquired by the settlor only in her "capacity as trustee." This loophole has been plugged by Congress.[3]

It is also possible for the settlor to reserve the power of reacquiring the trust property by payment of a relatively small consideration. Broad control over the sale of trust *corpus* may give the settlor an effective check on the fund. It may be that he holds broad powers to invade the trust *corpus* if income is insufficient. He may retain the right to borrow on easy terms from the trust. Sometimes he reserves the right to shift beneficiaries or to add beneficiaries. Then, too, there may be a contingent power of revocation that may be relinquished by the settlor, possibly in contemplation of death. Innumerable ways of setting up trusts may be devised to avoid taxes or at least to take advantage of the lower gift tax.

Randolph Paul sums up the revocable-trust problem as follows:[4]

[1] *Helvering v. City Bank Farmers Trust Co.*, 296 U.S. 70 (1935).
[2] *White v. Poor*, 296 U.S. 98 (1935).
[3] *Internal Revenue Code*, Sec. 811 (*d*) (1) and (2).
[4] Randolph E. Paul, *Studies in Federal Taxation*, 3d Series, Harvard University Press, Cambridge, 1940, pp. 293–294.

Death Taxation

When one views the whole panorama of revocable trusts, one becomes completely confounded as to what should be done A few things are clear. As a whole the tax avoiders have succeeded and from the revenue point of view the statute has failed.

What should be done is more than one person should venture to say. Certainly we shall have to begin all over again, reframing the statute with reference to hundreds of decisions and a new judicial attitude toward tax avoidance.

The Remedy. Integration of the estate and gift taxes would constitute a fundamental and probably the only fundamental solution of the problem. This would remove the motive to devise methods of tax avoidance. Settlors might arrange their trusts to accomplish various purposes without regard for tax consequences. The only issue would then become the *time* at which the transfer tax would be paid. The time factor would be of some, but not great, significance. Integration would solve the problem of revocable trusts far more effectively than the most careful revamping of the statute to plug individual loopholes. The trust with interests reserved in the settlor (in its simplest form, with life estate in the settlor, remainder to the children) would also be fairly treated under an integrated gift and estate tax. Donors now refrain from this type of disposition in order to escape high estate taxes.

Creation of Limited Interests in Property to Avoid Successive Transfers

Powers of Appointment. The power of appointment is a tax-avoidance device of a different character from those previously discussed. It seeks to avoid all taxes on one or several dispositions after an initial disposition. Today it is rare that a will or trust, involving the distribution of a large estate to two or more generations, is created without the use of one or even several powers of appointment. One authority describes this situation as follows:[1]

The power of appointment is the most efficient dispositive device that the ingenuity of Anglo-American lawyers has ever worked out.

[1] W. Barton Leach, "Powers of Appointment," *American Bar Association Journal,* Vol. 24 (1938), p. 807.

Its use is definitely on the increase. Lawyers in increasing numbers have discovered in the last twenty-five years that the power of appointment is the answer to more of the problems that face the draftsman of wills and trusts than any other device.

Outside of tax advantages, the power of appointment permits a realistic and flexible disposition according to need. Take the case of the testator who wishes to leave an estate to his daughter and to her children. He may choose one of three alternatives: (1) He might bequeath the property to his daughter outright. This disposition would be unwise both from the tax angle and from the standpoint of flexibility. There would be an estate tax when the estate passed to the daughter and another when it passed from the daughter to her children. (2) He could leave the property to his daughter for life and then to her children in remainder. This would protect the fund against loss by the daughter and it would not involve a second tax. (3) He could grant a life estate to the daughter with a power of appointment among her children. At her death, which under normal expectancies might take place 20 to 25 years after the testator's death, the daughter would have the opportunity of distributing the fund among her children according to their needs and circumstances. This disposition would have the advantage of flexibility and equity and there would be no tax when the estate passed on to the children. There would, of course, be a full estate tax when the testator in the first instance granted to the daughter.

A power of appointment is not an absolute right of property nor is it an estate. It creates in the donee no right, title, or interest in the property to be conveyed. Whether the power is exercised by the donee or not, the property subject to appointment is not a part of his estate. It can be said that the appointee really takes from the donor. The donee performs something in the nature of an administrative act for the donor. A general power is a power to appoint anyone, including the donee of the power himself. For example, a general power would read as follows: "To John for life,

Death Taxation

remainder to such persons as John shall appoint." John may appoint to himself, his estate, his creditors, or anyone else. This type of broad power, if exercised and if property passed under it, rendered the donee's estate taxable under the Revenue Act of 1926 and subsequent acts. Special powers restrict appointment to certain specified individuals, excluding the donee. For example, a special power might read as follows: "To John for life, remainder to such children of John as John shall appoint." Under these circumstances, no estate tax is ordinarily assessed on the donee's estate. In the case of general powers, the donee can dispose of property as if it were his own. Under special power, he is largely carrying out the intention of the donor.

Special powers lend themselves very well to long-run tax avoidance. The trust and the life-estate-remainder device can easily avoid one estate tax, but special powers, when combined with successive delegations of such powers, might succeed in avoiding estate taxes several times in as many successive transfers.

Let us try to reconstruct the tax avoider's paradise: Assume that A dies, leaving property in trust for his son B for life, with remainder to such of B's children as B shall appoint (a special power) with full delegation of that power in B (so that B can transfer the power to someone else). When A dies, his estate pays the original tax. When B dies, he appoints the property to his son C for life, remainder to C's children as C shall appoint, with full power of delegation in C of the newly created special power. And so on down the line. This means that the estate of A, created back in the 1930's, might not be paying death taxes in the 2020's. The limitation to the process is the rule against perpetuities. By the force of that rule, property interest appointed under special powers must vest in full (after creation of the power in the first instance at the death of A) within lives in being and 21 years. Just how long a period the will can cover depends somewhat on the astuteness of the draftsman. The lives referred to can

Postwar Taxation and Economic Progress

be any lives and need not be connected with the gifts. It is conceivable, therefore, that a period up to 100 years can be engineered, during which there would be no federal tax. In Delaware, the avoidance can go on *ad infinitum* because, in 1933, the Delaware legislature passed a statute declaring that the period of perpetuities as applied to property appointed under special powers was to be calculated from the time of its exercise and not from the time of its creation.[1]

The 1916 Act failed to make any provision for taxing property passing under powers of appointment, but the 1918 Act[2] provided for such taxation in a limited way. Only general powers were covered and, even here, the power had to be exercised. In *Helvering v. Grinnell*[3] the appointees under the power renounced their rights under the will of the donee of the power and elected to "take" under a limitation in their favor in default of appointment in the will of the donor. The Court held that the appointed property could not be taxed.

The sections of the Internal Revenue Code dealing with powers remained unchanged for over 20 years. Finally, in 1942, in response to urging by the Treasury, provisions dealing with powers of appointment were considerably revised and tightened. Present provisions of Sec. 811 (*f*) of the Internal Revenue Code may be analyzed as follows:

1. A tax which was formerly confined to only general powers has been replaced by a levy reaching "any power to appoint exercisable by the decedent alone or in conjunction with any other person," whether general, special, or hybrid, with the exception of two stated powers. The amendment thereby eliminates all speculation inherent in the phrase "general powers" and at the same time broadens the scope of the tax to include nongeneral powers.

---

[1] *Ibid*, p. 809.
[2] *Internal Revenue Code*, Sec 811(*f*), Cf. 1918–1921 Acts, Sec. 402(*a*), 1924 and 1926 Acts, Sec. 302(*f*).
[3] 294 U.S. 153 (1935).

Death Taxation

2. Property subject to a taxable power at the date of the donee's death does not escape the estate tax merely because the donee failed to exercise the power. The power is taxed, whether exercised or not, since the nonexercise of the power is in fact a way of effecting the transfer of the property. The relevant factor is the decedent's power to control the destination of the property.

3. Since the exercise of the power is no longer required to make the power taxable, appointees can no longer circumvent the tax by "electing" to take as if by default of appointment, even though the donee did exercise the power.

4. It is provided that if the power to appoint is exercised by the creation of another power to appoint, the first exercised power does not qualify as one of the powers exempted from taxation. This should eliminate tax avoidance by a "succession" of tax-exempt powers.

Two stipulated powers are exempted from estate taxes.

1. A power to appoint within a class including only spouse of the decedent, spouse of the creator of the powers, descendants of the decedent or his spouse, descendants (other than the decedent) of the creator of the power or his spouse, spouses of such descendants, and the donees of powers to make charitable appointments.

2. The power to appoint within a restricted class if the decedent did not receive any beneficial interest of any kind and neither he nor his estate could in any manner acquire any such interest—that is, where a trust company or a disinterested trustee is made the donee of the power.

Thus, although the extreme abuse of powers of appointment has been eliminated, it is still possible to avoid death taxes on every second transfer. This is about the same situation that prevails in the use of the life-estate-remainder combination. The 1942 Act fails to eliminate the use of powers of appointment to skip a generation or two of death taxes. Up to a point, it sanctions and even guides the way to successful skipping. The tax is entirely avoided if the power is entrusted exclusively to a trust company or if it is kept within the range of the relationship specified in the statute. Avoidance isn't quite so easy nor can it be carried so far as formerly.[1]

Life-estate-remainder Sequence. Closely related to powers of appointment, as a means of tax avoidance, is the use of the life-estate-remainder sequence. Where property is transferred by A to B for life, remainder to C, the transfer is viewed as a single disposition of A's full title to the property. Property law looks at A as the grantor of both B's and C's estate, and holds that legal title does not pass to C upon the cessation of B's life estate because it has already passed to him. Therefore, there is nothing to tax when the remainderman takes over. The inclusion of the "fee simple" (full title) in A's estate for estate-tax purposes takes care of both the transfer of the life estate to B and the fee to C. That is the technical and legalistic way to view these transfers. The emphasis is upon form and title.

For the tax treatment of the life-estate-remainder transfers, Sec. 811 of the Internal Revenue Code provides:

> The value of the gross estate of the decedent shall be determined by including the value at the time of death of all property . . . to the extent of the interest therein of the decedent at the time of his death.

Since the life tenant's interest at his death is zero, no federal estate tax is due.

If the estate tax is to be protected as a source of revenue, then the life-estate-remainder transfer must be weighed for what it really is—a fruition of the right to enjoy property. When that takes place as a transfer from one generation to another, it should be taxed with as little regard as feasible to the technical legal distinction as to the form of the transfer.[2]

---

[1] Louis Eisenstein, "Powers of Appointment and Estate Taxes," *Yale Law Journal*, Vol. 52 (June, 1943), pp. 551–552.

[2] Willard C. Mills, "Transfers from Life Tenant to Remainderman," *Taxes, The Tax Magazine*, Vol. 19 (April, 1941), p. 195.

Death Taxation

The British have gone much further than we in divorcing themselves from some old concepts of common law. Under the English estate duty, "all property" passing on the death of the decedent is taxed. The property passing includes not only that over which the decedent had power to control the devolution, but also property over which he was a life tenant in possession at his death, or property in which any person had a beneficial interest arising on his death, to the extent of the benefit so arising.[1] The expression "to the extent of the benefit so arising," when applied to a transfer from a life tenant to a remainderman, is interpreted to mean the full value of the property transferred, even though the immediate interest arising is but a life estate.[2]

In the United States, the problem of how to handle the skipping of death taxes for one out of every two generations is not a mere academic question. As far back as 1926, when estate-tax exemptions were quite high and rates were still relatively low, it was estimated that a full one-quarter of inherited property was being transferred by way of life estates with remainders.[3] In 1945, with estate and gift taxes higher, the use of property settlements of various kinds—trusts, life-estate-remainder, and powers of appointment—as means of avoiding the estate tax is apparently the common practice for most estates of $60,000 and more. Probably one-half of all inherited property is transferred so as to skip at least one death tax. The full fiscal effects of this practice will be felt more when the initial life tenants die and property worth millions of dollars will pass untaxed to later life tenants or remaindermen.

The view has been expressed that, unless transfers from life tenants to remaindermen are taxed, the base of the federal estate tax will shrink to the point where the tax will not serve

---

[1] British Finance Act of 1894, Sec. 1, 2 (1) (*b*).
[2] Mills, *op. cit*, p 196.
[3] William J Shultz, *The Taxation of Inheritance*, Houghton Mifflin Company, Boston, 1926, p 231.

Postwar Taxation and Economic Progress

a useful function in the tax system.[1] If this is the situation, legislative action on the issue must be forthcoming at the earliest possible moment. If the matter is permitted to drift for a number of years, it will mean that when action is taken it will very likely be retroactive in effect. Congress would be compelled to act retroactively upon a huge volume of past settlements in order to tax future settlements. To act non-retroactively would be both inadequate and inequitable; on the other hand, retroactivity bears heavily on the well-laid plans of the dead.

Conclusion Concerning Avoidance on Successive Transfers. The conclusion is that a tax must be brought to bear upon the transfer from the life tenant to the remainderman. On the assumption that the federal government will continue to employ the estate tax rather then a succession levy, an attempt to add a special acquisition tax on the remainderman does not seem feasible. The solution would be to apply the estate tax as the British do but to allow the life tenant's estate the right of recovering the tax from the remainderman. By so taxing transfers from life tenants to remaindermen, the problem of tax avoidance by the use of trusts, powers of appointment, and life-estate-remainders would be largely resolved.

Insurance

In the past, insurance has been a favorable field for avoidance of the estate tax, operating much like an irrevocable trust in this respect. A policy in favor of a specific beneficiary with no rights reserved to the insured (such as the right to change the beneficiary) has been interpreted as an *inter vivos* transfer. Between 1918 and 1942, a specific exemption of $40,000 was allowed in addition to the general estate-tax exemption. In the 1942 Act, the specific exemption was eliminated, although the general exemption was increased from $40,000 to $60,000, and Section 811 (g) of the Code was rewritten and expanded. As the law now stands, insurance

[1] Mills, *op. cit.*, p. 196.

Death Taxation

receivable by individual beneficiaries is included in the estate if the decedent either paid the premiums or retained incidents of ownership.[1] Some concessions were made to policies then in existence. However, for entirely new purchases and gifts of insurance after January 10, 1941, the proceeds of insurance on the life of the decedent are not taxable only when the premiums are paid by someone else and the decedent retains or acquires no incidents of ownership. The exception simply covers the case where some other person may have an insurable interest in the life of the insured and takes out an insurance policy accordingly. There is then nothing moving from the dead to the living. It is reasonable to conclude that insurance loopholes in death-tax legislation have been plugged.

Charitable Gifts, Bequests, and Trusts

Congressional policy in allowing tax concessions for various kinds of gifts and bequests to charitable, educational, and religious institutions has been very liberal. It has subsidized such donations both through the income tax and through the estate and gift taxes. This has been a conscious policy. President Eliot of Harvard once observed that if the state wants work done, it has but two alternatives: "It can do it itself, or it can encourage and help benevolent public-spirited individuals to do it. There is no third way."[2] The theory has been that if services were not rendered by tax-favored institutions, they would need to be performed by the state. It is an open question whether the state can administer them more efficiently and more in accordance with need than can private agencies.

When wealthy donors make large gifts to favored purposes, the funds so granted are those which would otherwise largely go to the Treasury. A charitable gift of $10,000 by a single

[1] *Internal Revenue Code*, Sec. 811 (g) (2) as amended by Sec. 404(a) of the Revenue Act of 1942.
[2] Randolph E. Paul, *Federal Estate and Gift Taxation, op cit*, Vol I, quotation p. 687.

man with a net income of $100,000 (before deduction of the gift), reduces his income tax from $64,060 to $55,784—a net cost to him of $1,724. If the same individual were to die with a net estate of $10 million, the federal government would take 77 per cent of the $10,000 gift were it left to individual beneficiaries. Taking into account the estate and gift tax together with the income tax, the gift to charity would cost the donor and the beneficiaries of his estate a net of $425. Actually the largest part of the gift is made by the federal government itself.[1]

The creation of charitable trusts does not always divest the heirs of the deceased from control of the property so distributed. For example, Mr. Andrew Mellon left an estate of approximately $100 million almost entirely to the A. W. Mellon Educational and Charitable Trust. The charitable deduction granted to the estate practically wiped out an estate tax of about $67 million and the property continues in the control of those nominated by Mr. Mellon,[2] namely, his son, son-in-law, and attorney.[3] The element of "control" in modern economic life is often of greater strategic value than bare legal title. Dominion and control may be almost as valuable as outright ownership.

An attempt might be made to limit the exemption of charitable donations to cases where both control and benefits are surrendered by those who might have a direct economic interest in the bequest. Should this prove impracticable, a top limit might be placed on the portion of an estate that may be exempt from taxation as a charitable contribution.

THE INTEGRATION OF FEDERAL ESTATE AND GIFT TAXES

The enactment of federal gift taxes has been in itself a move toward the integration of taxes based on donative

[1] Roswell Magill, *Impact of Federal Taxes*, p. 116.
[2] Erwin Griswold, *Cases and Materials on Federal Taxation*, Foundation Press, Chicago, 1940, p. 264.
[3] Paul, *op. cit.*, p. 689.

Death Taxation

transfers. The intent of the 1924 Act was to achieve a "unified scheme of taxation of gifts whether *inter vivos* or at death."[1] The 1924 gift tax was repealed in 1926. However, in 1932 Congress restored the gift tax to the federal revenue system. Again it was frankly stated that the new tax was auxiliary to the estate tax. But the purpose of both the 1924 and 1932 acts was also to implement the income tax. It was thought that the gift tax would reduce the incentive to make gifts, thereby dividing the interests in future income and reducing income-tax liability.

Although the passage of gift-tax legislation was a step in the right direction, it failed to recognize that gifts during life are not essentially different from gifts at death. Under existing law with two transfer taxes, the estate owner is free to use either or both, according to his particular advantage. It is quite convenient for him to make use of the exemptions and lower brackets of both and thereby escape the upper brackets of either. Thus the progressivity and revenue-raising capacity of both taxes are defeated. Both levies should be replaced by a single, cumulative transfer tax.

The plan of integration may be summarized as follows:

1. The integrated transfer tax base would be a single tax base made up of all transfers *inter vivos* and final transfers—cumulated over the gift-granting life of the donor.

2. It would provide a single system of exemptions to cover both forms of transfers.

3. It would make use of a single system of rates applied progressively to the cumulated rising tax base as more and more gifts were granted and the final transfers made.

There is serious doubt whether the policy of allowing a liberal exemption to any one donee each year should be maintained. A substantial specific exemption for a widow and dependent children should be allowed but it might well be reserved by law to apply only to the final transfer at death.

In building a rate structure for the combined base, the aim

[1] *Estate of Sanford v. Commissioner*, 308 U.S. 48 (1939).

should be to reach the great majority of transfers, applying a relatively low rate to the small ones and then progressively higher rates as the estates become larger. With a combined base and lower exemptions, the revenue would increase even if the rates were somewhat reduced.

The present law creates a powerful incentive to dispose of property by *inter vivos* gifts, and the integrated system should not go to the opposite extreme of making *inter vivos* gifts less attractive than death transfers. It may be advantageous from the personal standpoint to dispose by *inter vivos* gifts at a time when financial guidance and assistance can be given the donee by the donor. Sons and daughters may much prefer to receive their destined portions at a time when they are starting their careers. Gifts provide the state with early use of the tax receipts and reduce the risk of loss in principal. At the very least, a moderate discount to take account of differences in timing should be provided. The discount might be applied to the tax collected from the gift, the time factor being gauged by the life expectancy of the donor. The donor might also be allowed the privilege of postponing his exemption until death, thus ensuring a more adequate provision for dependents at that time.

Although the integrated tax would be principally beneficial to the government, it would afford the taxpayer at least one important advantage. It would greatly reduce the necessity of adjusting his plans to take account of the tax factor and it would give him much greater certainty as to what his final tax liability might be.[1]

MISCELLANEOUS CONSIDERATIONS

In addition to better integration of estate and gift taxes at the federal level, greater coordination of federal and state

[1] For a further account of the problem of estate-gift tax integration see C. Lowell Hariss, *Gift Taxation in the United States*, American Council on Public Affairs, Washington, 1940; Geo. T. Altman, "Integration of Estate and Gift Taxes," *Law and Contemporary Problems*, Vol. 7, Spring, 1940; Erwin N. Griswold, "A Plan for the Coordination of Income, Estate and Gift Tax with Respect to Trust and Other Transfers," 56 *Harvard Law Review* 335 (1942).

Death Taxation

taxes is needed. Some coordination was introduced in 1924 and extended in 1926, when state death taxes were allowed as a credit up to 80 per cent of the federal tax. The credit has been retained through many modifications of the federal tax but it is still attached to 1926 rates and exemptions and does not apply to the new gift taxes. The credit is in need of modernization. It should be expressed in terms of the latest rates and exemptions and it should be extended to cover the gift tax.

As previously indicated, the states have much difficulty in determining jurisdiction to tax estates, and considerable multiple taxation results from overlapping levies. The federal government might well use its crediting device to assist the states in the elimination of this evil.

Considerable inequity arises in estate taxation because of irregular intervals between deaths among successors to the same estate. The law recognizes this inequity to some extent by exempting a second transfer within a 5-year period. A large improvement could be made to solve this difficulty by allowing liberal exemptions to spouses and by preventing avoidance through the life-estate-remainder device. Some consideration might be given the application of a rule providing a percentage exemption for property reinherited within 30 years. This might be accompanied by an extra levy if property did not pass through the death tax mill before the end of, let us say, a 50-year interval from the previous tax. The principal difficulty here would be that of distinguishing an original estate at the time of a subsequent transfer.

A better basis of allowing for the time factor might be to weight exemptions in terms of the differentials in age between the deceased and the legatee. A 30- or 40-year differential would be regarded as standard. An age differential of zero might be sufficient ground for disregarding the transfer for death-tax purposes completely. Age differentials between zero and 30 or 40 might allow a fractional weighting. For example, a 10-year differential would support an exemption of two-thirds or three-fourths of the estate. A differential of more than 30 or 40 years would result in a weighting of more than 100 per cent or an increase in the base over the amount actually transferred. The application of the age differential to the gift tax should present no special problems. If it is thought that the heir who is of the same age as the donor should pay some tax because of the former's probable tendency to spend the substance of an estate, this could be allowed for in the weighting. Exemptions to allow for the time factor would be in addition to those allowed to care for dependent relatives. This fundamental reform might avoid the necessity of other reforms, such as those connected with life estates and powers of appointment. Some new and bold thinking in the field of death taxation is definitely needed.

CONCLUSION

It has long been recognized that, in spite of very stiff rates and occasional onerous burdens imposed by the federal estate-tax law, the results of the death-tax system are fiscally disappointing and its impact highly capricious. The following have been recommended to increase the effectiveness and improve the economic effects of the death tax:

1. The estate tax should be integrated with the gift tax. Capricious and undesirable results follow from the fact that, for example, the owner of an estate of $100,000 can make a 90 per cent saving by disposing of his estate through *inter vivos* gifts.

2. Notorious loopholes, particularly those relating to the disposition of property by means of trusts, powers of appointment, and life-estate-remainders, are in urgent need of repair.

3. A period after death (3 years), during which the executor of the estate may choose the time for valuation of its assets, should be allowed.

4. Exemption of $60,000 at a time of urgent revenue need is, to say the least, unwise.[1]

[1] Of course, both the social and the personal interest in providing for the

Death Taxation

5. Exemptions should be granted to the estate on the basis of the relationship of the beneficiary to the deceased.[1]

6. Exemption of charitable bequests should be redefined to eliminate abuses or some limit should be imposed on the proportion of an estate allowed tax exemption because of disposition for philanthropic purposes.

7. Attention should be given the possibility of including time between successive transfers of estates as one of the dimensions of an estate-tax base.

It is recognized that the death-tax field is highly intricate, with many possibilities for discriminatory anomalies. It is important to make the tax more equitable as well as more productive. Again, the example of the British may prove helpful although the British, too, have badly neglected loopholes associated with gifts. Still, the British, with lower top rates than ours, have succeeded in making their death-tax system relatively much more productive.

Both the income and the death tax involve complex mechanisms and present difficult administrative and avoidance problems. It is evident, however, that many of these complexities are not inherent and can be resolved with adequate effort. This must be done since, if these complexities and difficulties are not held within reasonable bounds, simpler but less equitable and economically less desirable forms of taxation may have to be substituted.

---

security of dependent relatives must be recognized For this and other reasons, widows and minor children of deceased estate owners are entitled to special consideration

[1] *Ibid*

X. SPECIAL EXCISES AND GENERAL SALES TAXES

INTRODUCTION

WE HAVE already noted the strong trend toward business taxation in the federal tax system and have recommended that the trend be reversed. This poses sharply the question of alternatives: What kind of revenue system should we establish? Our recommendations point in the direction of a more personal tax system. It would be possible, however, to move in the opposite direction toward an impersonal, indirect, consumption-tax system. If this were the goal, the proper procedure would probably be to retain business taxes but to broaden their base. Instead of using net income as the base of the business tax, we could use net operating income (interest not deductible), or "value added," or gross income. Perhaps eventually we would arrive at retail sales taxation as the mainstay of federal revenues.

Consumption taxes, like many other kinds of taxation, assume various forms. General consumption or sales taxes can be levied at any one of the several stages of production; they are usually applied at the manufacturing, wholesaling, or retailing levels. The retail sales tax has received most recent attention. A manufacturers' sales tax and a wholesalers' tax are regarded as considerably easier to administer than a retail sales tax, but they are less personal in their impact and less certain as to incidence and effects. The retail sales tax can be so applied as to give the consumer specific information on the amount of tax he is paying. The closer to the consumer the levy is applied, the less likely is pyramiding of prices (adding more than the tax).

Special excises differ from general consumption taxes in

Special Excises and General Sales Taxes

that the former are applied to the sales of a specific commodity or service, such as tobacco or electricity, whereas the latter apply to all or a large part of goods and services purchased.

FEDERAL EXCISES BEFORE AND DURING THE WAR

During the period from 1935 to 1939, federal excise, sales, and documentary stamp taxes (but not including custom duties) on the average accounted for about 32 per cent of total federal revenues raised each year. Of course, at that time federal revenues amounted to only $5 or $6 billion per year as compared with a postwar budget that will probably be three or four times this figure. In 1939, at relatively low rates (as compared with those now applied), the alcoholic beverage tax and tobacco tax alone raised $1.168 billion.

Federal excises have been greatly expanded since 1939. These taxes are listed in condensed form in Table XXVI. They now include "admission and dues taxes," with the rate about 20 per cent. The manufacturers' excise taxes, usually based upon manufacturers' sales prices, include a long list of items such as automobiles, gasoline, radios, and electrical appliances. These carry rates ranging from 5 to 25 per cent. In addition there is a retailers' excise tax, based on retail sales and covering cosmetics, toilet preparations, furs and fur articles, jewelry, and luggage. These are taxed at rates of about 20 per cent. Another set of excises apply to uses and services, including the automobile and boat use tax, and levies on electric energy, communications, and transportation of persons and property. Liquor taxes are $9 per gallon of distilled spirits and $8 per barrel of beer (with similar rates for liquor in other forms). Tobacco products also carry high taxes; the levy on the ordinary package of cigarettes is now 7 cents. There are also some occupational taxes and a considerable list of miscellaneous excises, such as the tax on playing cards. In addition to all these excises there is, of course, a whole system of custom duties that produced $300 to $400 million of federal revenue before the war.

TABLE XXVI
Federal Excise Taxes on Common Consumption Items

Item	Rate or Amount of Tax
Admissions to theaters, athletic events, etc	1¢ for each 5¢ or major fraction
Dues, membership, and initiation fees	20%
Cosmetics, toilet preparations, furs, jewelry, and luggage	20%
Manufacturers' excise taxes	
Automobiles, passenger	7%
Auto parts and accessories	5%
Auto radio and components	10%
Business machines	10%
Cameras and photographic equipment	25%
Electric, gas, and oil appliances	10%
Electric-light bulbs and tubes	20%
Gasoline	1½¢ per gal.
Lubricating oils	6¢ per gal.
Matches, ordinary	2¢ per 1000
Matches, fancy wooden	5½¢ per 1000
Musical instruments	10%
Phonographs, parts and records	10%
Radio receiving sets and parts	10%
Refrigerators, household	10%
Sporting goods and equipment	10%
Tires	5¢ per lb
Tubes	9¢ per lb.
Taxes on uses and services	
Auto use tax	$5 per yr
Boat use tax (depending on size)	$5 to $200 per yr
Electrical energy	3⅓%
Local telephone service	15%
Railroad, bus, and other transportation tickets	15%
Transportation of freight	3%
Liquor taxes:	
Distilled spirits (including brandy)	$9 per proof gal.
Beer and other fermented liquors	$8 per bbl.
Still wines (according to alcoholic content)	15¢ to $2 per wine gal.
Champagne	15¢ per ½ pt.
Liqueurs, cordials, etc	10¢ per ½ pt.
Imported perfumes (containing distilled spirits)	$9 per gal.
Tobacco taxes:	
Tobacco and snuff	18¢ per lb.
Light cigars	75¢ per 1000
Heavier cigars (depending on retail price)	$2.50 to $20.00 per 1000
Ordinary cigarettes	$3.50 per 1000 or 7¢ per pkg
Heavier cigarettes	$8.40 per 1000 or 16¢ per pkg.
Miscellaneous taxes:	
Playing cards	13¢ per pkg.
Sugar (manufactured in U.S. or imported)	0.465¢ per lb.

Source: Compiled from the Revenue Act of 1943 (passed in February, 1944).

Special Excises and General Sales Taxes

For the year 1944, the yield from all federal excise taxes was estimated at about $5 billion. This is almost as much as the yield from our entire federal revenue system before the war. It is reasonable to estimate that all federal consumption taxes average from 5 to 6 per cent of the total consumption expenditures—in other words, from $50 to $60 per thousand of such expenditures. A wise revision of consumption taxes offers a first-rate opportunity to relieve tax burdens for low-income groups and to improve the prospects for postwar markets.

ARGUMENTS FAVORING CONSUMPTION TAXES

A consumption-tax system has vigorous proponents and can be supported on some plausible grounds. Consumption taxes that are shifted to the consumer may cause no diminution of profits and, in that event, they would not affect enterprise incentives. The main alternative, taxation of net income, can affect the motivation to risk-taking and enterprise, especially if the tax is levied on a progressive scale and progression is carried to excess. Consumption taxes are a means of reaching areas of income which the more equitable income tax, for administrative and political reasons, seems obliged to ignore.

Consumption taxes are often defended on the ground that they are relatively painless and convenient to pay. They are usually collected a few cents at a time—"as the leech, the calf, and the bee take their food"[1]—and often are concealed in the price of the goods purchased. Closely connected with the foregoing point is the claim that consumption taxes are easily collected and yield substantial revenue. They may also afford an opportunity to collect some revenue from those who evade the income tax. It is often contended that consumption taxes make everyone contribute to the government and that everyone should make some payment for the benefits

[1] Quoted by Mabel Newcomer, *Taxation and Fiscal Policy*, Columbia University Press, New York, 1940, p. 22.

he receives. Citizens will be less prone to support extravagant public expenditure if they all contribute to it.

Further, consumption taxes are often more or less sumptuary in character—that is, they tend to discourage certain types of consumption generally recognized as harmful. This is particularly true of the liquor tax. There is strong and valid support for the view that cheap whiskey would not be socially desirable. Although the same argument applied to tobacco would have less support, the fact that a tax on the latter leaves the taxpayer an alternative quite compatible with his health and citizenship places such a levy in an entirely different class from a tax on bread.

Finally, it is argued that sales taxes could be justified if they were earmarked for governmental outlays of special benefit to poor people, which would not be made except through the provision of adequate funds by means of this type of levy. This argument rests on the assumptions (1) that the expenditures thus financed, in addition to the other governmental outlays, would be in the social interest and would not be wasteful or political handouts; and (2) that the political resistance to direct taxation would be more than a wholesome restraint on government spending.

ARGUMENTS AGAINST CONSUMPTION TAXES

Consumption taxes bear a capricious or indifferent relationship to the financial circumstances of the taxpayer. The rich and the poor pay the same rate and, although the amount of tax varies with the consumption of the commodity or service, it is not at all proportional to the means of the taxpayer. There are no exemptions to conserve the living standard of the "little fellow." Those with small incomes are compelled to spend practically all of (and sometimes more than) their earnings for consumption goods. All sales taxes ignore savings and the tendency of the wealthy to save a larger proportion of their incomes than do the poor. It is true that the regressiveness of these taxes can be avoided to

Special Excises and General Sales Taxes

some extent by exemptions, but it cannot be avoided entirely without sacrificing the advantages of simplicity and ease of administration, which are among the chief "virtues" claimed for this type of levy. The more regressivity is eliminated by the addition of special features, the more the tax comes to resemble the personal income tax and to rival it in complexity and administrative difficulty. A cardinal point in a tax program to foster production is that the human resources of a country must be conserved. Consumption taxes can impinge heavily on the health and morale of the poorest third of the population.

Consumption taxes are hidden and for this reason they are conducive to governmental extravagance. The discipline involved in direct personal taxes promotes tax "consciousness" and a demand for restraint in government spending. It was not accidental that Mr. Townsend chose a sales tax to pave the way for his old-age pension program. Public budgets should be scrutinized as carefully and with as much proprietary interest as private budgets. Of course, the tax system is not the only factor affecting the development of such public attention, but it is a factor of great importance.

Moreover, the sales tax involves administrative problems of its own. This would be especially true of a federal retail sales tax. It would entail checking the accounts of hundreds of thousands of small businesses, just as does the income tax. The possibilities of avoidance, with resulting unfair competition, would be abundant. The sales tax "on any close examination, will be found to teem with arbitrary, unintelligible distinctions, elaborate yet crude stop-gap expedients, unprincipled exclusions and inclusions."[1]

Finally, sales taxes, because they are a direct charge upon spending and fall heaviest upon the poor, may be ill-suited to a high-consumption economy. They constitute a threat to postwar markets.

[1] Henry C. Simons, in a memorandum to the author.

Postwar Taxation and Economic Progress

CONSUMPTION TAXES AND THE FUNCTIONING
OF THE ECONOMIC SYSTEM

Consumption Taxes: A Remedy for Inflation?

The sales tax was strongly advocated during the war on the ground that it would be an effective aid to price stabilization. War tax policies are not our present concern, but the threat of inflation is likely to continue for some time after the war. During the early stages of the postwar period, the problem will probably be that of achieving levels of production sufficient to satisfy the pent-up demand. It is at this point that the threat of inflation will be most dangerous. Some effort to hold consumption "down to" production may be required. In the longer run, the task will probably prove to be that of stimulating consumption to keep pace with our greatly expanded capacity to produce. This, of course, will involve no problem of inflation. But, for the inflationary phase of the postwar period, the sales tax could be offered as a means of price control.

The sales tax has both inflationary and deflationary effects,[1] and balancing the two is not easy. On the deflationary side, the tax withdraws spending power from consumers. In addition, the willingness as well as the ability to spend would be affected; many persons would probably cut down their purchases rather than pay the tax. On the inflationary side, the tax would take the form of an increase in the price of goods. As a prescription for inflation, this seems highly questionable. Moreover, taxes added to the prices of essential goods and services might become the basis of insistent demands for wage increases. An epidemic of strikes for higher wages might aggravate the inflationary trend by checking production.

It would probably not be possible to confine the retail

---

[1] Marius Farioletti, "A Federal Retail Sales Tax as a Fiscal Device for Curbing Inflation in War Time," *Curbing Inflation through Taxation* (Symposium), Tax Institute, New York, 1944, p. 63.

Special Excises and General Sales Taxes

sales tax to individual consumers and exclude all agricultural, commercial, and industrial sales. Certain important business-cost items, such as fuel, seed, and fertilizer might be exempted; but many other such items could not be excluded without creating unnecessary administrative problems and sacrificing much of the revenue sought. Increases in production costs would result in new and unequal pressures on prices. Additional complications would attend the maintenance of parity for farm prices—a concept based on the relation between the prices of what the farmer buys and what he sells.

Taxes on durable consumption goods during the postwar transition period might be supported as a means of rationing a short supply and of raising some revenue. But this would unfairly penalize some purchasers, such as ex-servicemen, who will need these goods most.

A great danger in the use of the sales tax by the federal government is that it might continue in the tax system after the supposed need for it had passed. A regressive tax system need not be deflationary in an absolute sense; that is, it may simply involve the transfer of income from one group of the poor to another. But the market for goods is likely to suffer in the transfer. Certainly the market would suffer relatively more than it would through the imposition of the net-income tax.

The Maintenance of an Adequate Postwar Market

The maintenance of an adequate consumer demand, particularly for those goods that have a high social value, is threatened by a tax system which seeks a large part of its revenue from the lowest levels of income. This is of vital concern in the postwar period in view of the present and prospective expansion of productive capacity. The states, with their more limited fiscal resources, will probably maintain and perhaps develop the consumption-tax field. At all events, their tax systems are likely to remain regressive. The federal government should therefore stress direct personal taxation.

A concomitant of the underconsumption problem is the prospect of oversaving, discussed in Chaps. I and XIII. Oversaving is amenable to attack either through decreasing the supply of savings or through increasing the demand for capital. The latter might result from either increased consumption or improved incentives for investment. Unfortunately, it is difficult to devise a tax system that recognizes both of these interests. A broadly based personal-income tax, with moderate progression, would seem to strike the best balance possible. But heavy consumption taxes, in addition to a broadly based income tax, would be suspect.

SPECIAL EXCISES

Some retention of special excises, such as those on liquor and tobacco, is very likely; and these taxes, if not the best, are a tolerable element in the federal tax system. They mainly affect adults and do not penalize families as compared with single persons. A levy on liquor is a practical necessity for sumptuary reasons. The taxation of tobacco, as previously stated, allows the taxpayer an alternative to the tax that is quite in accord with the national interest. Indulgences such as those involved in the consumption of tobacco are at least a strategic point for "opportunistic" taxation. Moreover, a reduction of federal tobacco taxes might prove an invitation to the states to develop further this field, and the states are not in position to administer tobacco taxes effectively. A case can be made for a federal gasoline tax in view of considerable federal expenditures for highways. Some taxes, however, must be left to the states and this levy seems especially appropriate for that disposition. The tax is relatively easy to administer and can be integrated with property taxes and related to highway expenditures at the state level. Luxury taxes on goods consumed mainly by the wealthy, such as jewelry and furs, are tolerable but they

Special Excises and General Sales Taxes

provide little revenue and they are less equitable than income taxes. (They are not paid at all, of course, by people who do not consume luxuries, but there is no regular relationship in the higher incomes between income and the consumption of such luxuries.) In addition, they constitute a direct levy on the marketing of goods. With very few exceptions, the federal consumption-tax system should be confined to liquor and tobacco.

Detailed discussion cannot be given here to the special problems of liquor and tobacco taxation. Sumptuary interests would support a relatively light levy on beer and a heavy tax on hard liquor. The tax on hard liquor, however, presents a problem of administration, and it can be so high as to afford inordinate incentives for bootlegging. The cigarette tax, based on numbers rather than value, involves discrimination against low-priced products. The existing lighter levies on cigars than on cigarettes are difficult to explain except in terms of politics and because the trend in demand has been away from cigars. The present rates and classifications make these taxes considerably more regressive than is necessary. Low-priced products tend to be consumed by lower income recipients, and classification according to value with higher rates on more expensive products would result in a better distribution of the taxes. Even with the consumption taxes limited to the very few products here suggested, the field is not without problems and present practices are not without possibilities of improvement.

The excises do provide the federal tax system with an additional element of diversity. It would probably be rash and certainly unprecedented to burden the personal-income tax with, let us say, 80 per cent of a budget as formidable as that anticipated in the postwar era. On the other hand, some relief for postwar taxpayers in the lower-income brackets will be justified and, as between excises and the normal income-tax rates, the former are more appropriate for concessions.

Postwar Taxation and Economic Progress

Extended appraisal of custom duties is contemplated in other studies sponsored by the Committee for Economic Development, and this justifies confining our own comments to one or two observations. Insofar as customs are designed for protection, they represent the sort of indirect subsidies that have been criticized throughout this book. Insofar as they are designed for revenue, they represent consumption taxes that must be accepted or rejected like other consumption taxes. In the main, their retention is not recommended and they are included in our revenue estimates only on the ground that a proposal for free trade in the foreseeable future seems unrealistic. Nevertheless, considerable reduction in tariff rates can and should be made.

THE SPENDINGS TAX

Something may be said for a postwar spendings tax to curb extravagant and wasteful expenditures. This type of "sales" tax differs considerably from the usual sales tax. It is based on total rather than on specific expenditures and would be administered through personal reports like a net-income tax. Further features resembling those of a net-income tax are graduated rates and personal exemptions. It could include services purchased by consumers, an item that causes great administrative difficulty if included in the retail sales tax. It could also act as a check on avoidance of death taxes through wasteful spending. The tax accords with the view that the owners of large wealth must assume the role of "trustees." The spendings tax could be useful not only as a curb on extravagance but also as a check on inflation and as a supplementary source of revenue. It would constitute the most rational luxury levy.

Most important of the objections to this tax is the additional complexity in income-tax reporting and administration which would necessarily result. The personal-income tax is already too complex, and, if this new tax were added to it and the new tax returns were made even more complicated, both taxes would suffer from the resultant confusion of the taxpayer. Buehler suggests that these difficulties could be overcome by combining the normal and surtaxes into one schedule and dropping the earned-income credit of the income tax.[1] The latter change has recently been made and the former is desirable, but they should be accepted as an improvement to the income tax and not as a means of easing a new complication into it. Taxes based on personal reporting depend upon cooperation of the citizenry, and this addition might prove to be the "straw that breaks the camel's back." Unless the public cooperated fully in complete and honest reporting of disposable funds and deductions, the tax would fail hopelessly.

In the type of high-consumption economy anticipated after the war, checks on spending, except on that of a highly extravagant sort, seem inappropriate. Nevertheless, if administrative problems could be solved, there might be a place for an over-all spendings tax with a high (perhaps $5000) exemption.

CONCLUSION

Federal consumption taxes, in general, were tolerable during the past century when capital was at a premium and the citizen was not very conscious of his responsibilities to government. They are less appropriate today and will become still less appropriate as time goes on.

[1] A. G. Buehler, "Taxing Consumer Spending," *Bulletin of the National Tax Association*, Vol. 28, No. 4 (January, 1943)

XI. INCENTIVE TAXATION

INTRODUCTION

During the depression of the thirties, much was heard about incentive taxation, a term applied to the use of taxation as a system of rewards and penalties especially designed to encourage production and employment. During those necessitous times, inventiveness was at a high level and many original reforms were suggested. The period was characterized by an intensive (and in some cases almost pathological) tax consciousness. This combination produced many proposals seeking to solve the economic problem by ingenious use of the tax mechanism.

There is no disagreement concerning the fact that taxes can have stimulating or depressing effects upon enterprise. The basic purpose of every tax system is to raise sufficient revenue for the expenses of government, but it should contribute to rather than obstruct high levels of employment, production, investment, and consumption. This book is mainly concerned with tax modifications that would make the tax system noninhibitory to desirable economic activity, including consumption. These tax modifications include selection of, or more emphasis upon, tax A as contrasted with tax B. But, beyond this, taxes can be devised and arranged to offer *positive encouragement* to business undertakings. Such inducement can take many forms, of which the more common are exemptions, refunds, discounts, premiums, and credits. These inducements may be desirable at times, but care must be exercised lest they be at the expense of other equally desirable economic activities, and they should be discontinued as soon as the reasons for their adoption have disappeared. Finally, it is possible occasionally to use taxes as a "whip" to

Incentive Taxation

force certain types of desired economic conduct. This may assume the form of a penalty—much like a fine—which can be avoided by choosing desired, as against undesired, conduct. This type of taxation should at least be used sparingly and with the highest degree of precaution.

In Chapter I of this book, considerable discussion was given to avoiding inhibitory results in the use of the tax system. Here attention will be directed primarily to the use of taxation as a positive inducement or as a penalty to influence economic conduct.

SOME INCENTIVE TAXATION PROPOSALS

One of the most ambitious proposals that might be classed as incentive taxation was the Industrial Expansion Act introduced by Representatives Allen, Amlie, Maverick, and Voorhis in 1937. The bill proposed a comprehensive government plan for the coordinated expansion of production in the United States. A "processing tax similar to that employed in the Agricultural Adjustment Act" was to be employed to secure the full cooperation of major industries. The tax was to consist of a 25 per cent levy on "value added," with a 95 per cent cancellation of the liability if taxpayers complied with the terms of the Act. An Industrial Expansion Commission of seven members was to be appointed by the President, and a coordinator was to manage the program. The plan developed by the Commission was to take into account (1) consumer needs of the nation; (2) the capacity of our present industrial equipment to fill these needs; (3) desirable output of all types of raw materials and finished goods; (4) conservation of natural resources, minimizing of hazardous and harmful working conditions, reduction of waste, and consequent reduction of working hours; and (5) rehabilitation of the new unemployed population. Expansion programs, to be approved, would need to provide for an increase in the income of workers, and the increase in profits could not exceed 10 per cent of the sum of the pay roll increases plus the total amount saved to consumers by reduction in prices.[1] Any portion of increased production which proved unsalable would be taken over by the government, thus guaranteeing industry against loss.

The philosophy of this proposal was summarized by one of its sponsors[2] as follows:

It should be noted that this Act does not contemplate the socialization of industry, but it does contemplate the degree of cooperation from the federal government that is necessary to operate American industry at full capacity and give all of the American people a high standard of living. . . . If the machinery set up by the A.A A. and the N.R.A. were used to secure full production instead of restricted output, a minimum in goods and services equal to what $2500 a year will now buy, would be available for every family in the United States. . . .

It was acknowledged that some regimentation would be involved in this program but it was said that business ought not to object, since even while Hoover was in the White House, the Chamber of Commerce had favored a program similar to the NRA, which sought to ignore the Sherman Antitrust Act and allow "trade associations to restrict output."[3] Industry wanted to increase production but did not dare do so. Each industry's market depends on increased buying power on the part of workers in other industries, and expansion requires a central plan, so the argument ran.

According to a Swedish law of 1938, a corporation can yearly set aside a certain amount of its profit which becomes free of taxes. This money goes into two different funds: one for construction investments and the other for investment in inventories and stocks. In the first fund, 10 per cent of

[1] Industrial Expansion Bill H.R. 7504, 76th Congress, 1st Session, 1937, Sec. 5(f).

[2] Remarks of Hon. Robert G. Allen of Pennsylvania in the House of Representatives, August 16, 1937. *Recovery Plans*, The Temporary National Economic Committee, Monograph No. 25, Washington, 1940, p. 108.

[3] Remarks of Hon. Thomas R. Amlie, of Wisconsin, in the House of Representatives, August 21, 1937. *Recovery Plans, op. cit.*, p. 115

Incentive Taxation

profits or 2 per cent of capital and, in the second, 20 per cent of profits or 4 per cent of capital may be set aside. These funds cannot be used until the government gives authorization either to industries as a whole or to certain industries. If not used within 2 years, the corporation must pay the taxes that should ordinarily have been paid the year when the fund was set up, plus 6 per cent annual interest. Another Swedish law of the same date made it possible for a company to write off, without regard to actual depreciation, more machinery in bad and less in good years. Such transactions had to be approved by the tax authorities and assurances had to be given that, in case of corporate liquidation, funds would be available to pay postponed taxes.[1]

A somewhat similar proposal was made by Professor Hansen,[2] under which new investment would be defined by Congress with the help of the experts, the definition to make certain that only outlays which expand capital equipment were included. The portion of any income or inheritance so invested would be subject to a substantially lower tax than that otherwise employed. Applied to individuals, the proposal encounters the difficulty of tracing savings through insurance companies and banks. Applied to corporations or all business units, the scheme appears more plausible and is much like proposals granting special status to reinvested earnings. It is debatable, of course, whether the dollar that is invested in old investment, thus freeing another dollar for new investment, is less socially useful than the dollar which goes into new investment directly. All attempts to grant favor to new investment are to some extent at the expense of old investment and encounter the limitation that investors may see the possibility of future adverse discrimination replacing the present favorable one. An ounce of general

---

[1] Letter from Legation of Sweden, Washington, D C., received December 2, 1943.

[2] Alvin Hansen and Guy Greer, "Federal Taxes and the Future," *Harpers Magazine*, Vol. 184 (April, 1942), pp. 498–499.

confidence is probably worth a pound of special favor in the encouragement of new investment.

Proposals to apply a graduated tax rate inversely according to the pay roll or the volume of employment are numerous and assume many forms. Among the few cases of actual experience with special tax concessions to new investment or expanded employment is that of Germany under the so-called "Papen Plan" inaugurated in 1932.[1] A premium was offered for each newly employed worker (increasing the previous labor force), to be paid in tax certificates acceptable for the payment of certain future taxes and subject to discount for procurement of immediate cash. Among the other provisions of the plan was one which called for a reduction in wages for new employees below the terms fixed by collective agreements. The reduction would be conditional upon its application in such manner as to decrease hours and increase employment.

The plan was launched with high hopes and was accepted with enthusiasm by German business men. But instead of the expected recovery, unemployment again increased after being stationary for two months. A law in April, 1933, liquidated the premium for employment except in a very few cases.

It was said of the plan that on the surface it "was ingeniously constructed and seemed to justify confidence in its working."[2] Reasons cited for its failure were principally that German business was too monopolistic to allow it to succeed; the hope that one concern would expand heavily to obtain an advantage over its competitors proved unwarranted. Moreover, little attention was given to consumer demand, and this weakness may have accounted for the diffidence of business. The assumption that German budgets of the period could be balanced in spite of this additional strain

[1] Gerhard Colm, "Why the Papen Plan for Economic Recovery Failed," *Social Research*, February, 1934, p 82.
[2] *Ibid.*, p. 88.

Incentive Taxation

proved overoptimistic. The Papen Plan probably promoted the liquidation of private debts to some extent, but public debts were increased. It is not inconceivable that a subsidy program could start a wave of optimism in private business, but the uncertainties and problems involved are of serious proportions. The Germans were in a period of low morale, but in many other respects the conditions for the experiment were "not unfavorable."[1]

One of the most popular patterns of incentive taxation is that which proposes to tax idle money. A leading proponent[2] of this approach says that "the whole problem of government finance, like all other economic problems, depends upon the rapid turnover of money" and "taxing idle money is the key to everything." The tax would be designed to stimulate business rather than to provide revenue. If money were spent or invested rapidly, no tax would be collected. A tax on hoarded funds would, in effect, provide a negative rate of interest while they were held idle. Revenue would be raised largely by an over-all spendings tax (mainly an income tax with savings deductible). Further stimulation to the economy would be provided by varying the property tax inversely according to the degree of utilization of the property.

Some of the most comprehensive and ambitious plans for challenging the right to hoard and for depriving money of the power to "go on strike" have been proposed by Arthur Dahlberg. An early plan by this author called for a tax on both currency and deposits withdrawn from the productive process and awaiting better terms.[3] A monthly tax was to be levied on the demand deposits held by each depositor over a $300 minimum, exempt from the tax. Recognizing that paper money and bank deposits are alternative forms of money,

---
[1] *Ibid.*, p. 84.
[2] C. William Hazlitt, *A Dynamic Capitalism*, Harper & Brothers, New York, 1943.
[3] A. Dahlberg, *When Capital Goes on Strike*, Harper & Brothers, New York, 1938, Chaps. VII–VIII.

the necessity for the same or similar treatment of the two was conceded. It was proposed in effect that the currency become a "calendar currency" on which would be printed the value of the notes at a series of dates.

Numerous restrictions were proposed to prevent evading the tax. Conversion of bank deposits and paper currency into subsidiary coin would be prevented by making possession of more than $20 worth of coin illegal, except in the case of businesses with special needs. The use of foreign exchange as a means of tax evasion would be eliminated by making the hoardings tax applicable to the dollar balances held in the United States by foreign banks. Check blanks might carry a printed notice that checks would be automatically void or of reduced value if not cashed within a certain period. Similar means were suggested to prevent avoidance by conversion of currency and deposits into time deposits, matured drafts, short-term assets of banks, and so forth.

In later proposals, the author omitted the feature calling for a currency of changing value. Instead, it was proposed to provide for the distribution of a quantity of coin and currency before the imposition of a tax on deposits.[1] The government would then announce that when the total quantity of coin and currency in circulation had expanded to some preannounced figure, all coin and currency outstanding would be accepted at only a devaluated figure and, after the devaluation date, only new coins and currency would be accepted at par. The government would regularly announce to the public the changing value of outstanding currency. With a threatened penalty placed on excessive coin and currency expansion, owners of demand deposits logically would not seek undue expansion of holdings. If this were true, it would be unlikely that devaluation would ever be necessary. If devaluation were necessary, however, it would afford a profit to the currency-issuing banks—a profit which the government would divert to itself as federal tax revenue.

[1] *Recovery Plans, op. cit.*

Incentive Taxation

It is said that the tax system, by ignoring idle money and taxing productive investment, creates unemployment and that, in the interest of dynamic economy, this perversity should be corrected.[1]

INCENTIVE TAXATION PROPOSALS CRITICIZED

The author has strong doubts as to the effectiveness of these approaches in solving our economic problem, but they undoubtedly have been useful in calling attention to the necessity of concern for incentives in ordering the tax system.

Use of the tax system to penalize undesirable and reward desirable economic conduct introduces grave chances of political domination into the economic system. The Industrial Expansion Act would have reduced free enterprise to a shell. In fact, its proponents regarded the Act as a politically palatable form of socialism. If socialism is inevitable, many would prefer to take it directly rather than in disguise. Other proposals for bounties or tax exemptions contemplate no such high degree of political domination. But they are all a departure from the free market system and all of them involve reliance upon political supports. If business men are to "whoop it up" for free enterprise on the one hand and call for governmental bounties of some kind on the other, they cannot expect to be taken seriously by the American public.

There is something incongruous about taxing old enterprise to provide a lively incentive for new enterprise. It overlooks the fact that new enterprise becomes old and that the success of commitments already made is the strongest basis for confidence in new undertakings.

A free economic system, with proper governmental policing, should provide its own incentives. If it does not do so, something in the mechanism is out of gear. The proper procedure is to find the cause of the trouble and to correct it. Bounties and special tax incentives turn their backs on

[1] See George Richman Walker, "The Touch of Midas," *Harpers Magazine*, February, 1944, pp. 284–288.

this fundamental approach and seek to substitute political nostrums.

It seems highly doubtful that the economic virtues can be called into existence by negative treatment. People work enthusiastically, develop new ideas, and risk their fortunes on new enterprises when they have confidence in the future. That kind of confidence can hardly be engendered by taxing pessimism and by showing the potential investor two ways instead of one in which he can lose his resources. A heavy tax on idle property (the property tax) during the thirties resulted neither in payment of taxes nor in the use of the property; it resulted in heavy tax delinquency. Industry is a creative endeavor and it flourishes with the enthusiasm of its participants; such enthusiasm cannot be generated by application of a lash.

It may be that the economic system has developed such rigidities that it is no longer able to operate satisfactorily without an intermittent (or perhaps continuous) "shot in the arm" from government. But our experiences since 1929 have been too recent and too limited to give us a certain answer as to whether the defeatism engendered (even among business men) during that decade was warranted. Even if the answer is affirmative, there are other and probably better stimulants than can be provided by the tax system. Certa nly until the need for artificial stimulants is apparent, the tax system had better be designed to conserve such economic incentives as are naturally generated in the economic system rather than to provide incentives of its own.

It is true that the volume of currency and bank deposits increased substantially during the depression and the war and that the velocity of currency movement has greatly slackened. Undoubtedly the general spirit of economic diffidence has lead to a considerable amount of hoarding. On the other hand, were "timid money" forced out of hiding, it would probably go into the secure investment market where there is already a glutted supply. If more risk-taking and

Incentive Taxation

new enterprise are needed, a positive rather than a negative incentive is in order. It might be possible to force idle cash into consumption expenditure, but that this is the way to a healthy economic condition is extremely doubtful.

The specific programs described in the previous section are all open to other objections. The proposal to tax idle money, for instance, encounters the difficulty that banks lend credit rather than money. One could tax a bank for not lending up to the limit of its capacity. Presumably the bank will, as a matter of self-interest, accept such opportunities to lend money as are permitted by law and as are within the limits of prudence. We hardly solve our problem by forcing our banks to be reckless. It seems much wiser to try to make investment attractive rather than disinvestment unattractive. All proposals to tax hoarding miss the point that hoarding is at least as much a failure of demand for credit as a failure of supply. Moreover, any notion that hoarding is more than a symptom of the economic problem seems quite illusory. All the schemes thus far proposed for taxing idle currency and deposits have been highly complicated and cumbersome and have offered ample opportunities for technical loopholes.

If savings deposits in banks were to be exempt from the hoardings tax, the result would probably be an impressive expansion of savings deposits and a reduction of demand deposits. As a consequence, business transactions might be delayed. The investment problems of banks, already considerable, would be aggravated. Banks cannot indulge in the risk-taking type of investment. Such a tax plan might ultimately deprive small savers of an excellent saving device—time deposits. At least, banks would attempt to convert time deposits into a device much like demand deposits. The volume and frequency of withdrawals to meet current payments would be much greater than now. The banks would not be able to place as large a portion of their time deposits into long-term investments. They would need to maintain a high degree of liquidity in their time-deposit accounts. In more ways than one, the hoardings tax could injure the functioning and security of the banking system.

Of all the proposals here reviewed, that applied in Sweden seems by far the most promising. It works on the timing of investments and depreciation allowances. Similar recommendations can be found elsewhere in this report. We have also suggested tax concessions for small new business.

CLASSIFIED INCOME TAX

A proposal somewhat different from those just discussed is the adoption of a classified income tax with special rates, or weighting, for the kinds of income most sensitive to discouragement and most strategic for the maintenance of employment. It is argued that our present tax system is perverse in its favoritism to government bonds, earned income, and ordinary bonds, and in its special bias against stocks. Certain measures to eliminate this perverseness have been proposed here. But it would be possible to go further and classify the income-tax base with differential treatment for income according to source. Some case could be made for the especially heavy taxation of income from land on the argument that land is an inert factor of production with an inelastic supply needing no encouragement from the tax system. This will be considered in more detail presently.

A further suggestion is that dividends should be singled out for more favorable treatment than other income. It is plausibly argued that income from giving jobs should be treated less severely than income from the jobs themselves.[1] Supporting this view is the hypothesis, previously mentioned, that investment is more sensitive to attack by taxation than services compensated with salaries. Of course, stocks differ among themselves in the degree of "innovation and experimentation" that can be attributed to their owners. But a much stronger objection to the proposal is that the classified

[1] Sumner Slichter, "Social Security after the War," Winthrop Ames Memorial Lecture, Radcliffe College, April 4, 1943.

Incentive Taxation

income tax, departing as it does from the principles of universality and neutrality in taxation, leads back to the system of penalties and subsidies, which is so easily abused and from which we should seek emancipation. One "special privilege," even though warranted, is likely to lead to another, quite indefensible.

A favorable classification for dividends would raise the question of whether a similar favor should be extended to the business income of unincorporated businesses and farmers. Classification of income and graduation of rates according to the quantity of income are not a compatible combination and are likely to result (as in some European countries) in a tax system distinguished principally for its complication. Moreover, preferred treatment for dividends involves the element of income most given to concentration and most significant from the standpoint of economic power. On the whole, a reasonable reduction in the higher surtaxes—a move toward moderation—seems a better means of relieving the risk-taker.

FUNCTIONAL APPROACH TO TAXATION

One of the early proponents of what is now called the "functional" approach to economic problems was John A. Hobson. He contended that a sound tax system must not impair essential incentives to production or useful elements of consumption.[1] To discover the really taxable elements of income, those with a true "ability to bear," the origins or sources of income and the uses to which the income is applied must thus be examined. Hobson breaks down the concept of income into two parts: economically necessary payments for the use of factors of production (costs) and unnecessary or excessive payments (surplus). "Standard" wages constitute a necessary "cost," which has practically no ability to bear taxes. A minimum rate of interest as a return on invested capital is also a necessary payment, in this case to induce the saving classes to withhold enough of their spending power to supply

[1] J. A. Hobson, *Taxation in the New State*, Harcourt, Brace and Company, New York, 1920, p. 12.

such capital. A certain portion of profits is also necessary to stimulate initiative and energy for a thriving and growing private business.

Everything above these costs Hobson labels surplus income and designates as a proper object for taxation. Although the separation of costs and surplus is a difficult task and a considerable margin of error is inevitable, these limitations do not invalidate the principle. Hobson proposes his analysis as a theory of incidence as well as one of conservation. Taxes on costs will be shifted to surplus in any event, but the shifting process will involve waste and damage to production, extortion from consumers, and deception of the public as to the incidence of the levies. The surplus incomes can bear taxes without any shifting. Thus, economic rent could be taxed to the point of near confiscation, since the land could not be destroyed to avoid taxation. A tax on land appraised at its most profitable use would constitute a strong incentive to use the land most advantageously. Such use would be necessitated by the compulsion of meeting the tax bill.

Profits are packed with surplus because of the propensity of business to avoid competition through monopolistic practices and combinations. Monopolies set prices at the point of maximum net profits. This point would not be changed by the imposition of taxes on profits and, if it were, this would only indicate that insufficient skill and caution had been exercised in the imposition of the levies. It is suggested that a portion of reinvested corporate earnings might be exempted from taxation in the interest of adequate capital. But such exemptions would be limited in amount and confined to vital industries after a thorough scrutiny by the Income Tax Commissioners.

The doubtful feasibility of earmarking surplus, except for economic rent, is recognized, and Hobson would rely heavily on the general income tax as a first means of reaching income possessing real "ability to pay." This tax would make no distinctions, or at least not many or very elaborate ones, on

Incentive Taxation

the basis of income sources, but it would recognize the number of dependents that must get their support from the income. Income taxes would be supplemented by levies on estates, a surplus peculiarly fitted for taxation. The death taxes would reduce fiscal dependence upon the income tax and allow the latter to be kept within limits that would not obstruct the incentives to earn and save. Luxury consumption taxes might also have a legitimate place in a functional scheme of taxation, but most indirect taxes are ruled out as bearing too heavily upon those classes whose maintenance is a necessary social cost.

Thus Hobson conceived a scheme of taxation aimed at those elements of income which could be taxed without injuring the efficiency of production and subsequent decent living standards. His goal was revenue at no cost to economic efficiency and progress. His was a pioneering work on the subject of taxation and incentives and, although some of his conclusions are open to question, he offered a great deal of sound thinking on the subject, insufficiently recognized by many later public-finance writers.

Hobson's contemporary, Richard H. Tawney,[1] uses a similar approach to taxation, although this writer concerns himself less with specific proposals and more with the philosophy behind them. Tawney stresses the view that all riches are not a social gain, regardless of how they were obtained, and that all economic activity is not equally justifiable. Thus, part of the so-called "goods" annually produced are waste, because they consist of products that should not have been created until others had been developed in sufficient abundance, or should not have been produced at all. "If society is to be healthy, men must regard themselves not as owners of rights, but as trustees for the discharge of functions and the instruments of a social purpose."[2]

---

[1] Richard H. Tawney, *The Acquisitive Society*, Harcourt, Brace and Company, New York, 1920.
[2] *Ibid.*, p. 51.

Postwar Taxation and Economic Progress

Thomas Nixon Carver[1] follows the tradition of Hobson and Tawney but with more reservations and qualifications. Thus he observes that, whatever might be true if all men were willing to contribute tax payments according to their ability, the fact is that they are not willing to do so and that they will resort to avoidance devices to escape such contributions. However, he stresses the fact that any tax which represses a desirable industry not only imposes a sacrifice on the taxpayer but also one on those who are deprived of the services or the products of the repressed industry. He, too, looks to progressive taxation as a means of meeting fiscal needs with the least harmful economic effects. But he stresses the need for care lest the progressive scale reduce the energy and initiative required for economic progress. He proposes, as does Hobson, both the land tax and death duties as nonrepressive tax measures. A tax that is easily shifted and that therefore tends to diffuse itself widely throughout the community is suitable for temporary or emergency use only, whereas a nonshiftable tax is suitable for raising permanent revenue.

Few economists have laid more stress on the functional approach to taxation and other economic problems than John R. Commons.[2] In his view, individuals make the greatest use of their faculties and other resources *directly* in proportion to expected profits and *inversely* in proportion to taxes. He sets up a new canon of taxation in which there are two abilities to pay: the ability to serve, which varies directly with one's additions to the commonwealth, and the ability to pay, which varies inversely with such addition. "Taxes should be proportioned *directly* according to his ability to pay, and *inversely* according to his ability to serve the commonwealth."[3] Thus, one who gets his wealth by a mere rise in site values should pay proportionately higher taxes than one who gets his wealth through industry or agriculture.

[1] *Essays in Social Justice*, Harvard University Press, Cambridge, 1915.
[2] *Institutional Economics*, The Macmillan Company, New York, 1934
[3] *Ibid*, p. 819.

Incentive Taxation

Taxes regulate, regardless of intentions, for they determine in effect the directions in which people may become wealthy by determining the directions in which they may not become wealthy. In his specific tax proposals, Commons stresses the desirability of special levies on land and economic rent.

Qualitative and Quantitative Measures

All of these so-called functional approaches to the tax problem agree on the desirability of a qualitative rather than, or in addition to, a quantitative measure of income and wealth. Least favorable treatment should be given to so-called "unearned" as distinguished from "earned" income. These difficult terms have been analyzed by the author elsewhere as follows:[1]

It seems that differentiation of income for purposes of taxation might be based on any one or more of three different grounds The first is ethical in nature and labels some income as deserved and some as undeserved. The successful promoter of rackets will serve as an example of the recipient of unethical income. Almost everyone would agree that there are rackets and racketeers, some operating illegally and others (perhaps barely) within the law. Producers and distributors of "fake" remedies for human ailments would fall clearly within the class of recipients of unethical income. If we could single out racketeering income for especially heavy taxation, it would be the next best thing to stopping rackets. But the line between rackets and legitimate business is none too clear.

. . .

There can be no doubt that income does differ in moral character. But the differences are so subtle and so much a matter of opinion that differentiation on this ground for purposes of taxation would be very difficult to manage.

* * * *

A second basis of differentiating income is according to the effects upon future production which taxing it would have. This is a matter of necessary rewards for the incentives. Income may be

[1] Harold M. Groves, "Commons' Theory of Reasonable Value as Applied to Taxation," *Property Taxes*, Tax Policy League, New York, 1939, pp. 174–186.

regarded as a sort of "bribe" to induce economic activity and forbearance. "Bribes" should not be paid unless necessary and they should be kept at the minimum required. Here the case for taxing economic rent appears strongest. Its proponents claim that income from land values is the most conspicuous case of reward to a passive factor in production which might be taxed away without social detriment. God gave us 25,000 miles of the earth's circumference and we would still have it if all the landlords were taxed into the poorhouse.

Of course, land rent is by no means the only case of unnecessary or overgenerous payment of these economic "bribes" It was claimed by John A. Hobson in his *Taxation in the New State* that surpluses are rather general throughout the economic system. Hobson thought that they might be found in profits, interest, salaries, and even to a certain extent in wages. It has often been observed that a talented individual has in his capacities a more or less non-reproducible good, the return for which greatly resembles economic rent. This talent becomes negotiable when it takes the form of a patent or copyright. The corporation executive who receives $100,000 a year for his services may be worth to the corporation what he costs, but he may not be worth it to society in the sense that his services could not be had for less.

The difficulty in taxing surpluses (excess rewards) and sparing costs (necessary rewards) is that the two are distinguishable if at all only with the greatest difficulty. . . . It can be argued, of course, that land rent at any rate is a clear and distinguishable surplus and that it should be subjected to special taxes even though other and indistinguishable surpluses are not. There is some merit in this contention and we shall return to it later

The third ground for qualitative differentiation of income is that income from some sources is more potent than that from others. This is the basis for the present differentiation between earned and unearned income in the federal law.[1] The distinction looks not to the "deservedness" of the income, nor to the effects upon production which might follow from taxing it, but rather to the sacrifice involved in making payments. Thus it is said that income from service is less able than that from investments because the former is dependent upon the short and uncertain tenure of the human faculties. The

[1] Repealed since written.

Incentive Taxation

hazards of age and health have to be insured against before the security of the service income approaches that of the property income. Reliance upon investment may also involve hazards, but it is only a first line of defense with personal earning power available as a reserve. The distinction appears valid in the main, though its application in the federal law is highly arbitrary and may add more complications than its contribution to equity is worth.

The second of these bases of differentiation is the one that particularly concerns us here. "The definition of a privilege," says Tawney, "is a right to which no corresponding function is attached."[1] As an example he cites the urban landowner, of whom he says that no one supposes he performs any function; "he has the right of private taxation, that is all."

As previously suggested, the main difficulty in taxing "functionless supernumeraries" is to distinguish them. The two principal cases where the distinguishing seems feasible are inheritances and economic rent. The former are considered in a separate chapter, where we accept the view that heavy taxation of inherited wealth is justified.

Special Taxes on Economic Rent

The idea of a single tax on economic rent is primarily associated with the name of Henry George, although he was not the first to expound it. The essentials of his economic philosophy can be found in the writings of earlier economists,[2] but George was the first to make a land tax the center of an economic and social theory, a theory powerful enough to start a whole social reform movement.

The Georgian theory concentrated on the useless role of the landlord as the cause of all evils. Land was unique among the factors of production in its nonreproducible character, and this special characteristic was responsible for the fact that

---
[1] Tawney, *op. cit.*, p. 24.
[2] See basic works of Quesnay, Turgot, Adam Smith, Ricardo, Malthus, and John Stuart Mill.

only conditions influencing demand create land values. Since increased demand was a social phenomenon that caused the payment of rent, economic rent itself belonged to society. According to this theory, rent was an unearned payment resulting, not as a return for a productive service, but from the monopoly ownership of land. George proposed a tax on economic rent of 100 per cent and thought that this would provide ample revenues so that all other taxes could be abolished. Later economists who might be regarded as disciples of George did acknowledge other taxes, such as the inheritance tax, as feasible and practical, but the land-value tax was still emphasized as the basis of the tax system.[1]

The problem of incentives was involved in George's contention that the single tax on land would stimulate rather than retard production. If land were taxed at its full rental value, it would necessarily be forced into use. If the landlord could not use the land himself, he would at least be forced into letting others use it in return for a rent payment. The untaxing of improvements would also stimulate building and land development in many forms. Untaxing the earnings of labor would make the worker more industrious and ambitious. In contrast, a tax on monopolies would cost society nothing because the profit of monopoly is itself a tax levied upon production, and the government's levy would simply claim for the public treasury what the public must pay anyway.

The "single-taxers" claimed a great deal for their proposal, as indicated by statements that it would:

. . . solve the labor problem, do away with involuntary poverty, raise wages in all occupations to the full earnings of labor, make overproduction impossible until all human wants are satisfied, render labor-saving inventions a blessing to all, and cause such an enormous production and such an equitable distribution of wealth, as would

[1] See H. G. Brown, *Economic Science and the Common Welfare*, Lucas Brothers, Columbia, Mo., 1923, Part II, Chap. VI.

Incentive Taxation

give to all comfort, leisure, and participation in the advantages of an advancing civilization.[1]

It has long been rejoined to those who insist on the special taxation of economic rent that the distinctions between land and capital, as these terms are used by economists, are nowhere near as sharp as sometimes supposed. It is true that land in the sense of space is nonreproducible, but space is only one of the attributes of land. In many cases the developmental costs that make land usable—public utilities, for instance—are far more important than mere space. Nevertheless, although the distinction is one of degree, it does have some basis in reality. The supply of land is relatively fixed and inelastic. Taxes imposed upon land do accordingly tend to reduce land values rather than raise the prices of commodities.[2]

The discussion of the case for special taxation of land has been carried on in a rarefied academic atmosphere with little factual data to lend substance to the argument. One can hunt in vain for answers to the following questions: What is the proportion of land rent, or more particularly urban

---

[1] A N Young, *The Single Tax Movement in the United States*, Princeton University Press, Princeton, N J., 1916, pp. 260–261.

[2] "One of the frequent arguments for taxing land, especially urban land, is that such taxes are capitalized and tend to make land cheaper, whereas taxes on most other bases tend to be shifted forward to the consumer. It is the relative inelasticity in the supply of ground space which supports this view Inelasticity means that the supply will be forthcoming even though little or nothing is paid to suppliers The supply of rural land is influenced by the fertility element. . . Even urban ground space may be made available by the investment of labor and capital in such intangible improvements as filling and grading. But in spite of these qualifications, the supply of sites remains conspicuously inelastic. However, land investment competes with other investments and unrelieved special burdens attached to one class of investments tend to be discounted by purchasers This is the capitalization process which tends to diffuse the burden of land taxes among successive generations of owners. The widely accepted rule that land differs from capital in the incidence of taxation needs considerable qualification (more than can be here presented) but it appears to rest on solid ground." (Groves, *op. cit.*, pp. 183–184.)

land rent, in the national income? What is the ratio of "the developmental costs" of land to its value under different circumstances? What is the proportion of land increment to total capital gains? How effective is taxation (or might it be) in forcing the highest potential use of land?

Opposing the special taxation of land values is the fact that, even if one were to concede their uniquely unearned character, they have evolved so gradually with the development of population that they have been diffused with other values. In a young and growing country, many profit by the social and economic changes taking place in the community. But by the process of exchange and inheritance, these "unearned values" become diffused. For instance, a workingman may have spent his entire life laying up some savings to invest in a little land. After his investment takes place, is the income from his property "earned" or "unearned"? Moreover, a large amount of land is owned by relatively poor people; and it is probable that within certain ranges of income there is an inverse correlation between size of fortune and the proportion of it held in real estate. Although a particularly choice location is a monopoly for its owner in one sense, the public usually does have recourse to other desirable sites, and the differentials in site values can be reduced by improvements in transportation. The notion that land affords its owner a uniquely unearned income is based upon several abstract economic deductions and finds little support among most citizens, particularly those who are unreceptive to abstractions.

That heavy taxes on land tend to force its fullest economic use appears plausible, but this proposition is not supported by all the empirical evidence. Property-tax delinquency increased greatly during the depression of the thirties, either because of or in spite of high taxation, and the vacant lots on the outskirts of large cities constituted one of the most delinquent elements in the property-tax base. Whether the system of taxing land more severely than improvements (as in Pittsburgh) has acted as a stimulant to industrial growth is

Incentive Taxation

debatable, even among those close to the operation of the experiments.[1]

· Although the view that land is an especially proper subject for taxation is open to some objection and requires some qualification, it contains a large element of validity. This element is entitled to weight, at least in judgments concerning property-tax limitations, homestead exemptions, and other property-tax modifications. It also supports the contention that capital gains should be included in the base of the income tax.

SOCIAL SECURITY INCENTIVE TAXATION

Introduction

Our analysis of incentive taxation suggests the conclusion that a sound and sensible tax system is as practical a program for encouraging production as is likely to be found. However, taxation may also be applied as an incentive for business management to choose production policies desirable from the standpoint of the social interest other than in maximum production. A familiar application of incentives to promote a social interest has been functioning for several decades under our oldest type of social insurance legislation. Though workmen's compensation laws are rarely classed as tax laws, their practical effect is to *require* covered employers to pay premium rates or charges which vary according to their accident hazards and safety records. Such differential rates, whether paid to an exclusive state fund or to an insurance company, do result under compulsory statutes, one of whose major purposes is the prevention of work accidents and diseases. In short, the industrial safety movement is constantly supported by a system of incentives, backed by law and closely resembling tax inducements.

[1] Thomas C. McMahon, "Pittsburgh's Graded Tax on Buildings," *Proceedings of the National Tax Associatu n*, 1929, p. 134. See also E F. Daume, "The Graded Tax on Buildings," *Proceedings*, 1929, p. 140.

Postwar Taxation and Economic Progress

A differential pay roll tax for unemployment compensation is a more recent measure of this general character. Under the title of experience rating, this form of differential is now provided by the unemployment compensation systems of more than 40 states. But it is threatened by the opposition of the Social Security Board, which has included abolition of experience rating as one of the objectives in its proposal to nationalize the unemployment compensation program.

A major objective of the federal Social Security Act was to induce the separate states to enact employment security legislation; this end was to be attained by removing or at least reducing the fear of interstate competition. Competitive costs to employers were equalized by the imposition of a uniform federal tax, against which a state unemployment compensation tax could be credited up to 90 per cent of the federal levy. This law did prove effective in inducing state legislation, but the state laws and their objectives were far from uniform. Some states put the emphasis on the relief of unemployment; others were more interested in prevention; and still others attempted a combination of the two interests.

In the experience-rating states, employers may qualify for reduced taxes, within a considerable range from minimum to maximum, if they regularize their employment. In some states no tax at all is levied on stable companies, while unstable companies may pay as high as 4 per cent on their pay rolls. By the differential tax, the employer is given an incentive to keep men on the pay roll. The federal law does not provide for differentiation directly, since that is left for the states, but Secs. 1601 and 1602 of the Federal Unemployment Tax Act do provide for methods of computing the tax offset which enables employers to contribute to state funds at varying pay roll tax rates. Under these sections, the employer must pay to the federal government its 10 per cent of the full federal pay roll tax but may contribute to state unemployment funds at rates that fall below the other 90 per cent of the federal tax.

Incentive Taxation

Experience Rating in Unemployment Compensation

Objectives. Experience rating undertakes to allocate the cost of unemployment compensation in some degree, according to the unemployment records of industries and firms. This is based upon the propositions: (1) that unemployment can, to some extent, be prevented by management and that it is desirable to offer an incentive for such prevention; and (2) that regardless of the extent to which unemployment can be prevented, it is desirable to assess a portion of the cost on the specific firms and industries where it is incurred and to whom it can rationally be apportioned.

Prevention of Unemployment. As noted above, experience rating has long been applied in workmen's compensation, where it has played a substantial role in reducing industrial accidents and occupational diseases. Under workmen's compensation laws, pay roll premium rates frequently vary from 5 or 6 cents per $100 of pay roll for clerical work up to $30 to $40 for extremely hazardous occupations.[1] It may be conceded that unemployment is less within the power of business management than accidents, but management is far from being a negligible factor in either instance. In the case of unemployment, business executives can be particularly effective in reducing seasonal layoffs. It is quite appropriate, too, that management, as the risk-taker for society, should assume some responsibility for the regular maintenance of its own labor supply. If management is expected to pay its employees a dismissal wage, it can at least be allowed the privilege of using its ingenuity to reduce this social cost.

An argument against the use of a prevention incentive in unemployment compensation is that any tax differentiation which might be involved would be too small to affect the decisions of management materially.[2] It must be conceded

---

[1] Emerson P. Schmidt, "Incentive Taxation with Special Reference to Unemployment," *National Tax Association Proceedings*, 1941, p. 471.

[2] Moreover, it is thought that unemployment is chiefly the result of faulty

that the incentives offered by experience rating are minor compared to total pay roll or to overhead expenses that already provide motivation to maintain production and employment. But the effect of an additional consideration on the balance between regular and irregular production may have more weight than is apparent. Moreover, the psychological effect of an outside stimulus of this sort may be quite significant.

The management techniques open to progressive employers who desire to regularize employment have been enumerated as follows:[1]

1. Careful market analysis to provide workable estimates of demand and to lay the basis for improved production technique.

2. Reasonable diversification of output to fit new products into seasonal or predictable slack periods.

3. Simplification of the product and standardization of parts so as to permit production for stock.

4. Promotion of more regular consumption of products unduly subject to seasonal demand.

5. Careful planning of work, involving postponement of some work and advance completion of other work, to reduce fluctuations to a minimum.

6. Mechanical and chemical research to make possible off-season work.

7. Anticipation of technological changes to reduce labor separations to a minimum.

8. Training of workers for versatility and flexibility to permit transfer among jobs as different departments experience their ups and downs.

---

economic institutions and that amelioration should be a social rather than an employer's cost. See Walter A. Morton, "The Aims of Unemployment Insurance with Special Reference to the Wisconsin Act," *American Economic Review*, Vol XXIII (September, 1933), pp. 395–412.

[1] H. Feldman and D. M. Smith, "The Case for Experience Rating in Unemployment Compensation and a Proposed Method," Industrial Relations Counselors, Inc., New York, 1939, pp. 5–6.

Incentive Taxation

9. Varying of hours within reasonable limits to maintain a more constant force even though output varies.

10. Combining with other employers to dovetail requirements.

No useful purpose would be afforded by citing the considerable evidence[1] submitted by employers themselves of the influence of regularization incentives on management policies. Suffice it to say that the evidence far from confirms the view that the preventive power of experience rating is negligible.

It may be argued that pay roll taxes are shiftable and that, consequently, they are ineffectual as a penalty on irregularity or as a reward for regularity of employment. But a differential advantage obtained as a result of favorable merit rating is likely to be retained by the employer. Most competition consists of efforts to reduce costs below those of competitors and thus to get more business by underselling them in the market or more profit while selling at the same price. The differentials of merit rating fit quite nicely into this pattern.

Proper Allocation of Costs. The contention that costs of unemployment should in some degree follow their source rests upon the idea that goods should compete with each other on the basis of their true costs, including such social costs as can be allocated rationally. How can consumers know whether coal or oil is really the lower cost fuel if the cost of maintaining idle coal miners is paid in part by the oil refiners? Just as the consumer regularly pays for a certain number of unavoidable production accidents when he buys an automobile or a chair, so also he should pay for a certain amount of seasonality or other irregularity in the employment of labor. Decisions regarding technological improvements are made more intelligently if the social cost of these changes is considered. A business man's decision to introduce a new machine may be reversed, and properly, by the obligation

[1] Schmidt, *op. cit.*, pp. 464–477.

to take some account of the social costs involved. There is support for the view that unemployment ought to be regarded as a social overhead expense supported by taxes based on ability to pay. But there is plenty of room for the application of the ability-to-pay principle after all the costs that can be apportioned upon some rational basis are so apportioned. "To the degree that responsibility can be allocated, a burden is removed from the employees and the community. They will probably have burden enough left in caring for unemployment which cannot be allocated and which must be carried as a social overhead."[1]

Some Arguments against Experience Rating. Experience rating is criticized on the ground that the burden of differential taxes is in inverse ratio to ability to pay. This would be particularly unfortunate for declining industries, which would always be paying the full assessment simply because they were on the decline. To this the rejoinder is made that even declining industries should pay such costs as are fairly apportionable to them. No one would advocate that successful concerns should meet part or all of the wage costs of the firms that are unsuccessful.

As to the cyclical effects of unemployment compensation on the individual firm, it is also pointed out that substantial rate reductions might be granted in prosperity periods when the tax burden could easily be shifted to the consumer, whereas rate increases might be imposed in times of depression when adjustment of costs to falling prices would be imperative.[2] Thus, impetus to the downward phase of the cycle might be given by the mechanism of experience rating. This objection has some validity. However, there is nothing inherent in experience rating that makes it unadaptable to the requirements of business-cycle fiscal policy. By using a longer period

---

[1] H. M. Groves and Elizabeth Brandeis, "Wisconsin Unemployment Reserves Act," *American Economic Review*, Vol. XXIV (March, 1934), p. 43.

[2] K. Pribram, "Employment Stabilization through Payroll Taxation," *Quarterly Journal of Economics*, Vol. LVII (November, 1942), p. 150

Incentive Taxation

than one year as the basis for "experience" (most states now use 3 years) or by measuring the adequacy of reserves in terms of present pay roll, the cyclical effects of merit rating are subject to control. Undoubtedly much remains to be learned about this phase of the merit-rating problem, but the task is not so hopelessly difficult as some critics have contended.

It is argued that experience rating is ill adapted for postwar application because it discourages expansion by making employers loath to employ more men and thus increase their liability to unemployment compensation. This may have some validity, but it rests on the assumption that the employer should be spared a risk which is fairly attributable to his undertaking and which he has some power to minimize. The alternative is to assess the costs of unemployment without any regard to where these costs arise. The demoralization resulting from this pooling process would, in the opinion of most industrialists, prove much more of a dampener to enterprise and its expansion than the apportionment of costs by experience rating.

State unemployment compensation provisions need to be liberalized in many respects, as they may prove grossly inadequate to meet the needs of postwar reconversion. This is true in spite of the fact that the states have made substantial progress in improving their programs in the short time they have had for such improvement. Adequacy of funds is not the major problem, though added assurance of solvency might well be provided through the implementation and continuance of the federal loan fund recently authorized by Congress. As in the case of social security generally, coverage needs to be broadened and the program needs strengthening at many points. It appears that states have, in some instances, unduly restricted the qualifications establishing eligibility of employees to benefits.[1] It is unfortunate that the system is so immature

[1] See Ewan Clague and Ruth Reticker, "Trends in Disqualification from Benefits under State Unemployment Compensation Laws," *Social Security Bulletin*, January, 1944, Vol. 7, pp. 12–23.

at a time when it is likely to be subject to a heavy strain. But this does not create a conclusive case for abandoning its fundamental principles. Long-run objectives and the effect of the system on the individual should not be overlooked in a hot political scramble for higher benefits now.

Two Philosophies of Social Security. It is true that experience rating and state unemployment compensation systems stand in the way of a comprehensive national system of social security, supported through one big fund fed by a single system of taxes. Two rival philosophies of social insurance are now bidding for public favor. The one explained above in relation to unemployment compensation might be called the functional approach. The other approach might be termed distributional. The first puts great emphasis upon a setup that would encourage the effective functioning of the economic system; the second largely ignores these considerations and emphasizes minimum standards of living as its objective. The functional system would proceed pragmatically and with diverse procedures for different hazards (such as unemployment and old age); the distributional system gives great weight to the alleged necessity of a single logical plan of procedure.

The distributional approach to social security was given impetus by the Beveridge Plan in Great Britain. "Abolition of want" was declared to be the aim of the plan and this was to be accomplished by a redistribution of income through social insurance and children's allowances (the latter to supplement the earnings of employed workers).[1] A unified and uniform scheme was outlined. Benefits were to vary only with the size of family and status of age and sex. They were to be unlimited in duration. Costs were to be distributed as widely as possible; half the support was to come from general taxes and half from employer and employee contributions. Rates of contribution were to be uniform (except for factors

[1] Sir William Beveridge, *Social Insurance and Allied Services* ("The Beveridge Report"), American ed., The Macmillan Company, New York, 1942, pp. 7, 8.

Incentive Taxation

of age and sex), with no variations for the size of employees' earnings or for differences in industrial risk. A single payment was to cover all the social security obligation of the contributor. Even "workmen's compensation" for accidents was merged in the single program.

The Beveridge Plan thus aimed at a social security system achieved by cooperation between the state and the individual. Cooperation with industry was scarcely mentioned, and the implication was that industry and social security have no responsibilities toward each other. It has been suggested that the plan views social security "as the outgrowth or modern counterpart of the Elizabethan poor law, better administered and far more humane, but equally divorced from the going economic system."[1] The plan is laudable in its aim at a wide coverage and high standards of social security but, particularly for our own country with its widely varying conditions, a more pragmatic approach with more regard for incentives seems preferable.

Conclusion. The experience-rating feature of pay roll taxes levied for unemployment compensation provides a desirable incentive for stabilization of employment. It is also a desirable means of distributing a social cost in a manner most conducive to the effective functioning of the economic system. It should not be eliminated by either state or federal action.

CONCLUSION

In general, incentive taxation "gadgets" are not very promising means to achieve the goals of greater employment, production, investment, and consumption. Most of these schemes involve hazards of deliberate discrimination among economic factors or units; they often offer favors to one desirable activity at the expense of another; they do not go to the root of economic ills; and they ignore the necessity of a favor-

[1] Elizabeth Brandeis, "What Road Is Forward in Social Security?" *Problems of the Postwar World*, a symposium edited by Thomas C. T. McCormick, McGraw-Hill Book Company, Inc., 1945, pp 49–84 at p. 60.

able climate for business activity. Some of the incentive taxation proposals would fail to accomplish their ends and others, such as the tax on hoarding, would probably do much more harm than good. On the other hand, as previously stated, the use of accelerated depreciation as a stimulant and special treatment for the reinvested earnings of new small businesses seem measures well worth trying. The functional approach to taxation, which calls for the selection of taxes according to their incidence and the sensitivity of tax bases, has provided some sound tax doctrine in support of income taxes, death taxes, and land taxes. Experience rating in unemployment compensation provides a sound incentive for regularizing employment and a desirable basis for distributing part of the necessary costs of unemployment.

XII. STATE AND LOCAL TAXES AND THEIR BEARING ON PRODUCTION

INTRODUCTION

THUS far our attention has been confined largely to the federal tax system. State and local tax systems are also of great importance and they, too, affect production and employment. Except during war periods, state and local taxes have always occupied a predominant place in total governmental revenues in the United States. This was true even during the thirties, although federal revenues gained relatively in that period. In 1939, over 60 per cent of all taxes collected were levies by state and local governments. The United States is the only major country in which state and local finance has normally occupied such an important position. Although this predominance will surely not continue, the financial systems of these units will still hold an important place in the fiscal program of the nation.

Modifications in state and local taxation have been occurring for many years; but, under the extraordinary pressures of the depression in the thirties, the pace was so accelerated that the changes have been frequently described as revolutionary. Although the property tax continues to be the overwhelmingly important and sometimes the almost sole support for local governments, it is no longer the principal means of state support, and some states have discarded it entirely. Motor-vehicle taxes, state income taxes (two-thirds of the states), business taxes (under a great variety of names and formulas), special excises (particularly on liquor and tobacco), and general sales taxes (half the states), all scored important gains during the thirties.

Through both shared taxes and state aids, the states have

assumed a growing responsibility for local fiscal requirements. These transfers have resulted in some reductions of local property-tax burdens, particularly in rural areas. Cities have received relatively less support and, because of this fact and the development of new responsibilities (particularly for welfare), city property-tax rates have tended to rise rather than fall. Municipalities have sought new sources of revenue either in grants from the state and federal governments or in authorization to tax their own resources with new types of levies. A few, such as New York with its municipal sales tax and Philadelphia with its earned-income tax, have been successful in broadening their tax bases.

Property-tax curbs of one sort or another—tax-limitation statutes, constitutional amendments, homestead exemptions —made considerable headway during the thirties. Tax delinquency and resentment of high fixed charges upon farmer, homeowner, and business man, combined with the vigorous attacks of real-estate associations, precipitated what might be described as a general rebellion against the property tax. Following the curbs, many states hastened to adopt the general sales tax.

In contrast to what occurred at state and municipal levels during the twenties and at the federal level during the thirties, state and local indebtedness ceased to expand during the thirties and even showed some contraction. Local finances recouped substantially during the war; revenues flowed abundantly and there was a moderate amount of debt retirement and other forms of surplus financing.

Table XXVII presents a quantitative picture of state and local revenue sources in 1941.

Those who contend that important values are at stake in the preservation of decentralized initiative must view with some concern the propensity of government functions to gravitate to Washington. Obviously, not all functions can be managed effectively at the state and local levels. For example, the states are in no position to attack the business-

State and Local Taxes

TABLE XXVII
PERCENTAGE DISTRIBUTION OF STATE, LOCAL, AND TERRITORIAL REVENUES
(The revenue sources are of total revenues of each type of government)

Source	State	Local	Territorial
Total revenue	100.0	100 0	100.0
I. Nontax revenue	9 3	12 3	10.6
II. Tax revenue	90 7	87 7	89 4
A. Net income and death transfers	11 0	0.1	8 7
Individual incomes	4.7	. . .	2.9
Corporate income	3 8	...	5 3
Inheritance, estate, and gift	2.5	..	0 5
B. Property	5 0	80.4	17 6
C. Specific business	10 5	3 4	13 7
Corporation and public utilities	4 4	0.8	0 5
Alcoholic beverages	1 2	0.7	0 2
Insurance	2 1		
Severance and others	2 8	1.9	13 0
D. Sales, customs, and gross income	36 7	2 0	39 9
Customs	..		7.9
General sales	11 4	1 3	0 9
Alcoholic beverages	4 3		5 1
Tobacco	2 2	.	2 5
Motor-vehicle fuel	18 4	0 1	2 1
Miscellaneous excises	0 4	0 6	21 4
E. Pay roll	18 2	0 1	1.9
F. Other taxes	9 3	1 7	7 6
Motor-vehicle license	8 4	0 5	0 4
Licenses offsetting services	0 7	0 9	1 8
Poll and miscellaneous	0 2	0 3	5 4

SOURCE: Adapted from U S. Department of Commerce, Bureau of Census, *Financing Federal, State, and Local Governments* 1941, Special Study No 20, Final, September, 1942, Table 7, p 28

cycle problem. But a presumption in favor of state and local retention of authority may nevertheless be recognized.

CRITICISMS OF STATE AND LOCAL TAX SYSTEMS AS THEY AFFECT ECONOMIC PROGRESS

State and local tax systems are widely criticized as interfering with economic progress. More specifically, they are criticized because they are (1) irresponsive to federal fiscal policy, (2) regressive, and (3) repressive. Regressivity impedes economic progress by curtailing markets. Repressivity results from diversity and confusion in state business taxes and from their overlapping with each other and with federal levies.

Irresponsiveness to Federal Fiscal Policy

It is said that whatever strategy the federal government may employ to counteract business instability, the effects are likely to be nullified, in some degree at least, through opposite action by the states and municipalities. If the federal government reduces its taxation during a depression, state and local governments are likely to increase their levies; if the federal government enlarges its expenditures at such times, states and municipalities will curtail their outlays; and, if the federal government enlarges its debt in the hope of stimulating employment, states and municipalities will start reducing their indebtedness.

Some of this is the inevitable result of the fact that monetary powers are confined to the federal government and that states and municipalities are not free to follow countercycle fiscal policy. To some extent the federal government has, can, and will come to the aid of the states in emergency periods through subventions and direct assumption of responsibility for the alleviation of unemployment. To some extent the states and municipalities can cooperate with federal fiscal policy and will do so as they are made increasingly aware of their part in federal programs. Beyond this, state and municipal fiscal systems can be made somewhat more flexible by recasting tax and debt limitations and by improving techniques of surplus (reserve) financing.

Many states have little or no constitutional power to borrow, and municipalities are usually limited by statutes providing that indebtedness may not exceed a certain ratio to the property-tax base (assessed value of property). These municipal debt limitations are often ineffective and not accurately related to local resources or to the purposes of

State and Local Taxes

borrowing. A percentage of assessed value takes no account of ratios of assessed to true values or of other revenues the local unit may receive. A ratio of debt to average total revenue would be more appropriate. There is no good reason, either, why debt limits related to general resources should bar borrowing for a self-liquidating project.

Regressivity

It is alleged that state and local taxes are predominantly regressive and that they thus unduly restrict markets. A glance at Table XXVII will convince the reader that state income and inheritance taxes are comparatively minor revenue sources. The property tax is regressive because it is mainly a tax on shelter, for which relatively poor persons spend a larger proportion of their incomes than do the rich. Property taxes are supplemented mainly by sales taxes, which are at least equally regressive.

It cannot be assumed that regressive taxes are always deflationary. If these taxes take purchasing power from the stream, they return it to the same stream and quite possibly to persons no less likely to spend it. Of course, it can be argued that income and inheritance taxes would definitely improve the distribution of purchasing power whereas the regressive taxes would, at best, be neutral.

Income- and death-tax revenues could be given a larger role in state finance through one of two courses: (1) collection of the taxes by the federal government with distribution to the states, and (2) development of state income and death taxes independently levied. The first will be discussed in the next section. The second may now be considered.

The development of state income taxes encounters the following difficulties: (1) constitutional barriers, (2) the fairly thorough federal exploitation of the field, and (3) instability and insufficiency of revenue from this source, especially in poor and agricultural states.

Postwar Taxation and Economic Progress

Two possibilities for the enlargement of state and local income tax revenues are worth further exploration. The first is the development of state and local supplements to taxes centrally levied and collected. These taxes would be administered by the federal government or the states with the proviso that the states or municipalities might add to the rates. Additional revenue thus provided would be collected by the central government and returned to state or city, as the case might be, minus the apportioned cost of administration. An interim committee in Michigan recently recommended that Michigan municipalities be allowed to levy an addition of 0.5 per cent to state sales-tax rates. As applied to the income tax, this procedure might augment problems of jurisdiction and multiple taxation; but it would provide uniformity and simplicity of administration and it would bring within the scope of local tax systems a tax based on income above subsistence.

The second possibility is a new kind of income tax, independently levied. This might follow the model (with some modifications) of the present municipal income tax of Philadelphia: flat or conservatively graduated rate, deductions confined to expenses involved in creating the income, and no exemptions. This tax would have many advantages over the property tax, sales tax, or gross-income tax. It would less likely be passed on to the consumer than any of these alternatives. It would not be regressive, as are these alternatives; it would be a genuinely proportional tax. It would not charge the family man more than the single man. If applied at the municipal level and if assessed where income is earned, it would (unlike the property tax) collect substantial sums from those who work in the city but reside in the suburbs.

As compared with the more conventional net-income tax, the suggested type of levy would not be progressive, but it would produce more and steadier revenue. In a typical city, the tax at a 1 per cent rate could yield, perhaps, as much as 5 mills on the property-tax base (full value). It would not

State and Local Taxes

overlap the existing federal levy as seriously as does the conventional type of income tax.

Repressiveness

The third alleged adverse effect of state and local taxation on economic progress is the confusion resulting from diverse and overlapping taxes. The diversity is found especially in business taxation, which involves various types of levies—notably, capital stock, corporate excess, corporate income, and license fees. The overlapping includes not only that of federal with state tax systems but also the conflict of one state system with another. Territorial multiple taxation is a problem of large and growing proportions. Interstate business must be carved into artificial parts for state taxation, and frequently the whole and the sum of all its parts are not equal.

Looking toward simplification and economy in business taxation, the Royal Commission on Dominion-Provincial Relations in 1941 recommended federal collection, state sharing. The case for such action was stated as follows:[1]

> The present complexity [in business taxation] is beyond belief. The most important item is the corporation income tax, levied by the Dominion and most of the Provincial Governments. There are, in addition, taxes levied by one or more governments, on various bases such as capital stock, number of business places, gross revenue, physical volume of output, period of operation, mileage of tract or wire, mileage operated, note circulation, insurance premiums, investments, volume of deposits. . . They [these taxes] have grown up in a completely unplanned and uncoordinated way, and violate every canon of sound taxation.
>
> . . . As a result [of the uncoordinated system] investments in the same forms of business are taxed at different rates in the same Province; investments in the same kind of business are taxed at different rates in different Provinces; investments in business operating on a national scale are double or triple-taxed with no relation to earning power; certain forms of business can be and are

[1] *Report of the Royal Commission on Dominion-Provincial Relations*, Book II, p. 113.

singled out for discriminatory taxation; tax compliance costs are uselessly and unreasonably increased And again, it should be added that the same amount of revenue could be secured without imposing any of these discriminatory and inequitable burdens.

The business-tax situation in Canada in 1941 was not unlike our own at present. The Canadian report recommended a national system of business taxation and "national adjustment grants" to finance, partly, certain provincial expenses. Although the report has not been accepted as a program of action by the Canadian government, the income tax (personal and corporate) has been nationalized for the war period.

Coordination of federal and state business taxes to most people means federal collection, state sharing. The federal government might collect business taxes and distribute certain proportions to the states on condition that the states abstain from capital stock, gross income, corporate net income, insurance, and other business taxes.

This program sounds simple but it is replete with complications. It involves a separation of business taxes from property taxes, and these two are very substantially integrated at the state level. It encounters a difficult problem in federal apportionment to the states. Apportionment might be determined on the basis of origin, but there is no clear rule defining the origin of business. Actually, inauguration of such a program would probably create a demand for an equalization factor in the distribution system. This would be on the theory that state needs should be given weight in federal distribution. Once an objective standard were departed from, the apportionment formula could easily become a political football. A formula taking no account of state needs and disposition to spend might provide some states with excessive funds and leave others with acute revenue problems. It would be easy to waste more money through maldistribution of centrally collected funds than could be saved by eliminating overlapping taxes. Moreover, an issue of state independence and self-reliance is involved in federal

State and Local Taxes

collection, state sharing. Under this system, the federal government has discretion over the revenues of the divisions except for the expenditure of the funds. This subordinate status is one with which municipalities are familiar in their relations to the states, but there is no similar tradition in federal-state relations.[1]

Both aids and shared taxes involve a circuitous routing of revenue from the division to the central unit and return. In the course of this procedure, some loss occurs, much diversion takes place, and self-reliance suffers. Possibly aids should be confined to equalization—*i.e.*, to ensuring minimum services of government to underprivileged areas. And the wisdom of a highly developed system of shared taxes is at least equally dubious.

Valid and impressive as are the objections to federal collection, state sharing of business taxes, they must be weighed against the repression, confusion, unfair competition, and high compliance costs attending the present system. Unfortunately, we have no adequate picture of the handicap to business which these items represent.[2] It seems unlikely that the present system of state business taxation involves such impediments to business that a system of federal collection, state sharing, with its great hazards and objections, would be justified as a substitute. But the balance of advantage is not so uneven as to suggest that the issue be closed.

---

[1] Experience with federal collection, state sharing in Germany, under the Weimar Constitution, was none too happy. "The shared taxes led to state and local extravagance in the few years of prosperity in which they were being distributed, and in the time of depression they brought maldistribution of funds, since the neediest districts in general received the least. Constant revision was found necessary in order to keep the system functioning at all." (*Federal, State and Local Government Fiscal Relations*, p 158.)

[2] Concerning compliance costs, see Robert Murray Haig, "The Cost to Business Concerns of Compliance with Tax Laws," *The Management Review*, Vol. 24 (November, 1935), pp. 323-333; James W. Martin, "Costs of Tax Administration. Examples of Compliance Expenses," *Bulletin of the National Tax Association*, April, 1944, pp. 194-205, also "Costs of Tax Administration: Statistics of Public Expenses," No. 5, February, 1944.

Postwar Taxation and Economic Progress

Of course, progress toward a more coordinated federal-state tax system is not limited to the development of federal collection, state sharing. The foundation for such progress could be laid were the federal government to devise a rational system of business taxation for itself. The states could contribute by eliminating needless and fortuitous diversities in their tax systems. State income taxes should evolve toward a status where they are supplements to the federal tax, with single reporting and administration and with common rules and definitions. Development of a tradition of cooperation between the federal government and the states could lead to an attack on the multiple taxation problem that might achieve important results without coercion and without increased centralization. A federal-state agency might be helpful in attaining these results.[1]

Competition among states for the domicile of corporations has important consequences both for regulation of the corporate institution and for taxation. In regard to the latter, competition results because of the accepted legal rule that a state incorporating a company can tax all of its capital stock, irrespective of where its property may be located or where its business may be transacted. The location of a company's factory usually depends upon markets, labor supply, and sources of raw material. Even the head office, though less restricted as to location, is oriented to a large degree by economic factors. In contrast, a company's domicile is one of its most fluid elements and is likely to be determined by political rather than economic factors.

Evidence indicates that about 29 per cent of American corporations reporting to the Securities and Exchange Commission have their domiciles in Delaware and that, in recent years, from 35 to 53 per cent of new companies have taken out their charters in that state.[2] Although the *listed* corporations

---

[1] *Federal, State and Local Government Fiscal Relations*, pp. 5–8.

[2] Securities and Exchange Commission, *Statistics of American Listed Corporations*, Part 1, *Summary Report*, 1940, pp. 25–26.

State and Local Taxes

as a sample do not represent the corporate universe, the figures are indicative of the tendency of certain corporations to choose a favorable domicile.

Both because the states lack the perspective to regulate interstate corporations effectively and because the present system gives unfair tax prerogatives, it is recommended that the federal government assume the exclusive right to charter companies doing an interstate business. This would involve some shock to business in the transition period, but it would also be to the ultimate best interest of business. As usually happens in a change of this kind, vested interests would be involved and it might be necessary to compensate some states, such as Delaware, for the loss of even an unwarranted privilege. It is true that the Securities and Exchange Commission, with its regulatory powers over some business operations, makes federal incorporation less essential. But even on the score of regulations, federal incorporation could still play a useful role. The recent broadening of the legal definition of interstate commerce makes a step of this sort more significant. In general, the transfer of public functions from the states to Washington may have been overdone, but here is one instance where the case for centralization is overwhelming.

SELECTION OF A STATE BUSINESS TAX

Alternative forms of business taxation were discussed in Chap. V, and it was concluded that the corporate net-income tax is the happiest choice. The argument applied largely to the federal situation; conditions at the state level present many differences. However, these differences do not appear to justify a change in the conclusion. The outstanding fact is that a cost tax on business is ultimately borne largely by the consumer and, if the objective is to tax consumption, it can be done most simply and directly through a retail sales tax.

State business taxes, other than the corporate net-income

Postwar Taxation and Economic Progress

TABLE XXVIII[a]
STATE GENERAL CORPORATION TAXES
(January 1, 1944)

State	Net income	Capital stock	Corporate excess	Other
Alabama	X	X	X	
Arizona	X			
Arkansas	X	X		
California	X			
Colorado	X	X		
Connecticut	X			
Delaware		X		
Florida		X		
Georgia	X	X		
Idaho	X	X		
Illinois		X	X	
Indiana			X[a]	X[b]
Iowa	X			
Kansas	X	X	X	
Kentucky	X	X		
Louisiana	X	X		
Maine		X		
Maryland	X	X		
Massachusetts	X		X	
Michigan		X		
Minnesota	X			
Mississippi	X	X		
Missouri	X	X		
Montana	X[b]			
Nebraska		X	X	
New Hampshire		X		
New Jersey		X		
New Mexico	X	X		
New York	X	X[c]		
North Carolina	X	X		
North Dakota	X			
Ohio		X		
Oklahoma	X	X		
Oregon	X	X		
Pennsylvania	X	X		X[d]
Rhode Island		X[e]	X	
South Carolina	X	X		
Tennessee	X	X	X	X[f]
Texas		X		
Utah	X			
Vermont	X	X		
Virginia	X	X		
Washington		X		
West Virginia		X		
Wisconsin	X			
Wyoming		X		

[a] Prepared by the Tax Foundation
[b] Special additional 3 per cent tax on net income in final business year
[c] New York's capital stock tax is a minimum tax subordinate to the corporation net-income tax
[d] Corporate borrowing tax
[e] Rhode Island's capital-stock tax is a minimum tax subordinate to the corporate excess tax
[f] Gross-receipts tax
[g] Although the provisions for the taxation of corporate excess on domestic manufacturing, mining and road companies have not been repealed, this tax has been largely obsolete since 1920. Many of its provisions have been expressly or impliedly repealed by the act taxing intangibles

SOURCE: U.S. Treasury Department, Division of Tax Research, revised to date from Tax Systems

State and Local Taxes

tax, are all open to strong objections. A capital stock tax based on par value of stock, as most such taxes are, is so arbitrary and fortuitous that it hardly warrants a place in an intelligent revenue system. Corporate excess taxes[1] involve great administrative difficulties. The gross-income tax is objectionable because it involves duplication. If a "cost" tax is desired, probably "value added" would be the best base. But as previously stated, the consumer can be taxed more simply and directly through the retail sales tax.

The confusion of state business taxes is so great and the basis of levies in many cases so arbitrary that almost any logical procedure would be an improvement on present practices One such procedure, involving a multiple and alternative tax base (including net, gross, and a minimum tax) has been explained in Chap. V. It is open to some objections but far less than the present practices of many states.

Present application of major business taxes by states is presented in Table XXVIII.[2]

---

[1] Taxes usually partly or entirely integrated with property taxes, and based upon the difference between the total value of a corporate business and its tangible assets

[2] Space does not permit an elaborate description of business taxes as used by states The corporate excess tax is an adaptation of the levy on property, based on the difference between the capital value of corporations, as measured by par or market value of their capital stock (and, in some cases, bonds) and the actual or assessed value of their real and personal property for tax purposes. The original method of assessment by local officials has lost ground in favor of assessment by state officials If the corporate excess tax is levied on domestic corporations as a franchise tax on the privilege of doing business, then, in fairness, a supplementary privilege tax should be applied to foreign corporations. This is the rule in Massachusetts, Rhode Island, and Tennessee, but not in Illinois and several other states Although the corporate excess tax applies only to the intangible value of corporations whereas the capital stock tax applies also to tangibles, the two levies tap much the same value; and the use of both levies, as in Alabama and Tennessee, is difficult to justify.

In some states, particularly in the South, a great variety of special charges are imposed upon business. The outstanding characteristic of these occupation "taxes" is their arbitrariness To the outsider, it appears that the legislature simply procured a classified advertisement section of a telephone directory and assessed each occupational group an arbitrary amount—for instance, $50

Postwar Taxation and Economic Progress

TREATMENT OF DIVIDENDS UNDER STATE
PERSONAL-INCOME TAXES

The wide variation of procedures applied in state tax systems to integrate corporate and personal taxes is illustrated in the treatment of dividends. Although some changes have been made as a result of war conditions, a summary of this situation, as of 1941, will suffice for illustrative purposes:[1]

The treatment of cash dividends is . . . varied, ranging from exemption—which may take the form of an exclusion, a deduction, or a credit—to additional taxation. With minor qualifications, eight States exclude dividends from individual gross income to the extent that they are paid out of the income of corporations already taxed by them. Three States, Iowa, Missouri, and South Dakota,[2] aim at a similar but more equitable result by allowing a credit equal to the amount of the corporation tax on dividends paid out of taxed corporate income. Since the first two apply a flat rate to corporate income, they state the credit in terms of that rate. Four states, Alabama, Arizona, Idaho, and Wisconsin, employ the so-called "50–50 rule," whereby such dividends as are derived from corporations earning more than 50 per cent of their income in the taxing State are entirely deducted from the income of the individual taxpayer. Seventeen States, including three that do not impose a corporation tax, tax dividends fully, like other income. With the exception of Vermont, all States levying both personal income taxes and corporation franchise taxes measured by net income, as distinct from direct income taxes on corporations, fall into this group. Finally, two States, Colorado and Oregon, impose surtaxes on dividends, in

---

for advertising agencies, $70 for automobile body builders, etc Some states have hundreds of such levies.

The following states might be mentioned as examples of specific business tax systems: Wisconsin relies almost exclusively on the corporate net-income tax; Massachusetts features the corporate excess tax; Indiana employs a very broad gross-income tax; and Delaware depends upon a capital stock (franchise) tax. The latter state applies its tax to reach assets employed outside the state. Thus it is said that Delaware receives a grant-in-aid from other states in direct proportion to the distribution of shares of Delaware corporations in each state

[1] *Federal, State and Local Government Fiscal Relations*, pp 421, 422.

[2] The South Dakota statute was repealed in 1943; Chap. 295 Session Laws of South Dakota, 1943.

State and Local Taxes

addition to including them in full, like other income, under the regular income tax.

. The varying treatment of dividends in the State income-tax statutes may be associated with corresponding conceptions of the relation between corporation and individual income taxes.

Here we find described an elaborate diversity of practices, complicated enough to satisfy the most extravagant taste of those who believe that the states are desirable laboratories for experimentation with different legislative procedures. On the merits, the interest in universality in the application of the personal-income tax argues strongly against the exemption of dividends from this tax base. A credit to domestic stockholders for corporate taxes paid on dividends distributed is in accord with the view of corporate income taken here. A state in which an absentee-owned corporation operates is still allowed an opportunity to tax income earned in the state but distributed outside its borders. Unless a credit is also provided for stockholders not residing in the state, an element of double taxation will occur. Moreover, the credit applied only in the state where the corporation operates may favor home-owned over foreign-owned corporations. This is not desirable but, in the absence of a further allowance of credits by the domiciliary states or of some other division of the tax base, it can be avoided only by general double taxation of corporate income and dividends. The credit system is clearly preferable, but double taxation at relatively low rates is not intolerable and may be better than doubling up in the case of foreign holdings only. An agreement between states providing an equal division of taxes, based on income earned in one state and received in another, is the ideal solution of this problem. This would be difficult to arrange but well worth the attempt.

MIGRATION OF BUSINESS TO ESCAPE TAXES: SPECIAL INDUCEMENTS TO LOCATE

One of the great historical achievements of our federal system is the high degree of freedom it allows for interstate migration and commerce. If a person or a business does not like the climate in California, he or it is perfectly free to try Wisconsin! This freedom is advantageous both for its own sake and for economic efficiency. However, when a high degree of freedom is combined with a high degree of fluidity, it becomes difficult for state and local tax systems to operate. Special inducements for locating in a particular center, ranging from slight favoritism in property-tax administration to direct money gifts or "bribes," are likely to appear in the tax system. Although there might be some justification in a judicious use of the tax system for such purposes, the inducement programs in practice are about 99 per cent abuse and waste.

The facts regarding special inducements and migration may be summarized as follows:

1. Tax inducements occur principally in property-tax concessions to new business by local governments. The states set the tone of this competition by authorizing or even compelling such concessions. Sometimes, however, concessions are made in defiance of state rules.

2. More positive inducements are gifts in the form of money, buildings, moving expenses, and the like. These, too, are usually authorized by the state. Advertising is also used but this is a form of verbal persuasion rather than material inducement.

3. State tax systems are adapted (sometimes unconsciously) to take account of migration.

4. Open inducements to encourage business location are most commonly found in the South and in New England, but covert inducements are quite common throughout the country.

5. Cities with populations under 10,000 are especially prone to offer inducements, and the shoe, textile, and garment industries have been especially prone to bid for them. These industries are less fixed than most others by materials

and markets and are oriented in large degree by considerations of cheap rent and labor.

· 6. Inducements are not confined to the relocation of old industries but apply also to new industries and branch factories of old companies.

7. Territorial bidding for industries is no new phenomenon; it was prevalent even during the colonial era of this country and it has long been a matter of concern in Great Britain.

8. Studies of industry migration to escape taxation tend to minimize the phenomenon, but these studies deal with averages and general situations. For a specific company in a specific city, a tax incentive added to other reasonably attractive conditions may be very effective. Certainly many city fathers think so.

9. Undoubtedly, tax inducements were stimulated by the depression and by the necessity for larger relief expenditures as the alternative to industrial promotion. This problem will be considerably mitigated if the postwar period is one of abundant opportunity.

10. Not much conclusive evidence is available as to the ultimate success of industrial promotion through tax and other inducements. The records show many specific examples of industries that have failed to make good on promises of employment (given in consideration of tax concessions).

The whole story of inducements is an excellent exhibit of the use of tax immunities and subsidies for industrial promotion. If such a program were planned and executed with sufficient discrimination and restraint, it might conceivably be defensible. It would be similar in objective to the application of tariffs for infant industries. Some outside help would be given a new industry to counteract its handicap in competition with older and more established firms.

Actually, the inducement feature is far more likely to prove a curse than a blessing. Inducements lose their effectiveness when all competing cities offer them. They must be paid for by other taxpayers in the community—perhaps even to some extent by the competitors of the favored industries. In programs of this kind, the social interest becomes interwoven with private interests and the two cannot be disentangled. An industry coddled in its infancy may not show much propensity to stand on its own feet when it is full grown. Industries should locate, migrate, succeed, and fail as a result of their adjustment to economic factors, and the fewer political factors brought into the picture, the better. If new industries need assistance through the tax system, the federal government is in the best position to supply such assistance.

It is probably not possible to persuade all communities and all businesses that their long-run interests would best be served by foregoing immunities and other favors. Many are already convinced of this fact, however, and some others can be influenced by sufficiently clear reiteration of where tax-inducement programs lead.

Probably the most constructive way in which a community can promote its own economic progress is through the organization of community "banks," which would supply equity capital to promising new concerns and promising new ideas. Or an organization of a somewhat different character might serve effectively in an advisory capacity. This would be inducement without tax immunity. That it could function effectively has not been verified, but experimentation along this line merits consideration.

THE PROPERTY TAX

Introduction

The inequities of the general property tax as it operates typically in the American states have been so widely exposed that little new can be added. The inequities are important not only for their own sake but because of their bearing on production. Unequal competition caused by discrimination

State and Local Taxes

in the property tax is demoralizing. The tax in its present degree of application necessarily places a high fixed charge on the operation of business. But this is far less serious than the unequal application of the tax, resulting from bad administration and from multiple taxation. It seems hard to believe, but it is apparently true, that in Great Britain agricultural property (except farm homes) is entirely tax-exempt, and business property is two-thirds "derated." The British appear to appreciate more than any other people that, in the last analysis, all taxes come to the doorstep of "flesh-and-blood" citizens.

Assessment

With valuations made at the caprice of the assessor rather than according to definitely established rules and procedures, property-tax costs become a matter of political pressure; fair competition on the basis of business efficiency disappears. Moreover, if a business is not itself assessed according to law, its position in a legal action contesting a valuation may be prejudiced.

In some states and cities the real property of large concerns is relatively undervalued in order to prevent migration. In some cases, also, assessors underassess business property because they are either incompetent to handle large values or are intimidated by them. In other cases, the political power of homeowners results in assessments unfavorable to business. The infiltration of politics into the assessment of personal property, tangible as well as intangible, is notorious. The net effect of these influences is impossible to determine without an elaborate field investigation. It can be said with confidence, however, that business itself would be better off on the whole if the assessment standard were applied impartially.

This is not the place to examine in detail ways and means for improving property-tax administration. It is generally known that improvements can be had in two directions—either by devising better machinery for local property-tax administration or by developing an effective system of state supervision.[1] Civil service tenure for assessors is extremely desirable; short of this, appointment of assessors can be substituted for election, and long tenure can be offered in either event. Local board-of-review machinery needs overhauling. Good administration requires adequate financial support. Exemptions from the tax are often both too broad and too narrow; too broad in that much real estate, unconvincingly claimed to be serving a public purpose, is freed from tax; too narrow in that many jurisdictions attempt the impossible and demoralizing task of listing intangible property. Most important of all is a high degree of integrity in the conduct of local affairs.

Taxation of Intangible Property

Most states apply the property tax in some form to intangibles.[2] Intangibles such as mortgages, bonds, credits, and commercial paper have no inherent or intrinsic values. They merely represent interests or rights in tangible property, already (at least, theoretically) taxed. If the tangible property which these paper assets represent were destroyed, the intangibles would become valueless. Through the device

[1] Harold M Groves and A Bristol Goodman, "A Pattern of Successful Property Tax Administration The Wisconsin Experience," *Journal of Land & Public Utility Economics*, May, August, and November, 1943

[2] Common items classified as intangibles are stock, bonds, notes, mortgages, accounts receivable, life insurance policies, patents, copyrights, good will, trade letters, debentures, evidence of indebtedness, certificates of deposit, instruments evidencing an interest in property, bankers' acceptances, bank deposits, money, and credits of all kinds. For purposes of analysis, intangibles are divided by economists between representative and nonrepresentative intangible property. "A representative intangible is an item of intangible property which is at once the asset of one person and the liability of another, such as notes, accounts, mortgages, bonds, and shares of stock. Such intangibles as special franchises, goodwill, patents, copyrights and trademarks are nonrepresentative." (*Property Taxation of Intangibles*, Bulletin No. 21, National Association of Assessing Officers, Chicago) However, the status of intangible personal property is confused by many court rulings that stocks, bonds, certificates of deposit, money, and other items, are tangible property. Such rulings have considerable significance because of the jurisdiction given states thereby to tax such evidences of value in the place where the legal instrument merely happens to be kept.

State and Local Taxes

of the intangibles instrumentality, a value may be multiplied to an almost infinite degree. For example, real estate may be mortgaged, bonds may be issued based on the mortgage, a corporation may be formed and issue capital stock with these bonds as its asset, and so on. The intangibles tax is thus usually a levy on wealth which has already been counted in the property-tax base. An exception occurs when the levy is on copyrights, patents, and good will.

Property consists of physical objects and ownership rights attached thereto. If it all were assessed once, twice, or three times, no injustice would necessarily occur; but when different items are included at different multiples, the possibilities of grave injustice are manifold. It is a matter of uncertainty whether bad administration in this case compounds the inequities or (mercifully) corrects to some degree the errors resulting from a faulty conception of the nature of property.

Territorial multiple taxation of intangible property is superimposed upon that which prevails in a single jurisdiction. The present Supreme Court tends toward the view that property consists of many rights and privileges and, if any one of these is within the domain of a particular state, the latter has jurisdiction to tax. Corporate intangibles may be taxed at the legal domicile or head office of the corporation, the place where its other business operations are carried on, or (in some cases) the place where the intangibles are kept.[1] The Court recognizes the problem of multiple taxation involved in this position but holds that this is a matter for legislative bodies and interstate or federal-state negotiation rather than for court limitation.

A business and governmental problem associated with the taxation of intangible property is the transfer of such property to new locations at assessment date. In spite of no very serious effort to enforce the intangibles tax, withdrawals of

---

[1] *New Orleans v. Stempel,* 175 U S. 309 (1899), *Metropolitan Life Insurance Company v. New Orleans,* 205 U S. 395 (1907), *Wheeling Steel Corporation v. Fox,* 298 U.S. 193 (1936).

bank deposits in St. Louis before assessment day apparently run from 25 to 40 per cent of such assets. This may create a serious banking problem. In recent years, several states have substituted a special income tax on the income from intangibles for an *ad valorem* tax, either at general or special rates. The new form of tax avoids the hazard of migration of wealth at or about assessment day.

Low-rate taxation of intangibles, now in vogue in a number of states, probably has improved the level of property-tax administration to some extent but not enough.[1]

Rational support for the property tax, if any, rests mainly on the theories of special benefit and of the incidence of land taxes. Neither applies to intangible property.

Recommendations

The property tax should be confined to tangibles and perhaps to real estate. Some will object to this on the ground that wealth tends more and more to concentrate in the form of intangible property. The answer to this objection is that taxes ought more and more to be levied upon persons in accordance with their net income. Intangible property should be reached through this income tax. The change would eliminate several forms of vicious multiple taxation.

Administration of the property tax can and should be greatly improved by overhauling local assessment machinery and developing state supervision of local assessments.

Although space does not permit an elaboration of the point, it is possible to suggest further that the whole concept and basis of property taxation might well be reexamined. There is too much disposition to regard the general property tax as a fixed and permanent institution. The results are not good enough to warrant this complacency.

[1] Roy G. Blakey and Associates, *Taxation in Minnesota*, University of Minnesota Press, Minneapolis, 1932, pp. 216–217; *A Factual Analysis of the Money and Credits Tax Problems in Minnesota*, State Governmental Research Bulletin, No. 13, Minnesota Institute of Governmental Research, St. Paul, Minnesota, February, 1943.

XIII. FISCAL POLICY AND THE FUNCTIONING OF THE ECONOMY IN THE POSTWAR PERIOD

INTRODUCTION

MANY scholars think of fiscal policy as almost synonymous with statecraft. The term is used to cover not only the selection of tax measures that will least impede production—our main concern—but also the determination of policy with regard to balancing the budget; paying off, stabilizing, or adding to the debt; other matters of budget and debt management; public spending; banking and currency control; and foreign trade, investment, and exchange. Fiscal policy, so defined, is highly significant and might make or break the economy. This chapter deals mainly with the broad taxation aspects of this extensive field.

TAX AND FISCAL POLICY DURING THE LATER PHASES OF THE WAR

The key to good fiscal policy during war is a strong tax program. This is important to relieve the pressure on prices, to keep the debt within bounds, and to balance, to some extent, the sacrifices of persons in the armed services with those of civilians. If prices were not controlled, the deferred purchasing power vital to postwar prosperity would be dissipated. The opinion is widespread that our wartime tax burden was stabilized at the maximum which industry and labor could assume. This is open to question. The elasticity of the personal-income tax was not exhausted, and there were important loopholes in this tax that could and should have been plugged. During a war, when resistance to desirable change is at a minimum, the time is especially favorable to tighten tax laws. Even with the maximum feasible tax program, indebtedness may reach embarrassing proportions. At any rate, war taxation has erred on the side of too little rather than too much.

TAX AND FISCAL POLICY DURING RECONVERSION

Postwar Economic Developments

A number of forecasts have been made as to the transition period. Moulton and Schlotterbeck employ the method of historical comparison for this purpose.[1] A study of the transition periods following the three major wars—the War of 1812, the Civil War, and the First World War—reveals close parallelism. The postwar periods conform to the following general pattern: a few months of hesitance, a year or more of active business characterized as a replacement boom, a relatively short period of trade and financial readjustment, and finally a period of business prosperity extending over several years. Assuming that history repeats itself in the transition period following the recent war, the nature of the period might be described as follows: during the process of readjustment immediately after the end of the war, there would be a moderate business recession for perhaps 6 months; a rapid recovery and expansion due to the increased demand for consumer goods would follow; this replacement boom would end, in a little over a year, in a collapse of prices and an acute but relatively short depression; and this would be succeeded by a relatively long era of recovery and prosperity.

Speculation as to the probability that history may repeat itself in the postwar transition period is based on an examination of present conditions. Favorable and unfavorable factors include the prospect of a more orderly demobilization after hostilities cease; a large potential demand for both capital and consumer goods at home and abroad; a relatively

[1] Harold G. Moulton and Karl T. Schlotterbeck, *Collapse or Boom at the End of the War*, Brookings Institution, Washington, 1942.

Fiscal Policy in the Postwar Period

larger purchasing power, especially among wage earners and farmers; and less need for a downward readjustment of prices, resulting from the effectiveness of price control during the war. The return of many women and older persons (partly because of social security) to home life will remove some pressure from the labor market. Unemployment compensation and dismissal pay will help to bolster purchasing power during the transition.

On the debit side of the balance sheet, civilian jobs must be provided for the largest force of demobilized manpower in our history (about 9 to 10 million from the armed forces, 1.6 million from government service, at least another 6 million from war industries). A larger number of industries than in the last war must be reconverted to civilian production. Price ceilings have resulted in an unfavorable cost-price ratio for some manufacturing. The squeeze between cost and price will develop after the war when the volume of manufacturing shrinks without any corresponding reduction in wage rates and raw material costs. There has been substantial improvement in productive efficiency, which means more production per man-hour and less need, perhaps, for labor and capital. There has also been a large expansion in our heavy industries, such as steel, aluminum, shipbuilding, machine tools, and others. For some time, little additional expansion can be anticipated in these areas. Finally, there is the psychology of fear and uncertainty, part of which is a hang-over from the thirties and part a feature of war-boom towns like Detroit, Seattle, and others.

Balancing the favorable and unfavorable factors, Moulton and Schlotterbeck conclude that the outlook in the economy is somewhat less favorable than it was in 1919. However, as compared with the economy prior to the war, the prospects are distinctly favorable. Economic prosperity after the transition period will depend upon the solution of basic economic problems.

Other writers have approached the problem of postwar

prediction by analyzing the basic trends in the war economy.[1] Both the capacity and the manpower to produce on a large scale were developed and demonstrated during the war. In addition to the increase in manpower, there was a continuous rise in output per worker. It is estimated that the available manpower in 1946 will produce almost 50 per cent more goods and services than in 1940. But the mere existence of a skilled labor force, efficient plant and equipment, sufficient capital, and available raw materials is no guarantee that these factors of production will be employed to satisfy consumer wants. There are no automatic devices in the private enterprise economy that ensure markets. Research has been and is being conducted on this problem by the Department of Commerce and by a number of private corporations.[2] Predictions of the demand for specific consumer goods have been worked out in considerable detail.

One school of thought is skeptical as to the adequacy of postwar demand. It bases this reaction upon the alleged fact that investment opportunities are permanently curtailed by the maturity of the nation and the declining rate of population growth.[3] Others hold that private enterprise has at least an even chance of providing adequate investment opportunities after the war.[4] They lay stress on the relation between costs and prices, present and prospective; the willingness of inventors and business enterprises to embark upon venturesome undertakings in anticipation of demand; and

---

[1] See S. Morris Livingston, *Markets After the War* (reprinted by The Committee for Economic Development), U S Department of Commerce, Washington, March, 1943; Alvin H. Hansen, *After the War—Full Employment*, National Resources Planning Board, January, 1942, Alvin H. Hansen and Guy Greer, "Toward Full Use of Our Resources," *Fortune*, November, 1942, pp. 130–133, Sumner H Slichter, "Postwar Boom or Collapse," *Harvard Business Review*, Autumn, 1942, pp. 5–42

[2] Livingston, *op. cit.*, pp. 13, 23, 27–52.

[3] See Alvin H. Hansen, *Fiscal Policy and Business Cycles*, W. W. Norton & Company, Inc., New York, 1941.

[4] Sumner H. Slichter, "What Is the Outlook for Private Enterprise in America?" *Dun's Review*, April, 1942.

Fiscal Policy in the Postwar Period

the rate of technological change. Labor relations, tax policy, and outlay for research are factors which, according to this view, can greatly affect prospects.

Since demand is a key factor in the transition period, the attention of several writers has been focused on the deferred demand arising from shortages of civilian goods and the accumulation of purchasing power in the form of government bonds, bank deposits, and the liquidation of debts. To the deferred demand at home must be added the shortages abroad, a large but somewhat uncertain item. Other factors in the demand forecast are the increased number of marriages prior to and during the first few months of the war; the discontinuance, during the war, of growth in the number of business concerns; wartime movements in population; and the high rate of technological progress now prevailing. According to certain estimates[1] of this future prospective demand, the postwar market for goods and services will exceed the present demand for war materials. If the transition of production from war materials to civilian goods can be accomplished smoothly and without too much lapse of time, high levels of employment and output can, in all probability, be achieved and perhaps maintained for some time.

Surplus savings of individuals as a counterpart to the accumulated shortage of goods has also been analyzed. "The war is making both individuals and business enterprises far more liquid than they have ever been and is building up the largest accumulation of purchasing power in the history of the country."[2] Many of these assets are described as "hot" or "warm" in the sense that owners are able and ready to turn them into purchasing power.

On the basis of analysis made by both Livingston and Slichter, the surplus savings at the end of the war would

[1] Slichter, "Postwar Boom or Collapse," *op cit.*, pp. 7–10.
[2] Sumner H. Slichter, "Present Savings and Postwar Markets," reprinted from *Harvard Business Review*, Autumn, 1943, p. 69.

exceed decidedly the accumulated demand for goods. In this analysis, it was assumed that price control would be continued in the transition wherever it was reasonably necessary. Should price controls be allowed to lapse, the effectiveness of the accumulated purchasing power would rapidly disappear.

Considering previous experience and the factors involved, it seems likely that the postwar decade will be divided into at least three periods. These periods might be designated by the principal fears that will dominate them. The first, a matter of a year or two, would be dominated by the danger of another 1921; the second, immediately following, would confront the fear of another 1939; and the third, running considerably farther into the future, would encounter the prospect of another 1929. The psychological factors are an important and largely unpredictable element, and the real significance of the 1930's is not yet visible in true perspective. Necessarily all forecasts involve a considerable amount of guesswork.

As stated in the introductory chapter, whether private business is or is not successful in providing reasonably full employment after the war, tax policy should seek to ensure that business carry as much of the load as possible. If the effort is successful, so much the better. If it is unsuccessful, tax policy should at all events seek to minimize the problem of coping with unemployment. Whether inflation or deflation or both (successively) will become our principal problem is more important. Since no definite answer is possible, we need to prepare for both.

Tax Measures for the Reconversion Period

Considerable attention has already been given to the matter of war and postwar tax policies that would facilitate reconversion. In treating corporate losses and the excess-profits tax, attention was called to the present generous carry-back of losses and excess-profits tax credit introduced in 1942. A

Fiscal Policy in the Postwar Period

continuation of these provisions was recommended for as long as the effects of the war upon business remain important. A 2-year period should be sufficient to cover most of the war-caused postwar expenses.

The situation may call for retention of the carry-back feature of the excess-profits tax after the tax itself is suspended. The program cannot be significant without involving large refunds. This might seem unduly generous to prosperous corporations, but it is based on the eminently sound principle that war profits should be figured on actual and not fictitious earnings.[1] (However, it is also true that the carry-backs will allow the offsetting of postwar deficits not occasioned by the war and will invite some manipulation of income to take advantage of the tax laws.) The adequacy or inadequacy of war taxes themselves is an entirely distinct issue. As previously stated, the corollary to this policy is that the excess-profits tax should be retained as long as positive profits attributable to the war remain an important factor.

To illustrate the operation of the present carry-backs, if corporation A has earned large excess profits and has paid high excess-profits taxes throughout the war period but, because of repercussions of the war, barely "makes ends meet" in the first 2 years after the war, the returns of the last 2 war years may be reopened. The difference between the actual postwar earnings and the maximum earnings which would not be subject to the excess-profits tax may, in effect, be deducted from the income of the war years. This would entitle the company to a refund. The same would be true if corporation A had incurred a loss after the war, except that in this case the wartime net-income tax return as well as the excess-profits tax liability might be reopened. To some degree the system provides that the experience of the postwar

---

[1] "Assuming that war is something of an abnormality, a special excursion which business has been obliged to take, it tends to follow that both the cost of coming and going should be charged to war revenue." (William A. Paton, in a letter to the author.)

years may be averaged in with that of the war years in the ultimate determination of war income and profits taxes.

The carry-backs not only provide a means of fairly appraising relative war profits for tax purposes but in addition they may supply considerable postwar capital. The excess-profits tax statute provides, in addition to the carry-back and carry-over of unused excess-profits tax credit, a postwar credit of 10 per cent of excess-profits taxes paid. This will also be a source of postwar capital. Although the financial position of most corporations is strong, many of them, in adapting themselves to the postwar period, will need all the resources they can command. At the very least it can be said that if business is to have the benefit of carry-backs and refunds, they should be available at the earliest date possible.

The timing of tax reductions is a difficult postwar problem that will be considered in a later section. During the reconversion period, or at least during its early and most intensive phase, taxes should be maintained at their wartime levels.

TAXES AND FISCAL POLICY IN THE POSTWAR
PERIOD FOLLOWING RECONVERSION

Budget and Debts

A problem of great concern for the whole economy is that of postwar budget policy. Should this policy seek annual surpluses in order to start paying off the huge national debt? Should we merely seek to avoid annual deficits and thus prevent the debt from becoming larger? Should we tolerate some deficits in bad years, aiming to balance the budget over a period of years (cyclical budget)? Or should we go in for deficit spending as a regular policy, hoping thereby to bolster a "stagnant economy"?

Several considerations need to be weighed in answering these questions: (1) Business confidence is an important element in industrial expansion and such confidence would probably be considerably strengthened by a *successful* budget-

Fiscal Policy in the Postwar Period

balancing or debt-retirement policy. (2) Raising taxes and lowering exemptions in bad years tend to aggravate depression. (3) Budget-balancing will not be too difficult if the national income can be maintained at near to wartime levels. (4) Debt reduction would increase the capacity of the nation to borrow for future emergencies and would decrease fixed charges in the budget.

Placing the heaviest emphasis upon (2) and (3) above, the author recommends that we seek to balance the budget during years of good employment only; that we strive for a surplus during the best years; that we aim at least to balance the budget over a period of years (the cycle); and that we hope for such prosperity that the debt can be substantially reduced. Whether we should go further than to balance the budget over the immediate postwar years depends entirely on how successfully we achieve high economic levels during these years. These high economic levels are more important than debt retirement, but it may be possible to have both.

It is true that a cyclical budget-balancing program encounters important political difficulties. The objective assumes perspective and discipline on the part of Congress, which might not be forthcoming. It would be "easy" for Congress to incur deficits during the years of low production, justifying this conduct on the ground that such deficits have a wholesome economic effect. In the years of large output, the corollary of this action might be ignored on the ground that still greater production would be possible and should be realized before any attempt is made to obtain a budgetary surplus. This tendency could be counteracted to some extent by improved budgetary techniques. For example, a technique used by Sweden might be copied—that of carrying forward in the current budget, from year to year, budgetary deficits that are cyclical in nature.

Although the problems of balancing the budget over a series of years are undoubtedly impressive, they are at least not greater than those of attempting a budget balance "come hell or high water." Such an attempt may not only cause serious economic disruption but may fail to accomplish its objective where a more imaginative fiscal program might have been successful. No program of budget balancing that loses sight of the importance of the national income is well advised even from the sole standpoint of balancing the national budget. It is necessary to take some risks (public as well as private) if the common objective of a balanced budget is to be realized. Fiscal policy controls may seem dangerous and difficult but they are less so than the completely regimented economy that might follow without them.

On the other hand, the program here recommended admittedly takes some chances on a secular increase in the debt. If there is also a strong upward trend in the national income and the debt increase is no greater than that of the tax base, this need cause no alarm. Undoubtedly, however, there is danger of a runaway increase in the debt, resulting from a lack of discipline attending a relaxation in the resolution to balance the budget annually. The need for caution and restraint in public expenditures will be greater than ever before.

Much has been written on the deflationary effects of taxation to retire indebtedness, not all of which is plausible and little of which has been verified by the test of time and experience. Retirement of bonds held by banks is deflationary since it is likely to reduce the quantity of money or money substitutes in circulation. This effect may not follow in the case of individuals, although the retirement may have a deflationary effect on the assumptions (1) that oversaving is a problem and (2) that the bondholding class has a greater propensity and ability to save than the taxpayers. This argument might support conservative taxes and no debt retirement, but it also supports taxes on the higher brackets of income. It seems probable that retirement of Series E savings bonds could be accomplished with very little deflationary effect. In fact, the effect might be quite the reverse.

Fiscal Policy in the Postwar Period

Experience offers no definite answer as to the deflationary effect of government surpluses. As recently as the twenties, surpluses were managed without disastrous consequences and with little concern for deflationary results. During the thirties governmental deficits did not create the expected inflationary effects. However, these deficits were primarily the result of deficit spending and not of conservative tax policy. We cannot be sure that setting taxes "too high" would have an important deflationary effect. But, since the principal problem of the postwar period is the avoidance of a deflationary spiral similar to that of the thirties and since excessive taxation might aggravate this problem, we had best adjust our tax program to provide surpluses only at high levels of employment.

Attitudes toward the public debt vary all the way from holding that it is the great menace of our time to calling it a positive asset. The truth, as usual, probably lies between these extremes. Were the debt to disappear by some happy accident, certain substantial adjustments would be necessary, but it would hardly be an occasion for national mourning. However, the issue is likely to be confined to a little more or a little less debt, and elimination is not one of the available alternatives. To say that the debt constitutes no burden because it is all internally held is an oversimplification. It is true that the problem is less serious under these circumstances than were larger transfers to foreign countries involved. But transfers within a country create a strain on the tax mechanism. Just how much debt a nation can carry without too great a strain will depend on many factors, including the interest rate borne by the debt, the distribution of the debt, the distribution of income, the tax system, and, most important of all, the maintenance of a high aggregate income. The ideal internal economic order for carrying a substantial debt comfortably would be a large national income, equitably distributed throughout all income groups; a wide distribution of the debt; and a reasonably progressive tax system. The nearer we approach this ideal, the less difficulty will the debt give us. A debt of twice the normal national income is generally recognized as not so large as to cause alarm.

Countercycle Influence of Taxation

It is true that the tax instrument does not lend itself readily to the objective of cyclical control. "Control demands quick action, and tax bills do not go through Congress quickly and smoothly, as recent events should demonstrate. Moreover the collections lag far behind the legislation."[1] The proposal to delegate the taxing power to an administrative agency, instructed to use it for purposes of fiscal control, is mainly of academic interest. However, if tax rates are not increased during a depression, taxation automatically exercises a pronounced countercycle influence. This is the sort of countercycle taxation policy which is likely to prove most practical. It does not require that tax rates and the tax system shall be completely stabilized in the postwar period. New sources of expenditure will be knocking at the door constantly. Some of these demands should, and more of them will be, allowed admittance. Tax rates, and particularly exemptions, should be flexible enough to respond to these expansions. However, tax rates should not be increased because of a depression or decreased because of a wave of prosperity.

It would be logical to go a step further and recommend that tax rates be reduced during a depression and increased during a boom. This would be desirable from the viewpoint of fiscal policy and is, perhaps, to some extent feasible. The change to stable tax rates over the cycle would represent, however, a substantial gain for countercycle fiscal policy, especially in view of the fact that the kind of taxes recommended for the postwar tax system are very "cycle-sensitive." This program would be a sharp reversal of the policy followed

[1] Mabel Newcomer, *A Tax Policy for Postwar America*, New York University Institute on Postwar Reconstruction, November 10, 1943.

in the twenties and thirties, when tax rates were eased on the crest of a boom and sharply increased during the most severe depression of our history. If we can achieve stability of tax rates over the cycle, we shall have taken a long step forward. As previously observed, state and local governments can and should be urged to follow the lead of the federal government as far as their less flexible revenue systems will permit.

There should be an element of "contract" in our tax system. Enterprisers should have the "right" to "rely" on a fair measure of stability in taxation. This psychology is strategically significant, especially when the economy is endeavoring to pull itself out of a depression. Decisions must be made concerning new investment, expansion of existing plant, employment, and risk-taking. Enterprisers should at such times be free from the fear of rapidly rising tax burdens.

Is there a conflict between averaging income and the achievement of greater flexibility in the tax system for counter-cycle manipulation? If we contemplate constant changes to make the income tax serve as a stimulant and a narcotic at the right times, will this not make averaging impossible? Or conversely, if we accept averaging, will this not encumber the development of a flexible income tax as a tool of fiscal policy? If there is an irreconcilable conflict, which is more important—averaging or flexibility?

These are questions that cannot be answered definitely without more experience. Undoubtedly, averaging would be most easily applied if there were only one variable with which to contend—that of fluctuating as opposed to steady income. But if rate changes are considered, another variable is introduced. In calculating the tax on average income it becomes necessary either to apply two schedules or to choose one of them. Applying two rates would produce cases where fluctuating income pays less tax than steady income. It would preclude the levy of heavy taxes on incomes abnormally high in a particular year (as in wartime). And of course it would complicate the recalculation of taxes on average income. Use of a single schedule would eliminate a variable but might be arbitrary and produce capricious results.

For the present, the conflict between these two prospective modifications in the tax system is mainly of academic interest; we would need to establish greater stability of rates before we achieved a procedure for manipulating rates to counteract the business cycle. If the conflict should later prove real and vital, it might require a choice between two promising instruments of fiscal policy.

Most of the taxation program outlined here can be used during all phases of the business cycle. Some special stimulants and narcotics might be needed, however, in case of extreme fluctuations. These remedies should be associated with the factor of investment.

An appropriate tool as an investment control would be a special allowance for accelerated depreciation during extreme depression years.[1] This would encourage improvements and reduce current tax obligations during bad years, and it would exercise reverse or compensating effects during good years. As previously stated, tools of this character should be reserved for extreme conditions.

Timing of Tax Reductions in the Postwar Period

There is no clear consensus of prediction as to the pattern of postwar economic events. Nevertheless, it is possible to outline a probable pattern and to suggest the objectives of taxation and the appropriate taxation program that would attend each phase.

In all probability the first phase of the postwar period will be characterized by inflationary tendencies due to an inadequate supply of civilian goods to meet the demand. Considerable "bottle-neck" unemployment may result from the

[1] See Chap. VI.

confusion. The budget will still be substantially unbalanced, and further borrowing both from individuals and banks can be anticipated. Tax reductions, if any, should be conservative, and they should take account of the fact that the wartime tax program erred on the side of leniency. As previously stated, the excess-profits tax should be repealed, to become effective one or two years later.

During this period there will be an acute danger of rapidly mounting prices, especially for stocks and real estate. Should this danger materialize it might be followed, as in 1921, by a relatively short period of deflation and price adjustment. This and the early phases of the ensuing recovery would be an appropriate time for major postwar tax changes, such as integration of personal and corporate taxes, elimination of excises, and moderation of the personal income tax. As the tide of prosperity mounts, further reductions should be avoided and some increases in the personal income and social security taxes would be appropriate. If no deflationary setback occurs for several years after the war, major tax revisions can still be made when production has had an opportunity to adjust itself to peacetime conditions and when the danger of rapidly rising prices has been nullified.

If only for the probability of large windfalls, integration of corporate and individual taxes should wait upon full taxation of capital gains and the realization of such gains at death, which in turn should wait upon the development of an averaging system under the individual income tax.

Saving, Investment, and Spending

The relation of taxation to the problem of balancing saving, investment, and spending has been discussed to some extent in other chapters. The observation was made that there is no necessary relationship between what a nation's individuals and businesses desire and are able to save, and the opportunities to invest these savings. It was also suggested that we have no irrefutable evidence that oversaving is an important and persistent problem, even in a rich country like our own, but that there is enough plausibility in the contention to justify some consideration of it in formulating a tax policy.

However, the problem does not end with this conclusion. The supply of savings can be reduced by progressive taxation. The demand for them can be increased by tax policies which make investment attractive and by those which ensure a good market. Fostering investment by supporting incentives is based on the theory that expansion in anticipation of demand is of great importance. Fostering consumption relies on the theory that expansion follows demand and that this will be especially true in the consumption economy we are now approaching. How these factors balance out and what taxation policy would serve to ensure a proper balance is indeed a riddle of the first order.

Modifications in the tax system that would serve each of these interests have been suggested: reduced consumption taxes for the broad market; graduated income and especially death taxes for a check on the supply of savings; elimination of double taxation of profits, together with other changes, to improve investment incentives. Whether this combination will provide the golden mean that will produce the desired dynamic economy cannot be said with assurance, but it appears more promising than alternative tax programs.

The problem of maintaining a large and steady flow of private investment is certainly one of the most difficult in economics. Investment (at least replacement) sometimes follows consumption, though it often precedes demand and creates the latter. Expansion may be a function of acceleration in demand rather than of demand itself. There may be overinvestment as well as underinvestment. The counter-cyclical devices here recommended—stable tax rates, a rational tax system, carry-over of losses, and accelerated depreciation (in times of stress)—are all in the interest of large and steady private investment.

Fiscal Policy in the Postwar Period

Public Spending

. It has also been suggested that deficit public spending for public works can be anticipated if and when the economy falls short of providing adequate employment opportunity. The public has come to expect of its economy (and rightly) both a high standard of living and ample opportunity to earn a livelihood. It would prefer jobs in private industry to another WPA (even with improvements), but the latter is regarded as the minimum to be expected. Since deficit spending is a necessary relief measure in times of much unemployment, it is somewhat academic, perhaps, to argue whether it is a useful tool to pull an economy out of a deep depression. At any rate, it may be said that the manner of its use can greatly affect the likelihood of economic improvement.

First, it should be emphasized that all other reasonable efforts to revitalize business ought to take precedence over deficit spending. The use of stable tax rates as a countercycle device involves many problems but probably fewer than deficit spending. One of the main problems in the use of the latter device is that of maintaining enough confidence and morale in private business so that the effect of creating purchasing power is not nullified by a decrease in the velocity of its utilization. The selection of expenditures, budgetary techniques, and the administration of the programs are all important in avoiding this result. The expenditures should be creative but, as far as possible, in areas not in direct competition with private business. As much stress should be placed upon creating additional wealth as upon providing employment. Budgetary techniques should keep the public informed as to the nature of the outlays and should encourage the selection of self-liquidating or at least economically creative outlays. Administration should stress a dollar's worth of service for a dollar's worth of expenditure. In all probability, the use of deficit spending did not end with the thirties, and every effort should be made to lay plans for future application (when necessary) that will be as constructive and sensible as possible.

It can also be said that, as between a program to provide opportunity and a program to provide security (beyond a certain minimum), those who are interested in economic progress must, without any hesitation, choose the former.

Adequacy of Revenue; Priority of Taxes

An estimate of the yield of taxes here recommended is submitted in Appendix A. Also included is a summary of two studies of prospective postwar expenditures. No sufficient precision in estimating either the revenue or the expenditure prospects is possible to support the claim of a neatly balanced budget. Receipts in the vicinity of $18 billion, exclusive of social security taxes, are estimated. This should suffice to justify using the program as a working plan for postwar revenues. If more revenue is desired or if less reliance on the recommended taxes is deemed necessary, other sources must be used. Some consideration of the priority these alternatives deserve is in order.

The following discussion should not be interpreted as a conclusion by the author that these recommendations exhaust the elasticity of personal income, death, and undistributed profits taxation. In the last analysis, personal income and wealth represent all there is to tax. Limitations consist of (1) the political unwillingness to face the discipline required in direct application of the tax burden and (2) the government's inability to administer these taxes with an acceptable degree of equity and efficiency. The weight to be given these limitations cannot be determined until more effort has been exerted and more experience is available for guidance. In the meantime, if more revenue is needed, first priority must go to an increase in the effective rate of the personal income tax generally. This implies a higher withholding rate on

Fiscal Policy in the Postwar Period

corporate income, including the undistributed portion of that income.

. Included in our recommendations are special excises on liquor and tobacco at only slightly below wartime rates. Taxes on these indulgences are thus given a high priority rating. A federal tax on gasoline, yielding the equivalent of federal aid for highways, can also, for obvious reasons, be given a fairly high priority. Beyond these, the special excise field offers few possibilities that would not be arbitrary in their selection and unfortunate in their effects upon the postwar market. Most potential special excises and any general federal sales tax must be given the lowest ratings on the list of tax possibilities.

A special corporate franchise tax (beyond a withholding levy applicable to both distributed and undistributed profits) is irrational and objectionable in other respects (especially in its effect on incentives), but it would be less inequitable and less injurious to the postwar market than a general sales tax or most special excises. It follows the liquor and tobacco taxes in the author's priority rating.

Postwar Debt and the Social Security System

Introduction. Some nice problems of fiscal policy arise in the relationship of the Old Age Pensions and Survivors' Insurance System to the postwar national debt. One factor in determining the extent to which the debt can be reduced is the amount and form of the reserve fund for social security. This problem dates back to 1935 and the passage of the Federal Social Security Act.

Historical Survey. The Social Security Act called for combined pay roll tax rates levied against employers and employees as follows: through 1943, 2 per cent; 1944 through 1945, 4 per cent; 1946 through 1948, 5 per cent; 1949 and thereafter, 6 per cent. According to the original plan, it was contemplated that a 5 per cent regular tax payment would finance the program and that lower rates at the start, combined with a 6 per cent levy after 12 years, would maintain the financial integrity of the system. Early benefits to workers retiring before making a minimum number of payments to the fund were to be partial benefits only. This would permit accumulation of a reserve fund originally calculated to reach $47 billion by 1980. For example, in the budget submitted by the President for the fiscal year ending June 30, 1944, it was estimated that employment taxes would total $1,982,200,000 and, of this amount, $1,525,450,000 would be appropriated to the Old Age and Survivors' Insurance Fund. Only $456,750,000 would be needed for the current disbursements of the system. From the beginning of the system, the rates of tax have been inadequate to meet the actuarial cost of the benefits accruing to employees (though more than sufficient to cover the cash outlays required for immediate benefit claims). Appropriations not used for current payment would go into the reserve, interest upon which would help to pay benefits when the latter reached their full height. The fund was to be invested in securities of the United States.

Congress accepted this plan but speedily modified it following the sharp business recession of 1937. In 1939, the Treasury's position on the social security reserve was altered under the influence of the business recession and repeated attacks of critics, who condemned the reserve as deflationary. The new position was that the reserve should be accumulated in periods of good business and that monetary considerations should be given predominant weight in reserve policy. Congress in 1939 refused to increase rates and appeared to endorse the plan of accumulating a "contingency" reserve instead of one arrived at by actuarial calculations. Apparently for the purpose of limiting the growth of the fund beyond "contingency" dimensions, an amendment to the law was passed [Sec. 201(*b*) (3)] requiring the trustees of the fund to " . . . report immediately to Congress whenever the Board of Trustees is of the opinion that during the ensuing five fiscal years the Trust Fund will exceed three times the highest annual expenditures anticipated during that five-fiscal-year period and whenever the Board of Trustees is of the opinion that the amount of the Trust Fund is unduly small."

The new procedure contemplates substantial payments for social security eventually from general taxes. According to one estimate,[1] by 1980 annual disbursements of the old-age insurance system would be $4.5 billion; the contingency reserve accumulated at present rates would be $13.5 billion, earning 3 per cent or $400 million annually; and the remainder of about $4.1 billion would come from taxation. This, it was thought, would require an appropriation annually of between $1.5 and $2 billion from general revenue funds.

Arguments against a Reserve Program. Principal arguments against the reserve program are (1) that it encourages extravagance, (2) that it is deflationary, and (3) that it is meaningless. As to the first, the contention is that an excess of collections over outlays for social security tempts the government to balance the budget on a cash basis only and to use excess collections not to retire existing debt but to enlarge current expenditures.

The alleged deflationary effect of a reserve is based on the assumption that the government will take the opposite course of that stated above and will use the reserve to retire debt. Retirement of debt may be deflationary if it cancels credit extended by banks or if it takes purchasing power from those who have a high propensity to spend and distributes it to bondholders who have less propensity to spend. (Of course, a deflationary effect is not always bad. During the war, for instance, this alleged effect was used to support the reserve program.)

The contention that a reserve is meaningless is based on the notion that a closed economy can neither borrow from itself nor build a credit for itself in any true sense. Double-entry bookkeeping is involved. A credit simply means that future

[1] W. R. Williamson, "Federal Old-Age and Survivors Insurance," *The Annalist*, Vol. 56, September 5, 1940.

taxpayers will pay taxes to the social security fund indirectly through the interest they are obliged to pay on the assets of the fund.

Arguments for a Reserve Program. Proponents of the reserve program argue that present old-age costs are in reality much larger than present old-age disbursements and that, with our present tax schedule, we are "placing all confidence in the taxing power of the future." A reserve program, it is said, would at least serve to keep the record clear.

It is argued, moreover, that the reserve serves to keep the social security program on a contributory basis. At present many general taxpayers, such as farmers, professional persons, independent business men, and government employees, are not involved in the benefit program; and, although their inclusion has been contemplated and proposed, the feasibility of such expansion has not been entirely demonstrated. If the future program is financed as largely from general taxes as required by present procedure, the system will fall far short of the original goal of self-support. The original program recognized the time-honored principle that the citizen has a primary obligation to support himself and that this includes some obligation to save for old age. Payment of pensions generally (without a needs test) is an ambitious financial program.

It is also argued that the reserve need not be deflationary or that, in all events, its deflationary effects may be avoided by other government policies. For instance, purchase of bonds from banks by the federal reserve system could offset such deflationary tendencies, and the budget-balancing program need not be entirely inflexible. Moreover, social security saving is no more deflationary than saving through private insurance companies. To the contention that a reserve is mere bookkeeping, it may be answered that it is not meaningless for one part of the economy to borrow from another and that the social security group is by no means identical with the whole economy.

Fiscal Policy in the Postwar Period

Conclusion. Extended discussion of the relative merits of these arguments would be fruitless, perhaps, in view of the government's commitment to the use of a reserve in the minor role of a contingency fund. The issue still arises, however, in the matter of raising tax rates with, or perhaps ahead of, the outlay requirements for benefits. The position here taken—that tax policy should be so framed as to avoid all possibilities of its becoming an aggravating factor in deflation (or redundancy of savings)—is compatible with a reserve program only if the latter is flexible and contains offsets for its deflationary effects during certain periods. On the other hand, the incentive approach provides a lively interest in maintaining the social security system on a contributory basis. On the whole, a contingency reserve of generous proportions, managed with due regard for fiscal considerations, seems the best solution.

OTHER FACTORS AND CONCLUSIONS

As suggested at the beginning of this chapter, fiscal policy includes much beyond the scope of taxation, public finance, and this study. A few of these broader aspects can be mentioned in passing. It is assumed that rationing and price controls will be dispensed with as soon as (and not before) the conditions responsible for their creation have ceased to exist. Other controls, however, will need strengthening. Those designed to prevent monopoly and monopolistic abuses are particularly important. Objectives of full production and employment are usually impeded by monopolistic control of production. Monopoly will probably be our number-one economic problem after the war. Wise use of banking controls, so as to correct, for instance, an overexpansion of credit and installment buying, is needed. They are likely to prove more effective in the short run than the slower moving fiscal policy. It may be desirable for the banking system, or perhaps the government, to develop a credit system for small business. Broadening the social security program can help to provide a better and more certain consumers' market. Of course, international economic relations are extremely significant in the outlook for postwar prosperity. This involves adequate aid for and investment in reconstruction, a statesmanlike tariff policy (freer trade), and stabilization of currency and exchange relationships. Foreign investment supported by stable international cooperation could supply this country with an adequate "frontier" and a promising outlet for savings. A general policy among industries of reducing prices as much as circumstances permit would enlarge the postwar market. Economic groups must learn to plan and act in terms of their long-run interest, which is likely to be also the public interest.

The problems ahead are complicated and difficult—much more so than those of 25 years ago. But our knowledge of what is needed and the popular understanding of these problems have also improved. The outlook is certainly not one for smooth sailing, but the chances of keeping an upright ship are far from hopeless.

XIV. CONCLUSIONS

IN RETROSPECT, the following qualifications emerge as essential for postwar taxes:

1. Taxes should be fair; distinctions in tax burden should be based on reasonable principles and should not be arbitrary. This is important both for its own sake and for the morale of the taxpayer. Progress in taxation consists largely of moving from opportunistic to rational revenue sources.

2. Taxes should reduce inequalities in wealth, income, and power. Wide inequalities are abhorrent to democracy.

3. Taxes should conserve the human resources that "man the works."

4. Taxes should preserve a wide market; they should not aggravate oversaving.

5. Taxes should preserve incentives. They should leave enough margin between the return to the ambitious, on the one hand, and the slothful, on the other, to make ambition definitely worth while; they should allow enough return to the successful risk-taker over that to the "safe" investor so that risk-taking is definitely worth while. Particularly those who innovate and take responsibilities should not be singled out for adverse treatment by the tax system.

6. Taxes should be as direct as feasible; in general, taxpayers react most sensibly to what they see and understand.

7. Direct taxes should be widely shared. Wide participation in government is desirable on both the voting and the financial sides. Expenditures voted by the many and paid for exclusively by the few are demoralizing, certainly for those who pay and probably for those who do not.

8. Taxes should be adequate. We have had an unbalanced federal budget for 14 years.

Postwar Taxation and Economic Progress

9. Tax reductions and tax increases serve as stimulants and narcotics to business, and these drugs should be administered so as to mitigate rather than to aggravate business instability. Tax reductions should be reserved for depressions and tax increases should be applied, as far as possible, during prosperity.

It may seem that an attempt to follow so many objectives, some of which apparently conflict, is a case of "riding off in all directions." However, all the above principles bear directly or indirectly on production. Fairness, for instance, is essential to morale, which in turn is a vital factor in production. It may be necessary to compromise, to some extent, but none of these principles can be ignored.

These considerations sustain the view that the main source of support for postwar governments should be a direct personal income tax with a broad base, an adequate standard rate, substantial graduation, no loopholes, and much stronger administration.

Exemptions and deductions here suggested will provide an income-tax base of about 40 per cent of the national income; it will protect from direct taxation about a third of income recipients. This should appeal to most people as a reasonable scope for the direct tax system and as adequate protection for the postwar market. If anything, it errs on the generous side. Restoration of 1939 exemptions would (at $140 billion national income) cut the tax base about half, leaving around $29 billion to tax. This is less than some estimates of federal postwar revenue needs! It will be recalled that in 1939 we collected more from liquor and tobacco taxes than from the personal income tax. If the graduated personal tax is by far the fairest and least repressive of all taxes, as most forward-looking people believe, then we should not so restrict its scope that it cannot possibly play a major role in the revenue system.

Our state income taxes, with their high exemptions and nominal rates on low incomes, are an example of taxation

Conclusions

that provides mostly talk and very little revenue. We praise the income tax but rely on the property tax and sales tax to pay the teachers' salaries.

Loopholes become more important as the income tax increases in importance. Among the most conspicuous are tax exemption of the interest on state and local (and some federal) bonds, special concessions to capital gains, and the division of income among members of the taxpayer's family (separate returns). In the interest of both fairness and morale, these loopholes should be plugged.

A consistently and regularly progressive tax will not only tax a $25,000 income at a higher rate than a $5000 income, but it will assess all $25,000 incomes at the same rate. Our present system applies a much higher effective rate on an income of $25,000 consisting of dividends than on one consisting of interest, salary, or capital gains. It assesses no tax at all on $25,000 of interest from state and local government bonds.

To hold that taxes can be defended merely because rich people pay them, no matter how capricious the distribution, is to exemplify the sort of irresponsibility that threatens the successful operation of a mixed economy.

Because of the proposal to tax capital gains in full, the rate scale here suggested is much tougher on the higher incomes than it appears on the surface. Capital gains constitute about a third of the higher incomes. They are treated very favorably at present. The effective rate on a million-dollar income would be slightly higher under the proposed scale, with capital gains fully included in the base, than under the wartime scale without such provision. How steep and how high a progressive scale should go is not an easy question. One answer might be that it should not go beyond what Congress is willing to apply consistently and enforce effectively. Extreme rates can defeat themselves and accomplish no useful purpose. A range of tax rates from 18 to 75 per cent, applied without loopholes and supplemented by a really effective death tax, could do a far better and possibly bigger job of equalizing than is done now.

Loopholes in death taxes are even more conspicuous than those in the net-income tax. The death tax can be strengthened without much danger of injuring important economic incentives.

Business taxes should be largely confined to undistributed profits, an element reached by the personal tax system only after long delay. These taxes are uncertain as to incidence and they impose a double impact on profit income as compared with a single burden on interest, less than a full tax on capital gains, and no burden at all on interest from state and local government bonds. Some argue that corporate taxes are less repressive than individual taxes. But a corporate tax is an individual tax indirectly. Eliminating the double burden would be a relief to individual income taxpayers as well as to business taxpayers.

As for undistributed profits, our recommendation calls for the application of a personal tax rate to such profits when earned and an effective program for taxing such earnings when they are realized as capital gains to the stockholder. There is considerable following for the view that such earnings should be taxed to the shareholder on a prorata basis when the earnings are reinvested. Undoubtedly this method is right theoretically and perhaps it is practical, although it involves administrative and other difficulties and has no successful precedent anywhere. In any event, our proposals would go a long way toward elimination of the present discrimination in favor of undistributed earnings. As our war experience very well demonstrates, the present discrimination is an open invitation to corporate hoarding.

With wide markets a major concern after the war, consumption taxes will be particularly inappropriate; they should be confined mainly to liquor and tobacco. If administrative difficulties could be solved, an over-all spendings tax, with a high exemption, could fill a useful purpose. This view of

Conclusions

consumption taxes includes opposition to tariffs, which have an additional disadvantage in that they create bad international relations.

It is vital to all concerned that interest in state and local government be revived after the war. The states and particularly the municipalities need a wider choice of revenue sources so that they are not forced to go continually "hat in hand" to higher units of government for funds. We might seek to develop supplements to centrally levied taxes, under which the central units would collect taxes for the local units at cost. Or states and municipalities might develop a new kind of income tax, similar to that used in Philadelphia, allowing little or no personal exemption.

It is recognized that the difficulties of administration and of politics impose uncertain limits upon the application of a rational tax system. Taking account of this, we have ranked the undesirable sources in priority order. Definitely recommended for the federal system are excises on liquor and tobacco; beyond these and a tax on motor fuel, the excises (special or general) are given a very low rating. Following the recommended sources comes a special franchise tax on corporate income. This is preferred to the excises because the inequities involved and the probable effects on postwar markets are less serious.

Taxes that take from a fifth to a quarter of the national income can hardly fail to have important effects on production incentives. Their repressiveness can be reduced by (1) eliminating or deemphasizing business taxes, with their double burden on the risk-taker; (2) offering a concession to the reinvested earnings of new small enterprises; (3) allowing a carry-over of business losses and applying some system of averaging to relieve fluctuating personal incomes; (4) moderation of the income tax by substituting alternative and better timed levies; and (5) eliminating tax-exempt securities.

Our approach to the tax problem places much emphasis on the factor of timing. The approach calls for some con-

Postwar Taxation and Economic Progress

cessions to industrialists in the current levies of business and personal income taxes. This is to give them adequate tools with which to serve the social interest in production. When they sell out (capital-gains tax) or attempt to pass on their accumulation of funds (death tax), the tax system will catch up with them. This supports the view that the business man must function as a trustee and that the ladder of opportunity must be protected. It is in the interest of responsible business leadership and a dynamic economy.

An effort has been made throughout this study to avoid recommendations that attempt to promote economic progress by shifting tax burdens from the rich to the poor. It is by no means certain that such a shift would accomplish that purpose. The combination of reduced sales taxes, lower tariffs, higher estate taxes, plugging loopholes, moderation of income-tax rates, and the integration of personal and corporate taxes would result in a tax system at least more *consistently* progressive than our present one and probably equally progressive in degree. We ought not to be so exclusively absorbed with the problem of distribution (of economic rewards after taxes) that we pay no heed whatever to the effect of taxes on what there is to distribute.

Taxation may be regarded as nothing but warfare between the rich and the poor, each seeking to shift a burden on the other. However, this book has sought to view it as an attempt to evolve a program in the social interest—a program that will be to the advantage of all groups in the long run.

Although taxation may not be the conclusive element in postwar economic progress, it is an important factor. Formulating a tax policy favorable to economic development is a task involving many complications and some conflicts. The solutions here presented have the advantage that on the whole they make for a rational tax system and serve other social objectives as well as economic progress. However, high employment and improved standards of living will and should be a minimum achievement expected of our postwar economic institutions.

APPENDIX A

THE POSTWAR FEDERAL BUDGET

POSTWAR FEDERAL EXPENDITURES

THE postwar level of federal expenditures will depend largely upon factors that cannot be accurately predicted. Uncertain factors include international developments affecting our requirements for national defense, the postwar price level, the proportion of unemployed workers in the labor force, and the course of political action in this country in regard to various economic affairs. Nonetheless, we must have some idea of the magnitude of postwar expenditures if we are to formulate tax policy.

Since two careful efforts to forecast postwar federal expenditures have already been made, we draw upon their conclusions. The first of these by William Leonard Crum, under the auspices of the Conference on Research in Fiscal Policy of the National Bureau of Economic Research,[1] approached the subject with the objective of predicting those expenditures which will (whether or not they should) be incurred during the postwar decade. The other, by The Twentieth Century Fund,[2] predicted the "minimum needs for public service . . . to keep our economy and society in running order" for 1950 and 1960.[3]

[1] Data from Professor Crum's study are presented with the special permission of the National Bureau of Economic Research. The data have not been published by the Bureau except in a confidential and tentative mimeographed form.

[2] The Twentieth Century Fund study was submitted in confidential form in 1944, it is to form a chapter on "Government Expenditures" in a book, *America's Needs and Resources*, by The Twentieth Century Fund, to be published early in 1946.

[3] A third study that appeared after this was written is Lewis H. Kimmel and Associates, *Postwar Fiscal Requirements*, Brookings Institution, Washington, D C., 1945

Postwar Taxation and Economic Progress

The study by Professor Crum, dated January, 1944, assumed the end of military operations in Europe by the second or third quarter of 1944 and in the Pacific by the second quarter of 1945; a price level averaging close to that of 1942 (special calculations were also made on the assumption of a 25 per cent rise in the price level); and an earnest, intelligent effort to balance the budget before the end of the decade, if not on

TABLE 1
ESTIMATED FEDERAL EXPENDITURES IN THE POSTWAR DECADE ACCORDING TO W. L. CRUM

	Billions
Inescapable items:	
Interest on the public debt	$ 5–$ 6
Nonmilitary operations	1– 2
Military outlays	5– 9
Provision for veterans....	2
Aids to agriculture	1
Social security, present plan	1– 2
(a) Total per year............	$15–$22
Discretionary items (aggregate for decade)	
Foreign items	
Relief and rehabilitation	$ 1–$ 2
Peacetime lend-lease	1– 2
Currency stabilization	0
Investment abroad	0– 2
(b) Total for decade	$ 2–$ 6
Domestic items:	
Debt retirement............	$ 0
Public works	10–$15
Subsidies to transport	5– 8
Subsidies to other industry	0– 5
Further aid to agriculture	0– 10
Relief	5– 12
Further aid to veterans	5– 10
Further social security.....	5– 15
(c) Total for decade....	$30–$75
(d) Total discretionary items (b + c) for decade	32– 81
Estimated probable range, total of discretionary items for decade.	40– 70
(e) Annual average of discretionary items	4– 7
(f) Budget total (a + e)........	19– 29
Average	24

SOURCE: Adapted with permission from *Third Interim Report on Conference Project F. A Preliminary Survey of Fiscal Planning for Reconstruction and Peace*, National Bureau of Economic Research, Conference on Research in Fiscal Policy, December, 1943, p. 12

Appendix A

TABLE 2
MINIMUM NEEDS FOR FEDERAL PUBLIC EXPENDITURE, 1950
(As estimated by George B Galloway and Wylie Kilpatrick for Twentieth Century Fund, preliminary and confidential)

Summary of Expenditure		Millions of 1940–1941 Dollars
I. Expenditure from own sources		19,773
II. Intergovernmental transfers·		
A. Plus transfers received.	20	
B. Less transfers paid.	1,370	
III Results in net expenditure for own functions		18,423

Detail of Expenditure for Own Purposes

Total		18,423
General control.		476
War and protection		5,485
Armed forces	4,218	
Veterans' care	1,200	
Police	26	
Inspection and regulation	41	
Transportation		1,322
Highways	2	
Airways and airports	1,000	
Waterways and other	320	
Natural resources		1,280
Agriculture	965	
Forestry, floods, and other	315	
Health and sanitation		35
Welfare, hospitals and correction		340
Social insurance (including reserves).		2,890
Education		84
Libraries		5
Recreation.		36
Public employee retirement		180
Interest		6,000
Debt retirement.		—
Contribution to credit corporations and government enterprises		260
Housing subsidies.	152	
Miscellaneous		30

SOURCE: Adapted from a chapter on "Government Expenditures" in *America's Needs and Resources*, to be published by The Twentieth Century Fund early in 1946.

Postwar Taxation and Economic Progress

the average during the decade. The assumptions of The Twentieth Century study were that the war would end in 1945, that transitional problems would be liquidated by the end of the decade, and that the 1950 decade would be one of stable and relatively full employment and high productivity. The results of these studies are summarized in Tables 1 and 2 and in the following paragraphs. (A few comments of our own are added.)

1. The maintenance of the national debt was calculated by both studies to involve an annual fixed charge of from $5 to $6 billion. The principal at the end of the war was estimated (by Crum) at $245 billion and the average debt for the decade following was placed at from $250 to $260 billion. Interest rates were calculated at 2 to 2½ per cent. Neither study made any allowance for debt retirement (except, perhaps, through the investment of social security reserves and the sale of government plant). These estimates look conservative and plausible. It may be noted, however, that the interest-charge estimates made no allowance for the possible transfer of government debt from the commercial banks to the central banking system or for monetizing part of the debt as an anti-depression measure.

2. Military outlays were estimated at from $5 to $9 billion (by Crum) and $3.5 to $5 billion (Twentieth Century Fund). Both estimates were based on the assumption of a peace that would create a tolerable world stability but yet would not ensure us against war. It was also implied (certainly in the larger estimate) that the threat of another major war would remain and that no successful agreement to limit armaments would be achieved. This may be realistic, but it is more pessimistic than our best reasonable hopes. Even the smaller range of estimates contemplated the maintenance of an armed force at least four times as large as before the war. Prewar outlays for national defense averaged about $1 billion per year for the fiscal years 1935 to 1939.

3. Cost of nonmilitary governmental activities, including

Appendix A

operation of the legislative and judicial branches of government and nonmilitary functions of the executive branch, was placed at $1 to $2 billion (Crum). The lower figure is slightly higher than the outlay in 1941.[1]

4. Provision for veterans was estimated at $2 billion (Crum) and $1.2 billion (Twentieth Century Fund).[2] These estimates did not include bonuses but only the care of the disabled, outlays for wives and other dependents, and other rehabilitation expenses. Outlays for veterans were running somewhat more than $0.5 billion in the immediate prewar years. Variables include the probable casualty rate and the rate of benefits.

5. For aid to agriculture, an "inescapable" outlay of $1 billion was predicted by Crum, with an additional amount labeled as "discretionary." More optimistic critics would probably label both of these categories "discretionary." The Twentieth Century Fund study allowed $965 million for agriculture but this included the full appropriation for the department. It was assumed that only "minimum subsidies for selected crops were likely to be continued."

6. Because of "the growing tendency in some quarters to think of social security benefits as approximately chargeable against the general funds of the Treasury," among other reasons, the social security outlays were estimated by Crum as those payable without provision for reserves. The amount was placed at from $1 to $2 billion. This was labeled the "inescapable" portion and included allowances for considerable expansion in grants to the states but none for increased coverage of employees, liberalization of benefits, or other expansionary changes. Other possible social security outlays were included among discretionary items. The Twentieth Century Fund study placed the figure at $2,890 million, but this sum included some net additions to reserves as well as

[1] The Twentieth Century Fund study used a different classification and provides no comparable estimate.

[2] All Twentieth Century Fund figures used in the discussion are for 1950.

payments to beneficiaries. The figure does not include all expansions recommended by the National Resources Planning Board and others, but it does cover allowances for a substantial expansion.

7. Crum selected certain items of possible postwar outlay and labeled them "discretionary." These were estimated for the postwar decade as a whole and included relief and rehabilitation abroad estimated at $1 to $2 billion; a peacetime lend-lease program at $1 to $2 billion; investment abroad, $0 to $2 billion; public works, $10 to $15 billion; subsidies to transport and other industries, $5 to $13 billion; further aid to agriculture, $0 to $10 billion; relief and further social security, $10 to $27 billion; and further aid to veterans, $5 to $10 billion. The Twentieth Century Fund study, with a different classification and the use of annual figures, allowed $1,322 million for transportation (mostly for airways and airports); $315 million for conservation of natural resources; $340 million for welfare, hospitals, and correction; and $152 million for housing (confining the list to the larger items only).

As to totals, Crum found a figure of $15 to $22 billion annual outlay for the inescapable and $4 to $7 billion for the discretionary items, with a grand total of $19 to $29 billion and a figure of $24 billion selected as a probable average. The Twentieth Century Fund items added up to $19,773 million.

Crum's estimates were based on the 1942 price level, and it is stated that, with a 25 per cent rise in prices, both the revenue and expenditure sides of the budget would be substantially increased, the former considerably more than the latter. A possible figure of $28.5 billion was suggested for total expenditures under these conditions.

The Twentieth Century Fund study made no independent calculations on various assumptions as to the price level, but its estimates were in terms of 1940-1941 dollars.

Figures on estimated state and local needs were included in The Twentieth Century Fund study. Without covering these in detail, the sum figures of $7,605 million for state and

Appendix A

$6,271 million for local, and a grand total of $33,649 million (including federal), may be cited. This is an impressive figure, and, in the authors' opinions, it will run to from 25 to 30 per cent of the national income, compared with 21 per cent in 1940. Attention is called to the fact, however, that large and greatly increased amounts of the predicted outlay needs are for transfer expenditures. These items amount to nearly one-third of the total. The figures at least serve to warn us that we have not yet reached the happy state of abundance where waste and prodigality in public expenditures can be tolerated.[1]

Although these estimates obviously serve a useful purpose, they need not be fatalistically accepted as the inevitable pattern of future events. Various critics will quarrel with different items, contending that they are either too high or too low. For our present purposes, we may conclude that planning for the future would be rash if it did not reckon for revenues of at least $18 or $19 billion, exclusive of social security outlays, in periods of high-level employment. The tax system must also possess elasticity sufficient to provide some additional billions if governmental services are expanded or if the estimates of expenditures prove inadequate. Under the Crum analysis, the $18 to $19 billion would provide $3 to $4 billion annually for his discretionary items (assuming his lowest figure for the inescapable ones) and an extra billion to offset deficits of the less prosperous years. It would come close enough to The Twentieth Century Fund estimates to ensure a reasonable coverage of minimum needs.

YIELDS OF TAX PROPOSALS

The proposed federal tax structure is estimated to yield $18 billion at a net national income of $140 billion. The personal-income tax would raise more than half of this total. Corporate taxes would yield about $2 billion (more than half being

[1] The Brookings study estimates federal expenditures in 1949 ranging from a minimum of $18,862 million to a maximum of $25,840 million.

withheld taxes on dividends); excises on liquor and tobacco slightly more than $2.55 billion; and estate and gift taxes, customs, and miscellaneous receipts would provide somewhat less than $1 billion each. The estimated yields are summarized in Table 3.

TABLE 3

SUMMARY OF ESTIMATED YIELD OF TAX PROPOSALS AT A NET NATIONAL INCOME OF $140 BILLION

Type of Tax	Yield, Billions
Personal income tax (excluding withholding tax on dividends)*	$10.85
Corporate income tax (including withholding tax on dividends)†	2.10
Estate and gift taxes‡	0.90
Excises on tobacco and liquor§	2.55
Customs‡	0.80
Miscellaneous receipts‖	0.80
Total (excluding social security taxes)	$18.00

* For suggested tax-rate schedule see Chap VII, p. 181.
† See Statement on Assumptions, pp 387-389.
  This total includes the following   *Billion*
    Withholding tax on dividends $1.23
    Tax on undistributed earnings $0.87
‡ See p 389.
§ At 1942 tax rates.
‖ Includes stock-transfer tax, liquor-license fees, miscellaneous fees, etc., and an estimate of $400 million from disposal of government plants, equipment, and supplies. See p. 389.

It should be emphasized that these estimates are not forecasts of the amount which will be raised in taxes after the war. The actual yield will depend to a large extent on the level of national income achieved. The net national income figure of $140 billion at 1943 prices has been used as the basis for the estimates because careful studies by a number of independent agencies[1] indicate that approximately this income level

---

[1] U.S. Department of Commerce, S. Morris Livingston, *Markets after the War* (1943); E. A. Goldenweiser and Everett E. Hagen, "Jobs after the War," *Federal Reserve Bulletin*, May, 1944; "Transition to Peace: Business in A.D. 194Q," *Fortune*, January, 1944. These estimates are presented in terms of gross national product rather than net national income; the estimates in *Markets after the War* are presented in 1940 prices. Converted into terms of net national income at 1943 prices, the several estimates group rather closely around $140 billion.

Appendix A

will be achieved if a satisfactory high level of employment is attained for the years immediately after the war. This figure represents an important *goal* for the postwar economy; it is not presented as a *forecast*.

The assumption regarding the size of the national income is of great importance in determining the tax yield. For example, if the net national income were only $120 billion, the yield would be reduced by a full $3 billion; if the net national income were $160 billion, the yield would increase by more than $3 billion.

The estimates presented are also subject to appreciable margins of error. They will be affected, for example, by such factors as the way the national income is distributed, the extent to which taxes are evaded or avoided, and the volume of international trade accompanying a given level of domestic economic activity.

Technical Statement on Assumptions

Personal Income Tax. The estimates assume elimination of the 3 per cent normal tax of the 1944 law, which allows no exemptions for dependents; a personal exemption of $500 for each income recipient and each dependent, defining dependent in the terms of the 1944 tax law; deductions from taxable income (necessary expenses of doing business, taxes, contributions, etc.) as in the 1944 tax law; a rate schedule of from 18 to 75 per cent on net taxable income; no special concessions to persons in the armed services; and continued omission of the earned-income credit. The estimates assume, further, a moderate reversal of the wartime concentration of incomes in the lower brackets; continued reporting and collection at the source for wages and salaries, and extension of this principle to dividends; elimination of double taxation of dividend income by crediting such income with the personal tax previously withheld by the corporation; a 3 per cent reduction in tax yield for allowances due to the averaging of irregular incomes; and vigorous enforcement at all income levels and in all occupations to keep evasion at a minimum. No allowance is made for the effects on tax yields of the recommendations for the application of full rates to capital gains or the more generous deductibility of capital losses. The net effect would be extremely difficult to estimate. It is believed that, with a continuing high level of economic activity, the loss of revenue through more generous provisions for deducting capital losses would be much more than offset by the increased yield from capital gains coupled with the revenue gains resulting from the elimination of tax-exempt securities. Full allowance for these provisions should add several hundred million dollars of revenue not included in the estimates.

Corporate Taxes. The calculations assume repeal of the wartime excess-profits tax and the combined declared-value capital-stock and excess-profits tax; equalization of the corporate income-tax rate to the standard rate of the personal income tax; and elimination of the double taxation of dividend income by crediting the withheld corporate taxes to stockholders. Postwar corporate profits before taxes are assumed to be $13 billion exclusive of intercorporate dividends.[1] Taxable dividends to individuals and fiduciaries are assumed to constitute 50 per cent of total corporate earnings; in addition, 6 per cent of total earnings are assumed to be paid out to institutions and individuals not subject to tax.[2] Undistributed profits before taxes are assumed to be 44 per cent of earnings, and net corporate savings 37 per cent of earnings. In the calculation of taxes on undistributed earnings, a

[1] This estimate represents a rough average of what may be expected if a high level of employment is maintained. Corporate profits may rise somewhat above $13 billion when a high level of employment is first attained and may decline below $13 billion in subsequent years if a high employment level is maintained.

[2] Dividend estimates upon which withholding was calculated are based on a study of prewar distributions in relation to the national income. It should be noted that change in the corporate tax would in itself cause a change in the national income as that figure is now calculated (with business taxes regarded as an expense of production and personal taxes not so regarded). No allowance for this is provided in the figures.

Appendix A

reduction equal to 7 per cent of total earnings was made to allow for the carry-forward of losses.

Estate and Gift Taxes. The estimates of yields from estate and gift taxes are conservative in view of the proposals for plugging loopholes in those taxes. They are slightly more than 50 per cent above current yield figures.

Excises on Liquor and Tobacco. The Treasury has estimated the revenue from liquor and tobacco taxes under the 1942 law at $2.2 billion. In view of the general upward trend of consumption, a postwar yield of $2.55 billion seems reasonable.

Customs. Customs revenue ranged between $300 and $500 million before 1940. A figure of $800 million, with a restoration of normal and perhaps expanded trade at higher income levels, is not excessive.

Miscellaneous Receipts. This category includes such items as stock-transfer taxes, liquor-license fees, miscellaneous license fees, and revenue from the disposal of government plants, equipment, and supplies. The yield from this source in 1941 was $256 million and, in 1942, $441 million, exclusive of revenue from the disposal of government plants and supplies. The yield estimate includes an average amount of $400 million for plant and supplies disposal and $400 million for other miscellaneous receipts.

APPENDIX B[1]

TECHNIQUE EMPLOYED TO ESTIMATE THE PERSONAL-INCOME-TAX REVENUE

THE personal-income-tax base at assumed levels of national income payments, with designated personal exemptions and various schedules of tax rates, was estimated by two methods. One method was developed for individual net incomes below $5000 and another for individual net incomes of $5000 and over.

Net Income below $5000

Estimates for this lower-income group[2] involve three steps: (1) analysis of 1941 income-tax returns; (2) adjustment of 1941 returns by means of a study of the distribution of income made by the Division of Tax Research;[3] (3) inflation of the adjusted returns and income to the assumed level of national income.

Analysis of 1941 *Returns.* The 1941 returns were tabulated by exemption status to form three distributions: (1) family returns, composed of joint returns and returns of single individuals claiming head-of-family exemption; (2) separate returns of husbands and wives and community property returns; and (3) single returns of single and married individuals claiming single exemption. This tabulation was made directly from the tables presented in *Statistics of Income* for all returns on Form 1040. Since returns on Form 1040A were classified by gross income, they were redistributed into

[1] Prepared by Oscar Litterer and Charlotte McNiesh.
[2] This method was outlined by William Vickrey.
[3] Hart and Lieblein, Division of Tax Research. This study included cross tabulations between net income and exemption status. It is based on a sample of consumer incomes compiled by the Bureau of Labor Statistics.

Appendix B

net-income classes before being combined with returns on Form 1040. The redistribution was made on the assumption that the differential between gross and net income on the short form is 5 per cent.

Adjustment of 1941 Returns. To facilitate estimating the tax base with various schedules of exemptions, the 1941 distribution of returns was adjusted to approximate a distribution wherein all income recipients were required to file returns. To accomplish this, the three distributional patterns of 1941 returns were compared with similar distributions in the Hart study. To make this comparison, the arithmetic ratios between 1941 returns and returns in the sample were computed for each net-income class. No adjustment was necessary for the separate-return group since the ratios were relatively constant, indicating that no pronounced differences existed between the Hart sample and the actual 1941 returns. For family returns, the ratios were relatively constant, varying from 15.8 to 23.7 in income classes exceeding $2000 but showing a decrease in the $1500 to $2000 class.[1] To adjust for this decline in 1941 returns, the returns in the Hart sample for all classes below $2000 were multiplied by 23.7, the ratio in the $2000 to $2500 class; the resulting products provided the estimated potential family returns below $2000. Similarly, a decline in single returns was noted for the $750 to $1000 net income class.[2] Using 33.1, the ratio in the $1000 to $1500 class, potential single returns below $1000 were estimated. By this method it was estimated that, if no exemptions or credit for dependents had been allowed in 1941, about 54,359,000 returns would have been filed.

For the purpose of estimating credit for dependents, family returns were grouped by number of dependents, from none

---

[1] Individuals claiming head-of-family exemption, with gross or net incomes equaling or exceeding $1500, were required to file returns. Nevertheless, individuals with several dependents probably did not file returns, which may account for the dropping off in the number of returns.

[2] Individuals claiming a single exemption, with gross or net incomes equaling or exceeding $750, were required to file returns. The marked decline in the

Postwar Taxation and Economic Progress

to five or more, into six categories. This was done on the basis of a percentage distribution of dependents among family returns based on the Hart sample. Dependents entered on single and separate returns were ignored as negligible.

To minimize error in subtracting personal exemptions from net income, the class intervals were subdivided into $100 net-income classes for each of the eight distributions. The number of returns allocated to each $100 interval was estimated graphically with freehand curves.[1]

Inflation of Adjusted Returns. In inflating the 1941 adjusted returns, the basic assumption was made that a rise in national income results from an increase in the number of individuals gainfully employed and from an inflation of individual incomes. According to estimates made by Livingston,[2] the labor force may expand from 48.8 million in 1941 to 55.5 million in 1946. This was taken as the best estimate of postwar employment. However, the tax base was estimated for five different levels of assumed postwar employment to show the effect on the tax base (and thereby on the revenue yield) of a rise or decline in employment.

It was estimated that a labor force of 55.5 million individuals would produce a national income, in terms of 1943 prices, of about $140 billion. At other levels of employment, the national income was estimated on the basis of the relationship between employment and national income during the thirties and the postwar relationship estimated by Livingston.

In the development of the methods employed to estimate revenue, it was discovered that the income reported on

---

number of returns provides some evidence that many individuals apparently did not file returns in spite of the requirement.

[1] Double logarithmic graph paper was used to facilitate drawing and reading the curves. The returns were subtotaled starting with the $0 to $250 interval, each subtotal being plotted at the end of the interval. From the freehand curves drawn through these points, the subtotals were read at each $100 interval. The differences between the successive subtotals represent the estimated number of returns in each $100 interval.

[2] S. Morris Livingston, "Postwar Manpower and Its Capacity to Produce," *Survey of Current Business*, April, 1943, pp. 10–16.

Appendix B

returns correlated more closely with national income payments than with national income. Therefore, income payments were used to inflate or deflate the income reported on returns. The difference between the two measures was estimated so the final results could be stated in terms of national income.[1]

The ratios used to adjust for changes in national income and employment are summarized in Table 4. These ratios or factors were used as follows: If a given distribution of 1941 returns included 10,000 returns, the number of returns in this distribution, with employment at 55.5 million, would be 11,370 (55.5 ÷ 48.8 = 1.137; 10,000 × 1.137 = 11,370). Using the income factor, assume that a specific tabulation of 1941 returns aggregated $20 billion. This same tabulation, with national income at $140 billion, would aggregate $29.32 billion (135.2 ÷ 92.2 = 1.466; 1.466 × 20 = 29.32). Using the level factor (income per return), a taxpayer whose income was $1048 in 1941 would, with national income at $140 billion, have an income of $1351 (135.2 ÷ 92.2 = 1.466; 1.466 ÷ 1.137 = 1.289; 1048 × 1.289 = 1351).

To arrive at estimates of net taxable income at any assumed level of national income, all preliminary calculations were made in terms of 1941 values which were then expanded to the assumed level of employment and income. Table 5 illustrates the detailed procedure for estimating taxable income at $140 billion national income, using a hypothetical distribu-

---

[1] National income payments include the transfer payments from government, i.e., transfer benefits actually paid to the unemployed, to holders of old-age insurance claims, and to retired employees under the above funds and systems; the soldiers' bonus and war service pensions, and subsistence payments, i e., general relief, payments to recipients of special types of public assistance (old-age assistance, aid to dependent children, and aid to the blind), emergency subsistence payments to farmers, the value of surplus food stamps, and allotments to dependents of military personnel [Marvin Hoffenberg, "Estimates of National Output, Distributed Income, Consumer Spending, Saving, and Capital Formation," *The Review of Economic Statistics*, Vol. XXV (May, 1943), p. 118.] These transfer payments are not included in national income However, the retained earnings of business corporations are included in national income and not in national income payments.

Postwar Taxation and Economic Progress

TABLE 4

National income, billions	National income payments, billions	Estimated employment, millions	Returns factor (3) ÷ 48.8*	Income factor (2) ÷ 92.2*	Level factor† (5) ÷ (4)
(1)	(2)	(3)	(4)	(5)	(6)
$ 70	$ 70.0	44.3	0.908	0.759	0.836
100	97.4	49.2	1.008	1.056	1.048
120	116.4	51.9	1.064	1.262	1.186
140	135.2	55.5	1.137	1.466	1.289
160	153.8	56.5	1.158	1.668	1.440

* For 1941, employment was estimated at 48.8 million and national income payments at $92.2 billion.

† The level factor was used to inflate or deflate the personal exemption per return and the limits of the income classes.

tion of 1941 potential single returns. Having estimated the distribution of potential returns in $100 net-income classes, the personal exemption was subtracted as shown in columns (3) and (4). Before making this subtraction, the $500 allowable exemption was deflated to 1941 dollars, using the appropriate level factor from Table 4. If the number of returns in column (3) were multiplied by the mid-points in column (4), the product would be the net taxable income in 1941 dollars. However, calculation of the tax was facilitated by distributing the income into brackets by the method illustrated in columns (5) to (7). The double cumulation of the returns from the upper end of the distribution, with the two adjustments made in the last column, distributes the cumulated taxable income among the brackets. The double cumulation of returns multiplied by $100 (the size of the bracket) would be the cumulated taxable income if the returns in each bracket were at the upper limit. To adjust the income so that the average amount reported on the returns would equal the mid-point of each bracket, the singly cumulated returns were multiplied by $50 and this amount was subtracted for each bracket. The first bracket contains the total taxable income, the second bracket all taxable income

Appendix B

TABLE 5
ILLUSTRATION OF METHOD USED TO ESTIMATE TAXABLE INCOME BELOW $5000 NET INCOME

(Hypothetical distribution of 1941 potential single returns inflated to estimate taxable income of single returns at $140 billion national income)

Net-income classes, 1941 dollars	Estimated number of returns	Estimated number of 1941 taxable returns	Taxable-income classes corresponding to (3), 1941 dollars	Column (3) cumulated	Column (5) cumulated	Taxable income $100 × (6) − $50 × (5), 1941 dollars
(1)	(2)	(3)	(4)	(5)	(6)	(7)
$ 0–100	1000					
100–200	1100					
200–300	1200					
300–400	1300	156†	$ 0–100‡	12,472	104,674	$9,843,800
400–500	1280	1280	100–200	12,316	92,202	8,604,400
500–600	1000	1000	200–300	11,036	79,886	7,436,800
1600–1700	300	300	1300–1400	2127	12,746	1,168,250
1700–1800	270	270	1400–1500	1827	10,619	970,550
1800–1900	250	250	1500–1600	1557	8792	801,350
1900–2000	235	235	1600–1700	1307	7235	658,150
3200–3300	23	23	2900–3000	99	329	27,950
3300–3400	18	18	3000–3100	76	230	19,200
3400–3500	15	15	3100–3200	58	154	12,500
3700–3800	10	10	3400–3500	17	24	1550
3800–3879*	7	7	3500–3600‡	7	7	350

CALCULATION OF NET TAXABLE INCOME BELOW $5000 NET INCOME

1941 level §		$140 billion level ‖	
Taxable income exceeding	Amount	Taxable income exceeding	Amount
0	$9,843,800	$ 0	$14,431,011
1552	658,150	2000	964,848
3103	12,500	4000	18,325

* The 1941 potential distribution is "cut off" at $3879 since $5000 at $140 billion national income is equivalent to $3879 at the 1941 level ($5000 ÷ 1 289 = $3879).

† According to the present law, a single person's exemption is $500 Since $500 at $140 billion national income is equivalent to $388 at the 1941 level, no returns with net incomes less than $388 would be taxable. Of the potential returns in the $300 to $400 class, 12 per cent would exceed $388.

‡ Actually the first and last classes are not $100 intervals However, the errors incurred by using $100 intervals are partly compensating and assumed to be negligible

§ Since the tax-rate schedules have increasing rates at $2000 intervals, it is necessary to know the taxable income in excess of $2000 and $4000. These amounts deflated by the level factor to the 1941 level equal $1552 and $3103 In the interest of simplification these amounts are rounded to the nearest $100 and the taxable income read from column (7), thus $658,150 is the taxable income in excess of $1600 rather than $1552 Some error is incurred by rounding but it is assumed to be negligible.

‖ To determine taxable income at the $140 billion level, inflate 1941 taxable income by the income factor, 1.466

· 395 ·

reported on each return above the first $100 of income, etc.

The final calculation inflates the 1941 dollars of taxable income to the assumed level by applying the proper income factor, 1.466, listed in Table 4.

The revenue was computed by applying the basic rate to income in the first bracket and only the differential rates to income in the other brackets. For example, with the normal rate 18 per cent and surtax rates advancing 1 per cent for each additional $100 of taxable income after the first, the amount of income in the first bracket would be multiplied by 18 per cent and the amount in each succeeding bracket would be multiplied by 1 per cent. The sum of the products would equal the total tax.

Net Incomes of $5000 and Over

The method devised for net incomes of $5000 and over was based on the relationship between the major sources of income (for example, wages, profits, rent, etc.) and national income payments. The income from a given source, tabulated in *Statistics of Income*, was plotted against total national income payments from 1933 to 1941 inclusive. A separate chart was made for each broad net income class (for example, from $5000 to $10,000, from $10,000 to $25,000, etc.). A linear trend was discernible for salaries, wages, commissions, etc.; business profits; partnership profits; rents and royalties; dividends; and income from fiduciaries. The trends, fitted to the above sources of income by the least-squares method,[1] were then projected to the assumed level of national income payments.

The total net income (*i.e.*, total income less the allowable deductions) was estimated by broad net-income classes, using the multiple correlation technique. The combined trends for the five major sources of income, namely, salaries, wages,

[1] The 1941 figure for rents and royalties was omitted in fitting the trend line, for it is obviously an atypical figure.

Appendix B

commissions, etc.; business profits; partnership profits; dividends; and rents and royalties, were used to predict this total net income.[1] In the multiple regression equations, the above sources of income constituted the independent variables and the total net income was the dependent variable. Nine regression equations were computed to cover the net income classes from $5000 to $1,000,000 and over.

There are two general types of error that may be incurred in this prediction. First, it is assumed that the historical trend between income payments and income reported on tax returns during the thirties is a valid basis for predicting future total income. Should economic relationships in the postwar period be quite unlike those of the thirties, the predictions would obviously be invalid. It is statistically impossible to estimate the probable error resulting from such factors.

The second type of error, which can be estimated mathematically, is the result of normal fluctuations in the data. Generally as the correlation between items increases, the reliability of predictions also increases. However, even with a high correlation the estimates are subject to some variation. The reliability of the estimates of net income was determined by variance analysis. For incomes from $5000 to $500,000, the net income was estimated with a possible range of error of less than 10 per cent.[2] From $500,000 to $1,000,000, the possible range of error increased to 18 per cent as a result of the small number of returns; and for incomes over $1,000,000,

---

[1] At the assumed level of national income, the total reported income from minor sources, namely, interest on bank deposit, notes, mortgages, corporation bonds, and government obligations, income from fiduciaries, capital gains, and other income, may be estimated indirectly from the total net income and other relevant information. Allowable deductions for individuals with net incomes of $5000 and above were estimated between 15 and 20 per cent. With a figure for the aggregate total reported income, the residual which is not attributed to the five major sources is the aggregate of the minor sources. The allocation among the latter sources can be made on the basis of the pertinent data available. However, estimates of income from minor sources have no direct bearing on the estimate of personal income-tax revenue.

[2] These ranges of error are based on three standard errors of estimate.

Postwar Taxation and Economic Progress

the possible error rose to 42 per cent. Since the latter income classes contribute only a small proportion of the total net income, the final result is not affected significantly by the unreliability of the estimate over $1,000,000.

The total net income estimated by broad income classes (for example, $5000 to $10,000, $10,000 to $25,000, etc.) was broken down into smaller classes on the basis of the 1941 distribution of total net income reported in *Statistics of Income*.

The number of returns in a given class interval was determined by dividing the estimated total net income by the adjusted mid-point of the class. The adjustment in the mid-point was made on the basis of the number of returns in the preceding and following classes.[1] The 1941 distribution of returns, tabulated in *Statistics of Income*, was used for this purpose.

The personal exemption and credit for dependents for taxpayers with net incomes of $5000 and over was estimated from the exemption and credit taken on the 1940 returns. The average number of different types of exemptions per return was computed. The types of exemptions are head-of-family, single individual, exemption on separate returns,[2] and credit for dependents. The respective average exemptions per return were multiplied by the amount to be allowed as a personal exemption and credit for dependents. The sum of the four products equals the average amount of exemption and credit for dependents allowed per return.[3] The returns in

[1] National Resources Committee, *Consumer Incomes in the United States and Their Distribution in 1935–1936*, Washington, 1938, p. 88. The adjustment to be added algebraically to the mid-point is: $\frac{(f'' - f')c}{24f}$ where f = frequency for class for which adjusted mid-point is being estimated; f'' = frequency of class immediately above; f' = frequency of class immediately below; and c = size of class interval.

[2] The exemption on separate returns over $5000 averaged 52 per cent of the head-of-family exemption on the 1940 returns.

[3] This is a modification of the method outlined by Vickrey in "Estimating Income and Estate Tax Yields," *Studies in Current Tax Problems*, The Twentieth Century Fund, New York, 1937, pp. 152–158

Appendix B

each net income class, multiplied by the average amount of the exemption and credit for dependents per return, equals the total personal exemption and credit for dependents per net income class. This amount was subtracted from the total net income to arrive at net taxable income.

The tax was computed on the basis of the average net taxable income per return. The tax per return was multiplied by the number of returns to secure the total.

In the 1944 Revenue Act several changes were made that will reduce the aggregate amount of net taxable income. The definition of dependents was broadened to include more individuals. The use of the short form was extended to individuals with adjusted gross incomes up to $5000. The percentage allowed for deductions on the short form was increased to 10 per cent of adjusted gross income. It was estimated that these changes would reduce the tax base approximately $1 billion if the national income were $140 billion. The amount deducted from the tax base at other levels of national income or with different provisions for personal exemption and credit for dependents was determined on the basis of proportional relationships. The estimated reduction in net taxable income was distributed over the net-income classes according to taxable income and the amount taken in personal exemptions and credit for dependents.

TECHNIQUE EMPLOYED TO ESTIMATE CAPITAL GAINS AND LOSSES[1]

An estimate was made of the aggregate amount of both capital gains and losses at an assumed level of national income. The estimate of capital gains was made in terms of actual net gains. Actual net gain is the difference between total gains realized from the sale of capital assets, regardless of the time they were held, and total losses incurred from the sale of such assets. In other words, it is a net gain figure for each taxpayer before the statutory percentages are applied to

[1] These estimates were used to compute the statistics for Table XXV, Chap. VII, p. 183.

ascertain the amount of gain recognized in the income-tax base. Such a tabulation, made by the United States Treasury[1] on the basis of the 1936 federal returns, reported an aggregate net gain of $1,224,861,462. This figure was inflated by the difference between national income payments of $68.1 billion for 1936 and $135.2 billion—the assumed postwar national income.[2]

Inflation of capital gains by the above method is very conservative. During a period of rising national income, capital gains tend to increase faster than total national income payments. From 1924 through 1933—a period when provisions for taxing capital gains were left unchanged—these receipts tended to increase at a constant rate while national income tended to increase at a constant amount. However, an exponential trend fitted to the data by the least-squares method and extrapolated to $140 billion of national income results in an unreasonably high figure for aggregate net capital gains. As the national income rises from $100 to $140 billion, the trend of these receipts probably levels off. Since it is extremely precarious to fit a trend line to these data and extrapolate the line to $140 billion of national income, it was concluded best to estimate the increase in aggregate net capital gains on a basis proportional with the rise in national income payments.

Having established an aggregate figure for net capital gains at the assumed level of national income, it was necessary to distribute these receipts by net-income classes. In order to arrive at a distribution comparable to the one devised for the total net income of income taxpayers, a typical prewar distribution was developed. From tabulations of short-term and long-term capital gains by net-income classes in *Statistics of Income* for the years from 1938 to 1941, inclusive, the per-

[1] U.S. Treasury Department, *Statistics of Income Supplement Compiled from Income Tax Returns for* 1936, Individual Incomes, Sec. IV, Capital Gains and Losses.

[2] It is assumed that $135.2 billion in national income payments is equal to $140 billion in national income. No estimate was made of capital gains reported on returns below the 1936 personal exemptions.

Appendix B

centage distribution of gains in broad net-income classes was computed. Since the concept of a short- and a long-term capital gain in the 1938 Revenue Act differed considerably from the provision for such receipts in the 1934 Revenue Act, the years prior to 1938 are not comparable to the subsequent ones. Moreover, a comparison of the distributions of short- and long-term capital gains for the years from 1938 to 1941, inclusive, indicated that those for the first and last years were clearly atypical. The change in the provisions of the 1938 Act may have had a differential effect on the realization of these receipts by taxpayers in the various net-income classes. During 1941, the effect of the European war on the national economy also may have had a differential influence. Consequently, the above 2 years were eliminated and a typical distribution was computed from the 2 remaining years by averaging percentages in each net-income class.

An aggregate figure was established for net capital losses by determining a typical proportion between total gains and total losses. From data tabulated in *Statistics of Income*, the ratio of total losses to total gains was computed for 1924 to 1933, inclusive. Although there was a wide range in these ratios, it was concluded conservatively that net capital losses tend to aggregate about one-fourth of the amount of net capital gains during a moderately prosperous year. The aggregate amount of net capital losses was distributed by net-income classes according to an average capital-loss distribution. The tax was computed separately on the short- and long-term capital gains.

A NOTE ON
THE COMMITTEE FOR ECONOMIC DEVELOPMENT
AND ITS RESEARCH PROGRAM

The Committee for Economic Development was organized in August, 1942, by a group of business leaders who were convinced that the attainment and maintenance of high employment after the war dare not be left to chance. To seize the opportunities for unprecedented peacetime prosperity in the postwar era and to avoid the real perils of mass unemployment or mass government employment, they believed that individual employers, while in no degree relaxing their efforts toward military victory, must begin to plan promptly, realistically, and boldly for rapid reconversion and vigorous expansion after the war.

There is widespread agreement among economists that American prosperity after the war calls for the sustained employment of 7 to 10 million more workers than in 1940, our banner peacetime year hitherto. The only sound road to such increased employment is the enlargement of production and sales of goods and services to a level some 30 to 45 per cent higher than that of 1940. This meant that business men had to plan for postwar business on a greatly expanded basis as compared to any known peacetime year.

To assist them to make their maximum contribution toward this goal, the Committee for Economic Development—through its Field Development Division—has been working locally in more than 2900 counties and communities in all states of the union. More than 65,000 business men have been serving as members of these committees, aiding as many as possible of the nation's 2 million private employers in the planning of their postwar production and employment.

No pattern or over-all program has been imposed on these

local committees. Each is autonomous, since each understands the peculiar problems of its community better than can any outsider. Yet the problems they had to meet and the tools they needed were in basic respects the same.

Therefore, tested procedures for making both postwar production and employment plans have been supplied to them by the national C.E.D. office. In addition, the country's outstanding specialists in industrial management, in product design, in advertising and selling, and in training of sales personnel have placed their skills freely at the service of all cooperating business men, through handbooks, films, training courses, business clinics, and forums for the local committees.

To plan for the future, the businessman needs particularly some measure for estimating postwar demand for his individual product. Another important service of C.E.D. was its postwar market analysis, conducted with the cooperation of many trade associations and leading industrial firms and covering more than 500 finished-goods products. The findings of this two-year study were made available to business and to the public in a report, *American Industry Looks Ahead*, issued in August of this year.

Even with the best of tools the businessman knows he cannot be wholly successful in carrying out plans for postwar expansion unless national policies prevail that make business expansion possible. To define what these national policies of government, business, and labor should be to encourage higher production and more jobs is the special task of the C.E.D. Research Division. This is the purpose of the research reports, of which this volume is the tenth.

To the long-range economic questions involved in this undertaking have been added the particular economic problems arising out of the war. Both areas have been studied. It is hoped that the reports, as a group, will provide the information that many have been seeking concerning problems intimately related to the life of each of us, as well as to the future of our society.

The Committee for Economic Development

The authors of these reports have already won distinction in their own fields. Perhaps more important is the fact that their previous work has demonstrated not only the competence but the vigor of thought which these complex problems demand. Knowing, however, that the problems that would be scrutinized—demobilization of the war economy, taxation, monetary policy, international trade, agriculture, and the like—are not separate ones, but are integrated and must be studied in relationship one to the other, the C.E.D. sought to make possible an exchange of information and views by the experts and, equally important, between the scholars and businessmen.

What may be a unique scheme of conferences was established, the objective being to blend the practical experience and judgment of the business world with the scholars' knowledge of the action of economic forces. A Research Committee consisting of representative successful business men was set up; to this group was added a Research Advisory Board whose members are recognized as among our leading social scientists; and finally, the persons who would be responsible for the individual reports were named, to comprise the Research Staff.

The subject matter of each report is discussed by the members of these three groups, meeting together. "Discussed" is an inadequate term. "Earnestly argued, and for long hours" does more justice to the work. The author of the report therefore has the benefit of criticism and suggestion by many other competent minds. He is able to follow closely the development of the reports on other economic matters that affect his own study.

No effort is made to arrive at absolute agreement. There is no single answer to the problems that are being studied. What is gained is agreement as to the determinative factors in each problem, and the possible results to be achieved by differing methods of handling the problem. The author of the report has full responsibility, and complete freedom, for proposing whatever action or solution seems advisable to him. There is only one rule—the approach must be from the standpoint of the general welfare and not from that of any special economic or political group; the objective must be high production and high employment in a democratic society.

Since the author is free to present his own conclusions and does not speak for the Research Committee or for the Research Advisory Board, the Research Committee will issue, for each study, where desirable, a separate C.E.D. *policy statement*. This may endorse all of the recommendations arrived at by the author, or it may disagree with some.

The research studies already under way divide roughly into two parts:

A. *The transition from war to peace:* the problems involved in the early *attainment* of high levels of employment and production;

B. *The longer-term fundamental problems* involved in the *maintenance* of high levels of productive employment after the transition period has passed.

The subjects to be covered by the individual monographs in the two series are:

A. *The Transition from War to Peace:*

1. *The Liquidation of War Production*, by A. D. H. Kaplan, The Brookings Institution (already published). The problems involved in the cancellation of war contracts and the disposal of government-owned surplus supplies, plants, and capital equipment are weighed quantitatively as well as qualitatively. How much war plant has the government financed, and what part of it could be put into civilian production? What criteria should prevail in selecting the producers to be released first from war manufactures, as the war production program is curtailed? How and when should surplus

The Committee for Economic Development

goods be sold? Rapid resumption of peace-time production, with conditions favorable to high levels of employment, is the gauge by which the recommendations are measured.

2. *Demobilization of Wartime Economic Controls*, by John Maurice Clark, Professor of Economics, Columbia University (already published). When and how should the wartime controls be removed? The interdependency of the wartime controls of production, manpower, prices, wages, rationing, credit policies, and others is made clear. How relaxation of each control may affect the peacetime economy—in terms of demand and supply, and therefore in terms of job and production levels—is weighed. The conditions that can be expected to prevail at different stages of the transition from a wartime to a peacetime economy are outlined, with emphasis on the variables with which we must be prepared to deal. Professor Clark does not overlook the significance of attitudes and objectives.

3. *Manpower Demobilization and Reemployment*, by Robert R. Nathan, Consulting Economist, and Emmett H. Welch, Chief, Economic Statistics Unit, Bureau of the Census. The relationship of demobilization policy to reemployment. Recommendations are made for a program that would avoid long-period joblessness among returning servicemen as well as war workers.

4. *Providing for Unemployed Workers in the Transition*, by Richard A. Lester, Associate Professor of Economics, Princeton University (already published). An estimate of the size and the duration of transition unemployment. The efficacy of public works employment, relief employment, the adequacy of unemployment compensation, wartime savings, dismissal pay, and the like are appraised. A program is developed to provide for the maintenance of workers who will be out of jobs in the transition from war to peace.

5. *Financing Industry during the Transition from War to Peace*, by Charles C. Abbott, Associate Professor of Business Economics, Harvard University. The sources upon which business has relied for its capital are examined, along with the current financial condition of large and small corporations. These two are weighed against the likely needs of financing by industry for reconversion and expansion in the transition years following the war.
6. *Monetary and Banking Policies in the Postwar Transition Period*, by John K. Langum, Vice-president, Federal Reserve Bank of Chicago. What monetary and banking policies can do to encourage production and employment. Federal fiscal policy is analyzed in its relationship to the financial requirements of business in reconversion and expansion. The significance of monetary policies prior to the war and the money and banking conditions that will stem from war financing are reviewed. The relationship of business spending to other money flows and the resultant production pattern is discussed.

B. *The Longer-term Fundamental Problems:*

1. *Production, Jobs and Taxes*, by Harold M. Groves, Professor of Economics, University of Wisconsin (already published). A study of the federal tax structure as it affects the creation of jobs. The present volume, *Postwar Taxation and Economic Progress*, concludes Professor Groves' analysis of the relationship of taxation to economic development, and presents an approach to taxation that would make for constructive tax policy. The second report inquires into the problems of state and local, as well as federal, taxation.
2. *Agriculture in an Unstable Economy*, by Theodore W. Schultz, Professor of Agricultural Economics, The University of Chicago (already published). An investigation going to the roots of the "farm problem." The

significance of excess labor resources on farms, the failure of price mechanisms to induce shifts of resources out of agriculture, the differences between the farm and industrial sectors in responding to reduced demand. The importance to farmers of continued prosperity in business. A solution to the farm problem without resort to price floors or restrictions on output.

3. *International Trade and Domestic Employment*, by Calvin B. Hoover, Dean of the Graduate School of Arts and Sciences, Duke University (already published). An examination of the kind of foreign trade policies and mechanisms we can adopt that will increase our gains from international trade and also contribute to world peace. A statement of the requirements in terms of the economies of other countries as well as our own.

4. *Business Arrangements in Foreign Trade*, by Edward S. Mason, Professor of Economics, Harvard University. A study of cartels and other forms of international business organizations.

5. *Minimizing Business Fluctuations and Unemployment*, a major series of studies which will be undertaken during the coming year, by John Maurice Clark, K. E. Boulding, M. de Chazeau, Albert G. Hart, Gardiner C. Means, Howard B. Myers, Theodore O. Yntema, and others to be appointed.

6. *The Special Problems of Small Business*, by A. D. H. Kaplan, The Brookings Institution, assisted by J. K. Wexman. An inquiry into the competitive position and the needs of small business.

7. *Providing Adequate Incentives for Enterprise*, by C. E. Griffin, Professor of Business Economics, University of Michigan.

8. *The "Billion Dollar Questions."* By Theodore O. Yntema, Gardiner C. Means, and Howard B. Myers. An economic primer posing the basic economic problems to be faced in a free enterprise system.

Postwar Taxation and Economic Progress

C. *Supplementary Papers:*
   1. *The Economics of a Free Society,* by the Hon. William Benton, Assistant Secretary of State. (Published in October, 1944, issue of *Fortune* Magazine.)
   2. *Personnel Problems of the Postwar Transition Period,* by Charles A. Myers, Assistant Professor of Industrial Relations, Massachusetts Institute of Technology (already published). An examination of the problems that will confront employers in connection with the rehiring of servicemen and war workers, and issues that will arise in the shift of the work force from wartime to peacetime production.
   3. *Federal Tax Reform,* by Henry C. Simons, Associate Professor of Economics, The University of Chicago. The development of a basic philosophy of taxation to simplify the federal tax structure and distribute the tax burden among individuals in relation to their incomes.
   4. *Incidence of Taxation,* by William Vickrey, formerly Tax Research Division, Treasury Department.
   5. *World Politics Faces Economics,* by Harold Lasswell, Director of War Communications Research, Library of Congress (already published). A discussion of the interrelationship of economic and political factors shaping the world political structure, with particular reference to the future relations of the United States and Russia.
   6. *Changes in Substantive Law, Legal Processes and Government Organization to Maintain Conditions Favorable to Competition,* by Corwin Edwards, Professor of Economics, Northwestern University.

These are the subjects so far authorized by the Research Committee of C.E.D. Others may be undertaken at a later date. These subject titles will not necessarily be the same as the book titles when finally published.

EXCERPTS FROM BY-LAWS OF THE COMMITTEE FOR ECONOMIC DEVELOPMENT CONCERNING THE RESEARCH PROGRAM

Section 3. Research Committee

It shall be the responsibility of the Research Committee to initiate studies into the principles of business policy and of public policy which will foster the full contribution by industry and commerce in the post-war period to the attainment of high and secure standards of living for people in all walks of life through maximum employment and high productivity in the domestic economy. All research is to be thoroughly objective in character, and the approach in each instance is to be from the standpoint of the general welfare and not from that of any special political or economic group.

Publication

The determination of whether or not a study shall be published shall rest solely with the Research Director and the Research Advisory Board. . . . A copy of any manuscript reported for publication shall be submitted to each member of the Research Advisory Board, of the Research Committee, of the Board of Trustees, and to the Chairman and Vice-chairman of the Field Development Committee. For each subject to be so submitted the Research Director, after consulting with the Chairman of the Research Advisory Board, shall appoint a Reading Committee of three members of the Board. Thereupon, as a special assignment each member of the Reading Committee shall read the manuscript and within fifteen days from its assignment to him shall signify his approval or disapproval for publication. If two out of the three Reading Committee members signify their approval, the manuscript shall be published at the expense of the Corporation. . . . In no case shall publication necessarily constitute endorsement by the Committee for Economic Development, the Board of Trustees, the Research Committee or by the Research Advisory Board of the manuscript's conclusions. Upon approval for publication, the Research Director shall notify all members of the Research Advisory Board and no manuscript may be published until fifteen days following such notification. The interval is allowed for the receipt of any memorandum of comment, reservation, or dissent that any member of the Research Advisory Board may wish to express. Should a member of the Research Advisory Board so request, his memorandum of comment, reservation, or dissent, which must be signed, shall be published with the manuscript. Any signed comment, reservation, or dissent which the Research Director may wish to express or have expressed by others shall at his request be published with the manuscript. . . . In the event the manuscript is not approved for publication at the Corporation's expense as above provided, the individual or group making the research shall nevertheless have the right to publish the manuscript.

Supplementary Papers

The Research Director may recommend to the Editorial Board for publication as a Supplementary Paper any manuscript (other than a regular research report) . . . which in his opinion should be made publicly available because it constitutes an important contribution to the understanding of a problem on which research has been initiated by the Research Committee.

An Editorial Board for Supplementary Papers shall be established consisting of five members: The Research Director, two members from the Research Committee, and two members from the Research Advisory Board. The members from the Research Committee and the members from the Research Advisory Board shall be appointed by the respective chairmen of those bodies. The Research Director shall be the chairman

The Committee for Economic Development

of the Editorial Board and shall act as Editor of the Supplementary Papers. . . . If a majority of the members of the Editorial Board vote for publication, the manuscript shall be published as one of a series of Supplementary Papers, separate and distinct from the regular research reports. . . . Publication does not constitute endorsement of the author's statements by the Committee for Economic Development, by the Board of Trustees, by the Research Committee, or by the Research Advisory Board.

RESEARCH COMMITTEE

RALPH E. FLANDERS, *Chairman*
President, Federal Reserve Bank
Boston, Massachusetts

CHESTER C. DAVIS, *Vice Chairman*
President, Federal Reserve Bank
St. Louis, Missouri

MARION B FOLSOM, *Vice Chairman*
Treasurer, Eastman Kodak
 Company
Rochester, New York

JAMES F. BROWNLEE
290 Hass Road
Fairfield, Connecticut

GARDNER COWLES, President & Publisher
Des Moines Register & Tribune
Des Moines, Iowa

DONALD DAVID, Dean
Graduate School of Business
 Administration
Harvard University
Boston, Massachusetts

JOHN F. FENNELLY, Partner
Glore, Forgan & Company
Chicago, Illinois

WILLIAM C. FOSTER, Vice President
Pressed & Welded Steel Products
 Company
Long Island City, New York

GEORGE L. HARRISON, President
New York Life Insurance Company
New York, New York

PAUL G. HOFFMAN, President
The Studebaker Corporation
South Bend, Indiana

ERIC A JOHNSTON, President
Brown-Johnston Company
 $^c/_o$ Chamber of Commerce of the
  United States
Washington, D.C.

ERNEST KANZLER
Chairman of the Board
Universal C.I.T. Credit
 Corporation
Detroit, Michigan

THOMAS B. McCABE, President
Scott Paper Company
Chester, Pennsylvania

PHILIP D REED
Chairman of the Board
General Electric Company
New York, New York

RAYMOND RUBICAM
444 Madison Avenue
New York, New York

BEARDSLEY RUML
Chairman of the Board
R. H Macy & Co.
New York, New York

R. GORDON WASSON, Vice President
J P. Morgan & Company
New York, New York

RESEARCH ADVISORY BOARD

SUMNER H. SLICHTER, *Chairman*
   Lamont University Professor
   Harvard University

ROBERT DE BLOIS CALKINS
   Vice Chairman
   Dean, School of Business
   Columbia University

DOUGLASS V BROWN
   Professor of Industrial Relations
   Massachusetts Institute of
     Technology

DAVID F. CAVERS
   Professor of Law (on leave)
   Harvard University

NEIL JACOBY
   Professor of Finance
   School of Business
   The University of Chicago

HAROLD LASSWELL
   Director of War Communications
     Research
   Library of Congress

THEODORE W. SCHULTZ
   Professor of Agricultural Economics
   The University of Chicago

RALPH YOUNG
   Professor of Economics
   University of Pennsylvania

Research Director
THEODORE O YNTEMA
Professor on leave from School of Business
The University of Chicago

*Associate Research Director
and
Executive Secretary of Research Committee*
HOWARD B MYERS

Associate Research Director
GARDINER C. MEANS

Assistant to Research Director
SYLVIA STONE

INDEX

A

Ability to pay, 22n, 26
  corporate, 84
  theory of, 84–85
Accountants, 128
Accountants' Handbook, by Paton, 156n
Accounting, depreciation in, 155, 160–161
  inventory in, 148n, 152
Accounting, Principles of, by Kohler and Morrison, 207n
Acquisitive Society, The, by Tawney, 309n
Adams, T. S., 21, 21n, 23, 49, 49n
"Administration, Costs of Tax," by Martin, 335n
Administration, tax, 129
Admission tax, 285
Advertising, 78
Agency, federal-state, 336
Agricultural Adjustment Act, 297, 298
Agriculture, aid to, 383, 384
Alabama, 339n, 340
Alcoholic beverage tax (*see* Liquor tax)
Allen, R. G., 297, 298n
Allowance, depletion of, 162
Allowances, depreciation, 45, 144
  obsolescence, 45
Altman, G. T., 280n
American Telephone and Telegraph Company, 53, 90
America's Capacity to Produce, by Nourse and Associates, 47n
America's Needs and Resources, 379n
Amlie, T. R., 297, 298n
Amos, J. E., 45n

Analysis, bracket, 174n
  classes-of-income, 174n
Anderson, W. H., 243n
Antitrust Division, 77
Appeals, Board of Tax, 129
Appointment, powers of, 269–274
"Appointment, Powers of," by Leach, 269n
"Appointment and Estate Taxes, Powers of," by Eisenstein, 274n
Arizona, 240, 340
Assets, capital, 206n–208n
  depreciating, 257–258
  "fixed," 207n
Australia, 70n, 144
Automobile Industry, Financial History of the American, by Seltzer, 46n
Automobile-use tax, 285
Averaging, 233–236, 361, 377
  system of, 226–228
Avoidance, Prevention of Tax, 191n
Avoidance, tax, 42–44

B

Ballentine, H. W., 90n
Ballentine on Corporations, by Ballentine, 90n
Bankruptcies, 112
Banks, Federal Reserve, 48
Base, business income-tax, 130–164
  personal income-tax, 165–170
Beer, tax on, 293
Belgium, 69n
Beneficiary, 266
Benefit theory, 23, 24, 115
Bequests, charitable, 277–278
Berle, A. A., 56n
"Betterments," 155n

Beveridge, Sir William, 324n
Beveridge Plan, 324–325
Bingham's Administrator v. Commonwealth, 254
Blakey, G. C, 33n
Blakey, R. G., 33n, 348n
Blockage problem, 253–257
"Blockage rule," 254, 255
Boat-use tax, 285
Bonbright, J C., 89n, 252n
Bond financing, 31–35, 114
Bondholders, 31
Bonds, government, 200, 306
  local, 200n
  ordinary, 306
  series E savings, 358
  state, 200n
Bonds, Problem of Tax-exempt, by Thompson, 202n
Bonus, veterans', 50
Bonuses, 124
Book income, 51
"Boom or Collapse, Postwar," by Slichter, 352n, 353n
Bounties, system of, 14
Bracket analysis, 174n
Brandeis, Elizabeth, 322n, 325n
Brass Mill Products Association, 149
Bribes, 312
Bridges, 248
British tax system, 62–64
Brown, E C., 159n
Brown, H. G., 314n
Budget, cyclical, 356
  postwar federal, 379–389
Budgetary instability, 112
Buehler, A. G., 45n, 69n, 295n
Buildings, 248
Bull v Smith, 256n
Bunn, Charles, 120n
Burr, Susan, 190n
Business, 8
  big, 27, 98, 111
  competitive, 26–27, 97–99
  decisions in, 13
  developing new products in, 26–27
  interstate, 333

Business, migration of, to escape taxes, 341–344
  new, 26–27, 97–105
  private, 2
  small, 26–27, 48, 53, 74–106, 111, 130–131
  taxes on size of, 105
  unincorporated, 117
"Business in A.D. 194Q, Transition to Peace·," 386n
Business Be Taxed, How Shall, 68n, 119n
"Business, Births and Deaths in," by Mitchell and Hayes, 97n
"Business, How Big is Big," by George, 98n
"Business, The New York State Tax on Unincorporated," by Rauh, 119n
Business, Problems of Small, 97n
"Business' Births and Deaths," by Thorp and Rothmann, 97n
"Business and Cigarette Tax, Connecticut's Unincorporated," by Goodrich, 199n
Business combinations, supervision of, 77
Business Funds and Consumer Purchasing Power, The Flow of, by Mack, 155n, 156n
"Business, The Taxation of," by Adams, 21
Business taxation, 24
  state, 333
"Business Taxation, Toward a Theory of," by Studenski, 22n
Business taxes, 17, 18, 19, 24, 70–71, 111, 117–119, 125–127, 376
  Canadian, 334
  coordination of state and federal, 334–337
  corporate, 117–119
  incidence of alternative forms of, 108–111
  multibase, 116
  rational system of, 71
  state, 327, 337–339

Index

Business taxes, "theoretical" basis of, 20–27
  theory of, 22
  (*See also* Income tax, corporate; Excess-profits tax)
Business Week, 52
Butters, J. Keith, 6n, 32, 32n, 135n, 142n

C

California, 240
California Fruit Growers' Association, 121
Campbell, H A , 240n
Canada, 44n
  business tax situation in, 334
Capital, distinctions between, and land, 315
  provisions for impairment of, 154–155
Capital Goes on Strike, When, by Dahlberg, 301n
Capital-gains tax, 59–62, 378
Capital-stock tax, 114–115
  genuine, 83
  state, 333, 339, 339n
"Capital Stock Tax, The Federal," by Drake, 115n
Capitalism, A Dynamic, by Hazlitt, 301n
Carnegie, Andrew, 246
Carr-Saunders, 122n
Carry-back of losses, 140, 145–146, 354–356
Carry-over of losses, 138, 139, 141–146, 154n, 160, 206, 226, 377
Cartel agreements, 77
Carver, T. N., 310
Chain-store tax, 100
Chile, 69n
Chudson, W. A., 33n, 91n, 147n
Cigarette tax, 197n
"Cigarette Tax, Connecticut's Unincorporated Business and," by Goodrich, 199n
Cigars, tax on, 293
Clague, Ewan, 323n

Coates, W. H., 38
Collapse or Boom at the End of the War, by Moulton and Schlotterbeck, 14n, 350n
Colm, Gerhard, 21, 21n, 51n, 53n, 67n, 68n, 69n, 91n, 144n, 198n, 300n
Colorado, 340
Colwyn Committee (*see* Debt and Taxation, British Committee on National)
Commerce, Chamber of, 298
Commons, John R , 2, 310
"Commons' Theory of Reasonable Value as Applied to Taxation," by Groves, 311n
Communications, tax on, 285
Compensation, unemployment, 318, 319–325
Competition, 76
Connally, Senator, 240
Connecticut, 119
"Connecticut's Unincorporated Business and Cigarette Tax," by Goodrich, 119n
Conservation, 3
  (*See also* Resources)
Construction, new, 4
Consumers, 29
Consumers' cooperative movement (*see* Cooperative movement)
Consumption, 3–4
Consumption taxes, 13, 17, 284, 290–295
  arguments, against, 288–289
  favoring, 287–288
  and deflation, 290–292
  and inflation, 290–292
  (*See also* Sales tax)
Control, price, 80
  social, 23n, 26
Coolidge, Calvin, 200n
Cooperation in Great Britain, Consumers, by Carr-Saunders, *et al.*, 122n
Cooperative movement, 7, 77, 119
Cooperatives, application of the tax system to, 119–125

Copyrights, 347
Corporate Enterprise, Taxation of, by Hynning and Colm, 51*n*
Corporate family, 88
Corporate Financial Structure, The Pattern of, by Chudson, 33*n*, 91*n*, 147*n*
Corporate Franchise as a Basis of Taxation, The, by Lindholm, 68*n*
Corporate and personal taxes, integration of federal, 20–39
Corporate Size and Earning Power, by Crum, 130*n*
Corporate taxes, 20–39, 385, 388
Corporate excess taxes, state, 333, 339, 339*n*
Corporation and Private Property, The Modern, by Berle and Means, 56*n*
Corporation Finance, by Mead, 46*n*
"Corporation Taxes, International Comparison of," by Colm, 67*n*
Corporation taxes, state, table, 338
Corporations, Committee of the National Tax Association on Federal Taxation of, 41, 108, 113, 118
Corporations, competition among states for the domicile of, 336
personal service, 55
treated like partnerships, 55–59
Corporations, Federal Taxation of, by Butters, 135*n*, 142
Corporations, Final Report of the Committee of the National Tax Association on Federal Taxation of, 41, 45*n*, 54*n*, 67*n*, 69*n*, 70*n*, 108*n*, 117*n*, 118*n*, 144*n*
Corporations, Financial Policy of, by Dewing, 9*n*, 47*n*
Corporations, The Financing of Large, by Koch, 45*n*
Corporations, Statistics of American Listed, 91
Cosmetics tax, 285
Costing, "flow" theories of, 147
Costs, 307–308

Costs, social, 22*n*
Court, Supreme, 42, 129, 347
tax, 129
Credits, 171–174, 296
Crum, W. L., 53, 53*n*, 130*n*, 241*n*, 379, 380
Crum analysis, 379–385
Curtis Publishing Company, statement of, 6
Curves, Lorenz, 194, 195
Custom revenue, 285, 386, 389

D

Dahlberg, Arthur, 301, 301*n*
Dams, 248
Dane County, Wisconsin, 230
Death taxation, 5, 62, 243–283
Death taxes, 13, 19, 40, 66, 165, 220, 309, 310, 376, 378
case, against, 244–250
for, 243–244
effect on incentives of, 245–250
evaluating assets of, 250–259
exemptions for, 259–262
forms of, 259–262
in Great Britain, 262
relation of, to monopoly, 248–249
to philanthrophy, 249–250
to risk-taking, 247
to savings, 246–248
treasury regulations of, 251–252
yield of, 262–278
Debt, funded, 32*n*
national, 356–360, 382
social security, 367–371
Debt limitations, municipal, 330–331
Debt and Taxation, British Committee on National, 38, 48*n*, 69
Debt and Taxation, Report of the Committee on National, 38, 48, 69*n*
Declared-value excess-profits tax, 50, 82–83
Deductions, 6, 170–171, 374
Deflation, 290–292
Delaware, 26, 272, 336, 337, 340*n*

Index

Delinquency, property tax, 18, 316
Demand, "acceleration," 131
  derived, 131
  "pick-up," 131
Depletion, 153, 161–164
"Depletion, Problems of," by Short, 162n
Deposits, savings, 305
Depreciation, 153–161, 257–258
Depreciation accounting, 155, 160–161
Depreciation allowance, 144
Depreciation and business-cycle economics, 157–158
"Depreciation A Neglected Chapter in War Taxation, Accelerated," by Brown and Patterson, 159n
Detroit, Michigan, 351
Dewing, A. S., 9n, 47n
Differentiation, 171, 172
Direct taxes, 373
Directors, board of, tyranny of, 46
Discounts, 296
Discrimination, tax, 40–42
Disincorporation, 118
Distribution, 2
Dividends, 29, 30, 35, 41, 340–341
  cash, 52
  "consent," 64n
  estimates of, 388n
  paid to individuals, table of, 86–87
  "patronage," 120–125
  preferred treatment for, 306–307
  security, 51n
  stock, 57
  tax on intercorporate, 64n, 91–94
  taxable stock, 58n
Domar, E. D , 10n
Dominion-Provincial Relations, Canadian Royal Commission on, 113, 333, 333n
Drake, C. A , 115n
Dues tax, 285
Duke, Doris, 247
Duplication in a gross-income tax, 110
  "value added," an alternative base for, 110

"Dwindling Dynasties," by Flynn, 249n

E

Economic Association, American, 49
Economic Committee, Hearings Before the Temporary National, 45n
Economic Fragments, by Robertson, 39
Economic morale, 3, 5–15
Economic motivation, 8
Economic Science and the Common Welfare, by Brown, 314n
Economics, business-cycle, 157–158
Economics, Principles of, by Marshall, 38
"Economy, mixed," 2
Eisenstein, Louis, 274n
Eisner v. Macomber, 42, 56
Electrical appliances, tax on, 285
Electrical energy, tax on, 285
Ellis, Paul W , 9n
Employment, postwar, 1–3
  techniques to regularize, 320 321
Employment, After the War—Full, by Hansen, 352n
"Employment Stabilization through Payroll Taxation," by Pribram, 322n
Enterprise, dynastic, 248–249
"Enterprise in America, What Is the Outlook for Private?" by Slichter, 352n
Enterprise, Effect of Federal Taxes on Growing, by Butters and Lintner, 6n
Enterprise, New Firms and Free, by Oxenfeldt, 98n
Enterprise, Taxation of Corporate, by Hynning and Colm, 51n
Equipment, 45
Estate of Leonard B. McKitterick, 256n
Estate of Sanford v. Commissioner, 279n
Estate tax, 17, 241, 259–260, 261–262. 278–282, 386, 389
  English, 275
  evasion of, 262–278
  federal, 278–282
  insurance for evasion of, 276–277

Estate and Gift Taxation, Federal, by Paul, 256n, 277n
Estate and gift taxes, integration of, 278-282
"Estate and Gift Taxes, Integration of," by Altman, 280n
"Estate Taxes, Powers of Appointment and," by Eisenstein, 274n
Estates, loss of value during settlement of, 252-259
"Estates and Inheritance Taxation, Economic Aspects of," by Mellon, 245n
Estates, Trusts, and Gifts, Federal Taxes on, by Montgomery, 264n
Excess-profits tax, 10, 17, 18, 33n, 38, 74-106, 354-356
"Excess Profits Tax, Immediate Future of the," by Adams, 49n
Excise tax, 16, 19, 284, 285, 286, 287
  special, 292-294, 327
Exemption, 17, 18, 171-174, 202-206, 296, 374
Expediency, social, 22n
Expenditure, Brookings study of federal, 385n
  federal public, 1950, table of, 381
  governmental, 14
  postwar federal, 379-385
  table of, 380
Experience rating, 318, 319-325
"Experience Rating in Unemployment Compensation, etc.," by Feldman and Smith, 320n

F

Farioletti, Marius, 290n
Federal Taxation, Cases and Materials on, by Griswold, 278n
Federal Taxation, Studies in, by Paul, 268n
"Federal Taxes and the Future," by Hansen and Greer, 299n
Federal Taxes, The Impact of, by Magill, 23n, 128n, 278n
"Fee simple," 274

Fees, license, 389
Feldman, H, 320n
Fennelly, J. F., 241n
Field, Marshall, 11
Finance, Public, by Lutz, 115n
Finance Act of 1923, 69
  of 1927, 211n
Finance Acts of the United Kingdom, 262n
Financial History of the American Automobile Industry, by Seltzer, 46n
Financing, bond, 31-35, 114
  deficit, 112
  stock, 31-35
Financing Government, by Groves, 41n, 109n, 266n
First-in, first-out theory, 147, 148, 151
Fiscal Planning for Total War, by Crum, Fennelly, and Seltzer, 241n
Fiscal Policy and Business Cycles, by Hansen, 352n
Fiscal Relations, Committee on Intergovernmental, 196
Fiscal Relations, Federal, State and Local Government, 201n, 335n, 336n, 340n
Fiscal Requirements, Postwar, by Kimmel, 379n
Fisher, Irving, 41
Fitch v. Tax Commission, 227n
Flynn, J. T., 249, 249n
Ford Motor Company, 45
Forest resources, 13
Form 1040, 390
Form 1040A, 390
France, 69n, 144
Franchise taxes, 25, 367, 377
Friday, David, 130n
Fruit Growers Association, California, 121
Fur articles, tax on, 285

G

"Gains, The British Treatment of Capital," by May, 209n
Gains, capital, 178, 180-184, 206-223, 399-401
  casual, 225

Index

"Gains, Taxation of Capital," by Haig, 207*n*
Gains and losses, capital, 206–223
    reported by Wisconsin taxpayers in 1929, table of, 216
Gambling, 10
Gasoline tax, 18, 285, 367, 377
General Electric Company, 45*n*
General Motors Company, 45*n*
George, E. B., 98*n*
George, Henry, 313, 314
Germany, 67–68, 300, 335*n*
Gift and estate taxes, integration of, 278–282
Gift taxes, 262–278, 386, 389
    federal, 278–282
Gift-tax legislation, 279
Gift Taxation in the United States, by Hariss, 280*n*
Gifts, in contemplation of death, 263, 264–265, 277–278
Gilbert, J. H., 144*n*, 170*n*
Goff v. Smith, 256
Goldenweiser, E. A., 167*n*, 386*n*
Good will, 347
Goodman, A B , 346*n*
Goodrich, E. S., 119*n*
Graduation, bracket system of, 10
Grants, special-privilege, 25
Great Britain, 48*n*, 67–70, 122, 241, 324, 343, 344
Green, Edith, 229*n*
Greer, Guy, 299*n*, 352*n*
Griswold, Erwin, 278*n*, 280*n*
Gross income, 107
Gross-income taxes, 24, 107–108, 339
Groves, H. M., 41*n*, 102*n*, 109*n*, 266*n*, 311*n*, 315*n*, 322*n*, 346*n*
Guthmann, H. G., 52*n*

H

Hagen, E. E., 167*n*, 386*n*
Haig, R. M., 207*n*, 209*n*, 211, 211*n*, 335*n*
Hanna, F. A., 195, 195*n*, 213*n*, 224*n*, 225*n*

Hansen, Alvin, 299, 299*n*, 352*n*
Harbors, 248
Harding, Warren G , 200*n*
Hariss, C. L., 280*n*
Hart, 390*n*
    sample, 391, 392
    study, 391
Hayes, W., 97*n*
Hazlitt, C. W., 301*n*
Heiner v. Donnan, 265*n*
Helvering v. City Bank Farmers Trust Co., 268*n*
Helvering v. Grinnell, 272
Helvering v. Maytag, 255*n*, 256*n*
Helvering v. Safe Deposit and Trust Co, 255*n*
Hoarding, 304, 305, 376
    corporate, 65
Hoardings tax, 301–303, 305
Hobson, J. A., 307–309, 310, 312
Hoffenberg, M., 393*n*
Holding companies, 27, 44, 89–91
Holding Company, The, by Bonbright and Means, 89*n*
Holdings, taxing intercorporate, 89–96
Hoover, Herbert, 244
Hospitals, 384
Housing, 3, 5, 384
Houston, Secretary of the Treasury, 49
H R. 6358, Statement before the Ways and Means Committee on, by Paul, 201*n*
Hynning, C. J., 51*n*, 53*n*, 91*n*

I

Idaho, 240, 340
Illinois, 339*n*
Incentive taxation, 14, 221, 296–326
    proposals for, 297–306
"Incentive Taxation with Special Reference to Unemployment," by Schmidt, 319*n*
Incentives, 6–15, 30, 111, 373
Income, annual, 207
    British tax on corporate, 62–64
    casual, 218
    concept of, 307

· 423 ·

Income, annual, differentiation of, 311-313
  earned, 306, 311
  gross, 107
  irregular, 228-236
  national, 4, 166n
  study of Wisconsin, 228-235
  surplus, 308
  tax on operating, 108
  taxable, 51
  taxation of imputed, 237-239
  taxpayers', 18
  unearned, 311
    distribution of net taxable, by brackets, table for, 175
"Income, Estate and Gift Tax, etc., Plan for the Coordination of," by Griswold, 280n
"Income and Estate Tax Yields, Estimating," by Vickrey, 398n
Income, of Identical Taxpayers, 1929-1935, Changes in, 225n
Income, Taxable, by Magill, 209n, 210n
"Income, The Taxation of Imputed," by Marsh, 237n, 238n
Income payments, national, 166n
"Income Tax, Discriminatory Effects of the Annual Computation of the Corporation," 135n
Income Tax, The Federal, by R. G. and G. C. Blakey, 33n
Income Tax in Great Britain and the United States, The, by Spaulding, 70n
Income Tax, Report of the Royal Commission on the, 208n
Income Tax, Royal Commission on the, 68, 143, 207-209
Income Tax, Shifting and Effects of the Federal Corporation, 37
Income-tax base, 130-164, 165-170
Income-tax Commissioners, 308
Income-tax returns for 1936, Wisconsin, 195
"Income Tax Statistics, Critical Analysis of Wisconsin Individual," by Hanna, 224n, 225n

Income Tax Statistics, Wisconsin Individual, 191n
Income Taxation, Capital Goods Industries and the Federal, 132n, 133n, 134n
"Income Taxation, Conflicting Theories of Corporate," by Colm, 21n, 68n
Income Taxation, The Law of Federal, by Paul and Mertens, 95n
Income Taxation, Personal, by Simons, 202n
"Income Taxation and Risk-taking, Proportional," by Domar and Musgrave, 10n
Income taxes, 6, 13, 17, 18
  British, 39, 191, 214
  business, 135-141
  Civil War, 55
  corporate, 17, 18, 20, 27-29, 37-39
  personal, 40-42, 66, 165-242, 366, 374, 387-388
    administration of, 198-199
    analysis of 1941 returns, 390-399
    classified, 306-307
    credits for, 171-174
    deductions in, 170-171
    estimated postwar, chart of, 167
    exemptions in, 171-174, 202-206
    rates for, 174-177, 180-188
    returns on, 241
    simplification of, 236
    simplified reporting of, 236
    state, 340-341
    surtax levels of, 177-180
    yield of, 189-192
  Philadelphia, 332, 377
  state, 18, 327, 331-333, 374
  Wisconsin, 216
"Income Taxes and the Price Level," by Seligman, 38
"Income in Theory and Income Taxation in Practice" by Fisher, 41
Income War Tax Act, Canadian, 44n
Incomes in the United States and their Distribution in 1935-1936, Consumer, 398n

Index

Incorporation, 25
Index, price, 151n, 152
Indiana, 340n
Indirect taxes, 109
Industrial Conference Board, National, 9n, 37–39
Industrial Discipline, The, by Tugwell, 47n
Industrial Expansion Act, 297–299, 303
Industrial Expansion Commission, 297
Industrial Recovery Act of 1933, 82, 143
Industries, equipment of, 131
Inflation, 81, 290–292
Inheritance tax, 17, 246, 259, 260–262
  state, 331
"Inheritance Taxation and Maladjustment of National Income Taxes," by Woolfson, 244n
Institutional Economics, by Commons, 310n
Insurance for avoidance of estate tax, 276–277
"Insurance" against loss, 131
Intangibles tax, 346–348
Interest, 4, 28, 33n, 307
International Harvester Company, 90
"Inventories, The Cost Approach to," by Paton, 147n
Inventory methods, tax status of, 150–151
Investment, 3–4, 363–364, 384
Investment Trusts and Investment Companies, 48n
Iowa, 340

J

Jackson, R H, 93n
Jewelry tax, 285
"Jobs after the War," by Goldenweiser and Hagen, 167n, 386n

K

Kaiser, Henry, 247
Kimmel, L H, 379n

Koch, Albert, 45n
Kohler, E. L., 207n
Koshland v. Helvering, 51n

L

Labor, 29
Land and capital, distinction between, 315
Land, tax on, 308, 311
Land tax, 310, 313
  (*See also* Single tax)
Last-in, first-out theory, the, 147, 148, 148n, 149n, 151, 151n
Law, Canadian inventory reserve, 151
  workmen's compensation, 317, 319
  Swedish, 1938, 298–299
Laws, British income tax, 207–211
  changes in tax, 12
  community property, 239–240
  corporation, 56n
  for exemption, 172
  federal tax, 12
  incorporation, 25, 94
  Oklahoma, 240
"Laws, Consumers' Cooperatives and Price Fixing," by Bunn, 120n
"Laws, Cost to Business Concerns of Compliance with Tax," by Haig, 335n
Laws, Report of the Connecticut Temporary Commission to Study the Tax, 119n
Leach, W. B, 269n
Legislation, gift-tax, 279
Lend-lease, 384
License fees, 389
Lieblein, 390n
Life-estate-remainder sequence, 273, 274–276
"Lifo" (*see* Last-in, first-out theory of costing)
Lindholm, R. W., 68n
Lintner, John, 6n
Liquor tax, 17, 285, 292, 367, 376, 377, 386, 389
Litterer, Oscar, 130n, 165n, 390n

· 425 ·

Livingston, S. M., 167n, 352n, 354, 386n, 392
Local taxes, 327–348, 377
Lockheed Aircraft Corporation, 6n
Loopholes, 375
Lords, House of, 122
Lorenz curves, 194, 195
Loss "insurance," 131
Losses, business, 130–132
   capital, 181–184, 206–223, 399
   in capital-goods industries, 132–135
   carry-back, 140, 145–146, 354–356
   carry-over of, 138, 139, 141–146, 154n, 160, 206, 226, 377
   in consumption-goods industries, 132–135
   corporate, 45, 131, 354
   deduction of, 6
   fear of, 9, 130
   inventory of, 146n
   treatment of, 143–144
Louisiana, 240
Luggage tax, 285
Lutz, Harley, 115, 115n
Luxury taxes, 292, 309

M

McCormick, C T, 325n
McIntyre, Francis, 52n
Mack, R. P., 155n, 156n
McMahon, Thomas C., 317n
McNeish, Charlotte, 165n, 390n
Magill, Roswell, 23n, 128n, 209n–210n, 278n
Maintenance, 155n
Malthus, T. R., 313n
Management, 9, 46, 131, 319, 320–321
Managers, 30
"Manpower and Its Capacity to Produce, Postwar," by Livingston, 392n
Market, free, 303
   postwar, 291–292
Market fluctuations, 131
Market valuation, 147
Markets after the War by Livingston, 167n, 352n, 386n

Marsh, D B, 237n, 238n
Marshall, Alfred, 38
Martin, J. W., 335n
Marx, Karl, 1
Massachusetts, 339n, 340n
Maverick, M., 297
May, G. O., 209n
May v. Heiner, 266n
Mead, E. S., 46n
Means, G. C., 56n, 89n
Mellon, A. W., 245n, 278
Mellon Educational and Charitable Trust, 278
Mertens, Jacob, 95n
Metropolitan Life Insurance Company v New Orleans, 347n
Michigan, 332
Midland Cooperative Wholesale v. Ickes, 123n
Military outlays, 382
Mill, John Stuart, 243, 243n, 313n
Mills, W. C., 274n
Missouri, 340
Mitchell, Jr., W., 97n
Money, "timid," 304
Money and Credits Tax Problem in Minnesota, Factual Analysis of the, 348n
Monopoly, 25, 26, 47n, 53, 74–106, 248–249, 308
   checking, 89–96
Monopoly problem, 76–81
Monopoly profits, 76, 80, 88
Montgomery, R. H., 264n
Morale, economic, 3, 5–15
Morrison, P. L., 207n
Morton, W. A., 320n
Motivation, economic, 8
Motor-vehicle tax, 327
   (*See also* Automobile-use tax)
Moulton, H. G., 14n, 350, 351
Multiple taxation, 333
Musgrave, R. A, 10n

N

Net income tax, corporate, 24, 83–89, 107–108, 109, 337

Index

Netherlands, 70n
New Jersey, 26
New Mexico, 240
New Orleans v. Stempel, 347n
New York, 119, 328
New York Stock Exchange, 222
New York Times, The, 240
Newcomer, Mabel, 68n, 196, 196n, 287n, 360n
Nonmilitary governmental activities, cost of, 382
"Normal tax," 174n
Norway, 69n
Nourse, E G., 47n
NRA, 298
Nutrition standards, 3

O

Obsolescence, 153–161
Oil business, 10n
Oklahoma, 240
Old-age pensions, 367, 368
"Old-Age and Survivors' Insurance, Federal," by Williamson, 369n
Old-Age and Survivors' Insurance Fund, 368
Oregon, 340
"Output, Maintaining Productive," by Friday, 130n
Oversaving, 4, 8, 247, 292, 364, 373
Oxenfeldt, A. R., 98n

P

Packard Motor Company, 43n
"Papen Plan," 300–301
"Papen Plan for Economic Recovery Failed, Why the," by Colm, 300n
Partnership procedure, 55–59
Partnerships, treating corporations like, 55–59
Patents, 347
Paton, W. A., 127n, 147n, 156n, 355n
Patterson, G., 159n
Paul, R. E, 95n, 163n, 201n, 210n, 256n, 268, 268n, 277n

Pay roll taxes, 17, 107, 110–111, 318–325
Peloubet, M. E., 149
Penalties, system of, 14
Pennsylvania Railway Company, 9
Pension program, old-age, 289
Perpetuities, rule against, 271–272
Personal tax, 24, 30
Personal taxes, integration of federal corporate and, 20–39
Peters, H. W , 254n
Petroleum Industry, The, by Shuman, 11n
Philadelphia, 328
Philadelphia income tax, 332, 377
Philanthrophy, 249–250
Pickford v. Quirke, 209n
Pittsburgh, Pa., 316
"Pittsburgh's Graded Tax on Buildings," by McMahon, 317n
Plant, new, 45
Playing cards, tax on, 285
Policy, Conference on Research in Fiscal, 379
Policy, Effects of Taxes on Corporate, 9, 43n, 124n, 158n
Policy, fiscal, 349, 350–355
  postwar budget, 356–358
  reconversion tax, 350–355
Political Economy, Principles of, by Mill, 243n
Poll taxes, 18
Pollock decision, 200n
Postwar period, production and taxes in, 1–19
Premiums, 296
Pribram, K., 322n
Privileges, special, 22n
Problems of the Postwar World, ed. by McCormick, 325n
Producers' goods, public, 248
Product, gross national, 166n
Production, 38
  "all-out," 2
  effect of tax system on, 3–15
  in postwar period, 1–19
Production, Jobs and Taxes, by Groves, 102n

Profits, 8, 9–12, 28, 38, 145, 308
   casual, 209
   inventory of, 146n
   monopoly, 76, 80
   undistributed, 40–73
Profits, Federal Taxation of Corporate, by Butters, 32, 32n
Progression, 292
"Progressive," 197n
Progressive taxation, 310
Property, intangible, 346–348
   taxation of community, 237, 239–242
"Property Act, Developments Relating to the Oklahoma," by Campbell, 240n
Property tax, 18, 21, 125, 239, 301, 304, 327, 328, 331, 344–348
   delinquency in, 18, 316
   in Great Britain, 345
"Property Tax Administration, Pattern of Successful," by Groves and Goodman, 346n
Property Taxation of Intangibles, 346n
Price controls, 80, 81, 354
Prices, 27-28, 29, 38–39
Psychological factors, 354
Public works, 384
Purchasing power, 172
Purchasing Power, The Flow of Business Funds and Consumer, by Mack, 155n, 156n
Pyramiding, 90, 91

Q

Quesnay, François, 313n

R

Radio tax, 285
Rate scale, 375
   yield, 186–188
Rate structures, 83–89
Rates, business income tax, 135–141
   city property-tax, 328
   corporate tax, 17, 18

Rates, federal income tax, table of, 137
   graduated, 84, 85, 88, 104–105
   marginal, 176
   penalty tax, 42
   schedule of, 180–186
   standard, 174n
   surtax, 17, 18
   withholding tax, 13
Rauh, J. J., 119n
Rebates, 122, 124
   on irregular income, 228–235
Recklessness, 12
Reconstruction Finance Corporation, 48
Reconversion, tax and fiscal policy during, 350–355
   tax measures for, 354–356
Recovery Plans, 298n
Reductions, tax, 374
Refunds, 296
Regressive taxes, 165, 197n, 293
Regressivity, 329
Regulations, 37, 253
   estate-tax, 253
   gift-tax, 253
Rehabilitation, 384
Relief, 384
Rent, 28, 238
   economic, 308, 311, 312, 313–317
   land, 312
Repairs, 155n
Replacements, 155n, 158
   equipment, 157
Repressivity, 330
Research, Division of Tax, 213n, 390
Research in Fiscal Policy, Conference on, 379
Research, National Bureau of Economic, 379
Reserves, 45
   "contingency," 368
   inventory, 151–152
   social-security, 367–371
"Reserves Act, Wisconsin Unemployment," by Groves and Brandeis, 322n
Resources, natural, 3, 13, 384

Index

Resources, America's Needs and, 379n
Resources Planning Board, National, 384
"Resources, Toward Full Use of Our" by Hansen and Greer, 352n
Reticker, Ruth, 323n
Returns, compulsory joint, 241
 consolidated, 241
 separate, 241
Revenue, Board of Inland, 209
Revenue, Bureau of Internal, 127, 128, 150, 156, 158, 160, 240
Revenue, Joint Committee of Internal, 214
Revenue Act, of 1909, 33n
 of 1913, 20, 33n
 of 1916, 33n, 272
 of 1918, 33n, 272
 of 1921, 42, 95n, 207n
 of 1924, 268, 279
 of 1926, 115, 271
 of 1932, 95n, 279
 of 1934, 208n
 of 1935, 92, 92n, 93n
 of 1936, 17, 20, 33n, 50, 52, 69n, 92, 92n, 155n
 of 1938, 17, 42, 51n, 52, 92n, 148n, 208n
  Section 102 of revenue law strengthened by, 42
 of 1939, 182
 of 1940, second, 95
 of 1942, 92, 95, 208n, 272, 273, 276
 of 1943, 208n
 of 1944, 172, 182, 399
 of 1945, 74n
Revenue Act of 1938, Hearings before the Committee on Finance, by Peloubet, 149n
Revenue Code, Internal, 257, 268n
 Sec. 811(f), 272–273
 Sec. 811(g), 276
Revenue Revision of 1942, Hearing before Ways and Means Committee, by Paul, 163n
Revenue Revision of 1942, Hearings, by Schram, 222n

Revenue Revision of 1942, Hearings on, 201n
Revenue sources, state and local, 1941, table of, 328, 329
Revenues, adequacy of, 366–367
 customs, 285, 386, 389
 federal income-tax, 214
Rewards, excess, 312
 necessary, 312
Rhode Island, 339n
Ricardo, David, 313n
Risk-taking, 9–12, 30, 112, 373
Roads, 248
Robertson, D. H., 39
Roosevelt, Franklin D., 200n, 203
Rothmann, W. A., 97n
Rudick, H. J., 44n

S

Safe Deposit and Trust Company of Baltimore, Executor v Commissioner, 254
Safety movement, industrial, 317
St. Louis, Mo, 348
Sales, 38
"Sales Tax as a Fiscal Device for Curbing Inflation in War Time, Federal Retail," by Farioletti, 290n
Sales taxes, 66, 109, 110, 111, 165, 284, 285, 288–289, 327, 328, 331, 367
Saturday Review of Literature, 6n
Saving, 3–4, 40, 353, 363–364
 corporate, 44, 46–49
Savings, Economics of Corporate, by Amos, 45n
"Savings and Postwar Markets, Present," by Slichter, 353n
Schlotterbeck, Karl, 14n, 350, 351
Schmidt, E. P., 319n
Schram, Emil, 222, 222n
Schwab, Charles, 246
Seattle, Wash, 350
Second Model Plan of the National Tax Association Committee on State and Local Taxation, 116

· 429 ·

"Section 102 and the Personal Holding Company Provisions of the Internal Revenue Code," by Rudick, 44n
Securities, "listed," 252n
 "non-listed," 252n
 tax-exempt, 200–206, 200n, 377
Securities and Exchange Commission, 34, 91, 94, 149, 336, 337
Seligman, E R. A., 23, 23n, 38
Seltzer, L., 46n, 241
Services, general, 22n
 special, 22n
Settlor, 266
Sherman Anti-trust Act, 298
Shifting, 109, 110
Short, F. G., 162n
Shuman, R. B, 10n
Simons, H C, 33n, 60n, 202n, 225n, 227n, 289
Single tax, on land, 313–317
Single Tax Movement in the United States, by Young, 315n
Slichter, Sumner, 306n, 352n, 353n, 354
Smith, Adam, 16, 313n
Smith, D M., 320n
Social Insurance and Allied Services, by Beveridge, 324n
Social Justice, Essays in, by Carver, 310n
Social security, 4, 13, 111, 324–325, 367–371, 383, 384
"Social Security after the War," by Slichter, 306n
"Social Security, What Road is Forward in," by Brandeis, 325n
Social Security Act, Federal, 318, 367–369
Social Security Board, 318
Soss, Joseph, 256n
South Dakota, 340
Spaulding, H. B, 70, 70n
Spending, 356, 363–364, 365–366
"Spending, Taxing Consumer," by Buehler, 295n
Spendings tax, 294–295, 301, 376
Squier, Jr., F. S., 256n

Stamp tax, documentary, 285
State taxes, 327–348, 377
Statistics of American Listed Corporations, 91
Statistics, Critical Analysis of Wisconsin Individual Income Tax, by Hanna, 195n
Statistics of Income, 45n, 52n, 53n, 131n, 132n, 137n, 189n, 390, 396, 398, 400, 400n
Statistics, income-tax, 187n
Stock Exchange, New York, 222
"Stock, Fair Value of Blocks of," by Peters, 254n
Stock transfer tax, 389
Stockholders, 9, 27, 30, 46, 62–67
Stocks, bias against, 306
 capital, 115
 financing, 31–35
Stone, Harlan, 265
Strikes, epidemic of, 290
Studenski, Paul, 22, 22n, 119n
Subsidies, 13, 14, 384
Subsistence standard of living, 171
Subvention system, 205
Supreme Court, 42, 129, 347
Surplus, 307–308, 312
Surtax levels, personal income tax, 177–180
"Surtaxes," 174n
Surtaxes, income, 19
Survivors' Insurance System, 367, 368
Sweden, 69n, 357

T

Tarasov, Helen, 198n
Tariff, 16, 17, 77, 377
Tawney, R. H., 309–310, 313
Tax Association Conference, 1941, National, 127n
Tax Association, Proceedings of the National, 1941, by Paton, 127n
Tax Court, 129
Tax Policy for Postwar America, A, by Newcomer, 360n

Index

Tax Problems, Studies in Current, by Burr and Vickrey, 190n
Tax System of Australasia, The, by Gilbert, 144n, 170n
Tax Systems of the World, 262n
Taxation, Essays in, by Seligman, 23n
Taxation and Fiscal Policy, by Newcomer, 287n
Taxation in Minnesota, by Blakey, 348n
Taxation in the New State, by Hobson, 307n, 312
Taxes, Who Pays the, by Colm and Tarasov, 198n
Temporary National Economic Committee, 45n, 97n
Tennessee, 339n
Tennessee Valley Authority, 125
Texas, 240
Theory, ability to pay, 84–85
  first-in, first-out, 147, 148, 151
  "flow," 147
  Georgian, 313
  last-in, first-out, 147, 148, 148n, 149n, 151, 151n
Thompson, J. F., 202n
Thorp, W L, 97n
Timing, 377
Tobacco tax, 17, 285, 292–293, 367, 377, 386, 389
Toilet preparations tax, 285
"Touch of Midas, The," by Walker, 303n
Trade practices, supervision of, 77
"Transfers from Life Tenant to Remainderman," by Mills, 274n
"Transition to Peace: Business in A.D. 194Q," 167n
Transportation, 384
  tax on, 285
Trusts, charitable, 277–278
  nature of, 265–269
Tugwell, R. G, 47n
Turgot, A. R. J., 313n
Twentieth Century Fund Study, 379–385

U

Undercapitalization, 114
Undistributed-profits tax, 17, 49–54, 59, 83
Undistributed Profits Tax, The, by Buehler, 45n
Undistributed Profits Tax, 1937, 69n
"Undistributed Profits Tax, The Corporate," 51n
"Undistributed Profits Tax—A Note," by Guthman, 52n
"Undistributed Profits Tax—A Reply," by McIntyre, 52n
Unemployment, 319, 321–322
Unemployment compensation, 318, 319–325
"Unemployment Compensation Laws, Trends in Disqualification from Benefits under State," by Clague and Reticker, 323n
"Unemployment Insurance with Special Reference to the Wisconsin Act, Aims of," by Morton, 320n
"Unemployment Reserves Act, Wisconsin," by Groves and Brandeis, 322n
Unemployment Tax Act, Federal, 318
U S Bureau of Labor Statistics, 390n
U S. Department of Commerce, 352
U S. Patent Office, 104
U S. State Department, 77
United States Steel Company, 45n, 90
U S. Treasury Department, 37
United States v Wells, 265n
"Units-of-production" method of depreciation, 155
Utilities, application of business taxes, to publicly owned, 125–127
  to privately owned, 126
Utility commissions, state, 34

V

Valuation, cost, 147
  inventory, 146–155
  market, 147

Valuation of Property, The, by Bonbright, 252n
Valuation-date hardships, 257
Veblen, Thorstein, 1
Vermont, 340
Vested interest, 203, 204
Veterans, provision for, 383
Vickrey, William, 190n, 390n, 398n
Victory tax, 172, 236
Voorhis, Representative, 297
Voting process, 24

W

Wage control, 81
Wage earners, 28
Wages, 27, 29
  standard, 307
Walker, G. R., 303n
Wallace, Henry A., 6, 7n, 99n
War, of 1812, 350
  Civil, 55, 350
  First World, 17, 20, 350
  Second World, 18, 20
Washington, 240
Waste, 12
Wealth, 8
Welfare, 22n, 384
Wheeling Steel Corporation v. Fox, 347n
White v. Poor, 268n
Williamson, W. R., 369n
Wisconsin, 136, 191, 213, 225, 226, 238, 340, 340n
Wisconsin Tax Commission, 213n, 228
Wisconsin Tax Departments, 136n
"Wisconsin Unemployment Reserves Act," by Groves and Brandeis, 322n
Withholding tax, 13, 20, 62-64
Woodward Iron Company, 32
Woolfson, A. P., 244n
WPA, 213n, 228, 250, 365
Wyoming, 240

Y

Yields, of postwar tax proposals, 385-389
  rate scale of, 186-188
  of tax proposals, estimated, table, 386
Young, A. N., 315n